W9-CIR-304

Global Civil Society
and Global Environmental Governance

SUNY Series in International Environmental Policy and Theory
Sheldon Kamieniecki, Editor

Global Civil Society and Global Environmental Governance

The Politics of Nature from Place to Planet

Ronnie D. Lipschutz

with Judith Mayer

State University of New York Press

ed by
niversity of New York Press, Albany

in the United States of America

For information, address State University of New York Press,
State University Plaza, Albany, N.Y., 12246

Production by Diane Ganeles
Marketing by Bernadette LaManna

Library of Congress Cataloging-in-Publication Data

Global civil society and global environmental governance ; the politics of nature from place to planet / Ronnie D. Lipschutz with Judith Mayer.
p. cm. — (SUNY series in international environmental policy and theory)
Includes bibliographical references and index.
ISBN 0-7914-3117-7 (CH : alk. paper). — ISBN 0-7914-3118-5 (PB : alk. paper)
1. Environmentalism—International cooperation. 2. Community power—International cooperation. 3. World politics.
I. Lipschutz, Ronnie D. II. Mayer, Judith. III. Series.
GE 195.G558 1996
363.7'00523—dc20 95-52245
CIP

10 9 8 7 6 5 4 3 2 1

To Eric, Maia, and Mary

"Learn of the green world what can be thy place."

Ezra Pound, *Cantos*, LXXXI

Contents

Figures

Acknowledgments

Riddle: What is the difference between nuclear physics and discourse analysis?

Answer: In one, you split atoms; in the other, you split hairs.

This book is about discourse analysis, not nuclear physics. But now having done both, I have found the latter to be considerably more straightforward. Nuclear physics mostly involves keeping track of things that, notwithstanding the new quantum mechanics, are more or less there; discourse analysis is more akin to trying to find Schroedinger's Cat: even if you *can* put your finger on it, you are not at all sure that it is there. Yet, if we are trying to tease out and understand changes in collective human behavior and beliefs that are, in some sense, material while, at the same time, not measurable, we are caught in the same sort of dilemma. Much of politics has this character, especially at the global level. The conventional realist wisdom about anarchy and power—phenomena that can be tracked—leaves out much that is difficult to specify or analyze. Efforts to investigate these latter phenomena fall victim to uncertainty and intersubjectivity.

Researcher: "It this what you mean when you say 'x'?"

Interviewee: "Well, maybe. I'm not sure. Perhaps."

Still, these kinds of beliefs, ideas, indefinable interests—*discourses*—are linked to behavior and do influence how people act, both individually and collectively, locally and globally.

How could one go about studying such phenomena? Whom would you talk to? What would you ask? How could you *measure* what they have done? Anthropologists have long confronted such methodological questions, and many of them have adopted a more-or-less interpretative approach to the subjects of their research. While I have no desire to either become an anthropologist—my old man is not one; at least not professionally—or get bogged down in their epistemological and ontological battles, some of what follows is anthropology. It is also political science, sociology, geography, and cultural studies, with a little economics and ethics sprinkled in. It is an attempt to focus on an emerging group of actors in global politics—I call them, collectively, "global civil society," while others use different terms—focused on protection, preservation, and restoration of the environment, locally *and* globally. This realm of politics, I would argue, is not measurable by the conventional analytical tools of international relations—power capabilities, wealth, trade balances, telephone calls—but must be looked at interpretively. The reader will have to judge whether or not I have been successful.

Had I not been sensitized to this phenomenon through contacts and conversations with many colleagues, I might not have written about it. Having decided to write about it, I have had contacts and conversations with more people than I am able to remember. They have all, in one way or another, contributed to this book. In no particular order, these include Ken Conca, Gene Rochlin, Jesse Ribot, Nancy Peluso, James Rosenau, Luther Gerlach, Dan Deudney, Paul Wapner, Karen Litfin, Beverly Crawford, David Meyer, Peter Euben, John Brown Childs, Dimitris Stevis, Matthias Finger, Tom Princen, Robert Meister, William "Des" Desmond, Ida Miró Kiss, Elizabeth Shove, Michael Maniates, Nuket Kardam, Jan Black, John G. Ruggie, Daniel Press, David Goodman, W. Jackson Davis, Augus Sari, Pál Tamás, Zoltan Illés, Atilla Santha, the many friends and acquaintances I cultivated during the course of my fieldwork and interviews in Hungary, northern California, and Washington, D.C., who are too numerous to list, as well as the many colleagues, friends, contacts who helped Judith Mayer with her chapter, and three anonymous reviewers for SUNY Press. Thanks, too, to Chel Lipschutz for her careful and meticulous help. Research assistance was provided by Tamira Franz and Laura Mann and help with translations from the Hungarian by Ida Miró Kiss and Rita Aronson. My greatest thanks go to Zsuzsa Gille, Mark Nechodom, and Judith Mayer, who assisted, advised and, finally, taught me much more than would have been possible for me to learn on my own. Finally, I dedicate this book to my family—Eric, Maia, and Mary—without whose forbearance it would not have been possible.

Financial and other support for the research presented in this book was provided by the University of California Systemwide Institute on Global Conflict and Cooperation at UC-San Diego, the Center for German and European Studies at UC-Berkeley, the Social Science Division and Academic Senate at UC-Santa Cruz, and the Monterey Institute of International Studies in Monterey, California.

Various portions of this book have appeared in journals and edited volumes or have been presented as conference papers. These are noted below.

Chapter 2. "Environmental Dramas on a Hundred Thousand Stages: The Logic of Thinking Globally and Acting Locally," Netherlands Universities Institute for Coordination of Research in Social Sciences, "Current Developments in Environmental Sociology," June 17–21, 1992, Conference Center Woudschoten, Woudenbergseweg, Netherlands; and "Local Action, Bioregional Politics, and Transnational Collaborative Networks in Policy Responses to Global Environmental Change," Invited presentation on a panel on "Global Environmental Change: The International Perspective," at the 1992 Annual meeting of the American Political Science Association, Chicago, Sept. 3–6, 1992; "Bioregional Politics and Local Organization in Policy Responses to Global Climate Change," pp. 102–22, in: David L. Feldman (ed.), *Global Climate Change and Public Policy*, Chicago: Nelson-Hall, 1994. © 1994 Nelson-Hall Publishing Company. Reprinted by permission.

Chapter 3. "Learn of the Green World: Global Environmental Change, Global Civil Society and Social Learning," paper prepared for presentation for a panel on Social and Environmental Learning, Annual Conference of the International Studies Association, Acapulco, March 23–27, 1993. Published in *Transnational Associations* 3 (1993):124–38. © Union of International Associations. Reprinted by permission; "Reconstructing World Politics: The Emergence of Global Civil Society." *Millennium* 21, #3 (Winter 1992): 389–420. © 1992 *Millennium: Journal of International Relations*. Reprinted by permission; "Not Seeing the Forest for the Trees: Property Rights, Constitutive Rules, and the Renegotiation of Resource Management Regimes," pp. 246–73, in: Ronnie D. Lipschutz and Ken Conca (eds.), *The State and Social Power in Global Environmental Politics,* New York: Columbia University Press, 1993. © 1993 Columbia University Press. Reprinted by permission. "Networks of Knowledge and Practice: Global Civil Society and Protection of the Global Environment," invited presentation to the Conference on the Environmental Management of Enclosed Coastal Seas, Baltimore, November 10–13, 1993, in: L. Anathea Brooks & Stacy VanDeveer (eds.), *Saving the Seas—Values, Scientists and International Governance*, College Park, Md: Maryland Sea Grant College, 1996.

Chapter 4. "Local Action, Bioregional Politics, and Transnational Collaborative Networks in Policy Responses to Global Environmental Change," ibid.; "Bioregional Politics and Local Organization in Policy Responses to Global Climate Change," ibid.

Chapter 5. "Environmentalism in One Country? The Case of Hungary," paper presented at the SSRC Workshop on "The Social Consequences of

Liberalization in Comparative Perspective," UC-Berkeley, April 22–24, 1993, and the Spring Workshop of the European Political Relations and Institutions Research Group, Center for German and European Studies, UC-Berkeley, April 30, 1993; "Learn of the Green World: Global Environmental Change, Global Civil Society and Social Learning," ibid.; "Networks of Knowledge and Practice: Global Civil Society and Protection of the Global Environment," ibid.

Chapter 7. "Who are we? Why are we here? Political identity, ecological politics, and global change," paper prepared for presentation at the Annual meeting of the International Studies Association, Washington, D.C., March 28–April 1, 1994.

Chapter 8. "Who knows? The Place of Local Knowledge in Global Environmental Governance," paper prepared for presentation at the Annual meeting of the International Studies Association, Chicago, Ill., Feb. 22–25, 1995.

CHAPTER 1

Introduction

This is a book about global environmental politics and global environmental governance. It is not, however, about "global" as the term is often used. I deliberately use the term "global" in place of "international" to make the point that the politics of the global environment encompass much more than the interactions of states.[1] Instead, I write here about an emerging form of "global" politics and governance that is rooted in the civil societies of many different countries but is also, to a growing degree, transnational in its reach, articulated via a complex set of knowledge-based linkages and, at the same time, sensitive to differences among local places. The emergence of this global environmental "regime" is a response to what is often called an "environmental crisis," but which is more properly understood as a reaction to certain processes of social transformation at work upon human civilization and its constituent societies. It is for this reason that, as will be seen in chapter 2, I argue that "global environmental change" is best conceived of as a *social* rather than a *physical* phenomenon.

The arguments developed in this book therefore revolve around two somewhat different (and sometimes clashing) themata. There is, first of all, a framing theme rooted in the sociology of knowledge, which focuses on the ways in which the worldviews underlying broad social practices change, and how these changes play themselves out over the longer term (see chapter 3, below, and Lipschutz & Mayer 1993). What I analyze here, in this respect, is what is often called the "environmental movement," but is better understood as a transnational system of rules, principles, norms, and practices, oriented around a very large number of often dissimilar actors, focused on environmental protection, sustainability, and governance.[2] While this transnational "regime" is much too broad and diverse to characterize in a few words, I have chosen to use the term *global civil society*, in preference to other possibilities, for three reasons. First, the term provides a convenient sort of shorthand. Second, it underlines the grounding of this sector in societal processes as opposed to state-centered, institutionalized political ones. And, third, it suggests a form of social action somewhat parallel to the holism that one finds in some ecological models, without suggesting the indivisibility of the planet so characteristic of much environmental analysis.

The argument, as developed here, is that the environmentally-oriented sector of global civil society is, whether consciously or not, engaged in a longer-term project to modify what can be regarded as the underlying constitutive rule basis of modern civilization and to develop new modes of local as well as transnational governance.[3] In doing so, global civil society is laying the basis for broad institutional, social and political change, although I should add that success in this endeavor is by no means assured.

The notion of "civil society" is one with a long history, but it generally refers to those forms of association among individuals that are explicitly not part of the public, state apparatus, the private, household realm or the atomistic market (Cohen & Arato 1992; Walzer 1992, 1995; Larkins & Fawn 1996). Civil society is important in global politics in that it is a sector of the state-society complex where social change often begins; for a number of reasons, which I address in this book, actors in civil society are a force for social and political change, in both the domestic and global arenas (see chapter 3; Lipschutz 1992/96). This does not mean that global civil society is a unity; it is riven by many divisions, more than one finds in even the international state system. Nonetheless, there are segments of this global civil society that are oriented in ways that specifically promote social and political change.

The second theme of this book is a policy-oriented one.[4] This focus concerns the formulation and implementation of environmental policy and, in particular, the possibilities of carrying out commitments implied or required by the terms of international environmental agreements. I take it as a given that environmental protection and sustainable development are "public goods" to be provided through various mechanisms of national and global governance. While this point might be disputed by some (e.g., Rubin 1994), it is not a terribly controversial statement. Given that the state and its agencies, as well as markets, are primarily engaged in the maintenance and reproduction of social structure, under conditions of great stress and dynamic change, what is the likelihood of developing and implementing successful policies to protect the environment?[5] For that matter, how is a state, such as one typically found in the developing world, to make decisions about the allocation of resources (Ascher & Healy 1990)? How are markets, operating primarily to satisfy short-term individual interests, to take account of environmental externalities and future generations (Ekins & Max-Neef 1992)? This is especially problematic when administrative structures dedicated to exploitation are strong while those intended to protect or conserve Nature are weak. The dilemma is further complicated by the difficult, short-term tradeoffs to be made between high rates of economic growth, that often benefit only elites, and strategies of environmental conservation, restoration and sustainability, that promise greater justice for all but fewer resources to the well-off. These are obviously questions of great concern to those who would protect or sustain the environment.

Although these two themes are quite different in ontological *and* epistemological terms, they are not unrelated. The policy theme has to do with material practices; the sociology of knowledge theme with the social beliefs that underpin those practices. One has to do with changing material practices; the other with the fundamental changes in beliefs that would be necessary to embed changed practices in social institutions. Or, to put it another way, if policy is not accompanied by an explanatory framework that somehow accounts for the need for a particular change, it is unlikely that human behavior will change so as to make the policy an effective one. These ideas will be further developed below, and in the chapters to follow. The remainder of this chapter lays out the problem(s) addressed in this book and summarizes how I approach them.

Learning

In an oft-quoted passage—almost a throwaway line—Max Weber once wrote:

> Not ideas, but material and ideal interests, directly govern men's conduct. Yet, very frequently the "world images" that have been created by "ideas" have, like switchmen, determined the tracks along which action has been pushed by the dynamic of interest (Gerth & Mills 1946:200; see also Lipschutz 1989; Robertson 1992).

While Weber was never very clear about what, exactly, he meant by this formulation, it nonetheless captures one of the central puzzles of both the policy and sociology of knowledge aspects of this volume and, in particular, the first part of this book. Weber's statement also raises an ontological issue related to the question of determinism: Does the material base determine the ideological, as some historical materialists would have it, or do the arrows point the other way? Indeed, if we are to think about practice aimed at changing social structures—inasmuch as I will argue in chapter 2, it is these social formations that bear major responsibility for environmental degradation—where do we begin?

One place to begin is with policy, as it is being made. Much attention is being focused on negotiations and activities by states and international organizations at the international level where, it is hoped, the infrastructure for global environmental sustainability might be established (Haas, Keohane & Levy 1993). I do not take it for granted that the mechanisms likely to be proposed and implemented by states at the international level to protect the environment and promote environmental sustainability will necessarily make it possible to achieve these goals. There are a number of reasons for making this assertion and they are addressed in detail in chapter 2; suffice it here to say that the obstacles to successful implementation are to be found in the relationships between the "local" and the "international."

A primary obstacle, however, involves how we conceptualize global environmental change. As often as not, damage to the environment is described in terms of its *physical* characteristics—the declining numbers of a particular species, the loss of so many inches of soil, the presence of so much pollution in air or water, the increase in average global temperature or the decrease in stratospheric ozone concentrations—with the implication that policy should focus on the things that can be counted instead of the things that count. Rather than seeing environmental change as solely a biogeophysical phenomenon, as argued in chapter 2, we should also think of it as a *social* phenomenon. After all, it is the particular structure and features of our political, social, and economic institutions that lead us to abuse our environment, and this argues for a reconfiguration of institutions rather than more conceptually-simple and simplistic notions such as changes in the "numbers." But such institutional reconfigurations are already underway. They include efforts to create new institutions of governance based on the "construction" of common property (or common-pool) resource systems that rely on self-enforcing solutions to the collective action problem (Ostrom 1990; Hechter 1990; Lipschutz 1991a). They also involve the construction of the global "regime," mentioned above, through the transmission, via global networks, of knowledge about these schemes that can be replicated in many places.

Chapter 3 returns to the questions posed above about the relationship between the material and ideal where human society and Nature are concerned. Answers can be formulated in a number of different ways, and there are any number of philosophers and ethicists grappling with them (Reagan 1984; Sagoff 1988; Stone 1993). In chapter 3, I am less interested in the relationship between social systems and Nature—that point is taken up in chapters 7 and 8—than in the ways new bodies of knowledge help, in effect, to restructure and reconstitute these systems. I prefer this approach for two reasons: First, it acknowledges that neither society nor Nature are static. Second, such bodies of knowledge help to establish the basis for changes in beliefs and practices.

In chapter 3, two complementary frameworks are offered for understanding the process of change in social practices and systems. These can be seen as two parts of an "agency-structure" system (Wendt 1987). The structure part is based on the notion of "actor networks," a framework that has been developed by scholars of what are called "large technical systems." Such systems consist of both physical and non-physical components, hardware as well as rules, organizations as well as information (Bijker, Hughes & Pinch 1987; Hughes 1987).

The second framework is focused on the possibilities of agency. It has been formulated by Robert Cox (1987) and Stephen Gill (1993), and relates changes in modes and social relations of production to changes in what they call, borrowing from Fernand Braudel, "historical structures." These structures offer the materials with which agents can make choices, both individually and collectively, about their futures. Such structures are, as often as not, legitimated and maintained by both state and society; they are the mechanisms of social reproduction as well as social change.

At first glance, the two frameworks might appear quite different. To the contrary, they are closely related. Let me clarify this point (and play off Weber) with an example based on trains and tracks. These, I claim, are not just "hardware" that people have used to get from here to there; they are also constitutive of a body of knowledge that, in its day, helped to reconstruct social practice and structure.[6] The first trains appeared in Britain during the second decade of the nineteenth century. By the 1830s, steam-powered trains were in common use and, within forty years, networks of rails could be found crossing all of the world's continents.[7] Trains had fundamental effects on markets, politics, and the conduct of war. Not only did they alter material practices in these three realms, they also changed fundamental understandings of those practices and their rules of operation, too. Thus, I use the term "body of knowledge" to indicate something that has major material and ideational impacts on societies and the ways in which they function and organize themselves.[8]

In 1820, a world webbed *with* rails was hardly imagined. By 1900, a world *without* rails was hardly imaginable, even though new modes of transportation—the automobile and airplane—were already beginning to appear and would, within a matter of decades, become dominant. In essence, trains were a material factor—a large technological system—that changed people's worldviews. But to argue that they were the next logical step in transportation is to be too clever by half (and note that, even as late as the 1870s, urban rail systems were often horse-powered). And surely they were not immediately and unequivocally accepted by society at large. What then was the dynamic? What was the relationship between the material and ideational processes? Why did railroads penetrate so deeply while, more recently, nuclear power has met with such strong social resistance (Rochlin 1994)?

Robert Cox argues, in essence, that changes in the dominant mode of production in a society and, indeed, the world, bring with them changes in what he calls people's *intersubjective ethics* and *rationalities* (which I understand to correspond to my use of ideal, ideological, and ideational, even though these three are not identical). These types of changes do not coincide with political or even generational cycles; they are more closely linked to "historical structures" that change only very slowly. This does not mean that material change determines absolutely ideational change, although the causal arrows seem mostly to point that way in Cox's model. As presented in chapter 3, the arrows pointing the other way are important, too, and it behooves us to look more closely how the material and ideal are mutually constitutive.

However irrelevant it might seem to the environmental case, my invocation of trains is not. The difficult question is: what constitutes a contemporary parallel to the large technological system of the nineteenth century that was the railroad? "Environmental change" involves such a parallel. Let us regard industrial civilization's cumulative impacts on the environment not merely as a set of somewhat disjoint physical phenomena or even the aggregation of the outputs of a broad range of human practices. Consider them, instead, as the consequence of a globally-integrated material structure formed by the cumulation of ideas, practices and technologies. The emerging and corresponding "body of knowledge" then has to do with how this process is taking place and how it might be dealt with.

Such a body of knowledge is not only about describing, however; it is also forcing us to change our understanding of the world, where we belong in it, and how we act in it. In studying the ways in which this body of knowledge is being propagated through human societies, thereby changing not only their material features but their ideational ones, we may also come to better understand the dynamics of large-scale social change. In chapter 3, I draw upon the literature on the sociology of knowledge and the constructivist approaches to the problem of agency and action to suggest how this process is taking place before our very eyes, even though it is not immediately apparent from the parts.

In essence, chapter 3 shows that the activities of "environmentalists"—in both the scientific and political senses—within global civil society, are helping to change the ideational frameworks that support one set of constructions of social reality by replacing old intersubjective rationalities and ethics with new ones. Advocates of biodiversity do more than just bring animals, plants, and bugs into the charmed circle of human ethics and law;

they fundamentally change society's understanding of the relationship *between* humanity and Nature. Those who practice environmental preservation and/or restoration are motivated not only by utilitarian goals, they are also engaged in ethical activities. Those who organize in towns and cities to control industrial and automotive pollution are not only concerned for their collective health, they are also changing the connections between political economy and environment. They are all engaged in similar transformative activities. The result is that, slowly but surely, a "body of knowledge" is being adapted, adopted, and integrated into social practice and beliefs. This involves the negotiation of new meanings of Nature, in which process we are "reconstructing" Nature as well as ourselves (Evernden 1992).

At this point, the reader might rightfully ask: "What does this have to do with global politics, whether environmental or not?" My argument here has as much to do with the distinction *between* as the linkages *among* the local and the global. Rather than repeating clichés, or invoking Tip O'Neill (the U.S. Congressman and Speaker of the House from Boston who argued that "All politics is local"; see Salisbury 1993), I would only make two points. First, everyone's experience of the world is centered where they are: The "global" has no material existence except insofar as it impacts on the individual, who is ineluctably restricted to a single place at any one time (CNN, economic integration and global air travel notwithstanding). Second, however, everyone is aware that the world is much more than the place in which they find themselves: Each "local" is part of a number of globe-girdling systems through which actions in one place can be transmitted and made known to other places (Robertson 1992). More to the point, the activities we ordinarily describe as "international" have no effect except as they motivate changes in the behavior and practices of individuals, or groups, acting locally. And this is the crux of my claim that this book addresses *global* environmental politics.

The Green World

How significant are these processes of social change? How can they be studied and measured? How can we "know" without experiencing such change? Can we be sure that change will be for the better? Major shifts in social beliefs and practices almost always occur at imperceptible rates and require long periods of time to become visible. Only when war or some other catastrophe substantially destroys the material base of society do we see rapid, radical changes in the belief structures of societies.[9] Even then, the "ruins" of earlier periods may remain discernible, even if only faintly so. As Georgi Derlugian puts it, "History is an enormously inertial process"

(1994). Otherwise, such changes take generations, if not longer, and occur in and through historical structures.

In the final part of this book, I will return to these questions and the policy and framework issues raised above. Chapters 4, 5, and 6 represent the empirical core of this book, presenting studies of global civil society and its environmental practices in three different parts of the world: California, Hungary, and Indonesia. The framework developed in the first part of the book influences, but does not determine, the stories told in these three chapters. I eschew the more traditional inductive or positivist approaches of social science in describing and understanding the types of phenomena discussed here. Instead, I operated along inductive-deductive-inductive lines in thinking, researching, and writing; hence the shift, at this point in the book, to place-specific "data."

The logic of the three research sites is, perhaps, not immediately apparent. They have as much to do with expediency—particular funding opportunities, the availability of graduate students with appropriate interests, language, and expertise—as a critical comparative element. The first research site is an industrialized society in the "West"; the second, an industrialized society in the old Soviet Bloc (or "East," as we used to call it); the third, a developing society in the "South." At the same time, all three cases are representative of "developmental" states, in the sense that the exploitation of the resource base of each has been and is legitimated by the state and has been and is central to social reproduction. But each state as a whole is not really at issue here; the specific focus of these chapters is much more the local than state or "nation," and what emerges is a fairly high degree of diversity even within each country. Hence, I maintain something of a fiction in calling each of these studies characteristic of the country within which they are found, but it is a fiction that is necessary, if not entirely precise.

Beyond this, however, there are a set of common characteristics that serve to unite the three cases, and that provide the basis for the fieldwork behind the chapters. First, although I had originally conceptualized "global civil society," in its local and national manifestations, as independent of or in opposition to the state, it became increasingly clear during my research that this was not the case. In contrast with some romantic views of the "new" social movements, and the academic literature focusing on and describing them, environmentalism and the environmental movement cannot be seen as, somehow, being fully autonomous from the state. Indeed, as John Walton (1992) makes clear in his study of water politics in the Owens Valley of California, states and social movements are part of a mutually-constitutive relationship *between* state and civil society. This remains the case even when they seem set on opposing tracks.[10]

Ultimately, these cases focus on the role of place—of specific places or regions—centered in larger, historically-contingent, state-driven political economies, as well as the actions of individuals and groups in those places, and the linkages between groups in those places and agents in other places. This is not to say only that people in Indonesia, California, and Hungary are in contact with one another; it is to say that, through the networks of global civil society, they are all participants in a shared episteme (Ruggie 1975), exposed to similar material factors, ethics, and intersubjective rationalities. "Tree-huggers" and "water-lovers" in Indonesia, California, and Hungary (there are very few of the former in Hungary) are all linked by a globally-shared system of symbols, knowledge creation and transmission, even though their practices are driven by the histories, politics, and ecologies of the places in which they act.

The research design utilized in the construction of these chapters draws on work in rural sociology elaborated by Norman Long and Ann Long (1992), and their collaborators, and described in detail by Andrew Long (1992): discourse and situational analysis.[11] As he puts it:

> [D]iscursive forms are the socio-historical product of actors' practical engagements with their world that combine many factors. . . . The definition of a particular discursive form, whose parameters are diffuse, can only come from an understanding of a particular field context and those actors involved in that arena. The situational method concerned with norms or rules of conduct is in effect another way of talking about and identifying discursive forms. . . . [S]uch norms (discursive forms) are translated (by actors) into practices that are ultimately manipulated in particular situations to serve particular ends (A. Long 1992:165).

In the three regions, therefore, the application of this approach has involved beginning at a distance, interviewing individuals involved in environmental organizations and activities, reading and analyzing printed materials and, eventually, focusing on action in one or two localities. While each of the specific stories told here are still "in progress" and, hence, incomplete, they nonetheless illustrate the relationships between global and local, and the central importance of the local in the reconstruction of the global.

As might be expected, the three cases are, in many ways, very different, even though for the purposes of this book, similarities are central. These differences are a function of the individual histories and political economies of both locale and country. Through these differences, however, it is possible to see that the emergence of discourses centered on Nature and resource exploitation are a response to the specific crises facing each "developmental" state. In each instance, the state has been and is instrumental in allocating property rights over resources and providing a stable political context within which exploitation and development can take place (Mulgan & Wilkinson 1992:341–42). Consequently, as the material conditions of local life are threatened or undermined, there emerges the possibility of different developmental discourses coming into play. These threaten the legitimacy and relationship of state to society and, in turn, can undermine the political stability so essential to the development process.[12] The state, therefore, finds itself in the curious position of having to legitimize behavior that forces changes in developmental strategies.

The history of "environmentalism" in California illustrates this process. The phenomenon can be traced back at least as far as John Muir and Gilbert Pinchot, in the late nineteenth century, and the Progressive/Conservationist movements of the early twentieth century, that eventually led to the creation of National Parks and National Forests (Hays 1980; Yaffee 1994). The Sierra Club, Friends of the Earth, Earth Island Institute[13] and other well-known environmental organizations were launched in California, and many other groups have since established offices there. The state is home to thousands of small, local operations, whose interests extend from conventional, "Not in my Back Yard" (NIMBY)-type issues all the way to those of global extent and implication. Environmentalist ideology is well-represented not only in the state legislature but also in the state's bureaucracies in Sacramento. Indeed, it was the infamous Santa Barbara channel oil spill of 1967 that is often considered the first "shot" fired in the rise of environmentalism over the past three or so decades.

California is not, however, unique in the United States in terms of the profusion of organizations and activists. Indeed, in some ways it is paradigmatic for a pattern that could be traced in most, if not all, of the states and provinces of North America. Where California is, perhaps, unusual is in the efforts undertaken by the *state* to problematize the society-Nature relationship through bioregionalism, a process described in chapter 4.

"Bioregionalism" is a term without a very precise definition; Humpty-Dumpty would have liked it (see Andruss, et al. 1990). I use the term here in a broad sense, to describe conscious and concrete efforts to reconcile human social institutions and practices with what we think of as (but which are really not) systems of "Nature,"[14] and to do so in an integrated sense, that is, one that considers the relationships and interactions of resources and human institutions in a comprehensive manner. While there is an extensive historical record of resource management districts—water, air, soil, etc.—and even considerable experience with ecosystem-based coordinated resource management planning (or "CR[I]MP," as it is called in California), efforts to institutionalize a bioregional approach through localized politics are quite new.[15] If these efforts succeed in California, it is quite probable that they will be picked up and replicated elsewhere.[16]

Hungary presents a different story. Although the country possesses a history of nature conservation, oriented largely around water projects and agricultural development launched in the early- to mid-nineteenth century, the modern environmental movement is only about fifteen or twenty years old. The regimes of the old Soviet Bloc paid lip service to the observance of environmental standards and laws. They also found it expedient to profess a commitment to environmental regulation as a means of generating "credit," both economic and political, with Western countries. Throughout Central and Eastern Europe and the former Soviet republics, however, the material reality was quite different from the regulatory ideal (DeBardeleben 1991; Pryde 1991; Feshbach & Friendly 1992; DeBardeleben & Hannigan 1995). The price of such policy is now apparent, for example, in the declining life expectancies of Russian men (Specter 1995).

Human welfare and Nature played second and third fiddles to industrialism, resulting in concomitant pollution on a massive scale without, in the final analysis, very much in the way of economic success to show for the effort. Somewhat paradoxically, the environmental movements in many of these formerly-Socialist countries, Hungary included, arose not so much in response to such pollution—since data were closely held by the state—but as protests against the totalitarian, society-colonizing practices of the Party state. In Hungary, such protest developed in reaction to a foreign-financed, state-planned project to dam the Danube River—a pre-eminent symbol of Hungary and its history—for a product as mundane as electricity. The protest movement became a political "Trojan Horse"—oppositional politics by other means, so to speak—and played an important role in the gradual discrediting of the old regime.

After 1989, the force of this movement was largely spent, as participants flocked to join the many parties springing up to contest seats in the new Parliament. Those left behind found it necessary to rebuild the movement, and to make the case that the concerns motivating the *Duna Kör* (Danube Circle/Blue Danube) protests had not withered away. For reasons to be explored in chapter 5, however, these efforts have not, and are not, taking place in a vacuum. Budapest is to European environmentalists today as Lisbon was to European spies during World War II: a hotbed of activity. Why this is so is something of a puzzle, but the result is that many of the several hundred environmental and conservationist groups and organizations scattered about the country are connected not only to the goings-on in the country's capital, but also to organizations in Eastern and Western Europe and the United States.

Hungary is not a "green" country, but environmental awareness is, perhaps, as high as, if not higher than, any other of the post-bloc states. Of particular importance to the arguments presented in this book are the "on-the-ground" activities of many of these groups, organized around the preservation or restoration of various aspects of the environment, especially rivers and streams. This is, I argue in chapter 5, partly a cultural artifact of the country's environmental history, although it also grows out of the material role of rivers and streams in the everyday life of industrial societies. These projects act as a potential core of both environmental protection and awareness. The hope is that a gradual improvement in the former will lead to growth in the latter, which will provide broader support for the former, and so on. In a country under economic stress, as Hungary is at present, such dialectical processes are likely to be more effective than abstract appeals to ethics and humanity.

Indonesia presents still another model of the ways in which environmental beliefs and practices are adopted, adapted, and integrated into the political and social life of a country. Indonesia falls, of course, into the category we often characterize as "developing" or "Southern." Such a categorization tends to obscure vast economic, social, and cultural differences within the country. In many respects, the differences between cities in Indonesia and those in industrialized countries are smaller than the contrasts between Jakarta and parts of the archipelago such as Kalimantan; indeed, it is sometimes easier to get to the peripheral islands from the "outside world" than it is from the capital.[17] And, the political system of the country is such as to discourage the growth and freedom of organizations that dissent from official policies and postures, which include lip service to environmental quality and protection of indigenous resources, such as tropical forests. In practice, however, resource degradation and destruction are pervasive, abetted by patterns of ownership and contracting that are very attractive to international capital and often have as much to do with family ties as economic efficiency and profitability.

Yet, even here one finds an active and growing part of global civil society. As discussed in chapter 6, written by Judith Mayer, many of the groups in this network are as advanced in their sophistication and skills as any group in Washington, D.C., and they have extensive connections to organizations in other parts of the world.[18] And, as is the case in Hungary, such connections sometimes bypass the capital entirely. On the one hand, researchers and representatives from universities and organizations in the industrialized world travel to the provinces and trek into the jungles to make common cause with those peoples whose resource management strategies are threatened by Indonesia's integration into global markets. On the other hand, Indonesian activists often take short-term political and intellectual refuge from domestic pressures by spending time at foreign universities and in the foreign offices of international environmental organizations. It is in and through their activities in these regions that one begins to understand how global environmental networks have begun to make connections with sophisticated local activists struggling against the processes of underdevelopment and environmental destruction, even in very remote parts of the world.

Indonesia's official environmental policies and politics are, thus, under pressure from within and without. In a state where control of the periphery by the center is often tenuous, at best, the potential for relatively independent, localized strategies is great. Moreover, as was the case in Hungary prior to 1989, environmentalism in Indonesia offers a space in which political organizing and struggle can be undertaken. Increasingly, environmentalists are making common cause with human rights activists to pressure governments for greater political freedom. As a result, environmentalists in countries like Indonesia must walk a fairly narrow line, if they are not to be accused by the government of illegal or unpatriotic activities.[19]

In many ways, these three cases are typical of specific categories of states and the environmental groups and activities that develop in them and, therefore, they differ from one another. But the similarities between the three should not be overlooked. Both California and Indonesia are highly urbanized but also depend on the exploitation and marketing of rural resources in world markets. The Suharto regime bears important resemblances to the pre-1989 government in Hungary. And Hungarian and Indonesian environmentalists are every bit as well-educated and skilled as their counterparts in California. I would not want to exaggerate the similarities, but an important concern here is the way in which similar beliefs and practices have appeared in three very different settings. In the final section of this book, I turn to an exploration of why this is so, and the implications for policymaking with respect to global environmental issues.

What can be thy Place?

Many observers and scholars have made note of the growing prominence of environmental non-governmental organizations (NGOs) in international as well as local politics (Princen & Finger 1994; Wapner 1995a, 1995b, 1996). But one question remains: Does this movement differ from other transnational social movements, especially those of decades past, such as the labor movement? The question is an important one for the following alternative reasons: If the environmental movement is similar to those social and political movements of the past, it is essentially engaged in a project of reform and it can be described with much the same models applied to those earlier movements (Stevis 1995). If the environmental movement is similar to other social movements in existence today, it arises in response to the same fragmenting processes that are breaking down the social structures of industrial society and replacing them with new, atomized identities (Offe 1990; Hall 1991). But perhaps neither of these two is entirely accurate. Perhaps the environmental movement (and other elements of global civil society) incorporates some of the features of both but is also different in key respects. This would be especially true with respect to its generation by considerations of *place*.

I subscribe to the third alternative. As suggested in chapter 7, place is of growing importance to the actions of the environmental element in global civil society, for reasons having as much to do with practicality as with individual and collective identities. Places (or habitats or landscapes) are not abstractions, as are globalized concepts such as climate change or biodiversity. Environmental damage, whether triggered by biogeophysical changes or development, occur in specific places, in people's "backyards." Often, these also form the bases of their livelihoods and histories. It is for this reason that place is important.

More to the point, the meanings that people, acting collectively, give to Nature around them are critical to their sense of identity and location in the world, even as they are often central to their local modes of production and social reproduction. We all live and work in concrete places, not in some sort of abstract global space. This is a sentiment that does not seem terribly relevant in a time of increasingly globalized markets and culture, yet it is, I believe, a very specific reaction to the process of globalization. For better or worse, this sense of identity with place is not so very different from the recent rise of ethnic identities in many parts of the world, a point also explored in chapter 7 (see also Robertson 1992).

The identification with place has implications, moreover, beyond simply acting locally. To return to my earlier arguments about the developmental state, the control over processes of extraction and production, *in specific places*, is one element that legitimizes the state in the eyes of society. A state that loses such control is not only weak, it is also unable to "deliver the goods" that generate societal support. In other words, it begins to lose the capacity to govern (Lipschutz 1991b). Insofar as local action is also about local control over the development process, the state may find itself weakened or confronted by local political opposition. Hence, the process of attempting to return or regain some degree of control becomes one of finding ways to legitimize state involvement in local activities. Not all states manage to do this and some, confronted by decentralization and fragmentation, simply fall apart. Others find ways to compromise. In all instances, the central question becomes: Who decides? And this leads to the final chapter of the book, in which the issue of governance is addressed.

Surely, the reader may argue at this point, environmental organizations and lobbyists are powerful in the capitals of many countries and have had significant influence on law and policy but, in aggregate, the activist core constitutes only a small fraction of each country's citizens, does it not? And the activities of local groups, however many there are, cannot possibly influence global politics. Chapter 8 returns to the notion of global civil society in its environmental manifestation and the role of global civil society in environmental governance. There, I further develop the argument that global civil society represents the emergence of a form of global governance that is, in some ways, complementary to the state and state system and, in other ways, in opposition to them.

Inasmuch as national governments are either unable or unwilling to engage in the policies required to set right a broad variety of environmental problems, strategies for dealing with them must emerge elsewhere. The creation of common-pool property resource systems through, for example, restoration projects or bioregionalism, involves the construction of new institutions for governance. These institutions may or may not have the blessings of government, but they do regulate the use of the place or ecosystem with which they are concerned. Are such institutions mechanisms simply for reform, or do they represent agents of real social change? It depends. We cannot generalize across all societies nor make confident predictions about the future. Still, I believe that such arrangements will be essential if we, as a civilization, are to "make peace with the planet" (Commoner 1990), and find ways to live with each other, too.

PART I

Learning

CHAPTER 2

Governing Nature: Global Change, Social Complexity, and Environmental Management[1]

The so-called environmental crisis demands not the inventing of solutions but the re-creation of the things themselves.

(Evernden 1992:123; emphasis in original)

This chapter discusses the policy theme described in chapter 1. The questions and the tentative answers will make clear the inherent difficulties of formulating policies that address "environmental change" at any spatial scale. Policymaking, as Deborah Stone (1988) has described with considerable insight, is full of tensions. These arise because the policy process is, to a considerable degree, about telling persuasive stories and bringing people along. As Stone puts it:

> Because paradox is an essential feature of political life, politics and policy are beyond the reach of rational analytic methods. . . . Political reasoning is reasoning by metaphor and analogy. It is trying to get others to see a situation as one thing rather than another. . . . It is strategic portrayal for policy's sake. . . . Policy making, in turn, is a constant struggle over the criteria for classification, the boundaries of categories, and the definition of ideals that guide the way people behave (1988:5–7).

The domination of ideas, and the policies that follow, are therefore rooted in the persuasiveness of the stories being told—not necessarily in their inherent scientific accuracy or rationality—and it does not hurt the endeavor to have these stories authorized, or reinforced, by those who fill certain kinds of legitimated roles.[2] The legitimacy of stories can also arise from the historical and material circumstances in which people find themselves, a point taken up in chapter 3.

If policies follow from particular stories, different stories can also be told about the same situation. Consider, for a moment, the concept of "environmental change," which is widely used to refer to the collective human degradation of the environment. The very term suggests a deviation from some baseline condition that, presumably, was somehow more "suitable" or "natural." But suitable for whom, or what? Ecologists are beginning to tell us that there is no baseline (Yoon 1994), nor are there any pristine ecosystems on Planet Earth: humans have left their imprint everywhere, in jungles, deserts, prairies, oceans as well as cities. If a "change" is deemed undesirable, to what condition, then, is the environment to be restored? There is a growing body of research which suggests that some human efforts to restore ecosystems may actually have catastrophic, rather than beneficial, consequences (Woodley, Kay & Francis 1993). Who, therefore, is to make decisions about the scale and type of an intervention? And what are we to do if these interventions lead to patently inequitable or unjust results? The intent in asking these questions is not to suggest that we not intervene at all, only that the answers are not at all obvious, *and they are not to be found in the authoritative pronouncements of either political leaders or scientists.*

This chapter is structured as follows: it first addresses the concept of "environmental change," in its global scope, and examines its social content and implications. The chapter offers a means of thinking about global environmental change not as a "natural" transformation that is caused by human activities and affects human activities. Rather, the phenomenon incorporates many "social processes" whose causes and consequences are mediated through physical as well as institutional systems. Next, it points out the contradictions inherent in seeing states and the state system as the appropriate institutional locus for dealing with the problems of management that seem to follow from global environmental change. *Where* we draw boundaries when we discuss environmental change is a political, and not a scientific, exercise with serious implications for how we can or should act. Third, how precisely do the ways we analyze and understand global environmental change point to amelioration strategies that may not be either practical or effective? If, indeed, environmental change is a consequence of social processes, perhaps we would do better to think in social terms about the phenomenon. It is to history and political economy we must look for understanding. Finally, what sorts of strategies and policies does this change of perspective imply? The way to re-integrate history, political economy and Nature is through localized "resource regimes," which are similar in many ways to the common property or common-pool resources described by Elinor Ostrom (1990) and others (e.g., Bromley 1992). This will lead us back to political and policy making consequences.

Meanings and metaphors

What is meant by the term "Global Environmental Change?"[3] For the most part this concept has been treated as a physical one. For example according to one authoritative source, a National Academy of Sciences volume (Stern, Young & Druckman 1992) entitled *Global Environmental Change—Understanding the Human Dimensions*, prepared by the Academy's Committee on the Human Dimensions of Global Change,

> The earth has entered a period of hydrological, climatological, and biological change that differs from previous episodes of global change in the extent to which it is human in origin. To explain or predict the course of the present global environmental changes, one must therefore understand the human sources, consequences, and responses, some of which can alter the course of global change (1992: 1).

The report's authors later supplement this somewhat vague preamble with the following:

> Global environmental changes are alterations in natural (e.g., physical or biological) systems whose impacts are not and cannot be localized. Sometimes the changes in question involve small but dramatic alterations in systems that operate at the level of the whole earth, such as shifts in the mix of gases in the stratosphere or in levels of carbon dioxide and other greenhouse gases throughout the atmosphere. We speak of global change of this sorts as *systemic* in nature because change initiated by actions anywhere on earth can directly affect events anywhere else on earth. Other times, the changes in question result from an accretion of localized changes in natural systems, such as loss of biological diversity through habitat destruction and changes in the boundaries of ecosystems resulting from deforestation, desertification or soil drying, and shifting patterns of human settlement. Global changes of this sort we describe as *cumulative* in nature; we can consider them global because their effects are worldwide, even if the causes can be localized. . . . The boundary between systemic and cumulative change is not sharp; it depends on how rapidly an environmental change spreads in space (Stern, Young & Druckman 1992:25–26; emphasis in original).

Oddly enough, the human factor is almost absent from this latter excerpt. Aside from some vague references to "change initiated by actions" and "habitat destruction and shifting patterns of human settlement," one might as well be talking about catastrophic volcanic eruptions or comets striking the earth, neither of which is of "human" origin. We see, instead, in this description a set of phenomena whose origins are obscured by a focus on the *physical* mediations of the changes in question. This does not mean that the National Academy volume ignores the human element but, rather, that this, a relatively concise description of global environmental change, does.

This is not a minor error of omission, inasmuch as global environmental change is best understood as a *social* phenomenon, rather than a physical one imposed on nature. As a social phenomenon, environmental change results from specific human activities, or institutionalized practices, that, in many cases, have become ingrained by virtue of long years of habit. They have been made to seem authoritative and "natural" via social relations of power and production (Harvey 1990: 219, 345; Agnew & Corbridge 1995: ch. 3). These practices are not discrete and uncoupled; in many instances, they are embedded in a whole range of "nested" practices and institutions. Each of these appears, at least at first glance, essential to the more-or-less continued functioning of the societies in which they are found. Finally, if it is a social process, global environmental change must be understood as the result of human agency operating within social structures of human origin; this means that any attempt to address global environmental change must also confront the dynamics of human social change.[4]

The frequent focus on physical change that one finds in much of the literature rests on the fact that, however complex they may be, this dimension of nature is infinitely more simple than human social institutions and their relationships to and with Nature. Given sufficient memory and time, supercomputers can produce fairly credible, if crude, approximations of how climate might change under certain specified conditions. Outside of the science fiction world depicted by Isaac Asimov in *The Foundation Trilogy* (1983), in which the human future was fully predictable through "psychohistory," however, there are no computers yet in existence that could do the same for human societies. Even if such devices were developed, how could they take into account the meanings—the stories—that link humans to Nature, but are not reducible to rationality in any meaningful sense (Oelschlaeger 1991; Evernden 1992)?

Environmental change, whether global or local, is a much more complex phenomenon than its physical manifestations, in terms of both its causes and consequences. Indeed, the term "global environmental change" conceals as much as it reveals, since it seems to relegate "local" environmental problems to another realm of behavior and politics, and presumes that "global" problems can, somehow, be handled through a top-down process of centralized management.[5] To a major degree, this separation between "global" and "local" phenomena is the result of political boundary-drawing exercises, and not a consequence of nature.[6] What, after all, makes powerplant pollution in one part of North America a "transnational" problem even as, in another part of the same continent, not far away, it is a domestic one? Why should watershed degradation be regarded as a local problem if it is happening all over the world? Why, if toxic wastes are generated by an electronics firm whose markets are global, is their disposal a strictly local matter?[7]

From these perspectives, use of the term "global," as in "global climate change," for example, is not entirely accurate. First, global climate change will be a secondary consequence of a broad range of spatially-bounded human activities that, in turn, are linked to or will cause other forms of environmental damage as well (Clark 1989). Second, while global climate change is mediated via a physical system of planetary dimensions, in most instances its effects are likely to be highly localized, in physical as well as social terms (Lipschutz 1995). Add to this differences in the capacity of societies to respond to disruption within even very small areas, and it becomes clear that the *social* impacts could very well have very different consequences on scales even as small as one city block.[8]

The ways in which we conceptualize environmental problems thus have a great deal of influence on how we try to address them; more than this, particular approaches serve to reify and reinforce certain types of structures and biases that, by their nature, might be environmentally-damaging (Rubin 1994: 15–16). Global perspectives allow us to see the big picture, but they wipe out the micro-level details where agency meets structure, so to speak, and where people really live.[9] Dividing the world into "local," "national," and "global" lends itself to a division of labor where thinking about cause and response are concerned. It does not really illuminate the number or nature of inter-level social as well as other linkages. For that, we need a different way of seeing things.

I use the term "social complexity" as one way of thinking about these micro-macro linkages and their social consequences.[10] This term is meant to capture both linkages and consequences and to capture the intricate webs of institutional, social and production relations within human societies and among them. Such a framework is useful for this purpose, inasmuch as many of the relationships between local causes and global effects are not simply restricted to single "levels" (Singer 1961). Rather, they are largely the result of coupling between particular economic and political arrangements at the local, national, and global levels, and local ecosystems tied to them through complex, transnational networks of exploitation (of people and nature), transaction, and exchange, and vice versa (Agnew 1993).

Social complexity can be further elaborated in two ways, in terms of multiple effects and mediating systems. For example, deforestation, even in temperate regions of the world, results not only in net emissions of carbon dioxide into the atmosphere (so long as replanting does not take place), it also contributes to soil erosion, water pollution, and loss of habitat and biodiversity (Repetto 1990). Each of these *physical* phenomena can have very different *social* consequences that depend on the histories, political economies and social structures of affected groups and regions.

Second, complex connections among environmental problems themselves are mediated not only through physical systems but through social ones, too. Globally-linked biogeophysical systems can, of course, aggregate the effects of local sources of pollutants. For example, consider the consequences of an increase in atmospheric carbon dioxide, coming from a multitude of fossil fuel-burning systems. Not only might we see global effects from this, the impacts could also vary dramatically with locale as changes in regional climate regimes alter precipitation rates over very short distances. These types of connections are widely recognized.

There are, however, other linkages of comparable or even greater importance. For example, when viewed in narrow physical terms, soil erosion can be seen as a *local* phenomenon occurring simultaneously in many places across the planet. But such local physical changes are linked to each other through various *global* connections of a social (or institutional) nature, both in terms of causes (such as through global markets in grain) and consequences (as might follow from fluctuations in global food productivity and distribution).[11] The rate at which carbon dioxide from fossil fuels enters the atmosphere depends, among other things, on the prices of various fuels, which can be a function of investment in supply, national or international political crises, and societal disruption in producing and consuming countries, among other things. Threats to biodiversity arise not simply because species are being killed intentionally, or for their "market value," but also as a side-effect of developmental pressures that destroy ecosystems. These processes of development are, as often as not, driven by forces originating in global social systems as well as national and local ones.[12]

Not all environmental problems are unbounded; there are places where lines can and must be drawn.[13] Although the *physical* environmental effects of certain activities may be manifested or mediated via open access resource commons,[14] the activities contributing to these impacts tend to be bounded in social, economic, and even physical terms. As Ronald Herring points out: "[A]ll local arrangements for dealing with natural systems are embedded in a larger common interest defined by the reach of ecosystems beyond localities" (1990:65). We can thus envision local systems of production and action—the immediate sources of environmental damage—as being nested within larger ones. These, in turn, comprise *eco-*

nomic and social networks of resource users and polluters rather than either discrete or totally-aggregated arrangements. These networks, moreover, are embedded in overlapping but not necessarily coterminous, social, political, economic, and physical spaces.[15]

Global environmental change can thus be understood as a social process in the sense that, as the cumulation of interlinked phenomena, it is intimately bound up with common, everyday social practices and institutions in a large number of societies, at different levels of analysis, and varying spatial and temporal scales. This does not mean that all societies are equal per capita contributors to global environmental change; it does mean that environmental change is integral to social processes, and not something that happens exogenously to them. It means that human beings are deeply implicated in the production of Nature, as well as its alteration, for better or worse. As anthropologists, ecologists and rural sociologists are increasingly coming to recognize, even "Nature" is rarely natural; where human beings have lived, they have, inevitably, engaged in a continuous pattern of transforming what they have found there (Cronon 1983; Peluso 1992). Environmental change itself is, consequently, not a new phenomenon; if we regard the demographic consequences of the European expansion as a form of environmental "change," even its global reach is not new (Crosby 1986; Jones 1981).

The articulation of global environmental change in these terms implies an approach to understanding and dealing with it not as an exclusively *international*, or even national, problem as it is commonly thought to be (a point to which I return, below). Instead, in keeping with Herring's notion of "nesting," environmental change is better understood as the outcome of what can be thought of as the operation of tens, if not hundreds of thousands of resource-using institutions—"resource regimes"—which function at varying geographic and social scales and level.[16] These are interlinked in the sense that the inputs of some are outputs of others. Richard Norgaard notes the implications of such relationships:

> While institutions will have to be locally tailored to support ecosystem-specific technologies, local institutions, nonetheless, will still have to mesh with regional and global institutions designed to capture the gains of ecosystem management on a larger scale and to prevent untoward broader consequences of local decisions (1988:609).

This argument has important ramifications for our attempts to "manage" our impacts on Nature.

Environmental change and international relations

Most scholars of global environmental change and its politics study them on the basis of analytical frameworks rooted in the concepts and practices of international relations.[17] As Richard Benedick, chief U.S. delegate at the negotiations leading to the Montreal Protocol on Substances that Deplete the Ozone Layer, puts it:

> Because of the nature of ozone depletion, no single country or group of countries, however powerful, could effectively solve the problem. Without far-ranging cooperation, the efforts of some nations to protect the ozone layer would be undermined (Benedick 1991:4).

The example of ozone diplomacy, claims Benedick, can "be examined as a paradigm for new diplomatic approaches to new kinds of international challenges" (p. xiii).

How should we regard his assessment? And what, if anything, does it miss or ignore? Benedick is only partly correct in making this argument, as we shall see, below. The exercise of formulating and implementing environment protection[18] strategies is particularly difficult where "global" environmental problems subject to international negotiation are concerned.[19] Most analyses of responses to large-scale environmental degradation take as their primary focus the role of the nation-state in addressing and ameliorating the problem (Young 1989, 1994a; P. Haas 1990). The argument is, by now, a familiar one: Because so many of these problems are transnational in nature, they can only be dealt with at the international level. Moreover, the logic of the "tragedy of the commons"—that a shared resource lacking controls on access and usage will inevitably be degraded—requires that states accept regulation—in Garrett Hardin's words, "mutual coercion mutually agreed upon"(1968)[20]—which mandates, first, collective action and, second, the yielding up of some degree of sovereignty in the name of the global good. Thus, unprecedented cooperation among countries at the international level is presumed to be a *sine qua non* for the successful control or amelioration of global environmental change in those manifestations defined as "global": climate change, tropical deforestation, biodiversity, population and ozone depletion.

According to the logic of this international relations-based framework, the sources of most, if not all, forms of environmental degradation are caused by a vast number of individual and collective activities that take place *within* specific countries. But because the distribution of impacts remains highly uncertain, the logic of international anarchy requires coordinated action by all countries, including those whose contribution to the problem is minimal. Consequently, most, if not all, countries will have to take actions, commensurate with their abilities, to ameliorate the effects of change, or to adapt to them, without any guarantees that they will benefit from the results. Such efforts will inevitably come into conflict with the sovereign desires and goals of individual countries and their polities (Putnam 1988; Evans, Jacobson & Putnam 1993). As the on-going negotiations over climate change have demonstrated, it is extremely politically-contentious to allocate specific responsibility to individual countries for their contribution to this "global" problem (*ECO* 1995; *Earth Negotiations Bulletin* 1995).

These tasks are difficult to accomplish but not impossible. The process leading to the Montreal Protocol and its amendments seems to have worked and is being offered, as Benedick hoped, as *the* model for international environmental agreements. The ozone agreements have been ratified by most of the countries of the world and include provisions for the transfer of technology and resources to Third World countries that might otherwise find themselves put at an economic and technical disadvantage by the ban on ozone-depleting substances. During March 1994, the United Nations Framework Convention on Climate Change (FCCC), modelled after the ozone agreements, came into force, having been ratified by the required number of states. The broad expectation is that similar binding commitments will, in due time, come to be made by the signatories to the FCCC, and that other conventions, covering other problems, will follow.[21]

There are two difficulties with such logic. The first is that the ozone problem is hardly typical of *most* environmental problems, including those affecting "commons," more accurately described as "open access resources." There are significant differences between the problem of controlling chlorofluorocarbons (CFCs) and most of the other substances that are the major contributors to ozone depletion, for example, and that of limiting the myriad of sources of the more numerous and voluminous "greenhouse" gases that will contribute to global warming. The variety of practices and customs that could be viewed as contributors to climate change and related problems increases the complexity of the global warming problem manyfold. The ozone agreements deal with substances produced by a fairly small number of firms (even though the protocols are framed primarily in terms of limits on *consumption* and *trade*). They include a fairly straightforward arrangement by which developing countries commit to reductions in the use of these chemicals in exchange for financial and technological assistance from developed countries in deploying substitutes. By contrast, the only international instrument so far in place to address global environmental change comprehensively, including global warming, is the Global

Environmental Facility (GEF) of the World Bank, whose precise role seems somewhat marginal and remains a topic of some dispute (Mott 1993; Rich 1994; Wells 1994). The ozone agreements are a model of clarity and straightforwardness by comparison.

The second, and more important, problem with arguments regarding the primacy of international collective action is that of actual implementation. International agreements are almost always phrased in terms of a national government's commitment to limitations on certain types of practices, as often as not without precise specification as to the means of implementation.[22] The hypothesis here is that management of environmental problems, however they manifest themselves, fall within the purview of national governments. This is so because only national governments have the authority and the tools to manage resources in a rational fashion and to mediate among those interests that find themselves in conflict over how resources and the environment are to be exploited. Individual governments are presumed capable of drafting, legislating, and implementing appropriate plans and programs (and, if not, then "technology transfer" is assumed to provide the necessary capabilities). Finally, there is the general expectation that a passive citizenry will willingly comply with whatever legal directives are sent down from the national capital (McEvoy 1988:223).

There are good reasons to question such assumptions. It may even be that the state, and its administrative organs, stand as *obstructions* to environmental protection and conservation.[23] Robert Wade has observed for developing countries that:

> Already over-stretched states in developing countries may not be able to provide the necessary resources to make [private property or state control regimes] work across myriad micro-locations. A malfunctioning approximation to a formalized system of state control or private property rights, based on a distant authority only dimly aware of local conditions, may be worse in terms of resource management than a strategy which aims to improve, or at least not impair, local systems of rules (1987:105).

Ronald Herring has argued, with specific reference to South Asia (but generally true elsewhere, as well), that:

> States in the region mock the theoretical states of academic discourse, dissolving into society with distance from the center, much as blood vessels diminish in size with distance from the heart until they disappear into spaces around cells (1990:65).

This is also true of industrialized states, as we shall see, below.

Resources, development, and the state

Why might states and governments find it so difficult to follow through on the effective implementation of international agreements? There are several reasons. First, a government must have the "political will" to see a deal through, which requires a convergence of interests among contesting groups and elites that may be difficult to achieve.[24] Second, assuming that state agencies and decisionmakers can generate such consensus at the legislative and executive level, they must still, as noted above, possess or find the necessary administrative and enforcement "capabilities" to pursue the commitment, as well as technical competence, financial, and other resources essential to implementation. Even if these first two conditions are met, a convergence between the interests and activities of the government and the interests and needs of those who utilize the resources in question will be necessary (Ascher & Healy 1990:17–30; Gallopin, Gutman & Maletta 1989). Although this last requirement might seem self-evident, it is not. Too often, "environmental protection and conservation" projects consist of plans and programs that pay little attention to conditions on the ground, with failure or unanticipated consequences the result (see, e.g., Ascher & Healy 1990; Shiva 1991; Peluso 1992; Rich 1994).

We can explain these outcomes from three different perspectives: externalization, relations of "affection," and marginalization. In resource-rich[25] industrialized, capitalist states, the environment is *externalized* with respect to the economy.[26] Thus, not only are the "incorrect" price signals sent to the economy (thereby commodifying the environment as well as creating externalities in the conventional sense), the environment is further abstracted from society by being regarded as a simple, exogenously-generated input to production. This has two consequences: first, Nature is made interchangeable with capital—and, in some optimistic views, with technology—and considered only as something useful if it produces a "return on investment." Second, as can be seen in discussions of "transferable pollution rights," it also has the effect of offering Nature up to the highest bidder (Passell 1994).

In formerly-socialist countries, still subject to scarcity of inputs and, in many instances, now driven by what Michael Burawoy and Pavel Krotov have called "primitive bartering among enterprises" (1992:18), the environment has been largely subordinated to an *economy of affection* necessary to fulfill basic industrial requirements. In this instance, resources are appropriated for purposes other than just production (Block 1990:25–29). Any signals intended to modify environmental exploitation that might be sent by the authorities to enterprises are lost in the noise of primitive exchange. Either they are disregarded, being too small and ineffectual, or they stand as an obstacle to output. The state's right to control and allocate resources is no longer merely contested; it is almost wholly non-existent. Central planning has been replaced by barter; property rights have been altered, but not in a way that promotes environmental conservation (or even efficient production).[27]

In less-developed countries we find the phenomenon of "marginalization." We are presented with state institutions that are fragile and lack legitimacy (a problem not unknown in developed countries). The weakness of developing country governments and states has been recognized generally as involving lack of "capacity," an inability to intervene effectively in various areas of socio-economic life (Evans, Reuschemeyer & Skocpol 1985:351–52). Two reasons are usually offered for this shortcoming: first, state agencies may lack "autonomy" in that they have very little wherewithal to independent action. Second, the state may be a "captive" of society (rather than the more-commonly imagined converse). As a result, it is so riddled by elements of domestic society that it is simply another societal institution among many, and not an autonomous actor.

These two explanations are related. To the extent that the state is intertwined with society, its agencies will find themselves constrained in their freedom to act in the best interests of society at large or the "environment." The residual power and autonomy of the state then rests not on the independent exercise of capacities. Rather, it is a function of the degree to which agencies can distribute favors, extract resources via the market, and create or reinforce social obligations among domestic groups. In its effort to exercise control over resources, the state may use law and force to marginalize those who have been customary users of the resource. By declaring through law the state's ownership of resources, the right to exclude or restrict traditional users is established, and this right is, as often as not, enforced via the state's police powers.[28] Of course, the state is not literally, itself, the beneficiary of such acts; the likely winners will be political and economic elites who, alone or in league with foreign capital, are able to appropriate the resources for their own benefit (Peluso 1993; Ribot 1993).

Rather than having re-created a "strong" European state, in which law and market operate in parallel, most developing countries have had Western legal systems imposed on much older, often pre-colonial or even colonial social formations. In the struggle for domination, it is no surprise that the older system absorbs the newer one. The result is that legal efforts to protect the environment or pursue particular policies are undermined by older "webs of social relations" (Migdal 1988; Ribot 1990a, 1990b).

There is some reason to think that this problem extends even to industrialized states, albeit in somewhat different form. Even where states are strong, and there is a strong distinction between legal/bureaucratic systems and the market, state competence *and* autonomy are increasingly coming under challenge.[29] Furthermore, because the impacts of various types of environmental degradation are not uniform across national territories but, rather, unevenly distributed *within* those territories, national governments will be increasingly hard put to mediate and manage the resulting patchwork of effects and costs without discrimination among regions.[30]

One of the fundamental bases of state power is control over access to resources located within the national territory. Governments are in a position not only to grant property rights to resources but also to use them or allocate them to specific users for state-building or state-sustaining purposes. In Western, industrialized countries, this privilege has been internalized and the capability is pretty much taken for granted (although often railed against by both political right and left). Not only are national authorities in a position to control the flow and exploitation of resources to certain users, they also do so within the context of a well-developed legal system that has evolved in parallel to markets where property rights are bought and sold (Libecap 1989). State agencies can also tap into these markets and extract revenues and resources for their own purposes. In many countries, East, West, North and South, such interventionist behavior has, at times, accounted for a not-inconsiderable fraction of national revenues.

At the same time, these capabilities are not nearly so strong when it comes to *altering* deeply-rooted property rights systems so as to promote environmental conservation or protection, because such efforts appear to undermine existing property rights and social institutions. Governments can hardly command that new systems of property rights be instituted forthwith and not expect resistance from those whose property rights have been modified or annulled (see chapter 4). Hence, there is a fundamental problem with state and government *legitimacy* that arises in the effort to alter patterns of resource management. This problem must be addressed.

All of this is not to say that states or governments are irrelevant in the face of global environmental change; to the contrary, at both the international and domestic levels, state involvement is essential. It does, however, suggest a need to change our focus of analysis to take into account potential and existing bureaucratic and institutional incapacities, and imagine how these shortcomings might be addressed. We need to understand how to "mesh" the structure and organization of environmental protection, preservation and restoration with the structure and organization of local societies and groups in affected areas. This means that these communities must be central actors in planning efforts, and must not be treated as unwanted externalities to those efforts.

To put this point another way, effective responses to global environmental change, in all of its manifestations, require a far better understanding of the webs of social and productive relations that characterize communities, greater knowledge about the ways in which these local systems are linked into global ones via systems of exchange, institutions, and norms, and vice versa, and a much better understanding of how to "couple" global agreements with local needs and conditions.[31] This understanding cannot be acquired until we have a clearer idea of the causal relationships between social processes and changes in Nature.

Environmental change and resource regimes

The ways in which we conceptualize environmental problems thus have a great deal of influence on how we try to address them. This may seem obvious, but the choice of one analytical framework over another can mean the difference between success and failure when the time comes to implement policy. Global environmental change is especially problematic in this respect. It is commonly viewed in terms of its most publicized manifestation, global warming. But global warming is a secondary consequence of a variety of localized human activities that result in other forms of environmental damage. The web of causes and effects are the result not of relatively straightforward physical relationships but complex social and natural ones. The analytical and policy literatures generally fail to pursue these latter notions of social complexity, even though they may have serious implications for policy and need to be addressed prior to the negotiation of international agreements.

This failure is understandable: the complexity of these sociospheric and biospheric connections often produces a confusion of causes, consequences, and linkages. More importantly, the complex linking of local and global means that some of the most important causes and consequences of global change—the sum of a myriad of individual human choices and actions, and the cumulative effects on a myriad of human lives—are inevitably distributed in an uneven fashion over a large number of nation-states, cultures, and societies, all of which complicates problem-solving. The very real existence of complex social linkages underlines a fundamental problem in thinking about approaches to environmental protection: if existing "borders" are a problem, where and how are we to draw boundaries for managing resources so as to facilitate such protection?

We take it for granted that ecosystemic boundaries have little correspondence to political, economic, and social institutions at the international level. This is one reason why international cooperation is seen as being so critical if global environmental problems are to be addressed. The same poor fit is true at the national and even local levels: the jurisdictions of virtually all governments match poorly to Nature. This suggests that environmental governance is problematic no matter where one looks. What, then, are we to do?

One solution might be the institutionalization of "bioregionalism." A bioregion is an area whose borders have been drawn, and governance components designed, so as to correspond to ecological boundaries. According to this logic, if we run our affairs in this manner we will have no choice but to act according to the constraints of the natural world, using only the resources available locally and eschewing conflicts arising from different natural factor endowments (Andruss, et al. 1990; Lipschutz 1991c; see chapter 4). But even bioregions are social constructs inasmuch as the natural world is better characterized by borderlands or ecotones than hard and fast borders. At any rate, what would be required to adapt existing institutional frameworks, or create new ones, in the effort to replace counties, states and provinces by bioregions? We would, in such a process, only be producing new situations in which society and Nature would be mismatched.

An alternative to bioregionalism is to look at the relationship between specific human systems of resource exploitation and the resources themselves: a political economy of Nature. An expansion of Herring's picture of "local arrangements for dealing with natural systems . . . embedded in a larger common interest defined by the reach of eco-systems beyond localities" (1990:65) is in order here. These "arrangements" can be regarded as resource-using social institutions or "resource regimes."[32]

A social institution is a management or social choice scheme for providing a collective good or dealing with a public bad; it is, in other words, a form of collective action (Hechter 1990; Hechter, Opp & Wippler 1990). It creates a "conjunction of convergent expectations and patterns of behavior or practice" through the rules and roles that make it up (in this sense, it is very close to the international political economy conception of a "regime"). The result of this conjunction is, as Oran Young puts it:

> [C]onventionalized behavior or behavior based on recognizable social conventions . . . [that] are guides to action or behavioral standards which actors treat as operative without making detailed calculations on a case-by-case basis (1982:16).[33]

According to Young, "Social institutions may and often do receive formal expression (in contracts, statutes, constitutions, or treaties), but this is not necessary for the emergence of or for the effective operations of a social institution . . ." (1982:18).

From where do such arrangements come? There is no reason to think that, *contra* the conventional wisdom about international regimes, social institutions are always—or even very often—the product of negotiated bargains among participants (Hechter 1990). Recent scholarship has focused on the deliberate construction of international regimes under conditions of anarchy and the process of negotiation among states,[34] but many resource-using social institutions are the outcomes of decades, even centuries, of material production, ecological change, and social interaction (McEvoy 1988).[35] They are historical and cultural artifacts, arising out of long-held customs, the structure of society, and the nature of the resource being managed. To be sure, such regimes are a reflection of power relations as they have developed within a society, but these are not wholly unfettered or one-way relations of power. Rather, it is their historical constitution *within* a society that legitimizes such power relations and often leads to the reification of the institutions themselves.

If we regard international agreements to protect the global environment as representing the "peak regime," in a system of many thousands of smaller-scale resource regimes, the difficulty of generating responsive action through these regimes becomes immediately apparent. It is not even clear that such international diplomatic efforts are linked to anything meaningful, since they cannot begin to alter the fundamental rules, roles, and relationships that constitute these micro-level regimes. *This may be the case not only in developing countries but in the industrialized world, as well.*[36] Fiscal and regulative levers may be able to reach into these institutions in some places, thereby modifying activities that are environmentally damaging. They are, however, likely to be next to useless in others. This raises the question: What then?

One answer is to reconceptualize our view of the relationship between society and Nature and our understanding of the relative roles of agency and structure in these relationships. We are all, in many ways, part of and implicated in such relationships, even though we may be quite unaware of them. To change these relationships—to do so consciously and collectively—is to act in a way that not only changes our *material* relationship to Nature but also *reconceptualizes* our place in Nature. This involves "reconstructing" resource regimes.

The social (re)construction of resource regimes

As an example of this process, consider Redwood Summer, the effort in 1990 to protect old-growth redwood stands in northern California. In many media accounts, Redwood Summer was tinted by somewhat rose-colored recollections of the 1960s. It became, almost, a "happening," pitting old political activists and new environmentalists against the capitalist, multinational "despoilers" of nature. Supposedly dedicated to civil rights for trees, it was consciously modeled on the Freedom Summers of three decades ago.[37] The circus atmosphere of the proceedings, and the way in which clashes between participants and loggers were portrayed in both organization journals and the public media, led many outside observers to expect either thrilling victories or agonizing defeats. Thus, it was not surprising that, after the dust had settled, Redwood Summer was assessed by many as having been unsuccessful: No grand movement emerged, no mass conversion of the blue-collar inhabitants of the region took place, and not much happened to indicate that the old-growth trees would, in fact, be protected (although, more recently, there has emerged a recognition that, as an exploitable resource, the old-growth forests of the region are on the verge of disappearing; see chapter 4).

Nevertheless, Redwood Summer could be seen as symptomatic, and symbolic, of an increasingly common transformative process in modern society that is altering the nature of political transactions and activity. This process has not only local and national implications and consequences, but international ones, as well. The participants in Redwood Summer were engaged in an effort to change the very basis of the relationship between trees and people, between Nature and society, by redefining the constitutive rule structure of the "resource regime" put in place so many years before by state and federal governments, in concert with railroad and lumber companies (see chapter 4; Hays 1990). If it had been a success, Redwood Summer would have led to the creation of a new social choice structure[38]—or governance arrangement—within which would apply new types of property right relationships. These would alter not only the nature and locus of control of the forest resource, but its legal and ethical "standing," as well.[39] At the same time as this process was taking place, participants in Redwood Summer were making a conscious effort to generalize the legitimacy of these new constitutive rules into the global arena—even if only symbolically—in an effort to extend the principles of Redwood Summer into the realm of global politics (Lipschutz & Mayer 1993).

In order to understand this process of renegotiation or social reconstruction of resource regimes and Nature, we must first consider the question of "property rights." Property rights used here, delineate the right of actors to behave in particular ways in various arenas, establish liability for actions, and convey rights to ownership and exploitation of physical goods.[40] These rights can also be defined in terms of systems of rules, customs, norms, and laws that specify relationships between actors and their political, economic, and physical environments (Lipschutz 1989: ch. 2; 1991a). Gary Libecap writes:

> Property rights are the social institutions that define or delimit the range of privileges granted to individuals to specific assets. . . . Property rights institutions range from formal arrangements, including constitutional provisions, statutes, and judicial rulings, to informal conventions and customs regarding the allocations and use of property. . . . By allocating decision-making authority, they also determine who are the economic actors in a system. . . . (1989:1)

Although property rights, according to Libecap's definition, designate *who* the "economic actors" in a system are, they say nothing about *how* these actors come to occupy their positions of economic or more general social and political power. Nor is there any suggestion whether those positions might be changed or undermined by forces other than either markets or revolution. In point of fact, the positions of economic actors can be affected by forces other than these two.

Property rights come in two forms: constitutive and regulative. *Constitutive* rules are fundamental organizing principles of social institutions and politics (or social choice mechanisms, in John Dryzek's terms). Rather than *regulating* behavior, constitutive rules establish *qualifications* for engaging in particular types of behavior. Constitutive rules grant to actors the authority to act and, rather than specifying rules of play, they prescribe frameworks for play.[41] Constitutive rules delineate eligibility requirements including who constitutes a legitimate actor within a particular social arrangement and what the criteria are for this designation of legitimacy. *Regulative* rules define norms of behavior within a specified social arrangement in which legitimate actors are already identified or given and specify how, and how much, of a given behavior one might engage in (Ruggie 1989:23; Dessler 1989:454–58). In some sense, constitutive rules, by defining *who* has a right to play, also define *who one is*. In other words, constitutive rules literally constitute identity which, in any event, only exists within a social context (see chapter 7).

We might look at a particular fishery regime, for example, and note that only certain qualified individuals (or actors) are eligible to participate in the exploitation of the resource, and then only under very specific conditions or strictly limited times. The right to participate might be purchased—as in the case of fishing licenses—or it might be usufruct—acquired through familial or other ties (Acheson 1989). Such required qualifications are *constitutive* of the fishing system (as well as those who fish, it might be noted). Given eligibility, rules may also exist for the taking or dividing of the resource—how much at one time, when during the year, open and closed areas, etc.—but these rules are regulative.[42] An actor, in other words, must be eligible before being allowed to exploit the resource.

This entire system of participation and exploitation constitutes a resource regime; indeed, on a larger scale, such systems not only constitute regimes, they legitimate the very idea that such arrangements can exist, as David Dessler illustrates with an example drawn from arms control:

> [W]hen two nations sign an arms control treaty, they not only adopt a set of operative arms control regulations, but they also reproduce the rules associated with the underlying practice of sovereignty (rules that give the nations the very identity required to make treaties possible) (1989:469).

The authority to act under such circumstances derives not only from the relative power or wealth of actors, but also from the legitimacy conferred on them through the constitutive rule system. A powerful actor can, of course, violate the rules, but potentially at the cost of having others decide to defect, to not participate in the arrangement any longer.[43]

How are these ideas relevant to the arguments regarding the reconstruction of resource regimes? Resource regimes are ordinarily embedded within larger social institutions—communities of stakeholders—and constitute only a part of the material base of that community. But such regimes are not only material, they are also *ideational*, involving collective cognition, ideas and explanations. These regimes place resources and Nature in a particular relationship to the community, thereby constituting the meaning of the resource as well as the identity of the community. To put this another way, the identities of logging and fishing communities are bound up with their relationships to the resource (and what happens to this identity when the resource is gone?).

Resource regimes are, consequently, not determined only by the material conditions of production, they are also a consequence of the means of social reproduction, as well as being integral to such reproduction. Such regimes can therefore be changed by the depletion of a resource as well as by ideational or cultural redefinition—a process that Luther Gerlach (1990) has called the "cultural [re]construction of the commons". Through this, the constitutive rules of social choice mechanisms for resource management are changed as a result of contestation not only within the public domain but, often, outside of the bounds of the authoritative political process.[44] John Dryzek points out that:

> The concept of social choice is not coterminous with governmental authority systems: governments constitute just one category—or, in some cases, just one component—of social choice. . . . It should also be noted that social choice mechanisms can have informal as well as formal components. Thus, social choice in most political systems proceeds in the

> context of constitutional rules; *but in addition, all such systems possess informal channels of influence and communication, without which they could hardly operate* (1987:8; my emphasis).

It is a common error—particularly among policy makers and some political scientists—to think that such a process, or the change that results, outside of constitutional channels is somehow illegitimate or necessarily represents a wholesale challenge to the legitimacy of a political system.[45]

In principle as well as in practice, there is no reason that the constitutive base of a social choice mechanism—or, in this case, a resource regime—must remain fixed, or subject only to change through state-sanctioned, institutionalized procedures. As Charles Lipson has noted, constitutive rules, such as they are, are never fixed permanently because one of their central purposes is the "rationalization and maintenance of social relations" in the domestic arena, as well as the international one. Therefore, observes Lipson:

> [C]hallenges [to constitutive rules] are important because . . . they do not have fixed meanings of decontextualized significance. Rather, [the rules] . . . are continually reproduced and redefined in the dispute process as the actors use or resist existing standards (1985:32).

At the domestic level, the development and application of constitutive rules in social choice systems or regimes incorporate not only interests and authority, but also socio-cultural rules and values. Concepts of property thus arise out of the economic *and* political history of a society—the history of its political economy—and are reflected in institutionalized relationships within the society. The principles used to explain these rules reflect and justify social and class structure and the distribution of wealth and power as they exist within that society (Augelli & Murphy 1988). Among different societies and states, the explanations for such distributions will vary and the basic constitutive rules will differ. Inasmuch as the roots of these rules, and their explanations, are not only legislative but also, to a large degree, cultural (in the sense of having historically-contingent origins), change often takes place via cultural transformations rather than legislative procedures.[46] Thus, Gerlach notes that:

> The participants in a global-resource management controversy . . . inhabit and may officially or voluntarily represent nation-states or other territorial units. As such, they possess particular cultures of adaptation that shape the way they view the problem and contribute to its resolution (1990:327).

What conclusions follow from the notion that cultural change can affect the constitution of what, at first glance, appear to be institutionalized and unchangeable resource regimes? At one level, what we might characterize as "environmental conflicts" can be seen as attempts by established interests to protect their claims to various types of resources and to resist efforts to change these rights. At another level, however, súch controversies involve efforts to redefine the constitutive basis of an existing regime for resource management. In chapter 3 the latter point is developed. Here, the argument is examined that action must first of all, be directed to those aspects of Nature with which we are the most familiar: the local.

From the global to the local

There is a growing body of *functional* evidence that suggests that environmental protection, restoration and conservation of resources might be accomplished more efficiently and effectively through more concentrated efforts at the local and regional levels (international coordination problems, discussed below, notwithstanding). There are also *analytical* grounds for a more localized approach, based on the structure and nested nature of resource regimes. These arguments rest on the notion that people are more likely to act collectively when their personal experiences and surroundings are implicated in a process than they are to respond to directives from a distance or abstract predictions of future dislocations.

More than this, the "stickiness" of large-scale social institutions makes changing them a difficult proposition, for a number of reasons. If we regard a social institution as, first, the embodiment of power relations within a society and, second, having as one of its primary goals social "reproduction" over time, the potential for significant, large-scale reform in the absence of major crisis would appear to be severely circumscribed, as suggested above. Such institutions can be changed, as indicated in the history of environmental regulation over the past three decades; conversely, the rise of the "Wise Use" movement in the United States demonstrates that resistance by those whose interests are affected by abstract and distant reform can become quite powerful.[47]

Similar conditions apply at the international level: collective action emerges only when someone's interests appear to be threatened by changes in the *status quo*.[48] Environmental regimes are negotiated by states, who are highly resistant to imposing on themselves an enforceable obligation to alter domestic social institutions in a serious way. Indeed, this is why so much attention is paid to economic "incentives" that alter relative prices as a means of changing consumer behavior on a large scale. Not only are such incentives "naturalized" by reference to market "efficiency," they also leave untouched fundamental structures and relationships within society. In many instances, they also impose costs on those who are sorely put to challenge the reforms.[49]

Moreover, incentives legislated at a distance may produce behavior or outcomes quite different from what is intended (McEvoy 1988). In reproducing social institutions through legislative and fiscal mechanisms, one is, in essence, recreating the relationships that caused the environmental degradation in the first place. In other words, we can see regimes and social institutions as mechanisms intended as much to *maintain* or *restore* structural relations of power as arrangements to facilitate collective action and cooperation (as is more commonly assumed).[50]

We need to ask what might be the appropriate level and scale for efforts intended to reconstruct collective behavior and social relations not only *instrumentally* but also *structurally*.[51] It is at the *local* and *regional* levels, that is, at the level of the operating resource regime itself, that we must focus, where people's awareness is part of the conditions of their existence, and not merely an abstraction.

The functional argument for focusing locally rests on five points: (1) scale of ecosystems *and* resource regimes; (2) assignment of property rights; (3) availability and location of social knowledge; (4) inclusion of stakeholders; (5) sensitivity to feedback.[52]

Scale of ecosystems & resource regimes

Although the environmental effects of certain activities may be manifested or mediated via a commons resource, these activities tend to be bounded in social, economic, and physical terms. While it is true that, even on a local level, political systems rarely overlap with natural ones, there is, nonetheless, a logic to the scale of systems of production that argues for thinking in terms of such limits. What we are confronted with are problems of, on the one hand, *collective action* at a limited spatial scale and, on the other, *coordination* among units at larger scales. This, in effect, separates the combination of collective action and coordination that is undertaken together in international regimes.

Social institutions for appropriation of resources and production of goods, while coupled into systems of national and global extent, are physically localized: factories, farms, forests and cities are all spatially-limited. Lumber mills draw mostly on local forests and labor; cities have regional impacts. While it is true that factories which produce electronic goods, such as VCRs, consume mostly intermediate goods that may come from the other side of the world, any particular factory will also have l vironmental impact, drawing on a localized labor force and helping to reproduce one part of a local community.[53] The factory is linked to other localized sites of production in other places, where impacts are also largely localized. Even though the demand of the first factory drives the pollution generated by the others (which, in turn, may drive similar impacts elsewhere), we find, once again, the nesting described by Herring (1990:65).

Assignment of property rights

Standard neo-classical economic analysis argues that degradation of resources and the environment result from the inappropriate "assignment" of property rights.[54] Absent well-defined, contract-based, preferably private rights, property will remain open access and subject to overuse and destruction. Only if a user can base the exploitation of a resource on firm expectations about its future availability, goes this argument, can she make a rational decision about both the pattern of resource use over time and the rate of use that will maximize economic return without destroying the resource in the case of renewable ones or undermining efficiency in the case of non-renewable ones (Smith 1981; Anderson 1991). The world is full of examples that invalidate this particular hypothesis, although such failures are usually explained away by reference to improper pricing, political intervention into markets, or outright "market failure."

The assignment of appropriate property rights to resources is not, however, simply a matter of auctioning rights to the highest bidder, in the expectation that the user will then find it in her rational best-interest to exploit the resource in a sustainable or maximally-efficient manner. Flows of energy and other inputs into ecosystems change across time periods, and may be variable across a large number of such cycles. Consequently, ecosystem productivity or populations of species can vary as a function of a large number of biogeophysical variables that are, for the most part, unpredictable (Yoon 1994).[55] Indeed, it seems likely that, without basic information about the nature of a resource, including but not limited to its extent, its reproduction cycle, its relationship to other resource systems, and so on—information that often cannot be acquired easily or quickly—any strictly economic assignment of property rights is likely to lead to degradation of the resource.[56]

The question of property rights becomes especially problematic in attempting to distinguish between "formal" and "informal" property rights systems. Formal systems assume the penetration of both legal and market relations throughout a society. When necessary, revisions to or enforcement of property rights occur via legislative and judicial means although, for the most part, contracts between parties and the legitimacy of the system are sufficient for it to be maintained. Informal systems of property rights are less formalized, more flexible, and highly diverse. Efforts to formalize such systems, as in the Dutch colonial and Indonesian state's codification of *adat*, privilege some groups over others, with different types of customary laws (see chapter 6). In addition, because formal property rights systems are generally based on individual or corporate appropriation, whereas informal ones are often collective, collisions between them can lead to the malfunctioning of both (Peluso 1992; Ribot 1990a, 1990b).

Availability and location of social knowledge

The issue of knowledge is central here: what is required to manage or sustain a resource? The information required for "sustainable" use of resources is frequently available as some form of "local knowledge and practice." It can be found in longstanding usage practices of indigenous peoples, who may have utilized the resource on the basis of exploitation and property rights systems that incorporate this information. This is not technical knowledge, as we commonly understand and apply it; it is a reversal of the argument made earlier: Environment and economy are "embedded" in society, which creates a "web of social relations" that binds members of a society to particular patterns of usage. Violation leads to sanctions; excessive use is, for the most part, not tolerated (Ostrom 1990; Hechter 1990).[57]

By this definition, local knowledge and practice as social knowledge is not restricted to antediluvian societies: Who controls resources and dispenses gifts in a community is an important bit of knowledge that cannot be measured by any technical or scientific means. A corporation's understanding of localized social relations can make a big difference in its being accepted by a community; "old-timers" may know things about local ecosystems—social as well as biophysical—that "new arrivals" or outsiders cannot.[58] Such knowledge may lie in the hands and activities of those who judge themselves to have a particular "stake" in the resource in question.[59] In either case, localized systems of property rights usage can be more closely tailored to the temporal and spatial variations of an ecosystem or, for that matter, relations between social system and ecosystem (a concept that sounds much like a "bioregion").

Property rights arrangements embedded in ecosystems can be regarded as localized "resource regimes," in the sense that they are social institutions "designed" to appropriate resources for specific purposes. Many such management arrangements have been documented in which various types of social, economic, and moral constraints, as well as an intimate knowledge about the character of a resource, restrict appropriation to levels that are sustainable over extended periods of time (Ostrom 1990: ch. 3; Berkes 1989; McCay & Acheson 1987; Bromley 1992). Some of these systems are found in "Western" societies (Miller 1989; Acheson 1989); others, as we shall see below and in subsequent chapters, are being newly "constructed" or "reconstructed" today. I do not mean to idealize such arrangements; under external pressures, they often prove less than robust, and the unregulated entry of growing numbers of users or changes in capture technology may also lead to resource degradation (McEvoy 1986). Nonetheless, the growing body of data on and case studies of such arrangements suggest that they are worth looking at more closely, especially in terms of their potential applicability to industrialized societies (a point to which I return below).

Inclusion of stakeholders

Participation in the functioning of a resource regime, by all who hold a "stake" in it, is essential to its maintenance. Such stakeholders are ordinarily local in some sense of the word.[60] Inasmuch as social knowledge is local, and in order to ensure equitable access and use, management schemes and decisions must be inclusive and participatory. Local participation is a buzzword in the development literature ("Sustainable Development" 1989; Korten 1986; Ghai & Vivian 1992; Burkey 1993), but there is an inherent logic in this notion that extends beyond the strictly economic self-interest of local users.[61] Social knowledge may be distributed among the users of a resource, and conservation or protection may depend upon its pooling. Attempts to maintain or change a local resource regime must be inclusive and participatory if such efforts are to generate the cooperation of all present and potential users and avoid defections. Finally, to the extent that collective action is based on non-economic factors, political solidarity and the creation of mutual social obligations among stakeholders would seem to be essential (Hechter 1990). This also argues for broad participation.

Simple access to technical information about the condition of a resource, while essential to the renegotiation process, is by itself an inadequate basis on which to generate a consensus within the user community about revising the rules of access and use. Although technical and scientific data are assumed to be the *sine qua non* for assessing environmental damage and devising schemes of protection or restoration, conclusions based on such data can be problematic because they are very often hedged with uncertainty. Consequently, not only is there disagreement among scientists about *technical* data and what constitutes *relevant* technical data, often there may be little consensus *within* a resource-using community itself about what constitutes proper social relations.

This raises the question about the relationship between science and politics. Science, by itself, cannot provide a community with values; only politics can do that. Resource regimes under stress include not only damaged Nature but also individuals who, along with their conditions of existence, are also under stress; to change patterns of use may require a change in values, as well. Only via an extended discursive process among stakeholders—a reconceptualization, as it were, of those conditions of existence—can knowledge be pooled and put to use to address such stress (Dryzek 1987). Because some resources—for example, water collection and distribution systems—have many and varied users, framing the use problem is likely to be a process of *social reconstruction*, rather than simply a matter of identifying shortfalls in supply or damage to wildlife or habitat (Gerlach 1990; Hawkins 1993; see also Anderson 1990).

A group of resource users acting through a resource regime is not merely an economic construct, it is an historically-constituted entity, a social institution. Consequently, it is characterized by specific relations of power, wealth, legitimation and affection (or disaffection) that have developed over time. Within such a regime, individuals are linked together through implicit and explicit bonds of social obligation, and their access to the resource is based upon patterns of access and distribution devised in the past (McCay & Acheson 1987; Berkes 1989; Ostrom 1990).[62] While these patterns may not be distributionally just, they do have the weight of history behind them.[63]

Feedback

Successful resource conservation, protection and restoration are very dependent on appropriate feedback, both social and technical. Such feedback requires a constant flow of information regarding, on the one hand, the condition of a resource and, on the other, the state of social relations among users. Some information can be obtained through technical monitoring and analysis—for example, air quality or water pollution monitors—but additional data are often only available from subjective observation by local stakeholders, who are in a position to observe the state of the resource (Ostrom 1990:79).[64] To the extent that "ecosystemic feedbacks"—knowledge about the changing condition of the resource—in the full, resource regime sense of the word, are observable only on a spatially-limited scale, this point represents an argument for a more localized focus where resource management regimes are concerned.[65]

Changing the internal structural relationships, rules and practices within a resource regime means, then, alterations in underlying (or constitutive) property rights, a process that is only possible through a renegotiation of these rights (Nuijten 1992). Inasmuch as the process of establishing or changing a localized resource regime is fundamentally political, it is also messy (Stone 1988: Conclusion). Legislation originating from "above" is rarely able to take into account the valid concerns of all stakeholders in a resource because of a lack of information about the institutional history and path dependency[66] of a resource management system, which are of critical importance to its revision (McEvoy 1988; Young 1989; Campbell 1992; House 1992). Moreover, the costs of altering this pattern can be significant; sunk costs are high and institutionalized paths are difficult to renegotiate (Libecap 1989). Resource regimes, in being created, reconstituted, or revised, *must* take into account such specific conditions if they are to have any chance of functioning in a sustainable fashion.

Restoring the commons

A focus on local resource regimes as the loci of action suggests a movement toward the "restoration of the commons." This is especially true in the sense that such a move involves a transformation of relationships between human beings and Nature based on the renegotiation of the rules governing a resource management regime. A common–pool (or common property) resource (CPR) is one managed and exploited by a limited group of users. Each user, by virtue of his or her membership in this group, is entitled to use or exploit the resource up to an amount determined by the group as a whole. Any member that repeatedly exceeds this quota can lose the right of access. The CPR is a "self-enforcing" system, in that each member has an interest in observing the rules and seeing that others observe them, as well, since repeated violations could lead to premature depletion (a point that applies not only to material use but aesthetic appreciation, too).

Moreover, because the users presumably also interact in a variety of different contexts, the desire to maintain good social relations also contributes to observation of the rules. A CPR approach to environmental protection is one that works best with a spatially-limited resource. If the extent of the resource becomes too great, or the number of users too large, the self-enforcement mechanisms become weakened or ineffective (Ostrom 1990; Bromley 1992). Restoring the commons—or constituting new ones—is, thus, about establishing new forms of management to replace older ones that are or have become ineffective in protecting specific resources from degradation. This requires, most importantly, the renegotiation of property rights, and this is no easy task,

A central problem with many systems of formally-constituted property rights to resources is that private ownership is a central tenet. The result is that such systems generally provide an unlimited individual right to *use* property as opposed to providing a limited right to use it in a fashion that protects the common interest. In other words, access to resources is framed simply as a right, rather than as a combination of rights and *responsibilities*. As a result, efforts to foster a common interest within a Western legal system take the form of restrictions that must be legislated in the face of conflicting and opposing interests.

If we choose to limit the harvesting of trees or mandate certain emission or mileage standards to be achieved by automobiles in the interest of controlling the production of greenhouse gases, we must do so by passing laws to this effect. Such laws, at first glance, would affect the interests of those served by their prior absence, so we might expect opposition to such projects. For the most part, in liberal political systems, the rights of individuals exist prior to the interests of the community (Orr 1992; Daly & Cobb 1989; Stone 1988: Part II). Similar resistance and conflict develops, however, even where resource regimes have been based on informal or "socialist" rules of property, as illustrated by the stories told in chapters 5 and 6.

The key question is: Can restoration of the commons substitute completely for international agreements on environmental protection? Clearly, they cannot, but they are important for two reasons. First, as argued above, material action to protect "global commons" must take place at the local and regional level; it must be reflected in the changed behaviors of people, all of whom are stakeholders in multiple resource regimes. Once it has been more generally recognized that environmental protection and resource regimes must be individually suited to local conditions, it will also become evident that such goals cannot be achieved through unilateral management or control by state bureaucracies or military or other forms of coercion (Peluso 1993).

Second, the reconstruction of resource regimes on a local and regional level provide both discursive and practical opportunities to transfer power away from state-based actors to local ones. Consequently, state agencies will have to become participants or stakeholders in a complex network of resource regimes and institutions, helping to coordinate among them, and fostering the creation of large numbers of "mediating organizations" whose purpose is to act as a buffer and filter between local contexts and these bureaucracies (Maniates 1990b; Carroll 1992; chapter 4, below). The model of environmental protection, conservation and restoration described here thus consists of a consciously-developed system of multiple layers and actors, linked loosely together in systems of political and social governance.

Conclusion

Global environmental change is a social process. It is a social process that is a consequence of the aggregation of a multitude of micro-level practices within what I call "resource regimes." These regimes are social institutions and, therefore, are based on rules, roles and relationships among actors and with the natural world. Dealing with global environmental change requires modification of these regimes, a task that may well be beyond the capabilities of international regimes and national governments. Change will have to be centered within these localized regimes, and it can come about only through a process of "renegotiating" the rules, roles and relationships that constitute them. Such renegotiations are becoming increasingly common and the result is a form of common–pool property resource in which stakeholders are invested by virtue of their participation in the renegotiation. The policy implications of this analysis differ greatly from the conventional wisdom which looks more to the national and international arenas as the foci of analysis and the sources of action or environmental damage. In the chapter that follows, we look more closely at the content of the renegotiation process, with a particular focus on the relationship between knowledge and practice, and their transfer through and application by global civil society.

CHAPTER 3

Linking the Natural World: Global Civil Society and Social Learning

Wilderness was never a homogenous raw material. It was very diverse, and the resulting artifacts are very diverse. These differences in the end-product are known as cultures. The rich diversity of the world's cultures reflects a corresponding diversity in the wilds that gave them birth.

(Leopold 1966:264)

What is the nature of environmental change? How is it transformed from an unconscious social process to a conscious political one? Who are the agents of such a process? How do they act, how are they constrained? This chapter is about modes of social learning about environmental change, global as well as local, and social and political action in response to such change. In chapter 2, I presented the *functionalist* argument for environmental protection, conservation and restoration through local resource regimes; in this chapter, I develop the *sociology of knowledge* theme promised in chapter 1. I argue here that such protection is being implemented, on a growing scale, by "global civil society." This can be conceptualized in terms of agents acting collectively through networks of knowledge and practice. Such agency operates both in opposition to and in concert with states and the international system, but always in terms of rules governing resource regimes. In a sense, global civil society can be seen as part of a growing system of global governance, rather than just an agent of reform, rebellion, or resistance.

As noted in chapter 2, environmental change is a *social* process, and not simply a physical one. It is a phenomenon that is socially "constructed" and "reconstructed" in specific ways, as human beings interpret, act, and come to grips with their impacts on Nature. Moreover, determining how environmental change is caused, how it could proceed, and in what ways it might be addressed are *political* exercises, and not just scientific or technological ones. Social processes and political exercises do not, however, simply occur in a transparent or non-problematical sense. It is one thing to explain how a small group of hunter-gatherers might have stumbled upon fire or developed flint tools; it is quite another to account for the transmission of bodies of knowledge and practice—technologies understood broadly—across centuries, continents, and cultures.[1]

All of this is important for policy-making around questions of environmental change and degradation because our understanding of particular technological problems has a great deal to do with how we address them. The process of learning about environmental change, (re)constructing the global environment, and acting in response is thus more complex than simple description or computer networking or the telling and retelling of stories or feedback cycles and equations. Rather, it is about the communication of bodies of knowledge and their subsequent application to real world circumstances. In this chapter, I propose that global civil society has become a central player in the process of social learning about local *and* global environments.

This chapter has three parts. The first presents a discussion and description of "global civil society" in order to make clear what it includes, as well as speculation on some of the reasons for its recent prominence. In the second part, I take up modes of social learning and argue that global civil society constitutes an emergent institutional framework for social learning, one that differs in important ways from "learning" in international regimes and governments and superficially similar concepts such as epistemic communities. Finally, in the third section I describe some of the ways in which practice becomes not only a method of communicating knowledge but also a means for changing the social structures through which global and local environmental change—both degradation *and* restoration—are taking place.

Global civil society: theory and illustrations

One of the most remarkable phenomena of the past ten to fifteen years has been the rise in global numbers of non-governmental organizations (NGOs), especially environment and development ones. By some estimates, there might be as many as several hundred thousand, although no one has actually counted them. Moreover, no one, to the best of my knowledge, has undertaken a really systematic look at whether the NGO phenomenon is really historically "different" or what particular confluence of agency and structure has caused this blossoming (but see Ghai & Vivian 1992; Ekins 1992; Princen & Finger 1994; Wapner 1996). Few observers seem willing, however, to gainsay the absolute increase in numbers.[2] Many observers have latched onto the concept of "new social movements" (NSM) to explain what is going on (Finger 1994). Some, such as James Rosenau (1990), place a heavy emphasis on the role of communications "hardware" and the enhancement of various skills to explain the rise of the "sovereignty-free" world of NGOs. Others suggest it is a consequence of "post-modernity" (Rich 1994). None of these approaches tries very hard to situate historically what it purports to explain and, if it does, it is often on the basis of some "crisis" or "legitimacy deficit" or alienation and so on. But "non-governmental organizations" and "social movements" have been in existence for some time. What makes this time different? Is it different?

I use the term "global civil society" in lieu of these other concepts and accounts. What, exactly, is global civil society?[3] First, global civil society is more than just a transnational phenomenon or a set of actors that deal only with the state system. It includes: (1) organizations or alliances that practice at the international or global level (Greenpeace, Climate Action Network) or across national borders (Ford Foundation, World Resources Institute); (2) organizations that provide technical assistance to local groups engaged in resource restoration (Global Rivers Environmental Education Network, or GREEN) and individual groups themselves; (3) individual groups that belong to national (WAHLI in Indonesia) or transnational alliances (Asia–Pacific People's Environmental Network); and (4) groups and organizations "in touch" with their counterparts elsewhere around the world or simply sharing an ecological epistemology.

Second, although the majority of the groups within global civil society are non-governmental organizations (NGOs), there are situations in which this distinction is not quite so easy to make. Because the sources of funds and technical support for groups and organizations are so varied, even "non-governmental organizations" (NGOs) are often linked to the state. One can find situations in which the staff of governmental administrative agencies are facilitating the practices of non-governmental groups or are in charge of mixed working groups and coalitions. One can find "revolving doors" between government, industry, and NGOs (leading to some muttering about another "Iron Triangle"). And some organizations, such as the Worldwide Fund for Nature, act as, in effect, sub-contractors for government agencies. As I shall argue in chapter 8, this has important implications for global environmental "governance" (see also Drabek 1987; Ghai & Vivian 1992).

Finally, although the "environmental movement" as a social movement can be seen as part of global civil society and is often conflated with it, the two are not the same if we go by the academic definition of a "social movement." Scholars of the new social movements tend to look at them either as an expression of frustration with institutionalized politics or as a manifestation of "post-industrial" identity politics.[4] Global civil society is more than this. To explain it, we have to look at the changing nature of global politics. Ken Booth has argued that:

> Sovereignty is disintegrating. States are less able to perform their traditional functions. Global factors increasingly impinge on all decisions made by governments. Identity patterns are becoming more complex, as people assert local loyalties but want to share in global values and lifestyles. The traditional distinction between "foreign" and "domestic" policy is less tenable than ever. And there is growing awareness that we are sharing a common world history....The [metaphor for the] international system which is now developing...is of an egg-box containing the shells of sovereignty; but alongside it a global community omelette is cooking (1991:542).

Booth's omelette includes a variety of ingredients: international regimes, international society, diplomatic culture and neoliberal institutions, all the components of what Barry Buzan might call a "maturing—if not mature—anarchy" (1991:174–81). Why should global civil society be added to what is, already, a fairly piquant recipe?

All of these concepts are, in the final analysis, overwhelmingly state-centric (Wapner 1995b). All are part of the menu of choices available to national governments as they struggle to retain elements of their sovereignty that are slowly diffusing away. Although the concept of international regime has not, after twenty years of debate, been clearly defined, international regimes do seem to be artifacts of state power, inasmuch as they serve the specific interests of state and governments (Krasner 1983; Litfin 1993). Hedley Bull, of course, wrote about an "international society" and, although he suggested that alternative future world orders might be "neo-medieval" in form, his conception of international society remained centered on states (1977:13, 264–76).[5] Diplomatic culture is an idea whose use and utility seem to have waned. Once it could be applied to an elite society of cultured, educated diplomats, who as representatives of their states' interests frequently met in a variety of different venues to deal with a wide range of issues. While even today such diplomats can still be found, most have been replaced by technically competent experts whose knowledge and experience are limited to very few issue areas and who do not have the cultural background evident in the old diplomacy.[6] Neoliberal institutions, according to Robert O. Keohane, simply represent the increasing socialization of states, such that "much behavior [in international politics] is recognized by participants as reflecting established rules, norms, and conventions, and its meaning is interpreted in light of these understandings" (1989:1). But who, except the most shortsighted realist, has ever suggested that states were never socialized?

Global civil society differs from all of these. The notion of civil society—from the Latin *civilis societas*—was originally used to refer not to those societies that existed within individual states or organized polities, but to the condition of living in a "civilized" community sufficiently advanced to have its own legal codes—*jus civile*—above that of individual states. Thus, barbarian and pre-urban cultures were not considered civil societies.

Subsequently, the concept underwent a bifurcation as it was adapted to meet the needs of various political theorists. Locke contrasted political or civil society with the paternal authority of the state, whereas for Hegel and Marx, civil society, or *burgerliche Gesellschaft*, referred to the state of human development reached by advanced peoples, where the economic and social order moved according to its own largely selfish principles and ends, independent of the ethical demands of law and political association. Unlike Locke, Hegel and Marx thought civil society to be self-seeking and lacking in the moral cohesion of primitive societies. Current usages focus mostly on the social, cultural, economic, and ethical arrangements of modern industrial society considered apart from the state, and they regard civil society as a realm that is somewhat autonomous of state control and, in particular, totalitarian control.[7]

Global civil society interacts with states but tries to maintain some degree of autonomy from them. It is never completely insulated from states, since it tends to occupy those "spaces" not directly controlled by states. The code of global civil society denies the primacy of states or *their* sovereign rights over the "sovereign" rights of individuals and communities.[8] Civil society is thus "global" not only because of those connections that cross national boundaries and operate within the "global, nonterritorial region" (Ruggie 1989:31), but also as a result of a growing element of global consciousness in the way the members of global civil society act.

Why should a "global civil society" be emerging at this particular juncture in world history and politics?[9] In my view, the answer to these questions lies in the political economy of the cold war period—military, political and economic—and its effects on global social and economic organization and associated modes of production (see also chapter 8). First, the cold war helped to bring to fruition the European project of universalizing the state as the ultimate form of political institution, through decolonization and reinforcement of state structures via military and economic assistance. Because the ideological division of the world was supportable only as long as there was also a matching territorial division, states became the ultimate unit of "keeping score." Alliances were preferable to territorial empires, moreover, because they more readily lent themselves to domination by leaders.[10]

Political and economic organization were, moreover, mutually constitutive.[11] The pursuit of the "Open Door," albeit in a somewhat different form, through GATT and the Bretton Woods system, brought virtually all societies in the "Free World" into the system of global economic liberalism (Ruggie 1983b). There was some recognition that such a system was, of necessity, a dynamic one, and subject to change. But there was also a widely-held belief that it had, more or less, attained a fixed form in terms of the number of states and their economic relationship to one another, except that the system would have to experience continuous economic growth in order to avoid a repetition of the Depression and instability of the 1930s.

This pattern of politics had two effects, one material, the other ideational. They have only been reinforced by the end of the cold war. A strictly functionalist explanation would suggest that environmental "externalities"—air and water pollution—and accidents—oil spills and nuclear mishaps—have led to the popular mobilization of interest groups or social movement organizations concerned about threats to health and survival and generally dissatisfied with the ways in which governments are dealing with them (Szasz 1994; Lipschutz 1991b). While I would not downplay this explanation, it seems to me to be incomplete insofar as it reduces actors and organizations to mere interest groups.

Robert Cox, and his colleague Stephen Gill, provide an analytical framework that I find much more illuminating.[12] Robert Cox (1987) writes about the idea of social and material transformation from the perspective of a historical materialism based on the writings of Antonio Gramsci. He argues that historical shifts in what he calls "ethics" and "rationalities" indicate social and material changes of major scope, and that these shifts originate with global changes in the means and modes of production. "Production," according to Cox:

> [C]reates the material base for all forms of social existence, and the ways in which human efforts are combined in productive processes affect all other aspects of social life, including the polity. Production generates the capacity to exercise power, but power determines the manner in which production takes place (1987:1).

This is the basis for his understanding of world order and how it changes. Elsewhere in his work he characterizes his approach as one based on the notion of historical structures, one that:

> [F]ocuses on the structures that constitute the framework or parameters for action and that shape the characters of individual actors. . . . Actors are conditioned by the resources, norms, expectations, and institutions of the

> societies in which they grow up. They are limited by the social–economic and military–political pressures of their environment. They are products of history (1987:38).

Historical structures are those institutional practices—or, in the language I use above, various social institutions—that make up the fabric of any society. They prescribe what is expected and proscribe what is forbidden. They condition human behavior, if not its nature, and exercise a constraining influence over the possibilities for individual action in history (Cox 1987:38; Lipschutz 1989: ch. 2; Thompson 1984:135). Historical structures, according to Cox, exist in the *longue durée* described by Fernand Braudel. Cox also suggests that:

> Participants in a mode of social relations of production share a mental picture of the mode in ideas of what is normal, expected behavior and in how people arrange their lives with regard to work and income. . . . Specific social groups tend to evolve a collective mentality, that is, a typical way of perceiving and interpreting the world that provides orientation to action for members of the group.

The first set of ideas are "ethics"; the second, "rationalities" (1987:22, 25). Ethics and rationalities are "intersubjective" in that they can only be really understood from within the classes and social groups that practice them. Traditional Marxism would argue that ethics and rationalities are simply superstructure determined by the material substructure. But Cox and Gill argue that the process of social change is as much a function of "progressive self-consciousness" as of structural constraints and material conditions (Gill 1993:36–37; Cox 1993).

As an example of this, Cox points to the potential emergence of "whole segments of societies [that have] become attached, through active participation and developed loyalties, to social institutions engaged in collective activities" (Cox 1993:272). He and Gill call them "counter-hegemonic" or, drawing on Gramsci, "historic blocs." This is happening, according to Gill, because the contradictions of economic globalization and political change have created a crisis of the old hegemonic structures and forms of political consent, which are now coming apart and providing an opportunity for, among other things, the emergence of a transnational civil society (Gill 1993:32–33). Ultimately, according to Cox,

> The condition for a restructuring of society and polity in this sense would be to build a new historic bloc capable of sustaining a long war of position until it is strong enough to become an alternative basis of polity. This effort would have to be grounded in the popular strata. The activities that

> comprise it will not likely initially be directed to the state because of the degree of depoliticisation and alienation from the state among these strata. They will more likely be directed to local authorities and to collective self-help. They will in many cases be local responses to global problems—to problems of the environment, of organising production of providing welfare, of migration. *If they are ultimately to result in new kinds of state, these forms of state will arise from the practice of non-state popular collective action rather than from extensions of existing types of administrative control* (1993:272; emphasis added).

I should add that, while I find the general argument persuasive, I have my doubts about whether global civil society as described above is truly a counter-hegemonic bloc wherein lie the seeds for a new polity. I think Cox and Gill may give too much emphasis to the relations of production and not enough to the flexibility of the relations of *social reproduction* associated with political institutions, especially under the long-term conditions characteristic of many environmental problems. While the transformation of modes of production is well underway, a crisis of the global material base—the environment—is not immediately obvious, although it could well emerge over the next twenty-five to fifty years.

In the contemporary economic system, with all of its changes, the environment still largely remains a component of the material base that is usually treated as being exogenous to society. Resources are something to be incorporated, as raw material, into the production process. Experience suggests, moreover, that as resources are depleted, substitutes are found, either in the form of new raw materials or new ways of doing things.[13] Neoclassical economists will even go so far as to argue that renewable resources, once degraded, can be restored or replaced with "appropriate" technologies. If the problem is too much carbon dioxide in the atmosphere, once the problem becomes too "costly," the market will come into play and we will simply devise means of stripping the gas out of the atmosphere. Economists may, of course, be correct, but if they are not, the damage to society might well be incalculable. How are we to know?

There is no way of knowing for certain. Faced with technical uncertainty of this sort, society as a whole is unlikely to respond either quickly or willingly, especially if the types of adaptations implied by the crisis threaten existing historical structures. If the threat to the material base is not immediate, but emerges over the longer term, it is likely that structures of reproduction and legitimation will be challenged by those who are slowly becoming aware of this crisis as a result of their training and their relationship to the state. These individuals are the intelligentsia, the educated, and the "powerful people." From the source of social legitimation—social elites—

there emerges a challenge to the social order and to the Gramscian hegemony of other elites.

In the longer term, it is these types of challenges, and not only changes in the modes of production, that serve to alter political and social practices and the social institutions associated with them. And these challenges arise from a civil society emerging to provide the basis for new institutional forms. But—and this is the important point—these forms are not wholly-autonomous of the present system of government and governance. That system nurtures those who issue the challenge and, indeed, as we shall see, the state plays an important role in legitimizing such institutions, even those that appear to be in active opposition to the state. This apparent paradox arises because the "state" is not a single entity under the conditions posited by Cox and Gill; rather, states are multi-level, pervasive, and in constant conflict with themselves: legitimation can come from the state in its international, national or local manifestations, a point to which I return in chapter 8, but which is also evident in the following chapters.

Global Civil Society and the Environment: Modes of Action

In general terms, we can identify four modes in which global civil society is organized and engaged in the renegotiation and reconstruction of resource regimes so as to change the global landscape of local environmental practices. These include: (1) ecosystem management and restoration; (2) fostering of localized environment/development projects; (3) environmental education; and (4) participation in national and transnational networks and alliances.

Ecosystem management and restoration

There are large (and growing) numbers of quasi- and non-governmental groups and organizations engaged in the management and restoration of environmental resources, often on an ecosystem basis. For example, individuals working on a small-scale watershed restoration project in the Sierra Nevada foothills (where two hundred had been documented by 1992; Kennedy & Greiman 1992) or the Chesapeake Bay drainages might not think of themselves as being linked into global networks. But they often receive visitors from other parts of the United States and the world, who come to study the project as a model for restoring other watersheds.[14] Those projects, in turn, inform others, and so on (Berger 1990). There are also organizations with a wider scope, such as GREEN in Michigan and River Watch in Vermont, that help to support, technically and financially, such efforts in the United States as well as other countries (see chapter 5). Individually, such projects might not seem very significant, but in aggregate they are, for two reasons. First, each stands as a form of social organization that can be studied and reproduced elsewhere, from both the technical and social perspective. Second, each also fulfills an *educational* function and draws local community members into the regime reconstruction project. Thus, practice begets knowledge and knowledge begets practice, a point returned to later in this chapter.

Local environment/development projects

Throughout the world, in industrialized countries as well as developing ones, there are burgeoning numbers of small, locally-oriented organizations engaged in the provision of a vast range of services to marginal and neglected populations, that incorporate environmental concerns. Often, these projects are initiated in a wholly-local fashion (Schneider 1988) in a manner that is fairly autonomous of the overarching state (Drabek 1987; During 1989; Bonner 1990; Korten 1990; Broad & Cavanagh 1993; Rich 1994).

For example, Brazil is the site of growing numbers of urban-based groups, with roots in the Christian base communities that emerged during the military dictatorship, who now seek to link environmental concerns with problems of urban pollution and economic justice (Jamie Anderson 1994). Many of these groups also draw on technical and financial assistance through global networks and transnational alliances established with other organizations in industrialized countries and even with the agencies of developed country governments. One example of an alliance between a Northern NGO and local projects is a program called "From the Ground Up," administered by the Center for International Development and Environment of the World Resources Institute (*NGO Networker*). The World Wildlife Fund/Worldwide Fund for Animals also funds and supports many projects of this type, and the Ford Foundation provides direct programmatic and financial support to local groups in many countries.

Environmental education

A third approach depends on locally-based activists (local to specific resource regimes). These are the people who undertake education, demonstrations, and proselytizing on behalf of environmental protection as well as the conservation of specific resources. Some of these groups are engaged in an effort to revise the constitutive basis for relationships between human society and nature; others are less ambitious in their goals (Lipschutz & Mayer 1993). Although traditionally environmental activists have been urban and suburban, they are appearing in increasing numbers in rural areas where many of the resources of greatest concern are actually located.[15] This element is discussed in greater detail below.

National and transnational networks and alliances

The fourth element of global civil society is based on networks and alliances, national, transnational and global, linked together by what their members see as common strategies and goals.[16] All of these networks exist under the overarching rubric of a general environmental ethic—what might be called an "operating system"—although the specific form of relations through the network and structure of the actors at the ends and nodes of the network vary a great deal. Some of these networks are quite deliberately contra-state, others are oriented toward state reform; a few are both. Some networks simply ignore the state altogether (Zisk 1992).

For example, WAHLI is a network of some three hundred environment/development groups in Indonesia that sometimes works with state agencies and, at other times, directly opposes them (see chapter 6). Greenpeace is something of a global network in itself, with both contra-state and state-reforming tendencies (Wapner 1996), while a number of observers even tend to view Greenpeace as a purveyor of environmental "imperialism" (Seager 1993: ch. 4). The Asia–Pacific People's Environmental Network, based in Penang, Malaysia, includes both urban and rural organizations, and operates at the international and regional levels; the Climate Action Network, a loose transnational coalition of environmental organizations, has branches in Asia, Africa, North America, South America, Western Europe, Eastern Europe and the Pacific.

NGO activities associated with the June 1992 UN Conference on Environment and Development (UNCED) in Brazil, and the September 1994 UN Conference on Population and Development in Cairo were coordinated through extensive transnational alliances and networks of communication. Indeed, according to some participants, NGOs were instrumental in formulating the language for various agreements and charters under negotiation for presentation at the Earth Summit (Spivy-Weber 1992; Hackman 1992; *In Our Hands* 1992; Woods 1993). Participants in global environmental networks are also deeply involved in ongoing negotiations on the elaboration of the Framework Convention on Climate Change run by the Convention Secretariat based in Bonn.[17] Even so-called indigenous peoples are creating such networks (Childs 1992; Maiguashca 1994; Wilmer 1994). All of these networks are organized around the protection of Nature, yet they also address concepts of place, nationality, culture, human rights, and species (Porter & Brown 1996:50–59).

Each of these forms of activity involve, in one way or another, efforts by participants in global civil society to "renegotiate" resource regimes. What is impressive is the extent to which this is happening at a local level; one need look only at the anthropological or sociological literature on virtually any developing country to find stories of struggles over the control of common property resources reflecting a variety of approaches, both violent and non-violent (Schmink & Wood 1992; Peluso 1992; Rush 1991). But these examples are "global" not only in the sense that some involve action in international and transnational fora but also because they are linked through global and transnational networks, alliances, communications and a shared ethic (or "sensibility," as Wapner (1995a, 1996) puts it).

Culture and the meanings of Nature

Struggles over resources do not take place in an informational vacuum. The grounds for altering resource regimes may be expressed in cultural-historical terms—witness the frequent evocation of Mother Earth or Native American principles in many environmental conflicts—or, conversely, the principle that resource privatization leads to better management. There is, however, usually also a strong knowledge base to such struggles, even among those strongly oriented toward culture and history, since this is required by the technological-scientific nature of ecology.[18] That is to say, many of the participants in these dramas are quite knowledgeable about basic ecological principles and linkages within and among ecosystems, as well as understanding the potential consequences of environmental degradation and destruction. Indeed, many trained experts, in addition to those designated as "epistemic communities", (P. Haas 1990, 1992a) are actively involved in these conflicts. There are also ongoing efforts to redefine cultural practices into the realm of "indigenous" or "local" knowledge as a means of legitimating them within the technological-scientific realm. Hence, struggle takes place not only over cultural and political claims, but also knowledge claims and problem definition.[19]

The result is that meanings have to be *negotiated*. When the term "negotiation" is used, it is not my intention to suggest the sort of legislative bargaining or environmental mediation with which we are relatively familiar (Young 1989; Cohen 1991; Evans, Jacobson & Putnam 1993; Susskind 1994). Rather, I mean to suggest a social and political interaction that involves a fundamental reworking of the *cultural meaning* of things elemental to society (Gamman 1994: ch. 4; Tsing 1993). Such meanings are more than just symbols or representations. As suggested in the discussion earlier in this chapter, they can be thought of as the intellectual framework to which our material systems are anchored and which give social purpose to those systems and help to legitimate them.

My argument draws on, but is not the same as, the Marxian notions of substructure and superstructure. Whereas traditional marxism regards ideas and ideologies as epiphenomenal rationalizations of material substructures, I consider the two to be mutually constitutive of each other (hence, "false consciousness" finds its analogue in "false materialism"). What this implies, then, is that a change in the intellectual framework, or "superstructure," can drive changes in political economy—in this instance, the political economy of a resource regime—or "substructure," just as surely as the reverse. This is contrary to conventional historical materialisms that only see changes in the material base as driving changes in the ideational superstructure. Thus, when I say that people are (re)negotiating the "meanings" of Nature, I mean to suggest that the meanings that they have held are no longer consonant with Nature as they see or now understand it (Hannerz 1992:153–54).[20]

To illustrate this point more clearly, consider whales and how the meaning of "Whale" fits into the political economy of particular times and places. In ancient times, whales were seen as monsters of the deep. To be sure, the biggest of the whales were very big, but consider how this meaning might have fit into the political economies of sea-based or fishing societies. Large whales could swamp a ship and, presumably, sometimes did; the meaning of "whale" thus contained a warning for hapless mariners, along the lines of "See a spout, get on out!" In more recent centuries, whales were transformed into a resource, a commodity, something to be torn from Nature. While the Great White Whale retained something of the monstrous significance of earlier times, Melville's fictional account placed Moby Dick squarely within the political economy of the times. *Whales were either monsters or resources*, but nothing else. Establishment of the International Whaling Commission (IWC), which held its first meeting in 1949, symbolized the full commodification of Whale. The IWC was intended to regulate the taking of whales, since some species were visibly declining in numbers or on the verge of being wiped out. Whales were no longer monsters, they were now an economically-significant resource (Peterson 1992).

Even this did not put an end to changes in the meaning of Whale. During the 1970s and 1980s, the social meaning of whales—and, indeed, all cetaceans—began to change more rapidly as their numbers further decreased. They were no longer commodities to be torn from Nature and consumed by industrial society, but representatives of a new relationship with Nature, to be nurtured and protected (they were, we might say, ethically-superior versions of ourselves). As Robert Hunter put it in his history of Greenpeace, *Warriors of the Rainbow*,

> Soon, images would be going out into hundreds of millions of minds around the world, a completely new set of basic images about whaling. Instead of small boats and giant whales, giant boats and small whales; instead of courage killing whales, courage saving whales; David had become Goliath, Goliath was now David; if the mythology of Moby Dick and Captain Ahab had dominated human consciousness about Leviathan for over a century, a whole new age was in the making (1979:229).[21]

Today, whales remain a type of commodity, and they will continue to be so, but they are "consumed" by whale watchers as *cultural* icons rather than as whale burgers.

The struggle over the cultural meaning of Whale continues, however, within the International Whaling Commission, inasmuch as not all countries hold this latest view (although even Norway and Japan defend continued whaling by invoking both science and aboriginal needs, rather than crass economic ones; see Pollack 1993). This is in keeping with a post-industrial political economy, which is oriented around the provision of services and the consumption of culture, rather than the production of material commodities and manufactures. But note the following: The change in the meaning of Whale, and the way the concept fits into a new political economy, has been as much the result of a much larger process of changing meanings of Nature as the depletion of whale populations.[22]

Such meanings can be renegotiated at the "local" level, too. As noted in chapter 2, most systems of resource exploitation are spatially-limited. And, even though such systems are almost always coupled to larger arrangements, the local remains an important unit of social interaction and political economy. It is at this level that appropriation of a resource takes place and that, moreover, the meaning and significance of Nature is greatest. Although it is risky to generalize this point, people tend, by and large, to establish their strongest identifications with the place in which they live. The local is one of the most familiar and least abstract of the many "places" they inhabit (Orr 1992) and it is imbued with the greatest personal and social meaning. Locality is also the place where people work, consume, have families and neighbors, and move around. These are practices that give further meaning to their lives.[23] Finally, locality is often where the sharpest contradictions between "superstructure" and "substructure" are to be found.

Consider, for a moment, the case of a community whose political economy is built on logging. Such a community will have a long history of logging, a large number of families whose members work in the industry, and a variety of businesses dependent on the stream of income that flows into the community from logging. (Recognize also that, generally speaking, most of the revenues generated by logging either leave the community or, as part of the process of capital accumulation, depend on transactions taking place elsewhere.) All of the people who are part of this political economy confer a particular meaning onto the Forest as a result of their social relationship with it. At the same time, there may also be people in the community, still linked to the political economy, who are not explicitly part of the logging "infrastructure." Some may be "environmentalists." Others may depend on the *preservation* of the Forest for their livelihood. The Forest will have a somewhat different meanings for these latter groups. Up to a point, these different meanings may be able to co-exist within a single community but, at times, they may become the basis for nasty and even violent conflicts within the community (cf. Redwood Summer).

Why should such a community renegotiate the meaning of the Forest? So long as the resource is in fairly plentiful supply, and contradictory meanings are able to co-exist, the incentives for renegotiation are rather small. But none of these communities is isolated from larger social and cultural forces; even as they defend their meanings, new ones are percolating in via various channels of communication. Not the least of these may be the arrivals of "new" carriers of "culture." This occurred in many rural parts of the United States in the 1960s and 1970s, leading to the often-celebrated confrontations between "hippies" and "rednecks."[24] Eventually, as a resource is diminished or degraded, the substructure for the local political economy becomes shaky. Traditionally, in a "boom and bust" economic system, this is a time for capital—and, perhaps, labor—to pull up stakes and move on. Increasingly, however, mobility is not an option[25] and, at such a point, strong incentives can develop to change the local political economy. To do this requires that the Forest become something other than what it has been, and new "uses" for what is left must be envisioned. In other words, a new meaning must *precede* a new political economy.[26]

None of this is meant to suggest that the process of renegotiation is easy. Inasmuch as it involves changing not only the meaning of place but also the meaning of *self* in relation to place (that is, individual and communal identities, as I have suggested above), the struggles can become quite intense and even violent. Nor should it be taken to mean that such changes are allowed to occur without interference from extra-local agents, be they corporate, commercial, environmental, judicial or bureaucratic. These extra-local agents may have an interest in blocking the process of change, or in seeing it move in one direction as opposed to another (as, for example, wilderness vs. multiple use). Indeed, just because extra-local environmental organizations may have preferences regarding the future political economy of a region, this does not mean that *their* meanings feed into the future political economy preferred by the inhabitants of a particular locale. (Think, for example, about the disputes over the right of Inuits to take whales in the context of *their* meaning of Whale.)

To sum up: the social institutions within which we live, through which we produce, and which often rely on the appropriation of Nature, are constituted not only by the visible artifacts of production and consumption but, also, by sets of rules that define one's place within the institution as well as one's relationships to others *and* Nature. Identities are constituted within social institutions by rules, roles, and relationships, and by meanings. To change the meanings of relationships is to change identities; to change identities is to change political economy; to change political economy is to change society.

Social learning, communication networks and global civil society

What is social learning? The foregoing discussion suggests that processes of renegotiation are, by and large, local ones in which stakeholders develop and agree on new meanings in a process largely, if not entirely, untouched by exogenous influences or forces. Nothing could be farther from reality; to reiterate, once again, Ronald Herring's point: "[A]ll local arrangements for dealing with natural systems are embedded in larger common interest defined by the reach of eco-systems beyond localities" (1990:65). We might revise this by saying: All local political economies are embedded in larger ones (whether they like it or not). In other words, "local arrangements" are influenced by larger ones, and vice versa. But, in the context of a renegotiation of the meanings of Nature and resource regimes, what is the character of this influence?

It is, I claim, a particular form of *social learning*, mediated by a network-type form of organizational structure and culture. More to the point, such renegotiations over resource regimes are about the (re)constitution of a diverse set of environmental phenomena as being linked together conceptually. While there are, of course, physical connections among many of the phenomena of concern, it is the combination of *social* with physical characteristics that makes them a linked set. And, it is social learning about this process, and responding accordingly, that makes environmental change, both global and local, more than just a policy issue to be addressed by governments.

As suggested in chapter 2, policy must take into account social actors other than the nation-state, but those other actors are not simply other levels of government or various kinds of interest groups. Rather, these actors are both cause and consequence of the process of renegotiation. It is the integration of new conceptions of environmental phenomena—facilitated by particular organizational structures and cultures—into everyday worldviews and practices wrapped around what have, in effect, become common property resource regimes, and the ways in which this changes human-nature relationships that, ultimately, may allow us to address the problems of concern.[27]

What, then, is meant by the term "social learning?" All learning is, in some sense, social, since all learning is the result of social interaction. Here, however, I mean to suggest the transfer of a body of knowledge and practice from one distinct social entity or institution to another.[28] Ernst Haas applies the notion of "learning" to what he calls "consensual knowledge." He asks: "How does knowledge about nature and society make the trip from lecture halls, think tanks, libraries, and documents to the minds of political actors?" "Knowledge," according to Haas, can be viewed as "a social epistemology, as a shaper of world views and notions of causation. . . . " The dissemination of knowledge takes place through the transmission of "consensual knowledge," which involves "generally accepted understandings about cause-and-effect linkages about any set of phenomena considered important by society. . . . " Specifically addressing the case of individuals affiliated with international organizations, he proposes that:

> [A]s members of the organization go through the learning process, it is likely that they will arrive at a *common* understanding of what causes the particular problems of concern. A common understanding of causes is likely to trigger a set of larger meanings about life and nature not previously held in common by the participating members (1990: 20,21,22, 24).

The suggestion here is that one becomes socialized into organizational culture by learning from others. One learns, first, the organizational worldview—presumably a function of notions about causality—and, second, what is required to succeed within the organization. Presumably, new consensual knowledge is transmitted throughout the organization in a learning process, as well.

Emanuel Adler writes of the "cognitive evolution" of states in a similar vein:

> [W]e can find the sources of collective learning in international relations at the national level—more precisely, in processes of intellectual innovation and political selection—and that with increasing interdependence and diplomatic, political, economic, and cultural contacts, nations transmit to each other the political innovations that have been selectively retained at the national level (1991: 50).

Again, there is a notion of socialization present here: to succeed in international politics, according to Adler, one must learn about the worldview of states in the system and adopt a common epistemology. This, then, is the "language" of international relations which national agents must "speak."[29]

Peter Haas and his colleagues have pointed to "epistemic communities" as one type of agent important in this process of learning and cognitive evolution:

> [M]embers [of epistemic communities] . . . not only hold in common a set of principled and causal beliefs but also have shared notions of validity and a shared policy enterprise. Their authoritative claim to policy-relevant knowledge in a particular domain is based on their recognized expertise within that domain (1992b:16; see also Breyman 1993).

Members of epistemic communities, consequently, not only learn from their research and from each other, they also adopt a shared framework of interpretation and cause-effect relations that orients their individual behaviors in a similar direction.[30]

According to Ernst Haas, consensual knowledge is not fixed, since it is subject to "continuous testing and examination through adversary procedures" (1990: 21).[31] By the same logic, the understandings held by an epistemic community may change as new information and understanding emerges from their joint enterprise. The assumption in both cases is that policy and practice can and will change accordingly (presumably for the better, although who defines what is "better" remains problematic) in response to the findings of new research projects. But this view of knowledge and learning is largely concerned with instrumental action, whereas policy is about politics (Litfin 1994: ch. 2). Policymaking also presumes a more-or-less uniform set of social processes to which knowledge can be applied with an expectation of more-or-less uniform results.

From one perspective, this is obviously a valid assumption: the same scrubbing technology applied to the same model of coal-fired generating plant around the world will, for the most part, work in the same fashion. But the *social* context and impacts of that technology cannot be assumed to be the same. As the very different performances of generally identical light-water nuclear power plants demonstrate, different "cultures" of monitoring and maintenance, access to financial resources and goal structures (e.g., output vs. environmental impacts) may result in very different performances by identical hardware installed in two different places even within the same country. In other words, technology is as much about social organization as it is about nuts, bolts, and meters. More generally, this is true of social relations and modes of production everywhere.[32]

Indeed, once we get past the level of hardware, or a mechanistic view of society and Nature, we find ourselves in a world of enormous social diversity and difference. While there are obviously some general rules, both scientific *and* social, that apply no matter what the context, one cannot take much else for granted.[33] As this point has been made with respect to another, apparently biological, system:

> Health phenomena that have long been regarded as natural manifestations of universal biological processes are now understood to be—to a significant degree—*locally variable, culturally mediated, socially situated, historically contingent, politically conditioned and differentiated by gender and age* (Kessel 1992:65; emphasis added).

To clarify this point further, consider *ecology* as a science. There are certain ecosystemic laws and relationships that are universally applicable (so long as we restrict ourselves to Planet Earth), or are applicable to certain specified domains (fresh water, ocean, soil, atmosphere, forests, etc.). Nonetheless, ecosystemic structures may be quite different from one place to another—even at very small scales as, for example, we find from one tree to the next in tropical rain forests. In a similar fashion, specification of the economic structures and communities of a region or locale can only be accomplished through detailed field research in a particular place. Or, as Wolfgang Sachs puts it:

> The search for general laws...implies concentrating on a minimum of elements which are common to the overwhelming variety of settings. The appreciation of a particular place with a particular community loses importance (1992b:32).

Once we consider social processes and Nature *together,* we may find that difference comes to overwhelm much of the similarity we sometimes ascribe to ecosystems.[34]

When thought of in this way, knowledge—here used in a general sense—becomes more than just a set of cause-and-effect relations subject to repeated testing via the scientific method. It becomes central to the relationship between "facts" and "values." There may be good reason to believe that, within a specific social context, generalized principles can be formulated—after all, what is "tradition" but the repetition of certain practices intended to elicit identical outcomes?—but there is no basis for assuming that similarly specific principles apply even to neighboring *social* units within a larger society. To a significant degree, in other words, knowledge of resource regimes may be, as I suggested in chapter 2, "local knowledge." There it functions as something akin to a structural element in a social process, becoming embedded in everyday life as a set of beliefs (or meanings) about the operation of sets of social relations and relations of production.[35]

Examples of local knowledge are seen most clearly in the practices of "indigenous peoples," who are generally regarded as having lived in particular places for extended periods of time, but they can also be found in industrialized contexts. Every human society has its own system of beliefs (myths, norms, rules), social relations, and production practices that form a single, more-or-less coherent framework (this includes liberalism, too). Within each one's framework, these beliefs, relations, and practices must operate in a regular fashion if the overall fabric of the society is to remain intact and be reproduced over time. *What is important here, therefore, is knowledge of Nature as part of a social system and not alienated from its institutional context.*

In industrialized, market-based societies, local "differences" manifest themselves, to the extent that they do, in what we call "culture": the language we speak, the customs we observe, the way we dress, the stories we tell our children, the television programs we watch, the modes of production in which we engage, and our differing relationships to land and resources. Economic rationality, directed toward maximum efficiency or utility, is generally presumed by policymakers to operate everywhere (although this is a possibly heroic assumption). Thus, it seems sensible to impose regulatory restrictions or apply fiscal tools to resource use or pollution as a means of adjusting individual and group behavior. Because everyone in industrialized, market-rational society is assumed to relate to the material world in a more-or-less similar way, a single form of intervention should produce a similar result in people's behavior. The same cannot be said for much of the rest of the world (for that matter, it cannot really be said even of industrialized societies; see chapters 4 and 5). Economic rationality exists, to be sure but, as suggested in chapter 2, it is a rationality wrapped within a "web of social relations" (Migdal 1988:33-38). As a result, while scientific principles apply across time, space, and cultures, social principles do not (Ribot 1990a, 1990b, 1993).

The implications of this point for environmental policymaking are significant: it means, as suggested in chapter 2, that centralized policy formulation at the global, or even the national, level is more than likely to run into serious difficulties in implementation. Thus, no matter how much is learned about environmental change—understood as either a physical or *global* phenomenon—it will never be sufficient to "solve" the "problem(s)" of environmental change, as a social process, at any level. Only by reconstructing our understanding of the global environment as the outcome of myriads of micro-level practices—which, consequently, requires changes in micro-level practices—can we even begin to think about problem-solving. Needless to say, there is probably no way to conceptualize the aggregation of all of these micro practices in anything remotely approaching manageable terms. It may only be through the broad process of social learning, and the transformations it accompanies or generates, that we can begin to deal with environmental change as the social phenomenon it really is.

What is being learned? What, then, are people learning about environmental change? Besides the exercise of collecting data and modelling interactions within ecosystems, social actors are learning and disseminating a significant body of technological knowledge and practice. I call this body of technological knowledge and practice *Ecology*, in recognition of the social element and in order to differentiate it from the science of *ecology*. Understood as a conventional science, ecology is not much different from any other body of consensual scientific knowledge. But, from a different perspective, ecology is more than just a body of consensual knowledge; it is more akin to a body of *technological* knowledge and practice, one that is contingent, and not determinate.

In chapter 1, I proposed that trains and railroads were best understood not as hardware or metal but, rather, as a "body" of technological knowledge and practice. As made clear earlier in this book, by using the term "body of technological knowledge and practice" I hold to a conception of technology that goes beyond just hardware to include social organization as well. This implies principles that are more than merely instrumental and imply a worldview, and a set of beliefs and values and both prescribed and proscribed practices. This conception also implies power, inasmuch as those who possess such knowledge can not only transfer it to others but also impose it on them (Litfin 1994: ch. 2).

While the parallel with trains and railroads is obviously not exact, Ecology can be seen as a similar body of technological knowledge and practice. In a general sense, Ecology involves a set of principles and practices and, although it does not explicitly prescribe norms and rules of behavior, it does imply certain kinds of relationships between human beings and ecosystems. In using the term, therefore, I mean to suggest that Ecology can be viewed as more than an approach to the study of natural systems and the relationships of populations therein. It can also be regarded as something along the lines of a "large technological system" of material presence, hardware (in the form of instrumentation), institutions, and practices, with a historically contingent origin, that formulates research programs and asks questions in a particular way. Thus, Ecology is based not on facts as *data* but facts as *narratives* (Cronon 1992), a point that highlights its somewhat contradictory character. As Wolfgang Sachs puts it (in a somewhat rueful vein),

> Ecology is both computer modelling and political action, scientific discipline as well as all-embracing worldview . . . the science of *ecology* gives rise to a scientific anti-modernism which has succeeded largely in disrupting the dominant discourse, yet the *science* of ecology opens the way for the technocratic recuperation of protest (1992b:30).[36]

Ecology as a body of technological knowledge and practice is not, to be sure, characterized by highly visible physical networks or installations—these are implicit in its holistic and systemic nature—but Ecology is, nonetheless, a technical system.

What is the character of the beliefs and values inherent to Ecology? In *Ariadne's Thread*, Mary E. Clark, a biologist at San Diego State University, argues that:

> Societies can no longer treat their support systems as exploitable commodities, selling off the fertility of their soils (in the form of cash crops) or other crucial resources at the expense of future generations. Only when each society preceives [sic] the ecosystem it inhabits as a sacred and inviolable trust to be preserved and passed on to future generations will the survival of humankind be assured (1989:24–45).

Clark is obviously trying to communicate a particular normative point of view, and does not hesitate to make this clear. But even in so technical a volume as *Stability and Complexity in Model Ecosystems*, we find Robert May writing that:

> Until such time as we better understand the principles which govern natural associations of plants and animals, we would do well to preserve large chunks of pristine ecosystems. They are unique laboratories. Quite apart from *valid ethical and aesthetic considerations*, there are pragmatic reasons why we should query the increasingly universal replacement of natural ecosystems, with their long evolutionary history, by agroecosystems, which are usually intrinsically unstable (1974:174; emphasis added).

In other words, the "practice" of ecological principles appears to carry with it an ethic or worldview, as well as implications for the organization and practices of societies.

One does not have to be a trained ecologist, with an advanced degree and subfield specialization, in order to propagate and practice the ecological ethic (Miller 1991). One can argue with the ethic, offer different versions of it, claim that it is wrong, that it privileges non-humans over humans, that it is the new "Red Threat" (or "Green" one) as some do. But, increasingly, it would seem that to accept the logic of the scientific principles, one must also accept the normative ethic. After all, how many practicing ecologists, cetologists, entomologists, etc. favor the destruction of the creatures that they study? And to what degree do they ignore that which is destroying the "object" of their study?[37] In favoring preservation or protection, they are implicitly questioning existing property rights arrangements and exercising some judgement about political priorities and the rights of Nature.[38]

More striking than this, however, is the way in which many practicing ecologists embed an ethical and political worldview in discussions of their research or practical focus, and the degree to which they are shared (as the quotes above suggest). In other words, ecologists constitute something akin to an "epistemic community" in the sense defined by Peter Haas (1990, 1992a). What Haas and his colleagues seem to miss in their analysis, however, is the extent to which the "projects" of epistemic communities can, in fact, be the bases for political and social tendencies in society-at-large.[39] In this sense, they are more like the "epistemes" discussed by Michel Foucault and described by Ruggie (1975:569–70). The responses within society in this instance are manifested neither through interest groups nor social movements in the generally-understood sense; they are more akin to changes in the historical structures around which these tendencies are organized. Not all "epistemic projects" have this effect, of course; the outcomes depend on the extent to which the goals of a project have to do with changing—whether intentionally or not—fundamental modes of social organization.[40]

The gradual diffusion of the worldview associated with Ecology, in a variety of forms, is striking (Hastings & Hastings 1994; Inglehart 1995). Just to take two examples, environmental education curricula and "green consumerism" are becoming increasingly popular around the world. But why? And why through the principles of Ecology, rather than something else? The generalized value of Nature as a "good" is one that has existed in Western society since sometime in the nineteenth century, in parallel with the view that it was "bad" or "wild" and there to be conquered or domesticated (Marx 1964; Hays 1980, 1987; Gould 1988; Bramwell 1989; Evernden 1992). In recent decades, this value has been split: on the one hand, Nature is seen as a "resource," to be exploited, whether sustainably or not (Booth 1994) and, on the other hand, Nature is seen as something to be accorded rights to existence in some "intact" fashion.[41] And, whereas my generation (educated circa 1960s) learned about the mineral and agricultural products of diverse countries—that is, *commodities* as values—in a subject called "Geography," my children learn about forests, rivers, and animals—that is, *Nature* as a value—in a subject called "Environmental Education."[42]

Even though I do not believe that market-based incentives are sufficient to fully protect the environment, ecological worldviews are nonetheless being diffused through the market via green consumerism and popular culture, too. The concept of green consumerism can be criticized on a variety of political grounds—especially as the reduction of Nature to the commodified object of atomized consumer choice—but there is no gainsaying the extent to which environmental considerations have become an integral part of modern capitalism (Luke 1993). One has only to read the nearest package or piece of paper to discover that it is composed, to some degree, of recycled materials, or to look for the "Green Cross" or "der Grüne Punkt" to recognize that producers are quite aware of the influence and public relations advantages of Ecological perspectives. When I take my children to McDonald's, they may well get some sort of environmentalist trinket in their "Happy Meal" (such as the injection-molded elephant that sits on one of my office shelves) that will increase their Ecological awareness, if only by a minuscule amount.[43] And, any parent who has been forced to sit through *The Lion King* is well aware of the Ecological ideology in the film—among the many ideologies to be discovered in it—even if it is skewed, anthropomorphic, and glorifies elitism. All of these constitute forms of "social learning" about Ecology, although it is clear that there are different and widely-contrasting degrees and types of social learning at work here.[44]

In suggesting this perspective, I do not want to downplay or ignore the historical contingency of various versions of "Ecology as a body of technological knowledge," nor do I regard the process described above as one with universal applicability. Consider the first point: As Donna Haraway points out, bodies of technological knowledge represented as "science" almost always carry the imprints of their "founders" through many generations of practitioners (1991: esp. ch. 5). Ecology, as the term is used here, could be mapped over time to show the influence of its founders on and antedecents in the practices and values of today. That map would show that individuals, at different points in time, acting alone and together, had made specific choices that influenced the ultimate content of "Ecology." Ecology is, in other words, a contingent, and not a determinate, body of technological knowledge and practice.[45]

Second, the particular ways in which Ecology is understood and practiced in any one place is strongly influenced by local variables, both natural and social. That does not mean that there are no fundamental elements that are universally shared, regardless of locale. It does mean that both historical trajectory and ecological difference play a role in local knowledge and practice. At the same time, however, local knowledge and practice are, increasingly, influenced by knowledge and practices originating elsewhere. Indeed, it would also be a mistake to regard Ecology as most people seem to regard soil erosion: Something that happens in many independent and different places around the world. Rather, as is true with many similar bodies of technological knowledge and practice, the diffusion of principles and practices among locales and between levels is intense and intentional (Long 1992b:35).

This, of course, raises questions about power, imperialism, intervention, resistance and relationships between "insiders" and "outsiders." Norman Long argues that:

> Intervention [into a context by external agents] is an ongoing transformational process that is constantly reshaped by its own internal organizational and political dynamic and by the specific conditions it encounters or itself creates, including the responses and strategies of local and regional groups who may struggle to define and defend their own social spaces, cultural boundaries and positions within the wider power field (Long 1992b:37).

Power and domination remain potent. Outsiders can arrive, make claims in the name of Ecology, and try to impose their views on insiders (or locals). But Ecology can also be used to legitimate local resistance against power and domination, as we shall see in subsequent chapters.

Networks of knowledge and practice

A key element in the diffusion of Ecology are "networks of knowledge and practice." In this context, what do I mean by the term "network?" Our understanding of the term is, overwhelmingly, influenced by the image (and realities, however limited and banal) of electronic communication networks, through which bits and bytes flow between electron collection devices, replicating inputs on fax paper or computer screens (*The Economist* 1995b).[46] This image does not capture the essential qualities of the social and political networks characteristic of global civil society, which are more than simply communication systems.

The literature on social networks tends to focus on the positions of individuals relative to other individuals within social institutions such as villages or corporations. As one volume puts it, "[N]etwork analysis . . . [focuses] upon communication links, rather than on isolated individuals, as the units of analysis [and] enables the researcher to explore the influence of other individuals on human behavior" (Rogers & Kincaid 1981:xi). Strictly speaking, the focus of network theory is on the relationships between social roles and, as noted, the reciprocal influences that result. Moreover, because structural roles *within* a network are important to this type of analysis, such networks are, inevitably, about power and hierarchy.[47] Some of the literature on "new social movements" also addresses the network phenomenon, but fails to explore the dynamics of exchange through a network. Tarrow describes the "social movement sector" as "a communications network that facilitates the diffusion and testing of new action forms, organizational styles, and particularly ideological themes" (1988:432). Melucci acknowledges the centrality of networks to new social movements, especially for the ecological movement, but focuses primarily on the nature of the actors in the network (1989:97–98). None of these explore or explain the network—consisting of actors and linkages—as an emergent global system.

My use of the term "networks of knowledge and practice" is meant to convey more than these understandings of social networks. Such networks are not simply relational, they are literally channels for the transfer of the bodies of technological knowledge and associated systems of hardware, practice, and values described above. As such, they include much more than the "data transfer" capabilities of television, phones, computers, and faxes; they include, as well, *social knowledge*. This means that practices and organization that are developed and applied in one location can be adapted and transferred to another.[48]

In essence, the "structure" of the process—if a process can rightfully be said to have a structure—is the network (Annis 1992; Sikkink 1993). The term "network" in this instance remains a somewhat imprecise one, but it connotes here more than the flow of something between points, or nodes. The imprecision of the term can be seen in the variety of uses to which it is put. For example, the concept of "networking" generally refers to an almost ritualized exchange of social knowledge among individuals who ordinarily do not work together. Since individuals who are not already part of a "network" do not engage in "networking," the practice essentially involves the opening of new channels in an already-existing system. Networks are also a means of reducing the transaction costs of obtaining knowledge without the interposition of markets or bureaucracies. Rather than sifting through data bases, one taps the network for knowledge (Fukuyama 1995; Derlugian 1993a, 1993b; Alvesson & Lindkvist 1993). More critically, networks are a form of social organization. At each node in the network we find an organization or a loosely-linked set of individual actors, and between the nodes we find flows of knowledge, practice, people, money, and other resources in all directions.

In spite of the popular notion that the Internet is an anarchy and the "great equalizer" of individuals, the picture painted here should not be taken to mean that hierarchy has been banished from these networks. Some of the larger and wealthier environmental organizations certainly see themselves in a vanguard position, and they control a great deal in the way of resources and access to power.[49] Still, as "local" knowledge acquires greater cachet and credibility, and the sheer number of small-scale groups comes to overwhelm the highly-capitalized ones, the vanguards may fall back into the pack.[50] There is also an inherent tension between these global networks and the local organizations linked into them. By their very nature, the networks of global civil society tend to be cosmopolitan, in the sense that they are driven by Ecology, a shared, global worldview. But, as noted above, the world is characterized by ecological diversity, both physical and social.

As a result, there is a continual struggle between the global and the local, as the former tries to impose some part of its vision on the latter, and the latter resists yielding up its particular identity to the former. The local does have leverage, however, since those actors whose reach is "global" cannot succeed unless they have access to the knowledge, legitimacy, and social capital possessed by the local (Putnam 1993). Lest all of this sound too abstract and rarified, as we shall see below, this tension is quite visible not only in Indonesia, but also in Hungary *and* California.

Finally, it would be a mistake to think that there is a single such network. It might be more accurate to say that there are many such networks, accessible to one another by virtue of the multiple social and institutional roles filled by both organizations and individuals. Thus, some organizations deal with both governments and "local" groups; some individuals go through the "revolving door" from public to private life and vice versa. And some people and groups wear multiple "hats," moving from one to the other as seems appropriate.[51] This is not surprising: Michael Maniates has documented how NGO "effectiveness" is as much a function of flexibility in terms of roles and linkages as it is of anything else. As he points out in the case of India, being able to interact with government bureaucracies and village demands at the same time, while not easy, is essential (1990b). This seems to follow elsewhere as well.

How might we study and analyze these networks? Kathryn Sikkink describes such networks as follows:

> An international issue-network comprises a set of organizations, bound by shared values and by dense exchanges of information and services, working internationally on an issue. The diverse entities that make up the international human rights issue-network include parts of IGOs [intergovernmental organizations] at both the international and regional levels, international NGOs on human rights, domestic NGOs on human rights, and private foundations. Other issue-networks will include a somewhat different array of actors; but international and domestic NGOs play a central role in all issue-networks. . . . To have a strong network, it must have a certain size and density. In other words, enough actors must exist and be connected in order to speak meaningfully of a network (1993:415–16).

Human rights networks differ from environmental networks in terms of one central feature: their focus is primarily on the state, since it is the state that is the guarantor of such human rights, if they are to be guaranteed at all. While the actors in environmental networks have many dealings with states—indeed, with government at all levels—in the final analysis, there is a much greater, and growing, concern with ecosystems—that is, with the local or regional context of environmental preservation or protection.

This suggests that the networks can be traced by documenting connections among NGOS and other actors, and evaluating the effect and effectiveness of the knowledge and practices transferred between organizations. The problem with this approach is that the number of organizations and linkages is enormous, certainly exceeding 100,000.[52] In practice, therefore, it is only possible to trace a limited number of organizations and linkages—or one or two regional alliances—and to assume that these are representative of the whole. There is, however, a further problem with such an approach: the political contexts within which linkages are established are very contextual and contingent on politics at various levels of governance and government. Local, regional, and national histories and political economies do matter.

In the chapters that follow, I have chosen, therefore, to study selected, well-defined regions and groups, their activities and beliefs, and their relationships to other organizations outside of the locality or region. These regions are defined by the groups themselves, and the networks and knowledge transfers are those described by group members. Because her unit of analysis is the state, Sikkink focuses on the role of actors and networks centered on specific states. In the case of actors focusing on environment (and development), the spatial unit of action is defined intersubjectively, including already-existing political units, newly-defined resource districts, ecosystems, bioregions or culturally-distinct areas. There is no a priori way of specifying the unit without engaging in fieldwork focused on actors. This is a point to which I will return in chapters 7 and 8; suffice it here to say that the three cases in the next section of the book are based on this methodological approach.

Conclusion

The cold war, and its end, have thus had paradoxical effects. They have opened the state to challenge by other forms of social institutions, from above and below, and they have brought into question the legitimacy of the system of production that, combined with the politics of the cold war, served to reproduce relations of power within the system. In the West, this challenge originates largely from the realm of civil society; in the East, where the spaces were much smaller, it was through the very small openings permitted to the peace, environment, and human rights movements; in the South, it has been in the context of democratizing states. This process can be understood as the "politicization" of civil society, the result of which is that the realm of the private has started to become, once again, part of the public realm.[53] The growth of politicized civil society has been further expedited by technological hardware that has made easier the reproduction of various forms of social practice and organization, including television, communications and, most importantly, inexpensive international travel (Lipschutz 1992/96; Alger 1990). Hardware, however, hardly accounts for the phenomenon as a whole.

The results of this process is an emerging "global civil society," a realm of actors who increasingly engage in a transnational politics that is often, but not always, characterized by a high degree of autonomy from the states in which they are based. This does not mean that global civil society is *independent* of the state system; but neither is it wholly the creation or subject of that system. In some sense, as in domestic settings, the state system (or, perhaps, international society; see Larkins & Fawn 1996) and global civil society are mutually constitutive, and the transformation of the former cannot take place without the existence of the latter.

In any event, global civil society is increasingly influential in the politics of both local *and* global, and it is precisely this juxtaposition of the micro and macro that gives it influence.[54] A powerful example of such influence was visible in terms of the role played by environmental NGOs in treaty negotiations preceding the Earth Summit as well as a host of other international conventions; at the opposite end of the scale, the growing numbers of local NGOs, many of them linked via alliances, associations, and coalitions, both national and transnational, also appear quite significant in the politics of many places (World Resources Institute 1992b). All of this might seem naive or utopian; certainly, it might appear to explain too much by too little, or claim more than has so far been accomplished. My point is not to reify global civil society nor endow it with extraordinary powers but, rather, to suggest that this particular mode of transnational politics is significant in the environmental context.

The practical activities of global civil society are to be found in the three focused case studies in the next part of this book. There, I turn to specific places and the role of global civil society in them. While these places are broadly characterized as being in California, Hungary, and Indonesia, this is more a matter of convenience than an attempt to capture wholes through names found on maps; the places themselves are much smaller than the countries in which they are found. Still, the larger political units are not irrelevant to the stories told there: To a considerable degree, the histories and political economies of places have been structured by political, economic, and social forces that are, on the one hand, intimately linked to the state and, on the other hand, often have their origins elsewhere in the world. To tell the story of global civil society *and* places thus requires not only documenting what goes on in those places but also explaining how those places—society and Nature together—came to be.

Finally, the three stories told below are not finished ones; rather, they are "in progress." Hence, to specify "impact" or "outcome" is, as yet, difficult. Moreover, success in the terms set by the participants is not guaranteed, but then neither is failure inevitable. The cases should, therefore, be read as illustrative, rather than definitive. There are many such stories, each of them different, but each of them increasingly linked via the networks and alliances described in this chapter. They are on the other side of the world, but also in our own backyards.

PART II

The Green World

CHAPTER 4

"Guardians of the Forest": Renegotiating Resource Regimes in Northern California

The Mattole River on the "Lost Coast" of California is a rather short one. It rises in the forests at the base of the King Range, which runs parallel to the coastline, travels a distance of not much more than sixty miles through the counties of Mendocino and Humboldt, and reaches the Pacific Ocean not far from the small town of Petrolia, south of Cape Mendocino. The entire Mattole watershed of perhaps three hundred square miles is inhabited by no more than three thousand people. Historically, the economy of the valley has been based on resource extraction—logging, ranching, fishing—and not much else, in part because it is relatively inaccessible due to the poor roads linking it to the rest of the coast. Apart from its beauty and tranquility, the Mattole River valley has also acquired a reputation for the cooperative ventures of its citizens—ranchers, fishers, and environmentalists—working together toward restoration of the river's largely-depleted chinook salmon runs via organizations based in civil society.

This effort has become something of a model for similar projects in other parts of California and the rest of the world. In all of these projects, groups organized by concerned citizens, drawn from a variety of occupations and worldviews, are engaged in attempts to restore or protect the resources on which their communities once depended. They do this in the name of Ecology and local political economy, with the support of the state of California as well as some agencies of the federal government. The mechanisms through which these efforts are taking place are largely those of local governance, with the ultimate goal of creating a form of common-pool property resource regime in which all have a stake. My goal in this chapter is to describe and analyze this process.

The northern part of California—the foggy coast, the mountain ranges rising to the east, the flat Sacramento River valley, the rise again into the Sierra Nevada—is a region historically molded by resource extraction (Figure 4.1). It is, for the most part, politically conservative. It is a region that once voted to secede from the rest of the state. Given the current politics

Figure 4.1. Source: *California Biodiversity News* 3. #2, Winter 1996, p. 11.

of rural areas in the United States (Helvarg 1995), northern California seems an unlikely place for experiments in ecological sustainability. Yet, such experiments are underway there, the outgrowth of an epistemic union of intellectual musings by graduates of the 1960s counterculture, attempts by state and federal resource agencies to find a better way to "manage" public lands and resources, and the intense loyalty to place often felt by blue-collar workers—loggers, miners, ranchers—who find themselves unemployed as the tide of extractive production leaves them high and dry (Brown 1995; Snyder 1995).

The official name of the experiment, originally formulated by staff members of a group of ten—and later eighteen—state and federal resource agencies, is an unwieldy one: "California's Coordinated Regional Strategy to Conserve Biological Diversity." Most people call it the "bioregional" or "biodiversity" project. In some ways, state sponsorship represents an attempt to catch up with global civil society in California, whose members have undertaken hundreds of small-scale environmental protection and restoration projects throughout the state (as noted earlier, one survey in the early 1990s identified two hundred such projects in the Sierra Nevada alone; Kennedy & Grieman 1992). While agency administrators and staff in Sacramento tend to see the biodiversity project as a way to rationalize environmental protection and habitat conservation (Press 1995), it has the potential to be much more than that: It involves the renegotiation of resource regimes and the reinventing (or reimagining) of local political economies, as a means of reviving and sustaining communities that have been or would be otherwise devastated by resource depletion and left as sloughs of economic despair without much hope for the future.

At one level, the project is trying to foster the creation of governance structures that establish environmental sustainability and local social choice as joint priorities under "local" control—not only the control of municipal or county government but civil society, too. At another level, it is no less than an effort to conserve and protect California's environment by dividing it into ecological provinces—units of environmental governance based on ecosystem management. The participation of *both* state (at all levels) and society are critical to the project's success. Without civil society, the state cannot advance its goals and programs; without the state, civil society would be hard put to create and maintain such a project. Neither is entirely comfortable with this arrangement.

In this particular story, global civil society is implicated in environmental protection and conservation as a Foucauldian episteme of sorts, through the "ethics" and "rationalities" as well as the technical skills it brings to bear on the political economy of the region. These perspectives are rooted in a reconceptualization of the relationship between human societies and Nature, captured in, on the one hand, the technical term "ecosystem management" and, on the other, the more poetic notion of "bioregionalism." Both concepts take their organizing principles from ecological notions of "community" as an integrated biological system. The first, however, sees human beings as the managers of ecosystems; the second, as an integral participant in ecosystems.[1] What is central, in this instance, is that both conceptualizations involve some notion of a common–pool property resource, in which governance is shared among stakeholders. In this, they both attempt to transform certain types of social relations and relations of production within an institutional context. A commitment to either ecosystem management or bioregionalism is also a commitment to yield up certain rights in property to a locally-defined common good, with the result that those who manage, own, or live on the land are bound to each other via their ties to Nature and community, and their responsibilities to the specific place in Nature where they live.

The story I tell in this chapter is, at best, only a preliminary and partial account of the "bioregionalization" of parts of California.[2] Two central propositions are illustrated here: First, the transmission of knowledge and practice through various national and transnational networks that include individuals, non-governmental organizations, and state and federal agencies, has led to the formulation and implementation of a particular regionally-based strategy of Nature protection. Second, these experiments point toward the renegotiation of resource regimes and political economies *at the local and regional levels*—whichever is most "appropriate." In the first part of the chapter, the background to the emergence of California's bioregional project is provided. In the second, I discuss the elements of the strategy and its implementation. Finally, in the third section, I describe briefly some of the ecosystem management projects underway in several northern California communities. I also speculate on the longer-term political and ecological possibilities inherent in the strategy and the possible consequences of its dissemination beyond the borders of California.

One additional note: the lines of power, authority, and jurisdiction in northern California are exceedingly confused and confusing. There are multiple levels of "governance" operating here—only partly a consequence of American federalism—in which coalitions among levels and actors form and dissolve. This is a phenomenon not unfamiliar to scholars of American politics but it is also a phenomenon increasingly characteristic of environmental politics and struggles in many other parts of the world, including some where the state has been highly centralized (Hoberg 1993). As will be seen in chapters 5 and 6, even unitary states are finding themselves enmeshed within an increasingly "federalized" system of governance, as international conventions bind them from above to certain courses of action while actors in local jurisdictions—often in collaboration with outsiders and foreigners—struggle with them for control over Nature.

Boundaries: natural or social?

At first glance, the "Klamath Province" of northern California (see map) looks to be quintessentially Western: an area in which the defenders of the old ways of life—Native Americans, fifth-generation ranchers, loggers—must hold sway. Certainly, uproars over Northern Spotted Owls, marbled murrelets, salmon, old-growth forests, and Wise Use would suggest that this is the case. Yet, the province is no longer a culturally or economically "pure" region—if, indeed, it ever was. Here and there are to be found advocates and practitioners—in the urban refugees and members of the 1960s counterculture and even among some ranchers, loggers and others—of what has been called "post-materialism" (Inglehart 1990, 1995). Here also are retirees from the urban regions to the south, who, though conservative in many ways, nonetheless zealously covet Nature where they now live. Northern California is a place apart, its residents noted for their independence and distaste for the rest of the state. In 1992, they voted to secede from the "South"—which pointedly excluded both Sacramento *and* San Francisco. It is also a place whose economy has historically gone through booms and busts, in concert with the supply of and demand for lumber, raw materials and minerals, cattle, fish, and other resources.

Today, as is the case throughout much of the Pacific Northwest, the natural endowment of northern California is nearing the limits of sustainability. Once beyond that point, conservation or restoration will become extremely difficult. Forests have been over-harvested in response to housing growth and to pay off corporate debts incurred during the takeover boom of the 1980s. The anadromous salmon fisheries have been greatly diminished by over-fishing at sea as well as damage to spawning grounds, the result of dam building, clear-cutting and road-building along creek and river watersheds (Steelquist 1992; McEvoy 1986). Various species, the most notorious of which are the Northern and California Spotted Owls, appear endangered by indiscriminate destruction and development of habitat (Yaffee 1994). The decline in the extractive base has been a gradual one, but over the past decade, the rate of damage seems to have increased significantly.

These changes have not gone unnoticed by local, regional, and national environmental and preservation organizations. Beginning in the 1970s, and to a growing degree through the 1980s, regional groups such as the Oregon Wilderness Coalition, the Ancient Forests Alliance, the Environmental Protection Information Center, and local chapters of the Sierra Club, the National Audubon Society, and the National Wildlife Federation started to become active here (Yaffee 1994; Mitchell 1991a; Brown 1995). With varying degrees of success, these groups attempted to intervene in the policy planning process to try to slow or halt resource exploitation, using the Environmental Impact Review provisions of the National Environmental Policy Act and going to the courts to sue for enforcement of the Endangered Species Act. In Washington, D.C. as well as state capitals, these and other groups tried to foster legislation that would also serve to protect the environment, again with mixed outcomes. National, regional, and local groups did not always see eye-to-eye. Their individual agendas depended on the building of sometimes expedient political alliances at the national or local levels which, at times, tended to undermine cooperation. Overall, however, there was little concern for the question of purely local governance, especially inasmuch as efforts to protect the environment came into conflict with the economic viability of resource-based communities, engendering fierce resistance from loggers, miners, ranchers, and others (Mitchell 1991; Brown 1995).

Indeed, as various attempts to preserve and protect species and habitat have increased in scope and number, they have come face-to-face with the classic "environment-development" dilemma: jobs or Nature? Large tracts of land in the region are public, and therefore under federal and state jurisdiction; this makes it technically possible to put much of it off-limits to further "development." But whether to do so or not is a quintessentially political question: Do we stifle the economy to protect plants and animals at the expense of people, or do we bid farewell to plants and animals in order to keep people employed? Ecologists and environmentalists would prefer the former; the majority of loggers, ranchers, and miners seem to favor the latter. What to do? Some of the region's inhabitants have taken up the traditional American West response to bust-following-boom: they have moved onto "greener" climes or looked for other, mostly service-related employment. Tourism is a favorite; or, rather, servicing tourists is. But, there are few new places to move to, and the "green" in the places that remain in business is not much more attractive. Others have decided to fight. They are choosing to stay and make a last stand here.

But capitalism and culture are dynamic; change is ceaseless (Berman 1982). Even as one frontier closes, another one is opening. Ever since the 1960s, new arrivals have flowed into northern California in order to "get back to the land" or take advantage of the relatively low cost of living. A new version of Nature commodification, in the form of eco-tourism (Buckley 1994, Nelson 1994) provides some individuals with new livelihoods, although these are not as remunerative as the old ones. In some of the mountain ranges, especially within the so-called Emerald Triangle that encompasses three mountain counties, clandestine patches of high-quality marijuana are still to be found, in spite of the best efforts of police and politicians. Dope remains a good source of income, although there is always the chance that federal and state authorities will discover and destroy the crop.

Under such conditions of economic uncertainty, it seems unlikely that environmentalism, or ecology, would be very attractive either as philosophy or practice. Many people blame "environmentalists" for the decline in the region's economy, attributing it to over-regulation and the California Spotted Owl (cousin to the Northern branch). Feelings run high. Internet bulletin boards and Web sites buzz. Bumper stickers on pickup trucks are explicit: "Save a logger, eat an owl" (or an environmentalist). What to do?

The paradox in the Biodiversity Project—if there is one—is that while much of the impetus behind it has come from state and federal administrative agencies, whose directors and staffs have tried to manage the effort in a coordinated fashion, its success depends on the involvement of "locals"—whether Green or not—and a commitment to the process by local representatives of these agencies. As argued in chapter 2, however, such coordination and command cannot be imposed, *ex cathedra* from above. Local resistance and collaboration with other branches of the state, such as the U.S. Congress, could easily derail such efforts. Indeed, the fight over the forests of the Pacific Northwest has exactly this character. Hence, to actually engender local environmental governance requires something like the autochthonous emergence of new coalitions in civil society (or, even, class coalitions) that, under most other circumstances, would be regarded as highly unlikely, if not totally improbable (Foster 1993). There is another reason that northern California may be receptive to this process: it is the place where people have been talking and writing about bioregionalism for more than twenty years (Snyder 1992). While these ideas are often dismissed as impractical, their intellectual impact has been quite widespread. More to the point, bioregionalism is about local control, and this has broad appeal.

Some observers see implicit in this process the emergence of "true" democracies, along the lines of the Athenian *polis* or Jeffersonian yeomanry; others fear exactly such a result. Even now, some years after the project's launching, no one knows for certain what will actually happen in the longer-term. Whatever the outcome, the process underway in northern California can be seen as a model for what *must* happen if the renegotiation of resource regimes is to become a recognized and accepted approach to achieving environmental sustainability around the world. While social and natural conditions in countries such as the United States vary greatly even across very small distances, something of a shared political culture does exist from one community to the next. And, even though the differences between countries are great, as suggested in chapters 2 and 3, many of the forms evolving in the California effort are being transmitted through the networks of global civil society, adopted by groups in other parts of the world, and adapted to social and natural conditions in those places.

Conservation and the Biodiversity Project

In the conservationist tradition

Although the California Biodiversity Project appears, at first glance, to be quite original in conception, it actually reflects the long history of resource conservation in the United States. Where it *is* significantly different is in its assumption that technical capacity and scientific knowledge alone are necessary but not sufficient conditions for habitat protection. The protection of habitat represents something of an innovation in public policy, inasmuch as it goes beyond maintenance of individual species to consider the ecosystemic context in which Nature exists, as we shall see below. But ecosystems, unlike species, are "owned," and property, in the United States, is sacrosanct.

Thus, when representatives of ten California and federal resource agencies,[3] frustrated by an impasse in the state legislature over the terms of harvesting of old-growth forests, a federal judge's injunction against logging in the habitat of the Northern Spotted Owl—a wholly unexpected turn of events with major political consequences—and a generally growing disarray where management of other resources was concerned, met in 1991 to sign a Memorandum of Understanding (MOU), they hoped to cut a Gordian knot. Their intent was to protect habitat *and* property through cultural construction of a commons, in Luther Gerlach's (1990) terms, without fully socializing it.

The MOU was entitled "California's Coordinated Regional Strategy to Conserve Biological Diversity." According to the agreement's preamble:

> California is one of the most biologically diverse areas in the world. . . . Californians now recognize the need . . . to protect and manage ecosystems, biological communities, and landscapes. . . . To effectively conserve California's biological resources and maintain social and economic viability, public agencies and private groups must coordinate resource management and environmental protection activities, emphasizing regional solutions to regional issues and needs (MOU 1991:1).

Under the heading of "Strategic Principles," the memorandum proposed that:

1. Goals and strategies . . . be defined at the level of a bioregion.
2. Institutions and their policies . . . adapt to reflect a bioregional approach to the protection of natural diversity.

The ideas looked good on paper. Whether they could actually be implemented remained to be seen.

Despite its somewhat sudden appearance on the California environmental scene, the Biodiversity Project did not emerge *ex nihilo* from the minds of government bureaucrats nor was it an *ex cathedra* pronouncement by state policymakers. It was, rather, a consequence of three factors: first, it came after several years of intense social conflict over resource management throughout the state. Second, it was a response to a decline in and growing challenges to the logging industry in California. Third, it tried to address a growing sense that the "Conservationist" approach to resource extraction, as it had been practiced for almost a century, was losing legitimacy and no longer working very well (Hays 1980, 1987: ch.1; Ewing 1992). The resource agencies could, of course, have promulgated further administrative regulations, sending agents out into the field to check on compliance and threaten enforcement.[4] But they might well end up back in court, being sued by those who thought the rules too strict or those who felt them too lax. What was needed was a new approach; one that eschewed, or at least modified, the tenets of Conservationism.

One hundred years after its inception, Conservationism and its heroes have something of a mythical quality. But, the Conservationist movement was, as Samuel Hays put it in *Conservation and the Gospel of Efficiency*, a hard-nosed "scientific movement," whose "essence was rational planning to promote efficient development and use of all natural resources" (Hays 1990:2). Conservationism, especially as promulgated by Gilbert Pinchot, first director of the U.S. Forest Service, drew on European practices but then eventually spread abroad, as well, and became the model for state policies on resource extraction for much of the world (Hays 1990: ch.3).[5] It aimed to leave no stone unturned and no resource untouched.

The Conservationist movement had its organized political counterpart in the surge of Populism between 1880 and 1915 and the rise of Progressivism in response (Hays 1990: ch.13). Both arose in the context of a political and economic transition from craft-based industry to mass production—in some ways, parallelled by a similar transition today (see chapter 8; Gordon 1995)—and in response to what was seen as the uncontrolled depredation of the nation's forests and minerals by the corporate "robber barons" of the late nineteenth and early twentieth century.

But the Conservationist approach was not, in our terms, a "holistic" one. It did not look at integrated systems. To be sure, such notions were developing in the science that later came to be known as "ecology," itself part of the rise of philosophical and empirical positivism and the hardening of disciplinary boundaries that took place during the nineteenth century. But the adherents of Conservationism were relatively single-minded, focusing on individual resources—lumber, water, minerals, wildlife—and their replacement, if possible, with equivalent resources. They were aware of, but had little regard for, what we now understand as ecosystems. The single resource was sustainable, so to speak, for decades, so long as the "gospel of efficiency" was a dominant ideology, and the costs of resource depletion to Nature, as well as humans and their communities, were accepted as a part of the benefits of economic development. The sheer size of the American resource base made it seem, for a long time, that depletion would never be a problem.

There were a few dissenters from this ideology. George Perkins Marsh (1864) had already foreseen the problems inherent in such an approach. John Muir's conflict with Pinchot is legendary (Oelschlaeger 1991: ch. 6, 7). Another dissenter was Aldo Leopold (1966) who was trained in the principles and practices of Conservationism but, by the mid- to late-1940s, had begun to doubt them. There were not many others. The gospel of Conservationism did not meet its first serious political challenges until the 1960s and early 1970s, with the publication of Rachel Carson's *Silent Spring* in 1962, the emergence of environmentalism, and the organizations and activities spawned by that movement.

During its formative years, much of the newly-emergent American environmental movement tended to focus on the impacts on humans from pollution, resource depletion, and population (inspired, to no small degree, by Carson's book). The newer groups differed from long-established organizations such as the Sierra Club, the Wilderness Society, the National Wildlife Federation and the Audubon Society, organizations more committed to wildlife protection and Nature conservation in terms of specific species and landscapes. Their memberships differed, as well. The older organizations had been founded earlier in the century by "Brahmins" who tended to be rather well-off economically; the environmental movement drew from the middle-class and the protest movements of the 1960s.[6] Eventually, the two tendencies merged. But in the early 1970s, neither viewed Nature protection in terms of the protection of habitat; rather, they focused primarily on individual species—reflecting the then-current notion in ecology of "keystone" species—and the encroachment of development on parks and wilderness (Hays 1987:112).

Habitat is a diffuse concept. It differs from both place and ecosystem.[7] It does not have much emotional resonance. It encompasses multiple species and niches, some of which may be quite small or even ugly (most of the world's species are insects). And it does not privilege beautiful landscapes over less attractive ones. In terms of generating public support, individual species, mountains, and canyons—especially photogenic ones—arouse much more passionate commitments. As a result, in the 1970s the political objectives of environmental groups were usually expressed in terms of parks, bears, birds, butterflies, and dolphins, rather than more encompassing and ecologically-significant concepts such as habitat. This particular preference is evident in the Federal Endangered Species Act (ESA) of 1973, which is triggered by *numbers* of living individuals or pairs of a threatened species, rather than destruction of habitat, per se.[8] This particular point would, eventually, come to play a central role in the California drama.

While some, such as the current governor of California, Pete Wilson, regard the ESA as an unreasonable burden on human beings and their livelihood, the law nonetheless falls within the mainstream of U.S. legislation. By and large, it is a direct descendent of Conservationist and Progressivist tendencies, which remain strong in federal and state resource agencies such as the U.S. Forest Service (USFS), U.S. Fish and Wildlife (F&W), and the U.S. Bureau of Land Management (BLM). The Act offers a few words about habitat and puts forth an implicit argument about the ethical implications of species preservation. It focuses mostly on the status of individual species, establishing different categories of endangerment and protection.[9]

The listing of an individual species under the ESA depends upon the scientific assessment of its particular condition by biological specialists; economic or ecosystemic considerations are excluded.[10] In order to be listed, a baseline for the survival of a species must be established, which is usually framed in terms of a total number of surviving pairs, or some density of individuals per unit area.[11] This, in turn, requires intensive survey of the area inhabited by the species, differentiation between branches of the species (as, for example, between the Northern and California Spotted Owls), and some assessment of the conditions required for the species to reproduce and, if possible, to repopulate an area.[12] In most cases, such assessments come down to numbers and, as President Reagan once noted in a fit of absentmindedness, "facts are stupid things," especially when they require you to do politically unpopular deeds.[13]

Samuel Hays makes one other point about the ESA and associated regulations that is worth noting and which provides an interesting parallel to the civil rights movement. Whereas game management has, during much of the twentieth century, fallen almost entirely within the jurisdiction of individual states, the ESA, and the changes it has wrought, have essentially put protection of *all* species, and not just game animals, into the hands of the federal government (Hays 1987:114). Just as the federal government overrode claims of "states' rights" in the 1960s in an attempt to end segregation and establish the civil rights of African-Americans, the ESA has become a mechanism giving the federal government the authority to preempt local and state claims over resources and wildlife.[14] The rearguard tendencies of the Reagan administration where environment and conservation were concerned tended to yield some of this authority back to the states in the 1980s. By that time, however, the pendulum had shifted. Although state governments were not necessarily more protective of Nature than Washington, D.C., they were nonetheless more susceptible, through their administrative agencies, to the kinds of knowledged-based arguments associated with environmental protection. This, as we shall see, was and remains extremely important in the California case.

Forests forever?

In principle, the Conservationist ethic, as expressed in various state and federal regulatory regimes such as the Endangered Species Act, is intended to provide benchmarks; in practice, however, it is more likely to raise red flags. For example, under the California resource regime governing private timber harvesting in the state—a regime, firmly rooted in Conservationism—regulatory agencies look no farther in terms of impacts than the tract to be logged. For private tracts larger than three acres—those less than three acres are generally privately-owned and exempt from regulation—lumber companies must provide "timber harvest plans" (THPs) to the State Board of Forestry and the Department of Forestry and Fire Protection. Historically, these agencies have given such THPs cursory environmental review, opened them for a brief period of public comment, and approved them without a great deal of public involvement or modification.

Federal forests are governed by the National Forest Management Act of 1976, which mandates that the forests be managed for "multiple use," including not only timber harvesting, but water supply, recreation, fish and wildlife protection, as well as other societal objectives. In practice, the U.S. Forest Service has, more often, played down multiple use and concentrated on "getting out the cut," auctioning timber leases to lumber companies in return for a flat board-foot royalty. The process of multiple use management is further complicated by the checkerboard ownership pattern of many western forests, a consequence of land-ownership and sale during the era of the great Western railroads, which left alternating sections private and public.

Prior to the late 1980s, little effort had been made to look at larger patterns of timber harvesting or at the age of tracts. No consideration whatever had been given to the impacts of THPs and federal timber sales on species habitat or overall biodiversity in a tract or region. This shortcoming became especially evident during the 1980s when, under the pressure from financial markets and growing foreign demand, the rate of timber harvesting on private lands far exceeded growth rates, with yields dropping substantially as the decade progressed (Sample & Le Master 1992; Mitchell 1991a, 1991b). Leasing and logging practices on public lands began to come under harsh criticism from environmentalists, and the results became increasingly visible to those living near to and far away from many of the national forest lands. Political pressure to increase the cut was applied to state and federal bureaucracies, with some groups, such as the "Wise Use" movement, arguing for privatization of public lands. The continued clear-cutting of dwindling old-growth tracts along the North Coast of California and northward into Canada became increasingly alarming to others and began to generate systematic efforts by concerned individuals and groups of environmentalists to slow or halt the logging.[15] The Northern Spotted Owl controversy, while linked in the public mind and media to logging, actually developed in parallel to these protection efforts. In 1990, the two strands came together in California and the Pacific Northwest.

This was the context of "Redwood Summer" and the "Forests Forever" ballot initiative presented to the California electorate in 1990. Redwood Summer, as noted in chapter 3, was deliberately modelled on the Freedom Summers of the civil rights movement, devised to invoke a "civil rights" for trees. The parallel should not be extended too far, however: Freedom Summer was intended to bring the federal government into the Old South, but it is doubtful that many of those involved in Redwood Summer hoped for, or even wanted, federal intervention. Ironically, this has nonetheless happened, as we shall see, below. While Redwood Summer attracted far fewer participants than organizers had initially hoped, it did provide a highly visible backdrop to the growing conflict over logging in California. The Forests Forever initiative, which appeared on the statewide ballot in 1990, would have "placed a moratorium on the logging of old-growth forests, defined and mandated sustainable yield forestry, and required reorganization of the Board of Forestry to include representatives from the environmental community" (Nechodom 1992:10). The measure failed to win passage by a fairly narrow margin, but it nevertheless put the fear of God and the public into the hearts of timber industry and forest bureaucracy alike. As Luther Gerlach put it, "The shadow of Redwood Summer was cast over Washington [state]" (Lipschutz & Mayer 1993:264).

In Sacramento, California's capital, the response to this close call was a series of efforts by timber interests to push "compromise" legislation through the California assembly and senate. This was meant to hold off court challenges from environmentalists while still permitting industry to engage in logging, albeit at somewhat lower levels than had previously been allowed. Four "grand accords" were put together, with much public fanfare, and presented to the legislature, with the promise that they would put an end to "tree wars" (Kay 1989). Each accord emerged only after a complex and tedious negotiation between the interested parties, each ultimately failed to win legislative approval, as one group or another disavowed paternity (Lucas 1992). The pressures of pending legislation, the absence of authorized regulations, and the ever-present threat of legal action left agency administrators without guidance as to what to do. Together, these begat a coordinated reaction by state and federal agencies in Sacramento, who sought an administrative alternative to the legislative impasse.[16]

Apparently declining numbers of the Northern Spotted Owl and its close cousin, the California Spotted Owl, provided the other major impetus to the Biodiversity Project, through application of the Endangered Species Act (ESA) to northern California and the Pacific Northwest as a whole. The Spotted Owl prefers to nest in the snags and holes found in the dead or dying trees of old-growth forests although, if nothing else is available, the nesting pairs will settle for younger forests containing some "old-growth components" (Kay 1989:14, 16). Just how many Spotted Owl pairs remain, and what their distribution is, continues to be a subject of fierce debate. Estimates in the mid-1980s suggested that perhaps 1,500 nesting pairs remained in Oregon and Washington, while numbers in California were even less certain (Rosenbaum 1991:292; Diringer 1993; Yaffee 1994). More recent counts suggest that there may be as many as 10,000 pairs remaining throughout the Pacific Northwest (Easterbrook 1994).

The effort to list the Spotted Owl under the ESA and to apply the National Environmental Policy Act to federal timber sales, and the injunction against logging within 11.6 million acres of Spotted Owl "domain" put in place in 1991 by Federal Court Judge William Dwyer, triggered the so-called tree wars by putting off-limits, even if only temporarily, major tracts of mostly-federally-owned forests (Yaffee 1994; Hungerford 1994). In the late 1980s, these forests had supplied the lumber industry on the West Coast with the bulk of its raw materials, as private lands had been depleted (Mitchell 1991b; McKay 1991). The economic boom of the 1980s, and leveraged buyouts of several lumber companies, saw timber harvests from federal and private forests double. Reducing the cut, timber companies and labor organizations claimed, would have serious implications for the many communities in the region dependent on logging. Estimates of the economic consequences of such actions were thrown about with great alacrity. The federal government suggested that 4,500-9,500 jobs might be lost. *The Economist* suggested 30,000, and the industry, as many as 90,000 (Rosenbaum 1992:292; *Economist* 1991; Sample & Le Master 1992).[17] Other estimates were even higher, but it was clear that listing of the owl represented a serious challenge to business-as-usual (even if, as we shall see below, the job-loss analysis was not entirely correct).

Brought to inspect the battlefield during the presidential campaign of 1992, Candidate Clinton promised to convene a "Forest Summit" if elected, with a view toward negotiating a cease-fire, if not a peace treaty, in what was, by now, a growing and rhetorically-inflammatory conflict. Ultimately, under prodding from the Clinton administration, a National Forest Service task force developed what came to be known as "Option 9." This proposed to reduce the annual timber harvest in the Pacific Northwest, on federal lands west of the Cascade Mountains, from some five billion board-feet per year in the late 1980s—a level regarded by many as having been unsustainable—to about 1.2 billion board-feet per year during the period 1994-2004 (Healy & Richter 1993; U.S. Department of Agriculture, et al. 1993).

Option 9 placated no one, leading the timber and construction industries to raise dire warnings of imminent lumber shortages and more-costly homes, and environmentalists to threaten litigation, protests, and doom.[18] The plan also failed to propose establishment of permanent reserves of old-growth forests, as demanded by the environmental movement. This deliberate political omission generated yet more activity in the courts, as both sides attempted to overturn it (Healy & Richter 1993). Ultimately, all of these challenges failed. Option 9 was undermined, as well, its funding halted by Congress.

One person's property is another person's habitat

The whole Spotted Owl controversy had been criticized for focusing attention on species (Yaffee 1994:47–48), but one important result did emerge from this process: a growing recognition within federal policy that habitat is as important if not more so than the number of animals, a position reinforced by a 1995 U.S. Supreme Court decision (Lavelle 1995). Or, as Clinton himself proposed in presenting Option 9:

> This plan offers an innovative approach to conservation, protecting key watersheds and the most valuable of our old-growth forests . . . saving the most important groves of ancient trees and providing habitat for salmon and other endangered species (Swisher 1993).

The importance of the Northern Spotted Owl is, thus, less the species itself than incorporation into both federal and California policy what its threatened status is taken to indicate: the destruction of habitat, of ecosystems. Increasingly, the decline of particular species is being recognized *politically* as a sign that the places where they live are under stress from human intrusion and development. For every endangered species that is listed, other, less well-known species are likely to be threatened, too. For example, there may be as many as four hundred in the Cascades alone (Swisher 1993), and comparable numbers in northern California.

The centrality of habitat in the survival of species, and its importance as an organizing principle in efforts to develop mechanisms for environmental sustainability, cannot be emphasized too strongly. Habitats are not merely places; they imply relationships among the parts of an ecosystem. To give a simple-minded example, if prey die out, predators cannot survive. Since prey are predators at a lower trophic level, their disappearance signifies damage at that lower level, and so on. As a result, a commitment to protect one threatened species necessarily implies a commitment to protect or restore its habitat. In the case of the Northern and California Spotted Owls, this means imposing severe, and controversial, limits on the destruction of habitat (and which is why, for pro-timber interests, numbers become so important).

While ecologists have recognized for decades the importance to biodiversity of protection of ecosystems as a whole, the *political* implications of such an approach have only become really apparent over the past decade or so. These implications are explosive: to wit, habitat is land, land is owned, and ownership in the United States is, as often as not, private. But even where a large fraction of land ownership is public, as in northern California, conflicts over rights to use have become politically-contentious. Indeed, this point is the basis for the "Wise Use" movement, conflicts over grazing rights and fees, access to public lands by off-road vehicles, royalties from mining corporations, and so on.[19] In the United States, as well as in many other countries, private ownership—and, historically, many forms of access to public lands—convey the right to treat such property as the owner wishes, subject only to those constraints thought to be for the good of the larger community. Even these, often minor, restrictions may be regarded as constituting undue interference. So, while property owners may be prevented from engaging in activities that might threaten the public health or safety—and this could include restrictions on logging in order to prevent soil erosion or mudslides—the regulation of use to protect or maintain habitat goes much farther and is often described or presented in court proceedings as an illegal taking.[20]

This very point has been evident in recent years with regard to the protection of wetlands and marshlands in the United States. The U.S. government has acted, under the authority of the Clean Water Act of 1972, to designate what normally appear to be dry farmlands as areas whose modification must be approved by the U.S. Army Corps of Engineers. The qualification in this instance is that the lands be partially or wholly under water for as few as thirty days each year; the area in question includes Mississippi River bottomlands, which are subject to periodic inundation, but which have been privately farmed for generations; the result is that some farmers have been confronted with orders to restrict or cease their activities in these bottomlands (Robbins 1990). A similar situation in the Central Valley of California promises to replicate the Mississippi story: there, fairy shrimp are threatened with extinction by the destruction of the vernal pools, located on private farmlands, in which they live and breed. Should these shrimp be declared endangered, farmers will find themselves barred from using the lands where these pools are located. In part this is a regulatory process, in part the "cultural construction of the commons" (Gerlach 1990). The fight over the Spotted Owl and old growth forests has a similar character, a point to which I will return.

While the controversies over endangered species in the Pacific Northwest and northern California have affected access to public forests, the owl has been blamed unfairly for an outcome that would, in any event, have occurred by the end of the century: the demise of the timber resources from the current harvesting cycle along the central Pacific Coast (running from northern California to the Olympic Peninsula in Washington; the forests of British Columbia and the Alaskan Panhandle are headed the same way). The 30,000–50,000 loggers, the lumber companies, and the construction industry would all be humming the same tune by 2001 that they have instead been forced to sing in the early 1990s. The only difference would be that the threatened species would have vanished by then and could not be brought back to life (Sample & Le Master 1992). What angers so many is the seeming priority given to these species, over the livelihoods of those loggers, mill workers and others dependent on the industry. They see themselves as no less an integral part of the forest than the owls and, if anything, much more important to the political culture of the country than the environmentalists seeking to protect the Owl and its ecological associates.

The conflict over owls and forests, in other words, is as much about symbols and ideologies as it is about material things. And, although this is mentioned nowhere in the Memorandum of Understanding, it is the reconstruction of the relationship between human beings and Nature that is central to the Biodiversity Project, even if that goal is not immediately obvious to either the project's progenitors or its participants. What, after all, is underway here? In chapter 2, I proposed that the renegotiation of resource regimes involves the reworking not only of the visible elements of a political economy—technologies and workers—but also the cultural meanings of the parts and the roles of the players in old arrangements and whatever new ones might emerge. You can't have one without the other.

Herein lies the real significance of the California Biodiversity Project and its utilization of bioregionalism as an organizing principle: It provides the framework through which such a renegotiation can take place. Indeed, what happens in rural California may go far beyond the outcomes imagined by agency staff in Sacramento. As we shall see, the Biodiversity Project is as much a foil for those engaged in the renegotiation process as it is a framework. It not only allows the renegotiation to take place, it is also viewed suspiciously as an intervention and co-optation by those "outsiders" who, traditionally, have come into communities to exploit, extract, and leave. It is, like the ESA, a project with a potential far greater than the words in the Memorandum of Understanding to which agency heads put their signatures.

What, then, is the role of the state—California and federal—in this process? Earlier, I argued that the state, committed to a developmental strategy, is not in a position to radically change its management of environment and resources. Within California, the "state" is a much more ambiguous concept than it is ordinarily taken to be. Legal jurisdiction over resources is split among private landowners, individual as well as corporate, cities, counties, resource, air quality and water management districts, the state of California, the federal government and, to a growing degree, an emergent system of nongovernmental organizations (such as the Nature Conservancy) and international organizations and regimes. Hence, the possibility of actors at one level of jurisdiction building coalitions and alliances with those of another level against those in a third is always present. This constant struggle for control has led many observers to characterize the United States as a "weak" state, in contrast to others, such as France, which are much more centralized and less open to penetration or coalition-building.[21] Yet, what is evident in California, and in the two cases presented in chapters 5 and 6, is that even "strong" states can find themselves facing society-society, society-state and state-state coalitions that cross national borders, reach toward the international system and into other countries, and bring significant pressure to bear on political and economic institutions within the state, where the struggle over control and renegotiation is taking place.

This, then, is where the role played by global civil society is most evident. Such groups come to fill a number of functions that the state cannot, as well as some that the state prefers to avoid. As suggested in chapter 3, they are important in terms of education, through which they disseminate Ecology as both science and worldview, and via their membership in a globalizing episteme. As we shall see, when embedded in localized contexts, they can help to establish the basis on which antagonistic elements in a community can come together to negotiate. Finally, because of their technical and knowledged-based competence, they may also play a central role in the functional governance of the renegotiated resource regime, providing a venue for decision-making and program implementation legitimated by the very process through which the renegotiation takes place. These points will become more evident later in this chapter.

Paths to California Bioregions

The bioregional approach to ecological protection is not a new one in the state of California, although it has previously been on offer under a different name. For some years, state and federal resource agencies have been systematically applying such a strategy at the ecosystemic level, calling it by the less-glamorous term "Coordinated Resource Management and Planning" (CR(I)MP). As of 1993, there were fifty-nine CRIMP areas listed in a statewide registry ("California Coordinated Resource Management & Planning" n.d.). A CRIMP is

> [A] process designed to achieve compatibility between the uses being made of natural resources, energy and mineral resources, livestock production, watershed, wildlife habitat, wood products, and recreation; . . . [such] that such resources are improved, if necessary, and perpetuated in a condition of high quality for future generations. A coordinated resource management plan affects all ownerships in the planned area. All major uses of the areas are considered and coordinated to avoid unacceptable and unnecessary conflicts. *Each plan should become a coordinated management program administered by the principal owners, managers, and users of the resources addressed by the planning process* (Memorandum of Understanding 1990; emphasis added).[22]

The influence of the Conservationist credo is evident here: efficiency is degraded if conflicts predominate over coordination. What is less evident is how such a strategy plays itself out, either politically or on larger spatial scales that might cover several "ecosystems."[23] The CRIMP framework was designed to be applied to areas that are ecologically linked and characterized by varied ownership and jurisdictions but that are still spatially tractable. For example, a stream or river watershed might include parcels of land under private and corporate ownership as well as under the control of the Bureau of Land Management, the National Forest Service, and the California Department of Forestry and Fire Protection. A plan for such a watershed would include, however, only those stakeholders holding title to real property there, such as ranchers, farmers, miners, lumber companies, state and federal agencies, and so on. Nowhere does the CRIMP approach envision the involvement of "stakeholders" lacking such title (for example, city dwellers, rural renters, political conservatives, or environmentalists), inasmuch as it is presumed that the government agencies involved represent the interests of the public at large.

Yet, the extension of the CRIMP framework to bioregions carries with it an implicit commitment to broaden the range of stakeholders involved. After all, watersheds usually comprise, at most, only a small portion of a local or regional political economy, whereas a bioregion—however it is defined—may encompass several "local" or regional political economies.[24] The result is that the list of actual stakeholders includes not only property owners but also those who live in the area in question and, under some circumstances, those who live outside of the area, too. Not all of these potential stakeholders would, necessarily, choose to be involved in devising a coordinated plan, of course, but the number cannot be limited in any simple fashion. As we shall see, one consequence of applying the CRIMP strategy to the bioregional level has been to convert what was conceived of as an administrative planning process to a much more complex political one.

The Biodiversity Strategy, formulated in bioregional terms in the 1991 Memorandum of Understanding was, it appears in retrospect, not just simply an effort to short-circuit Sacramento politics; it was also a result of the confluence of at least three different streams of intellectual and regulatory activity within the state of California during the mid- to late-1980s. The first was a process set into motion via legislation that mandated a full-blown study of the forestry issue by an inter-agency group called the "Timberland Task Force." The second was an ecological "rationality," to use Robert Cox's term, with origins in the counterculture of the 1960s. By the late 1980s, this rationality had spread throughout American society and could even be found among the directors and staffs of the state and federal resource agencies. Its counterpart in California was to be found among what agency officials called the "real bioregionalists" (Ewing 1992; Kennedy & Greiman 1992). Finally, the attempt to utilize "scientific" principles of ecology and ecosystem management as a means of rationalizing administration of resources, encountered local environmental politics *and* global civil society, as it were. It is here that we see most clearly the relationship between the material and the ideational, the ways in which the seeds of potential social transformation emerge into a world of already-existing institutional structures and political economies.[25]

Timberland Task Force and sequelae

The Timberland Task Force was a state-level response to what, by the mid- to late-1980s, was already a major social conflict over forestry and habitat issues. The task force was mandated by amendments to an omnibus appropriations bill submitted to the California State Assembly in March 1989, based on an unsuccessful bill introduced earlier by State Senator Barry Keene (D-Benecia). Although Keene's district was far from the forested areas in question, his involvement reflected the broad and growing concerns throughout California about resource use and distribution.

Keene's bill would have set up an eleven-member group to consider the conflict between wildlife protection and timber production in California. According to the Legislative Counsel's Digest of the amendments, the task force was to have the following objectives:

(a) Develop a coordinated base of scientific information on the location, extent, and species composition of timberland ecosystems in California which does all of the following:

> (1) Accommodates a range of definitions for timberland habitats, including old growth timberland.
>
> (2) Permits evaluation of the cumulative impact of timber harvesting and other activities on the biodiversity of timberland ecosystems and on individual species.
>
> (3) Permits evaluation of the timberland habitat for its contribution, if any, to the overall maintenance of specific wildlife species in California.
>
> (4) Permits estimation of the economic impact of alternative mitigation measures (California State Legislative Counsel's Digest 1989:3).

In addition to these objectives, the task force was also charged to design and contract for a study that would "Identify critical habitat areas necessary to maintain and restore viable populations of species dependent upon specific timberland habitats for all or part of their life cycle" (California State Legislative Counsel's Digest 1989:3). Finally, the task force was directed to begin its studies in the "north coastal region," which later came to be called the "Klamath Province."

The task force staff put together a "Revised Work Plan" and, in doing so, recognized almost immediately the inherent contradiction in a habitat- or ecosystem-oriented approach to fulfilling the requirements of the legislative mandate. As they put it, "[S]ignificant problems remain in assuring the public that adequate environmental protection is being provided and in guaranteeing landowners that their rights to the economic use of their property are protected" (Timberland Task Force Staff 1990:2). These problems were enumerated as follows:

> First, there is a growing scientific and public recognition that adequate protection of wildlife species now requires a shift away from a focus just

> on management of single species to a land or habitat-based approach with a goal of conserving overall biological diversity. Second, there is a broadly shared realization that habitat and wildlife protection requirements fall across ownership lines and that several landowners or agencies may need to cooperate to provide comprehensive protection. Third, as we are faced with the challenges of considering the cumulative effects of management and the provision of multiple resource services, agencies with a single resource focus must define ways to work cooperatively. Finally, unavoidably, enhanced levels of wildlife protection are costly in terms of program administration and limitations on management options available to landowners. A fundamental equity question about how much protection to provide and the socially appropriate distribution of costs awaits a well reasoned answer (Timberland Task Force Staff 1990:2).

For better or worse, the task force itself did not have time to wait for the "well reasoned answer"; a sunset clause in the implementing legislation gave it only until January 1, 1992 to fulfill its mandate.

As its work progressed, therefore, the task force sought a means to continue the studies it had initiated and to begin to implement the coordination strategy outlined in the Revised Work Plan. At this point, an initiative emerged out of the California and federal resource agencies in Sacramento. It is here that we see, first, the cultural and political influences of the 1960s starting to surface and, second, the extent to which ecology, both as science and philosophy, was becoming central to the practice of "wildlife management" and "resource conservation." The initiative also illustrates the ways in which individuals act when faced with various institutional and structural constraints plus a number of possible responses to a specific situation (Long & Long 1992).[26]

The initiative was engineered in 1990 by the director of the California office of the U.S. Bureau of Land Management, Ed Hasty. He was asked by members of the Timberland Task Force to establish an ad hoc subcommittee that would help to bring together the work of the task force and the developing efforts to apply CRIMP in California. Hasty, in turn, asked representatives of the California Department of Forestry and Fire Protection, the U.S. National Forest Service in Sacramento, and the California Board of Forestry to take over this task. They, along with several other members of the subcommittee, formulated a set of seventeen principles intended to track the task force's objectives. Hasty and others on this ad hoc subcommittee accepted the principles, and Hasty then asked for an action plan, which was written by Department of Forestry and Fire Protection staff.[27] The seventeen principles became the core of the Memorandum of Understanding on "California's Coordinated Regional Strategy to Conserve Biological Diversity."

There matters might have rested if not for the fact that a new governor—Pete Wilson—had taken office at the beginning of 1991, offering what Hasty saw as an opportunity to institutionalize the committee's action plan. Although a Republican, Wilson's position on environmental issues was fairly liberal, as these things go. Wilson had named Douglas Wheeler, a former president of the Sierra Club and executive of the World Wildlife Fund, as well as an appointee in the U.S. Department of the Interior, to be the new head of the California Resources Agency. So Hasty brought the action plan to Wheeler and others, all of whom thought it a good idea. The result was the 1991 MOU which put "bioregionalism" front and center as part of the plan.

Old ideologies, new rationalities

How, one might ask, could such a strategy be formulated *and* approved by government agencies whose missions were still largely framed by the Conservationism of the early twentieth century? And how can we know that these agencies are not really "handmaidens" of the industries they were intended to regulate? Both questions can be answered by reference to two points. First, bureaucracies in the midst of conflict and uncertainty can offer certain kinds of entrepreneurial opportunities for staff to develop new programs and approaches, especially if framed in rational bureaucratic terms. Second, such situations are also conducive to fluid and sometimes unusual political alliances, in which interests temporarily converge.

In the case of the MOU, we see the growing influence of certain "rationalities," whose origins can be traced back to the political and cultural upheavals of the 1960s, *and* the emergence of ecology and ecosystems analysis as wholly-legitimated approaches to environmental protection and sustainability. Conservationism, as noted earlier, regards Nature as a repository of utilitarian resources that are to be managed in such a way as to yield a steady flow from what is, ideally, a stock whose growth rate over the time period in question is sufficient to replace what has been taken away.[28] The watchword, in this instance, is "efficiency," in the sense of reducing or minimizing wastage. In this schema, notions such as habitat or ecosystem do not exist; interdependencies between species are, for the most part, not recognized. And species, whether plant or animal, that have no utilitarian value appear nowhere in the Conservationist calculus. Conservationism was a response to an expanding industrial base and an effort to control the predatory accumulation of capital characteristic of the late nineteenth century; hence, it was an outgrowth of the industrial system and entirely compatible with it.

Bioregionalism is different, according to its proponents (see the following discussion). While the utilitarian possibilities of Nature are recognized, they are not privileged; rather, it is the survival and health of the whole that is important. This objective implies that an understanding and appreciation of ecological interdependencies are critical to the entire enterprise. Any use of Nature that undermines this holism is, by definition, unacceptable. Consequently, the "sustainable" exploitation of resources must take place at a much lower level than would be possible under a Conservationist scheme.

But bioregionalism is also about jurisdictions and borders: the boundaries of bioregions are, in theory, supposed to correspond to ecosystemic boundaries, rather than political, economic, or social ones. Nature acquires primacy over society, in this scheme; ideally, society must adapt to Nature, rather than trying to conquer it.[29] Is bioregionalism compatible with capital accumulation as practiced over the past 100-odd years? Perhaps, although this is not entirely clear: the relationship between bioregionalism and global industrialism has not only not been tested in practice, it has not even been worked out on paper (Lipschutz 1991c). As we shall see, this has led to some curious, and unpredictable, outcomes.

In the United States, state and federal resource agencies are still, to a large degree, directed by individuals whose belief systems run toward "Pinchotism," that is, applied Conservationism. This group of older, mostly white male supervisors in central offices is, however, being displaced by a growing cadre of middle managers and field staff who have been schooled in the science of ecology as it emerged in the 1960s and 1970s. Many of these individuals came of age during those years and were influenced not only in their beliefs but also in their professional career choices by the environmental movement of that period. Thus, they came to their work holding some notion of environmental protection as a desirable public good, with ecology as its intellectual basis.[30]

The result has been a gradual transformation in the self-proclaimed missions of individuals in many of these agencies and, more slowly, the agencies themselves.[31] Perhaps the most visible of these missions is the "New Forestry," epitomized in the person of Jerry Franklin, a plant ecologist for the U.S. Forest Service Pacific Northwest Research Station. He argues that forests should be treated as ecosystems and not simply as sources of commodities. Franklin's strategy emphasizes the importance of habitat protection and forest maintenance, rather than just extraction to meet the requirements of industry (Mitchell 1991b:94–95; Wallick 1992). This approach is gradually acquiring legitimacy in the forest agencies and has led to the establishment of groups such as the Association of Forest Service Employees for Environmental Ethics, which takes a deliberately global view of forestry.[32] A second trend is a growing orientation toward an approach based in conservation biology, which is more broadly oriented toward maintenance of biodiversity and ecosystems (Soulé 1986; Fiedler & Jain 1992). As individuals trained in these, and other, scientific approaches to environmental protection rise through the ranks of the agencies, their influence is becoming increasingly important in terms of what the agencies try, or are willing to try, to do (U.S. BLM 1993).

Thus, as noted earlier, prior to his appointment as current head of the California Resources Agency, Douglas Wheeler was active in several of what are now considered "mainstream" environmental organizations. As he put it, "I first heard about bioregionalism at the World Wildlife Fund. . . ."

> [I]f we've learned anything since the Endangered Species Act in 1973, it's that trying to save each species, one by one, as it goes into crisis, won't give us the certainty in planning we must have to sustain our economy. . . . So, long term, there's no way around looking at the habitats as a whole. That's why we seek to make this idea of bioregional planning relevant to resource planning in California (McHugh 1992:7).

Several of the resource agency personnel I interviewed admitted, quite frankly, not only that they had been influenced by the cultural changes of the last thirty years but that, in some instances, they were quite deliberately drawing on the ideas promoted by thinkers in the bioregional movement. Indeed, some suggested that the use of the term "bioregion" in the preamble to the Memorandum of Understanding on Biodiversity was a deliberate attempt to frame the issue in jurisdictional, rather than just scientific terms. In doing this, however, agency officials failed to anticipate the already-existing influence throughout California of what some called the "real bioregional movement" (Kennedy & Greiman 1992). These changes in rationalities would not be possible in isolation, especially insofar as they contradict the established ideologies of the agencies. But there was and is sufficient support for them outside of the agencies—in addition to growing evidence regarding the condition of various resources and species, especially in the terms of ecosystem management (Stevens 1993d)—to make the changes legitimate and possible.

The "real" bioregionalists

The authors of the MOU on Biodiversity apparently used bioregional language as a sort of shorthand; they anticipated developing regional strategies, along the lines of CRIMP plans, that would benefit from input and ratification by individuals, organizations, and politicians within the target regions (Ewing 1992). Their conception—and this remains largely the case with current formulations of ecosystem management—was scientific, technical, and administrative, and it did not anticipate political contestation.

But bioregionalism as a political-social concept was already widely-known throughout northern California, disseminated by Gary Snyder, who lives in the South Yuba River watershed in the Sierra Nevada foothills, Freeman House and his colleagues in the Mattole River watershed on the Lost Coast of California, Peter Berg at Planet Drum Foundation in San Francisco, and numerous others with "green" tendencies committed, either in theory or practice, to bioregionalism as a social strategy.[33] As Snyder put it,

> The term 'bioregion' was adopted by the signers to the Memorandum on Biological Diversity as a technical term from the field of bio-geography. I'm sure they couldn't have known that there were already groups of people around the United States and Canada who were talking in terms of bioregionally-oriented societies (Snyder 1992).

In this, as it turns out, Snyder was wrong; agency officials *did* know of bioregionalism, although they were less sure of its political content or implications.

What is a bioregion, anyway? As a scientific term, it denotes ecological-geographic provinces or regions, often oriented around creek or river watersheds, whose biological and physical composition are somehow distinct from those of a neighboring region.[34] Hence, it would be accurate, on the basis of wildlife, vegetation, geography, geology, and watersheds, to describe the Sacramento River valley as a bioregion distinct from, say, any of the dozens of creek and river watersheds on the Pacific Coast or San Francisco Bay Delta regions. These distinctions are, quite obviously, only approximate. Unlike human beings, Nature draws few sharp boundaries, preferring ecotones instead (Holland, Risser & Naiman 1991).

As a political and social concept, bioregionalism is this, and more. A collection of articles on the political, cultural, and social aspects of the concept offers the following: "Bioregionalism calls for human society to be more closely related to nature (hence, bio), and to be more conscious of its locale, or region, or life-place (therefore, region)" (Andruss, Plant, Plant & Wright 1990:2). Advocates of bioregionalism suggest that existing political units are artificial and bear no relationship to the land (an assumption that is only partly true, even in the United States, where many state boundaries were deliberately drawn so as not to correspond to natural features; see Deudney 1995a). They propose, therefore, that human societies and their politics be formulated around ecological-geographic areas such as creek and river watersheds. There are clearly some difficulties with this notion, especially insofar as a political/social bioregion is no more "natural" than, say, a county, and it can, at the extreme, reflect a form of environmental determinism.[35] Still, by appealing to Nature as "natural," the notion of a bioregion acquires a legitimacy that many find wanting in existing political institutions.[36]

Bioregionalism is also a concept with a resonance that extends beyond its devotees. It feeds into widespread visions of local autonomy, democracy, and even independence, inasmuch as it puts borders around the places that a region's inhabitants know best. County lines are mostly unmarked; bioregional boundaries correspond to rivers, mountains, and coasts. Places are culturally significant in a way that most political institutions are not. And such designations also allow people to draw distinctions between "insiders" who know and "outsiders" who don't. This sensibility extends even to the field staff of the state and federal agencies. Most of them have been trained in some subdiscipline of ecology and are quite familiar with the notion of bioregionalism. Many have "gone native." Because their place of work is regional, their sympathies are local and their loyalties to the center are often weaker than their commitments to their "homes." Political bioregionalism speaks to many people in a language they can understand and, as suggested in chapter 3, seeks to protect the same things that concern many practicing ecologists. Nonetheless, politics and science are engaged here in a constant struggle.

Science meets politics

As a political program, consequently, bioregionalism offers a set of guidelines for action and, many suppose, human social transformation at the collective level. By contrast, the scientific-technical concept is largely devoid of social factors, regarding humans as exogenous "disturbers" of ecosystems oriented around some type of equilibrium[37] and seeking to stabilize the political and economic system as it currently exists.[38] As one group of fisheries biologists has argued recently: "Resource problems are not really environmental problems. . . . They are human problems that we have created at many times and in many places under a variety of political, social, and economic systems" (cited in Stevens 1993c). The real political difficulty arises, consequently, in internalizing these "human problems" into an ecosystemic assessment conducted from a scientific perspective *without thereby implying a commitment to radical change in the social system.*

Moreover, the uncertainty inherent in predicting human behavior makes any kind of management strategy quite difficult, especially in the absence of such (mutually agreed to) social change. Whereas there is a great deal of uncertainty in predicting the year-to-year trends in an ecosystem, there is, at least, some predictability about the *behavior* of individuals and populations of animals and plants. Spotted owls will continue to make their homes in old-growth snags, and marbled murrelets will continue to fly inland to raise their young. Rational choice theory notwithstanding, human beings, alone and in society, are much less predictable, and they have the potential to alter their behavior in significant ways.[39]

The upshot of the tension between the technical and political bioregionalists is that the latter may have a decided advantage when it comes to negotiating the reconstruction of resource regimes and the modification of property rights, because they are not hobbled by scientific uncertainty. An ecosystems management approach to environmental protection and conservation—which, in this context, involves social choice and governance—acquires its legitimacy via the invocation of and recourse to a positivistic "science"; again, there is here some bureaucratic (as well as ecological) sense that what is "natural" must also be what is "right."[40] Science, it is believed, can provide a "true baseline" against which perturbations can be measured and their effects determined and managed—up to a point, anyway, inasmuch as paleobiology demonstrates the fundamental role of change rather than stasis in earth's natural history.[41]

But what do we mean by the notion of a "baseline?" Presumably, that would be ecosystems as they existed prior to 1492, although, even then, these ecosystems were already part of the human "environment." Outside of a few members of Earth First!, not even the most ardent advocates of bioregionalism propose to return to that baseline. Indeed, many environmentalists accept current conditions as being more-or-less acceptable, demanding only that there be no additional cutting of old growth or damage to other resources. Extractive industries, such as logging, fishing, mining, and ranching, find even this baseline to be too radical, arguing that there remains more than enough intact old-growth forest or other resource to permit some degree of future exploitation. In other words, the choice of a baseline from which to measure change, and with respect to which one would assess programmatic success, helps to determine the scale and scope of a management strategy. Choosing the baseline, however, is a social and political exercise, *not* a scientific one.

This raises problems for agency staff, who are trying to find and legitimate some sort of balance between the apparent requirements of ecological balance and the economic and political demands of their diverse constituencies. The emerging approach is, nonetheless, to frame management plans in technical terms and to propose detailed ecological assessments of individual provinces and tracts, focusing on those that are federally- or state-owned (regular access to private property remains problematic). This is to be done by using geographic information systems (GIS) and ground-based surveys that can be checked against each other and which, it is hoped, will provide detailed and easily accessible data bases that can be called up by anyone with a computer, a modem, and a minimal amount of training in ecology and GIS use (Moles 1993; Williams 1993). Such data bases will also, according to the plan, allow ethnobotanists and others to catalogue non-timber forest products that might become the basis for new forest use economies.[42] The implicit hope is that the entire enterprise, by adopting a scientific epistemology, will acquire a "respectability" that will help parties now in conflict to find acceptable compromises.

This hope may be a disingenuous one, inasmuch as the cataloguing and assessment process will be very costly *and* will not be completed for a number of years (if funding permits). Moreover, it is assumed that planning authority will rest with agency scientists and resource managers. This is, possibly, another faint hope, because even as the Biodiversity Project struggled through its first few years, several communities in the Klamath Province had already begun to overcome at least some of their internal antipathies, beginning their own planning process and seeking funding to support their proposed projects based, if possible, on forest clearing and salvage. Paradoxically, perhaps, the state of California and other public institutions have been fostering with one hand what they hope to prevent with the other: they have provided financial and technical support for community-based GIS analysis, and training, through quasi-NGOs (similar to what the British call a "quango") and outside of the purview of the agencies running the Biodiversity Project. One such example is the collaboration between the Klamath GIS Project in the Trinity Alps and public institutions and agencies, including the University of California, the U.S. Forest Service, the U.S. Fish & Wildlife Service, the California Board of Forestry and others (Klamath GIS Project brochure, 1994). The data from the Klamath GIS Project are available to regional watershed groups and forest collecting groups now, to meet their immediate needs.

What this suggests is that, first, while the agencies' GIS programs may, at some point, be gleaned for practical (or "useful") knowledge, they will not bear much in the way of useful fruit anytime in the near future. More important than this is the fact that within ten years, the timber-based political economy of the region will disappear almost completely and might, by that time, have already been replaced by locally-initiated alternatives. Consequently, the political process at the local level could well outrun the ability of the agencies to keep up, although they will continue to collect technical data with a view toward re-establishing *their* control. This could become a point of struggle between the local level, where participants are committed to local control and are willing to resist outsiders, and the state and national levels, which are legally- and politically-bound to assert and maintain control over what is, in large part, public property.[43]

It is worth noting that these local plans are, to a large degree, formulated in the language of ecology, but for political, and not technical, reasons. For example, one such proposal was, according to a newspaper report, formulated with the "aim to enhance the ecosystem of the . . . Shasta-

Trinity National Forest by employing displaced loggers and mill workers to rehabilitate roads and 'fireproof' the woods by tree thinning and burning forest litter during the spring and late fall."[44] In the same article, Nadine Bailey, the outspoken spouse of a northern California logger, who is also well-known for her dislike of environmentalists, was quoted as arguing that "The ecology of each forest will demand unique solutions" (Martin 1993). What this means in practice is not so clear; what *is* clear is that ecological and other science-based concepts and language are being used not to describe technical strategies but to legitimate political solutions. So long as a technical veneer can be maintained, local compromises are possible and common interests may be discovered. How these proposals will ultimately fare at the state and national levels remains to be seen; indeed, many urban environmentalists are less than happy with them.[45]

There is a final paradox in all of this. Those strategies that have been devised to address conflicts within communities and among resource users over environmental issues place their primary and initial focus on the process of discovering areas of shared interests, values and beliefs. They have little, if any, technical basis or content (Cruikshank 1987; Gamman 1994, 1991; Crowfoot & Wondolleck 1990). As John Gamman notes:

> In many instances it is difficult to identify how resource users and environmental NGO's [sic] share common interests. For example, when mining companies wish to explore biologically unique areas, it may be in conflict with the interests of NGO's [sic] which want to preserve them. However, this kind of conflict is rarely monolithic, involving only one issue. Rather than classifying the conflict as centering around one large issue, it is helpful to break out the larger issue into sub-issues, to find where tradeoffs can be made that satisfy both parties . . . (1991:49).[46]

Scientific and technical data enter into this process only as, first, a means of indicating that damage or degradation has taken place—although uncertainty in the data may provide support for opposing positions—and, second, after an initial agreement has been formulated (in the California instance, for example, an agreement to shift away from intensive resource extraction). The central process of finding shared interests, values, and beliefs is largely a political one, inasmuch as this involves establishing new constitutive rules for the local resource regime (see chapter 2).[47] The language, and even the numbers, of ecology will undoubtedly play a part in these discussions, but primarily as a means of legitimizing positions within a new framework of resource management and exploitation.[48]

As noted earlier, the California Biodiversity Strategy was initiated by resource agency staff in an effort to bypass a legislative gridlock and, in light of the Dwyer injunction, in the hope of avoiding further intervention by the courts. As one individual put it, the agencies, a product of Conservationism, were "out of synch" with the times and needed to become more innovative (Ewing 1992). Others expressed the opinion that, because the strategy was an administrative initiative, it would not have to come before the state legislature for ratification (Kennedy & Grieman 1992). By setting the context for the emergence of what might be called a new and local *polis*, these agencies were looking to stakeholders to formulate and ratify acceptable and "sensible" ecosystem management plans. Ironically, the resource managers were trying to do what environmental groups had been doing for years: bypass the state. But for California and federal bureaucracies, this tactic holds particular risks. Legitimating a *polis* in this fashion may, in fact, transfer power from the bureaucracy to the stakeholders, even if it is only the power of the veto. Outcomes may be quite different from those desired or hoped for by the initiators of the strategy.[49] As we shall see in the following stories, the agencies are, in some instances, struggling to keep up with the "people."

Applied bioregionalism: Three stories from the Klamath Province

The "Klamath Province" is huge (Figure 4.2). It encompasses an area of some 26,500 square miles (and, strictly speaking, includes a part of southern Oregon, as well). Its terrain includes coastal plain and mountain ranges, major inland mountain ranges and their foothills to the east, and numerous creeks and river watersheds that, in the west, flow into the Pacific and, in the east, the Sacramento River Valley. Ecologically, the region is characterized throughout by many similar plant and animal species, and watersheds often share many characteristics; at the same time, important ecological differences can be found over even very short distances (Jensen, Torn & Harte 1993). Socially and politically, however, there are major differences between the coastal plain, the mountains, and the eastern part of the province. These differences are a function of both the local political economy, recent history, and historical patterns of human settlement and in-migration from California's cities. The result is that the self-designated subregions of the Klamath Province—there are at least five—have somewhat different political and economic orders.

Generally speaking, each of the different physical landscapes in the province was historically constituted by different forms of capital accumulation and development, and dominated by a different form of resource extraction, although there was considerable intermixing among these. Along the coastal plains, the major sources of livelihood were fishing, sheep and

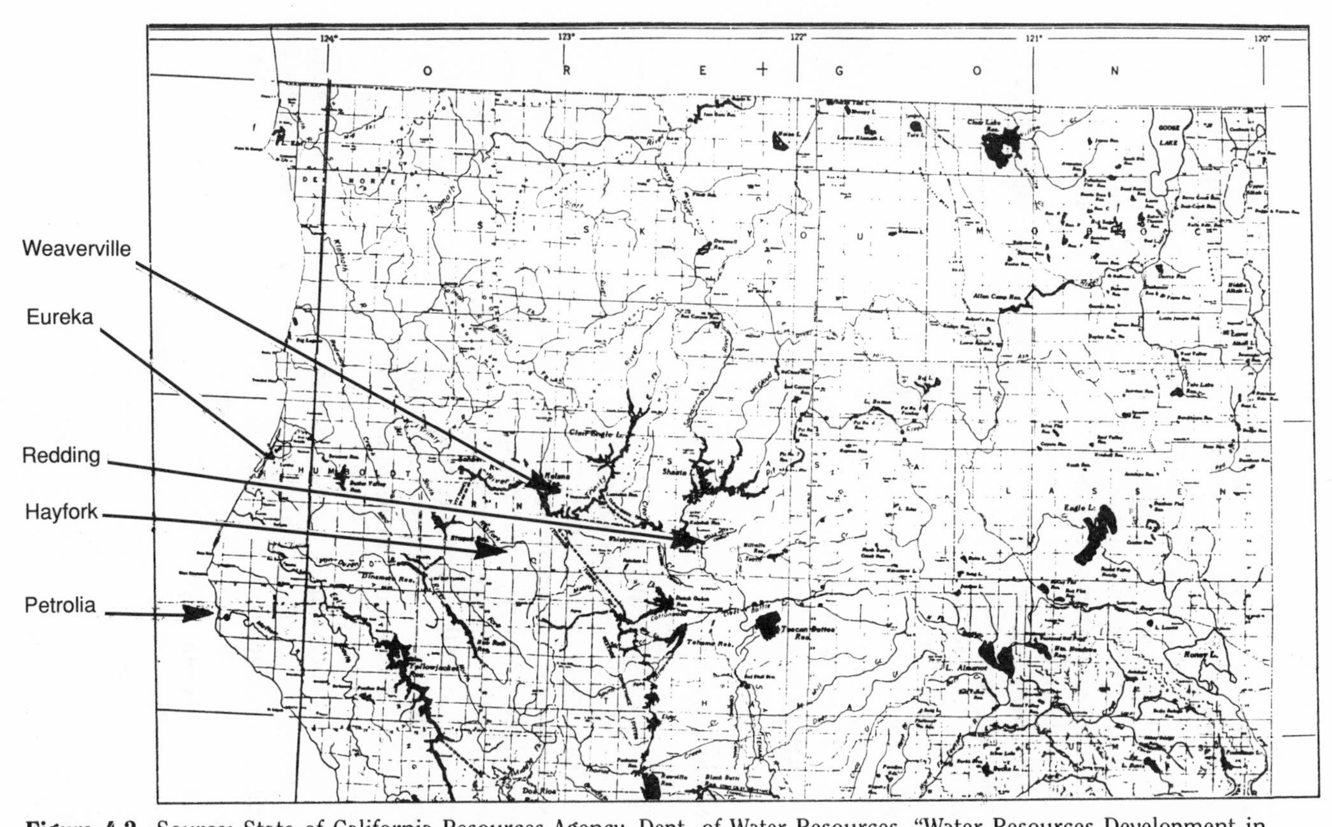

Figure 4.2. Source: State of California Resources Agency, Dept. of Water Resources, "Water Resources Development in California, Oct. 1970.

cattle ranching, and logging. The mountain ranges were dominated by logging and mining. The interior foothills were logged and grazed. In recent years, each of these extractive systems has begun to decline. The offshore commercial salmon fisheries have been subject to extreme variations in recent years.[50] Some ranching still goes on, although sheep ranchers often complain bitterly that they cannot compete with protected predators (coyotes, mountain lions, etc.; "Future Economics" 1992). Some mining still takes place, although mineral corporations contend that they have too difficult a time acquiring all requisite permits for new mines. And logging, of course, has been shrinking as a consequence of resource depletion, substitution of technology for labor, and competition in terms of the cost of other sources of lumber (Mitchell 1991a, 1991b; Sample & Le Master 1992).[51] Nonetheless, each of these industries has left behind political cultures whose adherents—some of whose families have been in the area for four or five generations—are fiercely loyal to their land, livelihoods, and "the way things used to be." Historically, there has been a considerable degree of intermarriage, as well, between Native Americans and old-time Anglo families. These old-timers are often locally prominent or community leaders or hold elective offices in the region's towns and counties, and many are also well-linked into California's politics.[52]

Overlain on this older demographic stratum are, as noted earlier, more recent arrivals, some of whom came as part of the "back to the land" movement of the 1960s and early 1970s, others who, as they put it, "escaped" the city, and those graduates of the local branch of the California State University who stayed after graduation.[53] These arrivals have brought all kinds of economic, social, and cultural innovations with them. Some have tried their hand at small-scale organic agriculture, although given local market demand, it is not an easy way to earn a living. Others are teachers, waiters, and craftspeople, with a few writers thrown in. They are mostly white, mostly of urban, middle-class origins, mostly environmentalists (with some survivalists—who may or may not also be environmentalist, but usually are not—present, for good measure). The environmental organizations in the province—there are two or three major ones and a larger number of smaller "watershed"-based groups—draw much of their membership from these "recent" arrivals. But, when one of the old-timers uses the epithet "environmentalist," it is usually these "recent" arrivals who are being conjured up (even though some have lived in the region for more than twenty years). There are a few members of the first group who have taken on some of the values and beliefs of the second, but only insofar as "environmentalism" represents a strategy to restore the past.

In recent years, the interior of the Klamath Province, centered on the city of Redding at the head of the Sacramento Valley just below Shasta

Lake, has become increasingly dependent on tourism, urban retirees, and health services. The resource extraction part of the local political economy has, thus, become somewhat more marginal to the area than was true in the past, and those involved with it seem to feel they are under attack (Kelly 1993; *SHARE* various issues). Some of the retirees have environmental sensibilities, insofar as they wish to limit further development in their neck of the woods (Williams 1993). They do not, however, support the wholesale social transformation advocated by some of the more radical environmentalists in the province. Those whose livelihoods have come to depend on tourism may not like what they see happening, but they cannot oppose it without threatening their own welfare. As we shall see, this rather heterogenous mix, resulting from a more homogenous and older rural political economy meeting a newer, more cosmopolitan one with urban origins, not only leads to odd politics but also to some unexpected contrasts between communities.

The accounts that follow, are centered in three of the communities within the Klamath Province. While they are all superficially similar, there is more difference than meets the eye. Indeed, the surprise is that the differences are so great across a distance of no more than about one hundred miles as the crow flies, going from Redding to Eureka via the Trinity Alps, and south a short distance toward the coast. More than this, the particular conjunction between changing demography and changing political economy has been responsible for the different outcomes in each community. These differences have a great deal to say about the necessary (but not sufficient) conditions for establishing a common–pool property regime in a particular area.

Mattole Watershed Alliance/Mattole Restoration Council

One of the first attempts to establish a bioregional "planning group" took place in the Mattole River town of Petrolia, on what is called the "Lost Coast of California."[54] The watershed falls within two different counties and districts of the California Department of Fish and Game (House 1992b:2). Historically, the economy of the area has been dependent on logging, fishing, and ranching, the ranches having been established late in the nineteenth century. The area experienced an influx of "new people" beginning in the 1960s, with an especially large number arriving during the late 1970s. The cash flowing into the region from marijuana cultivation, a cultural renaissance, and an influx of individuals engaged in craft-based and other types of work created something of an economic boom at that time.[55] Most of the land in the watershed is privately owned, although some twelve percent is within the Bureau of Land Management's 52,000-acre King Range Conservation Area (Walker 1992:225–30; Campbell 1992).

By the late 1970s, the salmon run in the Mattole River was in serious decline, and in the early 1980s, a number of the "new" arrivals in the region established the Mattole Watershed Salmon Support Group, a private, non-profit organization whose goal was the restoration of the chinook salmon runs. Among the group's founders were Freeman House and Dan Weaver, two of the "real bioregionalists" discussed previously, as well as several individuals with technical training in ecology and fisheries biology. The group went about its work very systematically. It surveyed salmon populations, spawning grounds, and nests. It looked for existing and potential causes of fishery decline. The group did whatever possible to maintain or restore salmon habitat in the river, including establishment of "homemade hatching and rearing facilities" (California Executive Council 1994:4; House 1992a; Zuckerman 1992). In the course of the group's work, it became clear that one of the major sources of damage to the fishery was erosion and the deposition of sediment into the river, via landslides, from road maintenance and activities associated with ranching. This meant, in the words of Vicki Campbell, then with the BLM office in Arcata, that salmon restoration had to move "out of the stream and up on the hillside" (Campbell 1992).

Consequently, in 1986, some of the local activists established the Mattole Restoration Council, which based its program on bioregionalism and took the watershed as its broader focus. It emphasized improvement of fish habitat and passage, reduction of sedimentation and restoration of vegetation, where possible. Inevitably, perhaps, the council's analyses and pinpointing of the causes of degradation, and the necessary responses, brought it into conflict with local landowners. These individuals saw the council not only as a hotbed of environmental radicalism but also as a threat to their property rights.

In January 1991, a regional meeting was arranged, at the behest of the council, to discuss how erosion into and sedimentation in the Mattole River was affecting the salmon fishery. The meeting was, by all reports, a "hot and heavy" encounter between ranchers and activists (Zuckerman 1992; Campbell 1992). Still, at the suggestion of then-University of California Extension Forester Richard Harris, participants agreed to "continue" the meeting at a later date. A new agenda committee was set up, including council members as well as six local ranchers but no governmental representatives (except the BLM, which, as a landholder in the watershed, later joined the committee). Discussions within the committee proved, in the words of one Petrolia resident, to be "transformative." Another public meeting was then held at the Mattole Grange in April 1991, at which the salmon problem proved to be the issue around which the very divergent interests of ranchers, environmentalists, and others could converge. During that meeting, the Mattole Watershed Alliance (MWA), with broader membership than the Restoration Council, was established.

The relatively narrow basis for consensus around which the MWA emerged proved enough to carry weight with both county and state agencies. The MWA was seen as representative of *all* stakeholders within the watershed, and not only environmentalists or lumber companies or ranchers. Hence, government agencies such as California Fish and Game and the Mendocino County Department of Public Works were willing to consider proposals that might otherwise have been difficult, if not impossible, to implement. For example, MWA members concluded that salmon restoration would require restrictions in the fishing season, and communicated this point to Fish and Game. Consequently, the agency agreed to close the Mattole to all recreational fishing and, later, to restrict commercial fishing off the river's mouth. In another instance, the MWA convinced the Mendocino county public works department to cease pushing debris cleared from a road into the river. The MWA was able to get state funding reinstated for its "backyard wild hatchery program" by the state committee responsible for such matters. Finally, it was also able to negotiate an agreement with salmon trollers to close the "commercial fishery at the mouth of the Mattole just during the time that the wild fish are gathering for their spawning run upstream" (House 1992b:3, 4). Not all of the MWA's early efforts were successful. When it came to discussing logging in the Mattole watershed, the major timber company, Pacific Lumber (PALCO, a subsidiary of Maxxam), refused to be bound by the MWA's wishes; the MWA, in turn, decided not to press the point (Markoff 1993).

On this last matter, however, the MWA most definitely did not represent the broad sweep of environmentalist opinion in the watershed (or the region), which is strongly dedicated to the preservation of old-growth forests, a tenet routinely opposed by PALCO. The company was acquired by Maxxam in 1986 in a $900 million leveraged buyout financed by junk bonds. Subsequently, PALCO was accused of greatly increasing its rate of logging on private lands of both second- and old-growth, far beyond the bounds of "sustainable yield," in order to pay the interest on the bonds. Earth First!, among other groups, made it a point of routinely challenging *all* actions by Maxxam and PALCO, and not just those affecting old-growth, in an effort to bring to public attention what was happening in northern California. Thus, the MWA's decision to not confront Pacific Lumber over the issue of logging in the Mattole watershed can be seen as a necessary part of the consensus-building needed to keep the group functioning.

Between 1980 and mid-1994, the Council, Salmon Group and Alliance undertook thirty-four restoration projects in the watershed, two-thirds of which were funded by state agencies and environmental NGOs such as the Coastal Conservancy (although there were, and continue to be, internal disagreements about the propriety of accepting governmental funds for these projects; California Executive Council 1994:4). These groups' roles in the Mattole Valley represent a mutually-transformative process of both community and state: the community, in finding the basis for collective action (albeit not without conflict), and the state, in recognizing the possibility of and necessity for local involvement in environmental restoration and governance. The Mattole-based effort represents one approach to bioregional organizing and is, by now, pointed to as a model by resource agencies in Sacramento and their staff in local field offices (California Executive Council 1994; Ewing 1992).

To some degree, the efforts of the organizations in the Mattole watershed reflect a transformation in the political economy of the area, as long-time residents are joined by "newcomers," some of whom make their livings in non-traditional ways. It demonstrates the diffusion of ecology, as a science, and Ecology, as knowledge and belief, into a local community via the networks of global civil society (Mattole Restoration Council 1995). It illustrates the reorganization of that community around new meanings and shared interest in a resource that many felt was changing beyond recognition. Finally, it seems to show, according to some observers, that even private landowners are coming to realize that their ownership rights in the land are not limitless and also include certain responsibilities (Campbell 1992). But the Mattole watershed is a unique place, as are all such places; it cannot be reproduced, in toto, even in the neighboring Bear River Valley watershed, where attempts were being made in 1993 to introduce a CRIMP project without much in the way of preparation.[56] Models are representations, not reality.

North Klamath Steering Committee

The North Klamath sub-region of the Klamath bioregional province provides a counterpoint to the Mattole. This region is centered on Humboldt County and the northern part of Mendocino County, from the Pacific Coast inland—it is, most definitely, not "lost." The major population centers, Eureka (27,000), Arcata (15,200), McKinleyville (10,750), and Fortuna (8,800), are strung out along Highway 101, the major transportation artery for the Pacific Coast from Los Angeles to the Olympic Peninsula in Washington. Historically, the region was highly dependent on extractive industries—mining, ranching, logging, and fishing—but, in recent decades, the area has begun to shift toward service industries (with concomitant impacts on employment and incomes; Martin 1994a). There is a branch of the California State University system, Humboldt State University, in Arcata. The influx of new residents since the 1960s has been significant here, too, and is most evident in Arcata, which has all the trappings of a California college town, including the requisite fans of the Grateful Dead. The pattern of land ownership in this part of the coastal region differs from the interior parts of the province. The percentage of privately-owned land is much higher, including a fair amount of uncut second-growth and smaller amounts of old-growth timber.

Here, too, the traditional industries have fallen on hard times. Logging is in decline, and several lumber mills have closed (including at least one noted for its violations of pollution regulations and sued by the Surfrider Foundation; the mill's owners decided to cease operations rather than clean up). Increasingly, as is the case along the Pacific coast into British Columbia and Alaska, whole logs are being shipped to other destinations, rather than being milled in the area. This, along with new lumber milling and manufacturing technologies, such as laminated beams, have also increased unemployment.

Commercial fishing is in serious trouble all along the California coast, too: In 1992, in an effort to restore the salmon fishery, and after several years of supply-shortened commercial seasons, the Pacific Fisheries Management Council banned all commercial salmon fishing along a 450-mile stretch from Point Arena in Mendocino County to Florence, Oregon; in 1993, there was no season at all (McKay 1992:3).[57] Many boatowners have berthed their craft permanently or have tried to sell them in Alaska; a few have even sold their fishing licenses to big corporations and signed on with them as waged labor (Dobson 1995).

Finally, from the perspective of outside capital, the north coast has all the disadvantages of poor access—it is a six hour drive from San Francisco—and relatively high labor costs. The most buoyant industry is easily "ecotourism" (although it is not usually called that). Highway 101 is heavily travelled, and the U.S. and state of California redwood parks strung out along several hundred miles of its length are a major tourist attraction, as are the beaches (often shrouded in fog) and the mountains rising to the east. But most of the people in the traffic that flows up and down the coast are "car camping" and not big spenders. The resulting service industry does not pay particularly well either (Buckley 1994; Nelson 1994).

Nonetheless, there seems to be little sense of either economic or resource problems here, although everyone is aware of the decline of the traditional industries (Martin 1994a). The evidence of economic trouble is not as clear here as in other places and, to the degree that the service industries located in the towns are able to survive, and even thrive, the direct experience of decline is not as strong as in the logging communities in the mountains. Finally, given that there is a considerable amount of second-growth timber in the hands of the larger lumber companies, there is still the possibility—however remote—that logging and fishing could be revived, if only "'environmentalists' would get out of the way" (Kay 1990; U.S. Senate 1995).

There are, to be sure, a surprising number of environmental organizations to be found in the North Klamath bioregion: fifteen are members of the North Coast Environmental Center (NCEC) in Arcata, including local chapters of Audubon and the Sierra Club, and there are others scattered throughout the region as well. NCEC functions as a clearinghouse, educational center, research sponsor, environmental consultant, and litigant in the courts. As with many environmental organizations in larger cities, NCEC has a historically-antagonistic relationship with the extractive industries in the region, especially timber companies. Relations with urban and national environmental organizations are not always smooth either. Even though NCEC's member groups share rationalities and ethics with their national and international counterparts, these latter organizations are sometimes seen as outsiders meddling in places they hardly know at all.

All of these factors combine to make the North Klamath subregion a difficult place in which to create a bioregional consensus; at the same time, that antagonistic actors have even managed to talk to each other represents a major accomplishment. Indeed, the subregion's Steering Committee includes ranchers, owners of large and small timber stands, representatives of Alta California (an organization run by an ex-timber public relations man, representing timber interests, among others), the Farm Bureau, the NCEC, the Sierra Club, and others. By 1993, this committee had been meeting for almost three years and had found it difficult to arrive at agreement on any type of shared interest, much less engage in a renegotiation of resource regimes. There was, according to one participant in the meetings, too much focus on process and not enough on projects (Stuart 1993).

Beyond this, the ongoing battles in the woods and the courts contribute to the maintenance of bad feelings and intentions among Steering Committee members and interest groups at large. Whenever a lumber company begins operations in one of its tracts—often, even with a timber harvest plan in place—it is likely to be hauled into court by nearby residents and/or environmentalists. For example, one meeting of the North Klamath subregion group took place in late November 1992, which just happened to be after the so-called Thanksgiving Day Massacre. PALCO, without having received official permission, began logging old-growth redwoods in the Owl Creek watershed of the Headwaters Forest (Headwaters was one of the stands at the focus of Redwood Summer). Environmentalists walked out of the meeting, and the episode left a residue of hostility for some time thereafter. Subsequent attempts by PALCO to log around Headwaters have also been contested in the courts. For the moment, not much appears to be happening in this area.

What this story suggests is that not only is the renegotiation of a resource regime a difficult task, it also requires a general acknowledgment that something more is at stake than just employment or environment. In the absence of a real sense of crisis within a political economy and community, buttressed by visible, material evidence that alternatives are lacking, the incentives to negotiate are weak. In particular, *meanings* are central to the effort to discover shared interests, and these are not evident in this subregion. In the absence of shared meanings, it is unlikely that any sort of consensus can be developed. The economy of the North Klamath subregion is sufficiently diversified, and the population apparently sufficiently large, that the material evidence remains unconvincing. Whether these visible conditions will change in the future remains, as yet, unclear.

Bioregionalism and Ecosystem Management in Hayfork

Hayfork is a very small town in the center of the Klamath Province. Surprisingly, some of the most active organizations in the area are to be found there, a direct result of the Memorandum of Understanding on biological diversity and "Option 9." The town is in Trinity County, amidst the Trinity Alps, two national forests, Shasta-Trinity and Six Rivers, and the 3,000 square mile watershed of the Trinity River. Some 70% of the watershed (1,340,000 acres) is included in the national forests. Of this, 69,000 acres are part of the Hoopa Valley Indian Reservation, and 45,600 acres fall within U.S. Bureau of Land Management jurisdiction. Fifteen percent of the watershed is owned by commercial timber companies, with towns and ranches comprising the rest. About 17,000 people live in the county's approximately 3,000 square miles, 4,000 in the county seat, Weaverville, 2,400 in Hayfork (Hayfork Economic Alliance, n.d).

As elsewhere in the province, the political economy of the region has historically depended on mining, ranching and grazing, and logging, with the last being the most important to Hayfork. Most of the lumber has come from the almost 80% of the county's land that is national forest, and so the Dwyer injunction had a particularly serious impact on the county. Weaverville has been less affected than Hayfork. Not only is it the county seat, it is also home to the local offices of several federal and state offices. Its location on the main east-west route through the Trinity Alps also means that it reaps at least some rents from tourist dollars. Hayfork is the location of one of the few remaining lumber mills in California able to mill large-girth, old-growth trees. Otherwise, it is "off the beaten path."

As has been the case in other parts of northern California, an influx of "newcomers" in the in the 1960s and 1970s began to change the economic complexion of the area. By the late 1970s, marijuana provided a major source of cash in the county, bringing with it a "mini-boom." The collapse in National Forest timber sales—from 220 million board-feet during the early 1980s to only 34 million by the early 1990s—occurred in tandem with state and federal efforts to halt pot farming. The result was a virtual regional depression (Martin 1995b). By 1992, some 30% of the people living in the local school district were said to be on public entitlements (Jungwirth 1993).

In 1989, in response to the first listing of the Northern Spotted Owl, which applied to the National Forests in the Trinity River watershed as well as in Oregon and Washington, private sector employers in Hayfork, with funding from the local Chamber of Commerce, set up the Hayfork Economic Alliance. The Alliance dedicated itself to re-establishing access to National Forest lumber. In early 1992, the Alliance, which could be characterized generously as "anti-owl," put together a plan called the "Trinity Watershed Forest Model," involving the

> [A]dministrative establishment of a state of the art forest model that looks exactly like the 1,908,000 acre Trinity River watershed. Using spatially planned, landscape forestry, structurally designed by professionals with best available technology to determine it's [sic] real potential and carrying capacity, the Trinity River basin is an ideal setting for a demonstration on a scale consistent with watershed and bioregional approaches (Hayfork Economic Alliance n.d.:2).

The Alliance quite deliberately included only landowners and private business in its membership, excluding, in particular, environmentalists and other "new arrivals." The latter group was rather more intent on stopping old-growth logging and, therefore, opposed to the Alliance's proposal. Efforts to find some basis for compromise between the two groups generally led only to intensified hostilities, although meetings began to take place during 1992, under the auspices of the state's biodiversity project.[58]

The break, so to speak, came with the Clinton Forest Summit in April 1992. Nadine Bailey (mentioned earlier), a Hayfork resident and chair of the Trinity County Concerned Citizens, a pro-logging group, was asked to give a presentation at the Summit. This provided her with a degree of visibility and credibility that allowed her to operate somewhat independently of the pro-logging bloc in town.[59] The Summit, moreover, provided a certain level of legitimacy to the public use of ecology-based concepts.[60] This, and a deliberate effort to avoid arguments over incompatible values, made it possible for a group of six individuals—three environmentalists, two loggers, and a miner—to formulate a set of proposals for the Trinity watershed that would, on the one hand, focus on ecosystem management and, on the other hand, provide employment to locals and even yield some lumber. The Trinity Bioregion Group (TBRG) proposals, estimated to cost some $139 million over a ten-year period, were intended to focus on tree thinning and forest litter removal for fire management, road maintenance, and rehabilitation aimed at controlling erosion into and siltation of creeks and rivers, and salmon spawning habitat restoration (Martin 1993). Eventually, according to the proposal's authors, these projects could be funded through selective harvesting of timber (Jungwirth 1994a).

To this end, in 1993, with a small amount of Forest Service funding, the TBRG established the Trinity Watershed Research and Training Center, a non-profit organization, to undertake such projects. As Lynn Jungwirth, one of the principals in the Center, put it:

> Our goal at the Center is to help with the new transition in forest management so that we end up with both healthy forests and healthy communities. With that goal in mind, we are working both with research, forest managers and economic development. We believe that eventually our forests will be managed both for communities of place and communities of interest. To me that means that the new sideboards of forest management on public lands will be to sustain bio-diversity. I believe that the community of interests will ask us to manage for carbon sink and power and water, within the sideboards of sustaining bio-diversity. That means, that the community of place, i.e. Hayfork, and the like must insist that we also manage for local economic stability within those same sideboards. When we can tie local economic and social health to sustainable bio-diversity we will make possible the kind of forest health management we've been describing for years. That means, to me, that we have to learn how to make a living off of the excess of a healthy forest in all successional stages (Jungwirth 1994b).

The TBRG proposal fit into President Clinton's "Option 9" for the Pacific Northwest—although many environmentalists through the region were not happy with Option 9.[61] That plan largely envisaged almost no logging on the western slope of the Cascades, with most of the cut coming on the eastern side. Among other things, the plan also included the creation of "Adaptive Management Areas" where activities such as those proposed by the TBRG would be undertaken; the only one of the AMAs included in the initial plan was located near Hayfork. Hayfork waited for the funds to arrive. Unfortunately, they never did, and Congress has since passed legislation, signed by President Clinton, authorizing salvage logging in the national forests. This has served, to some degree, to revive earlier antagonisms between environmentalists and others (Martin 1995b).

The arrival of money would not, in any event, have been sufficient to ensure success for the Trinity Bioregion Group, which depended more on the group's internal coherence. In early 1994—in part because of the financing difficulties—the TBRG suffered a split between the more political types and the more technically-proficient members—a split that also involved personality conflicts and led to the TBRG and Research and Training Centers going their separate ways. Nonetheless, the two groups have found it useful to cooperate on some projects, such as the Klamath GIS Project discussed above.

The TBRG and Watershed Research & Training Center provide another useful perspective on the process of renegotiating resource regimes. TBRG members initially included loggers, miners, environmentalists, a county supervisor, U.S. Forest Service, U.S. Soil Conservation, and U.S. Fish and Game staff, and others. Until the split, the entire group met approximately every three weeks (as the TBRG continues to do) to consider a fairly complex agenda oriented toward proposed and ongoing projects within the region. Conflicts over normative values did take place, but the group seemed united around its concern for management and sustenance of the forest, rather than the "sustained-yield" extraction of earlier years (which was not, in any event, sustainable).

Even those group members who were not foresters by training demonstrated a surprising sophistication when it came to ecological language and concepts. At a meeting I attended in September 1993, discussions took place, to a large degree, on the basis of technical considerations, rather than values or ideologies.[62] The importance in this context of the meaning(s) of Nature cannot be gainsaid. When I asked two group members, whose families had been long-time residents of Hayfork, what they saw as their role vis-à-vis the forest, they offered that they would like to be seen as "Guardians of the Forest." The image is, in some ways, laughable, except that it underlines the importance of changes in the *meaning* of the resource, and the extent to which community and individual identity are tied to land and Nature.

There is another important element here. Some observers dubbed the TBRG the "miracle of Hayfork," finding it hard to imagine that sworn ideological enemies might find a shared basis for cooperation (Martin 1993). But to a degree, these antagonists came together in opposition to outside regulation—for "outside," read resource agencies and environmentalists in Sacramento and Washington, D.C. Such coalitions are fragile, however, for they rely on the same "outsiders" for project funding and legitimation. The failure of Option 9 funds to materialize reinforces this weakness, and reinforces the sense that solutions must be formulated locally and reflect the unique quality of each locale. The state of California can legitimate the process (through the Biodiversity Project) and the federal government can legitimate the formulation (through the Forest Summit), but neither can unilaterally impose a solution. The result is that the Hayfork groups are being drawn into a process of governance of resources, in a way that no one had previously envisioned. This is a point to which I will return in chapter 8.

All of the bioregional groups in the Klamath Province are situated in a similarly awkward space. Having emerged from their local communities, in response to the state initiative and out of concern for livelihood and Nature, they are drawing on ideas and practices that, in some cases, originated in northern California and, in other cases, were first conceptualized and tried by global civil society in other parts of the United States and the world. These groups are not part of institutionalized politics, yet they are increasingly involved in a political process, the renegotiation of resource regimes. And the state, embodied in the resource agencies, is increasingly dependent on these groups to legitimize the practice of "ecosystem management," which is, somehow, supposed to reconcile economic demands with environmental ones. The pattern is not unique, although the solutions devised in each community are.

Conclusion

This chapter has looked at the role of global civil society in the renegotiation of resource regimes in northern California. The Klamath Province might stand as a model of the future of environmental protection and restoration, but not through some idealized version of bioregionalism. As sympathetic as I am to the concept in principle, bioregionalism is ahistorical where humans are concerned. To a considerable degree, so is "ecosystem management," although it, at least, recognizes that people own land (a very real artifact of history). At a conceptual level, we can afford to give priority to environment and ecosystemic boundaries; at a practical level, people are there, and they have been there for a long time. They have to agree to governance with Nature in mind, and if they have not been consulted, they are unlikely to agree. The state cannot mandate in such circumstances; it can only facilitate.

The Klamath Province is, on the one hand, undeniably a part of the "advanced industrialized world" but it has, on the other hand, historically played a subordinate and peripheral role in industrialization as a supplier of raw materials. The process of renegotiation in the Klamath Province is being cast in terms of the language and practices of ecology as a science. This, in turn, feeds into Ecology as a set of beliefs and practices, especially as framed by resource management agencies in Sacramento and Washington, D.C. But that process is actually being driven by two connected material facts of life: growing damage to Nature—the concern of environmentalists—and the decline of the traditional political economy—a concern of labor and business.

The state is playing a legitimating role in this process through its "Biodiversity Strategy," but it is ill-equipped to do much more, inasmuch as the legislature remains in deadlock and the executive agencies cannot impose their solutions on resistant communities.[63] If these renegotiations are successful—and it is too soon to be sure—they could actually lead to the creation of resource regimes that are protective of Nature as well as of the life and sustainability of human communities.

Global civil society, as conceptualized in chapter 3, is present throughout the Klamath Province of northern California. It is, in some ways, not as visible here, in the form of environmental NGOs, as in other places in the United States—although, here too, one finds evidence of transnational networks. What we do find here is a kind of "new environmentalism," based on Ecology and the "community of place." This has come into being through both a process of cultural diffusion from the outside and the commitment of those with longstanding roots to the survival of community. Global civil society here is linked to the "outside," although its relations with outsiders are sometimes prickly. In some ways, it is tactically-useful to establish coalitions against outsiders, be they environmentalists, bureaucrats, or Wall Street financiers. In the larger towns of the Klamath, however, such coalitions are more difficult to assemble; where they exist, shared interests are not always easy to find. The themes of local autonomy and particularism nonetheless sound loudly here, too, as the political economy undergoes the same kinds of wrenching, "post-industrial" changes that are affecting many other places throughout the United States and the world (Crook, Pakulski & Waters 1992).

CHAPTER 5

Environmentalism in One Country? Global Civil Society and Nature in Hungary[1]

It is said that Hungary was once covered by water (Figure 5.1). Rivers and streams flowed out of the surrounding mountains and toward the center of the Carpathian Basin, the Great Plain, where much of the land was seasonally-flooded, or even inundated year-round. The way of life of the people living there was adapted to its environmental peculiarities and not very expansive. The culture was seen as "backward" and, during the nineteenth century, disappeared (Bartos n.d. 1; Andrásfalvy 1989). Today, not more than one hundred fifty years later, most of the water is gone, diverted by decades of water "control," and there are predictions that, in the not-too-distant future, water might even run short (Molnár 1991; Bartos n.d. 2).

But efforts are underway to restore some aspects of this historical political economy, in a small part of Hungary called the *Ormánság*, lying around the confluence of the Danube and Dráva rivers. The *Ormánság* region encompasses approximately six hundred square kilometers in the southwestern part of the country, with a total population of some eighteen thousand people living in forty-six villages. Historically, the region was the site of what is now called the "water culture," a mode of production and life centered on the flood zones of the Danube and the Dráva. Much of this highly-localized mode of production disappeared long ago. But under the aegis of a regionally-based organization called the Ormánság Foundation, which draws for many of its ideas and projects on sources elsewhere in Hungary and the world, a cooperative effort is underway with the towns and villages in the region to restore some semblance of the historical landscape and culture. These efforts involve agriculture, animal husbandry, local infrastructural development, ecotourism and, most critically, hands-on environmental education and restoration. The *Ormánság* can never be returned to what it once was, of course—a region centered upon water. The project can, however, provide an important cultural basis for restoring the economic basis of local communities and preserving, in the process, some aspects of Nature.[2]

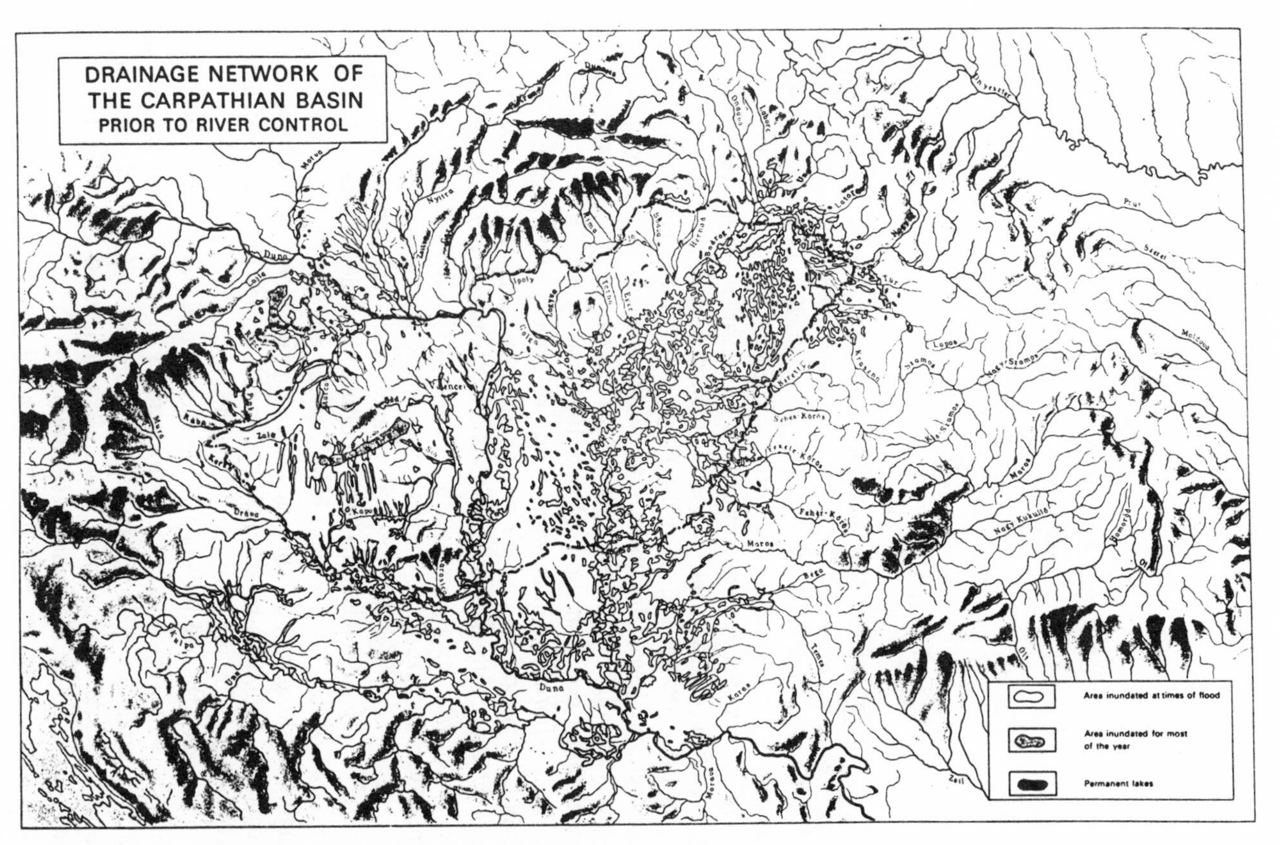

Figure 5.1. Source: *National Atlas of Hungary* (Budapest: Hungarian Academy of Sciences and Cartographia, 1967), p. 26.

Water was, once upon a time, of great symbolic and material importance in and to Hungary; it remains so today. But reinstating the central role of water in the environment of Hungary is not so easy. Of all the transformations of Nature undertaken by human beings, it might be water management that has been the most consequential. The diversion of mountain streams and rivers into reservoirs and aqueducts make possible both great cities and modern agriculture. The enclosure of free-flowing rivers behind gargantuan dams generates the electricity that lights and powers enormous industrial complexes. And the building of levees and straightening of river beds have brought under human control floodwaters that repeatedly drowned tens of thousands and terrorized millions. These things have happened throughout the world, and much the same is true in Hungary; indeed, it is with the social transformation of water that much of the country's recent environmental politics begin.

Although water is only one part of Nature, the almost-indiscriminate "taming" of water stands as representative of a particular kind of industrialism and development that existed, for a time, throughout Central and Eastern Europe, as well as in the former Soviet republics.[3] This form of industrialism was highly resource-intensive and not particularly mindful of Nature. Lenin once said "Communism is Soviet government plus the electrification of the whole country." To this formula, we might add "pollution," and lots of it. Natural resources were seen as "free" for the taking inasmuch as it was labor that gave things their value. In the process, Nature lost. The collapse of "really-existing" socialism between 1989 and 1991 revealed a degree of environmental degradation unimagined by even the harshest critics of the system; even today, the impacts have not been fully catalogued (Simons 1994; DeBardeleben & Hannigan 1995). But the extent of environmental degradation during the 1980s also had a catalyzing effect on society, especially in terms of the emergence of a civil society autonomous, to some small degree, of the centralized state. It was "local knowledge," as much as scientific data supplied by government-funded research, that revealed the degree to which human health and welfare, and the environment were suffering as a result of socialist industrialization. This knowledge became an important rallying point for oppositional movements and made a major contribution to the emergence of a civil society throughout the bloc. As a result, environmentalism became a tool for "politics by other means" (Vari & Pál 1993; Crook, Pakulski & Waters 1992: ch. 5).

Ironically, perhaps, socialist governments helped to engender this civil society and opposition. These regimes understood that demonstrating an interest in and concern for the *scientific* aspects of environmental protection could be used to establish a certain degree of legitimacy with the West. This included allowing selected groups to organize around themes related to environmental protection and conservation. At the same time, however, those governments seemed not to fully recognize the *political* potential of this process. Eventually, they were unable to exert total control over environmental organizing and activities. Civil society, as a result, became an important player in the *fin de siècle* drama of the old regimes' collapse.

The story of Hungary is particularly illustrative in this regard. During the 1980s, an emergent environmental "movement" in Hungary organized against a grandiose and environmentally-destructive dam project on the Danube River. The project was sponsored by the state, in collaboration with the government of Czechoslovakia and Austrian corporate capital. The movement was able to mobilize large numbers of people and to give voice to political dissidence through this mobilization. Some observers even gave the movement major credit in bringing down the old regime (Schapiro 1990). For a brief time, it seemed as though Hungary might be the first, truly "Green" country in Europe. That moment was lost, however, when much of the energy of that movement was drained away by the formation and institutionalization of new political parties. Since 1989, environmentalists in Hungary have struggled to reconstitute their civil society in terms of politics and practice. As is the case in California, this effort is not taking place in isolation from outside influences. As in California, there is much misunderstanding among outsiders about what *is* going on in Hungary. And, as in California, it is the reconstitution of local resource regimes that may, over the longer term, make environmental protection possible and practical.

What is lacking in Hungary is a state-driven legitimizing function akin to that provided by the resource agencies in California. Given the outcome of the 1994 Parliamentary elections, which saw a majority vote for candidates of the Socialist party (the renamed Communist Hungarian Socialist Workers Party), such legitimation is not likely to emerge soon. In fact, for a time there was discussion of eliminating the Environmental Ministry, and it was only as a result of the strenuous lobbying efforts of a small number of environmental activists that this did not happen (Illés 1994). Many groups look, consequently, to municipalities and counties for their legitimating function, a result of the former government's decision to pass responsibility for environmental regulation to the cities, towns, and counties. Some, however, are making efforts to influence government and lobby Parliament, thereby adopting a more American approach to environmental regulation.

This chapter begins with an overview of the environmental *problematique* in Hungary: the origins of pollution and health problems arising from Socialist industrialization. I then turn to environmental civil society and discuss its origins, its pre-1989 history, and its condition today. Finally, I describe several locally-focused projects that have been undertaken by global civil society in Hungary and place them in the larger context of environmental politics there.

The context of environmental degradation in Hungary

Environmental legislation in Hungary did not, originally, arise in response to civic action or protest about the impacts of production on health and Nature. In the early decades of socialism—the 1950s and 1960s—such problems were not acknowledged to exist. As was true in the West in the earlier part of the century, air pollution was a sign of industrialization, and industrialization was *good*: an indicator of growth, national strength, and prosperity. What, then, were the incentives for promulgating the environmental protection laws that began to appear in the late 1960s? First, official statements of concern about the environment were a response to the growth of environmentalism in the West in the 1960s, which led to the adoption of certain laws and principles. Second, in the 1970s the environment became one of several foci of the Nixon-era détente with the Soviet bloc, at the insistence of Soviet leaders. In both instances, the Hungarian government wanted to reinforce its "credit" with the West—especially with "progressive" environmentalists—and disarm domestic groups, which were beginning to appear in growing numbers. It was not particularly interested in environmental protection, per se. The results of these policies were, however, quite unanticipated. Governments and parties were found to be in brazen violation of their own laws—as the owners and operators of industry, they were, of course, polluters, as well. And, the issue of environmental quality provided a means for those inside and outside of the party to struggle for political reform and change.[4]

Indeed, the rise of environmentalism in the West had a kind of double-edged impact in the East. On the one hand, the critique by Western groups of the abuse of the environment under capitalism was readily picked up by Eastern media, who found it useful for propaganda purposes. On the other hand, Western protests against polluting factories also served to legitimate similar opposition in the East: "If they can criticize a steel mill in Pittsburgh, then we can criticize a steel mill in Miskolc." The growing scientific and technical focus on the environment in the West provided another channel into the East. Professional journals flowed freely through the Iron Curtain—although access to them was strictly controlled—and scientists could not help but see both the needs and the opportunities that might result from directing their research toward environmental concerns (Berczes & Attila 1992; Pál 1995).

Hungary was one of the first members of the Socialist bloc to pass legislation designed to protect the environment.[5] A few such laws were codified prior to 1970, having to do mostly with health standards, but most came later, as environmental concerns began to gain international prominence with the 1972 Stockholm Conference on the Human Environment. Although Hungary did not send a delegation to Sweden, the recommendations of the conference formed the basis for the regulations it did promulgate (Hungarian Ministry 1991b). It was also around this time that the environment first surfaced as an issue in negotiations over East-West relations, where it was seen by some as a "non-political" topic on which international cooperation could—and eventually did—take place. The culmination of this early period of environmental "detente" was the inclusion in the economic basket of the Helsinki Agreements, at the insistence of Soviet Party Secretary Brezhnev, of provisions regarding environmental protection and state obligations (Schreiber 1991:140).

Such legislation as was enacted by Bloc countries, however, had little effect on environmental quality or human health and welfare (DeBardeleben 1991; Pryde 1991; Feshbach & Friendly 1992). Not only did industrial production take a front seat to other concerns, enterprise managers found it expedient—and prudent—to ignore or subvert environmental regulations in the interest of acquiring needed inputs into production and meeting the constantly-increasing quotas set by central planners. The effect was a set of policies that appeared impressive on paper but were, in practice, mostly empty (Gille 1992). Nonetheless, the fact that these laws were unenforced and unenforceable did not mean that they served no purpose. Policies to protect the environment could be and were used to generate favorable views in, and even assistance from, the West. By the 1980s, a whole range of assistance and financial programs had been put in place in several countries—although not Hungary—by Western countries, intended to reduce the movement of pollutants into Western Europe and Scandinavia (French 1990:36). They could also be used to legitimate projects of "environmental colonialism," whereby Western corporations sought to ship hazardous and other wastes to legally-established dump sites in the East.

In general, environmental regulation in Hungary was not successful: Throughout the 1970s and 1980s, environmental quality declined. Between 1970 and 1985, age-specific mortality rates in Hungary increased, as did deaths by cancer, cardiac and vascular, and other diseases whose causes correlated with growing environmental degradation ("Hungary" 1990; Vukovich 1990:18–19). Toxic wastes were carelessly disposed of at production sites; waters were despoiled by a wide variety of chemicals, minerals, and wastes; air was heavily polluted by industry and transport. Numerous plant and animal species and their habitats were damaged or destroyed as the landscape was changed (Várkonyi 1992).

An assessment of the impacts of industrialization under state socialism was not fully compiled until after 1989. Even so, the data must be treated with caution, since the new non-socialist regime had an interest in discrediting its predecessor. Nonetheless, according to the Hungarian Ministry of the Environment and Regional Policy, as of 1991, 40 plants and 53 animal species within the country's borders had become extinct and an additional 1,130 were threatened. The economic loss due to environmental damage was estimated to be on the order of 3–5% of GDP (Hungarian Ministry 1991a:8). And, although authorities managed to collect two billion forints in environmental fines in 1988 and 1989 under the terms of existing legislation, most enterprises found it less costly to pay the fines than to reduce emissions (Kilényi 1990:38).[6]

Conditions did not improve enormously after 1989, in spite of widespread expectations that they would. Much of the fault lay with the first post-Socialist government, a conservative, nationalistic coalition of three parties dominated by the Hungarian Democratic Forum (MDF) and headed by Jozef Antall. Initially, the Antall government made some gestures in the direction of the environment—there were even a few active environmentalists in its ranks. It split the "Ministry for Environment and Water Management" and reorganized it into the "Ministry of the Environment and Development of Settlements." This had the effect of eliminating the very strong influence of the hydrology lobby over environmental policy. It appointed a well-known environmentalist, Zoltan Illés, to a position of Assistant Minister. And, the Antall government tried to push through a new environmental law. In the end, these efforts did not amount to very much. The new regime was more interested in foreign investment and industrial development than environmental protection. The ministry remained weak and ineffectual. For much of the post-1989 period, it consisted mostly of holdovers from the old regime who had lost the personal contacts and influence that were so important before 1989 (Assetto 1993; Gille 1993; Cole 1993). Illés was fired for his outspokenness. The new environmental law was never passed.

Things have not improved a great deal since the MDF was voted out of power. There remain some doubts that the MDF's successor—the reconstituted Socialist Party under Gyula Horn in coalition with the Liberal Party—is very much more interested in the environment. It tends to view economic growth and environmental protection as being in direct conflict, and therefore does not seem much more eager to pass legislation or implement policies. There are laws on the books, but only limited effort is made to enforce them. Moreover, the claim of lack of funds, due to the never-ending budget crises, to monitor environmental performance of industry and other activities serves as the pretext to not even try to enforce them.

The national environmental law has been redrafted at least seven times. Intended to establish a framework for regulation, enforcement, and liability, it has languished in Parliamentary Committee for years (Assetto 1993), although there is an expectation that it will be presented to Parliament during the term of the current government (Fülöp 1995; Roe 1995). At the same time, much jurisdiction over environmental protection has been passed from national to county and municipal authorities. These, as might be expected, are ill-equipped to enforce such laws and standards as exist.

The impact of changes in the economy have been less than originally expected, too. Even though Hungary continues to attract a great deal of foreign investment (*The Economist* 1993), the deployment of "environmentally-friendly" technologies that should have accompanied privatization and foreign capital has been slowed by a general reluctance of investors to underwrite any ventures so long as liability for the cleanup of old industrial sites has not been prescribed by a new environmental law (Simons 1992). Predictably, the costs of such cleanups are far more than the state can afford even though, as the previous owner of these sites, it is technically liable.

The lack of a large national constituency mobilized around environmental issues means that there is little pressure on either Parliament or government to regulate. Indeed, the Hungarian public seems largely indifferent to environmental quality except when it impinges directly on them—this, at least, is the impression conveyed by public opinion polls. Although there was a great deal of concern expressed about the environment, no one responding to a Gallup poll conducted in Hungary in 1992 thought that it should be a top priority (Okolicsanyi 1992:67; Hastings & Hastings 1994). A 1992 survey of sixteen hundred people conducted by a group of Hungarian environmental organizations showed widespread awareness of specific environmental problems but high levels of ignorance regarding causes and solutions. Even local authorities, on whom much responsibility for environmental protection now rests, were quite unsure about what they should do. When respondents were asked who could solve the country's environmental problems, they offered a wide range of possibilities, including Parliament and the Green Party. Surprisingly, even though it hardly existed at the time, the Green Party had very high public recognition and a high rating; by contrast, the Environmental Ministry received a very low rating (*Magyar Természetvédők Szövetsége* 1992; Persányi 1992). More recent *Eurobarometer* polls have indicated a much greater concern for the state of the Hungarian economy than for its environment (Pál, 1995), and public support for Greens in the 1994 elections was virtually nil.

Awareness is not, of course, the same as action. Hungary's recent history of centralized organization and control has meant that, since 1989, people have been generally unaware of how they might actually express their concerns and participate in the general process of creating new institutions and political practices. Moreover, there seems still to be a tendency to expect direction and directives to come from above (see, e.g., Hastings & Hastings 1994:647–48). As these are not forthcoming, a sense of political stasis or stagnation has been evident, at times providing some impetus to right-wing nationalism and xenophobia.[7]

Things are not uniformly grim however: since 1989, some environmental conditions have improved as many of the dirtier enterprises that were the pride of the old system have been forced to shut down or gone out of business (Hardi 1992; Kerekes 1993). And, there are some signs of improvement in regulatory terms, although the incentives come from without rather than within. As part of the long-term move toward hoped-for membership in the European Union, Hungary has found it expedient to adopt and implement the EU's environmental regulations. This has contributed to the internationalization and intellectual authority of the Environmental Ministry because oversight of the regulations is vested there (Pál 1995). Given this situation, global civil society in Hungary might be able to play a major role in the democratization process either via mass mobilization or through participation in party politics. That the former is not happening at all, and the latter only to a limited extent, is attributable to a combination of history and structure, as we shall see, below. Still, environmental civil society *is* manifest by way of projects focused on environmental protection and nature conservation; this may prove, in the longer term, to be as important as party politics or regulation from above.

Environment as politics

Enter the Party

As the discussion above suggests, domestic environmental conditions were not accorded priority among the concerns of the socialist regimes of Eastern and Central Europe.[8] This does not mean that the environment was not of *political* interest to the Hungarian Socialist Workers Party (HSWP) through its members. Indeed, environmental concern was expressed in two ways under socialism. First, those who were not party members sought to establish autonomous organizations, both legal and semi-legal. Of these, more will be said below. Second, those who were already members of the HSWP, or who were potential members, formed "interest groups" within the party and managed to get environmental concerns placed on its internal agenda. This was also a safer and more efficient route to environmental activism than the external one pursued by non-members. The party elites, in turn, saw this as a way to capture and keep in individuals who might, otherwise, leave and engage in political dissidence.

Thus, beginning in the 1970s, the party's rhetorical commitment to environmental protection began to acquire two, somewhat contradictory purposes. On the one hand, it was seen increasingly as a useful mechanism for social and political control. From the perspective of the HSWP, for example, environmental protection appeared to be an issue that did not—indeed, could not—threaten either the party's legitimacy or hegemony. It could, as noted above, be manipulated to bring into the official institutional structure individuals who might otherwise challenge the party. Taking advantage of the concerns of those who were already members, the issue could also be used to revitalize mass organizations under the aegis of the party, such as the National Patriotic Front (NPF) and the Young Communists League (YCL) (Persányi 1990:41). On the other hand, incorporation of such issues into the programs of such organizations provided a venue for "opening up" the political system to new ideas and practices not high on the agenda of the party elites (Miró Kiss 1994). Individuals, by accepting the constraints of party-sanctioned organizations, were thereby permitted to expand the arena of domestic political discourse.

Other regimes throughout Eastern and Central Europe adopted a similar approach, although their willingness to allow some degree of liberalization within structured institutions was, generally speaking, not as great. In general, the HSWP was never as unified or centralized as the parties in the other socialist states, although it, too, knew what constituted a threat to its hegemony. Thus, human rights movements, which seemed to strike at the heart of a regime's legitimacy, were suppressed, with individual members being kept under strict surveillance. Nature conservation and environmental education groups were not considered threatening and were allowed to organize with minimal interference, so long as they did so under the wing of the party (Schöpflin 1991:244; Pál 1995; a general description of the *modus operandi* of the HSWP can be found in Horváth & Szakolczai 1992).

To this end, in the early to mid-1970s, the NPF took on the task of focusing public attention on Hungary's environmental problems through various national congresses and appeals. One result was the 1976 "Act on the Protection of the Human Environment," which also created the National Office for Environment Protection and Nature Conservation (Kilényi 1990:36). Another consequence was an effort to create and/or bring under party control the various organizations and programs devoted to nature conservation and environmental education that had begun to emerge in response to the diffusion of the science of ecology and environmental awareness—a point to which I return below. For example, the NPF set up the National Environmental Protection Society, which involved scientists and other experts, but excluded those of a more activist bent. The Young Communists League established a series of Youth Councils—including one on environment—intended to represent the interests of different social sectors and to provide them with channels into the politics (Míro Kiss 1994).

In practical terms, the NPF's efforts to manage environmental activities within Hungary met with only limited success because the groups it did control did not see themselves as political activists, while those who considered themselves politically active refused to accede to the Front's rules. By the beginning of the 1980s, as a result, the NPF's environmental activities began to lose legitimacy as independent groups began to appear (Persányi 1992:81–82). Officially-sanctioned environmental organizations found themselves in a sort of competition with growing numbers of newly-formed, semi-autonomous environmental groups outside of party control. Once again, efforts were made by the authorities to either gain control of or suppress such groups, by offering funding and protection to them. These attempts met with limited success inasmuch as the groups' lack of a well-defined organizational structure and membership made it difficult for the HSWP to find political and economic leverage over them.[9] That such groups were able to exist even under these circumstances is evidence that, in Hungary at least, central control was never as total as it was sometimes made out to be; that the party did not recognize their political potential might have been, in retrospect, something of a fatal error.[10] John Walton (1992: ch. 8) can be invoked again here; as he suggests, in creating space for an environmental policy, however defined, the state may also confer legitimacy on those it does not—or cannot—fully supervise.

The state's efforts to manage the flow of and access to technical and scientific information about the environment also served, in the long run, to weaken its legitimacy. Longitudinal data on health and pollution were not plentiful, and certainly not widely circulated. Personal experience and anecdotal evidence, especially in heavily industrialized cities and towns, clearly indicated a worsening of local environmental conditions. The accumulation of such "local knowledge," which the regime could not manage, served as one impetus to the initial organizing efforts of a number of the semi-autonomous local groups. Eventually, many of these groups were mobilized into an independent mass movement largely focused on a specific environmental and symbolically-significant issue, the dam on the Danube.

How could the state have missed this dynamic; indeed, did the state miss it? There were, I would argue, two reasons for not regarding organizing around the environment as a political process. First, as we shall see, there were (and are) really two "Green" constituencies in Hungary, the "nature conservationists" and the "political ecologists." The former tended to be more conservative and middle or upper class, and were largely to be found in the smaller towns and cities outside Budapest. The latter was younger, upper middle class and Budapest-based as well as more politically radical, but was also either in the party or marginalized outside of it (Pál 1995). In both cases, matters seemed to be under control but were not.

The second reason was to be found in a fundamental misunderstanding of the ways in which discourses around symbolic issues (that often appear not to be so) may unexpectedly acquire political currency and authority. This is especially true when a discourse combines language with a high technical content—thereby making the issue appear to be one of *science* rather than *politics*—with culturally-significant symbols (a phenomenon that, I have suggested, is present in California, as well; Agnew & Corbridge 1995: ch.2). The distinction between environmental activism focused solely on "technical" nature conservation or quality-of-life problems, and that with a political focus, is often made by analysts and practitioners—by Hungarian, as well as other observers and practitioners of environmental policy and politics (with the political often being dismissed as "irrational").

According to the logic underlying the first approach, environmental protection activities should be "professionalized." In concert with the continuing emphasis on "real" science and hierarchy within the Hungarian academy, this means that scientific and technical strategies for environment monitoring and amelioration should be conducted only under the direction of experts.[11] As a result, many of those holding this view have tended to shy away from party politics.[12] The flaw in such an approach is that keeping the "politics" out of even technical programs is extremely difficult, if not impossible, since the logic of the scientific findings and arguments underlying environmental protection may also serve to undermine the social and political premises on which a social order is based.[13] Moreover, as Deborah Stone (1988: ch. 13) points out, selecting the terms of reference for any policy issue is, inevitably, a political exercise that can never be abstracted from the system of values and culture in which it is embedded. The distinction between "professional" and "political" approaches is, thus, not only a false one—and a real example of "false consciousness"—it is also a potential trap, inasmuch as it tends to disempower psychologically those who might otherwise be more active and effective through participation in the political process.

In *Autonomous Technology*, Langdon Winner (1977) analyzes, and finds wanting, the notion that a technological approach to social problems, without recourse to politics, is *the* way of "correcting" society's flaws. Winner proposes, instead, that technology is intensely political, not only for the power relations that it reveals (or hides) but also for the institutional patterns that it helps to reproduce through its existence as social organization. In other words, to control a technology is to control the politics of that technology, and to define the terms of debates about the technology is to exercise Gramscian hegemony over that form of control.[14]

The Hungarian Socialist Worker's Party, the National Patriotic Front, and the other party-linked organizations tried to do both. They attempted to manage the flow of data as well as the work of scientists by keeping both largely under their jurisdiction, thereby keeping all environmental discourses under the aegis of the party.[15] At the same time, however, because science was seen as being "above" politics it was not subject to the same degree of control by the regime as were political issues: scientific truths could not, it was thought, be molded to the demands of the party.[16] To be "professional," therefore had (and has) a double meaning. On the one hand, it was to accept the official ways in which basic questions were framed, analyzed, and debated; on the other, it was to challenge the party's right to control of technical knowledge. That "professionalization" continues to be an issue indicates ongoing political struggles at the core of environmental issues.[17]

In the case of Hungary, the state's efforts to control both science *and* discourse failed. The party could bottle up the data, but it could not contain the scientists nor could it wish away the "local knowledge" generated by people exposed to growing levels of pollution and environmental hazards. One result was the erosion of centralized political control and the eventual emergence of an alternative political "pole," both inside and outside of the party. While protecting the Danube was an important part of this process, those involved were really in the business of creating a new political discourse to challenge and delegitimize the old regime—which was, to some degree, complicit in this process. This is a tale offering some interesting insights that might have relevance for other authoritarian regimes.[18] But perhaps of even greater interest was the fact that the state was not entirely oblivious to the political organizing going on within, in particular, the movement to oppose the dam on the Danube. This is a point to which I will return below.

Is there a similar process in democratic (or pluralist) states? The apparent Western immunity to this process—evinced especially in the relative lack of success of Green Parties outside of Germany (Bramwell 1994; Dalton 1994)—is puzzling. One would think that the freedom to construct oppositional political discourses would help to undermine or delegitimate governments dedicated to protecting the environmental and political status quo. In the West, states and governments are less obviously involved in trying to manage political discourse than was the case with the party state in Hungary; the levers of manipulation are usually more subtle.[19] Moreover, since most political or social challenges in the West occur at the margins and are not aimed at overthrowing the existing order, it is relatively easy for them to be incorporated into mainstream politics, albeit with adjustments.[20] Technology and science are not means for proving or undermining the claims of authorities; rather, they allow for endless discussion of what the data really mean.[21] Hence, not only does "proof" become problematic, so does actual movement on the issues. These points are important in explaining the change in Hungarian environmental politics between 1988 and 1990 as we shall see.

To return to a point made earlier, then, the failure to recognize the close relationship between so-called technical and political approaches proved costly to the old regime in Hungary, just as it did in many other Eastern bloc countries (Jancar 1992, 1993). By regarding the environmental movement as one concerned about *technical* aspects of quality-of-life problems, the party largely missed the movement's *political* power until it was too late to be stopped. Seeing environmental activities as a diversion of political energies toward things of little or no interest to it, the regime ultimately found itself at the mercy of some of the very forces it had helped to nurture.

But, crucially, the party was also *complicit* in the challenge raised against it. In the late 1970s, and throughout the 1980s, social and cultural groups, such as those organized through the Young Communist League and the National Patriotic Front, provided "protected spaces" that were not rigidly policed and through which a certain degree of political discussion was possible (Míro Kiss 1992: 52–55; Horváth & Szakolczai 1992). In the 1980s, some of these very same groups became the focus of organizing by party members of a more liberal bent, as well as by opponents of the party. Both groups were unhappy with the system and hoped to generate a process of liberalization within the Communist regime. Similar struggles were taking place within the party itself, between "reformers" and "conservatives." Toward the end of the 1980s, the reformers managed to gain enough influence so that, by 1989, the party was engaged in negotiations with nascent political groups about the future of Hungarian politics. In Hungary, at least, the "revolution" was not wholly unexpected.

Enter global civil society

To comprehend the condition of civil society in Hungary and its role in environmental protection and conservation, it is necessary to know something about its particular history, and its relationship to the country's politics and economics (Szirmai 1993). Environmental civil society in Hungary, as indicated above, has two origins, one more conservative and scientific—usually self-named as "conservationist," the other more radical and politicized—usually called the "independents." Although this divide was a consequence of society's domination by the Hungarian Socialist Workers Party, in its various permutations and spinoffs over the forty-year rule of the old regime, it remains visible even today.

The conservationist branch developed out of the activities of scientists—ornithologists, biologists, and nature conservationists—who, perhaps reacting to the totalizing industrialism of the workers' state, sought in Nature what may have seemed to them a "safe" and largely non-political realm. Some were party members, but they tended towards conservativism and to come from the upper classes of the smaller peripheral cities and towns outside of Budapest. Many of the groups in this "conservationist" branch initially emerged independently of one another, as nature clubs in regional universities. Often, they acquired form as students followed charismatic teachers and professors "out to Nature." University affiliation offered official status to these groups, access to large numbers of potential members and resources available to students, and a degree of protection from politics (Persányi 1992:83–84). And, while these groups were not *of* the party, they were permitted and sanctioned *by* the party so long as they did not become too activist. Because of restrictions on communication and mobility, interactions among the conservationist groups were quite limited until 1974. In that year, the Hungarian Ornithological Society (MME) was established, with official sanction, in order to bring as many of these groups as possible under one umbrella. The MME also provided a means of "networking" within a country where phones were not always available and communication was sometimes quite difficult. Today, the MME is one of the largest environmental groups in Hungary.[22]

The independent element in environmental civil society began to emerge only in the early 1980s, in part as an increasingly-polluted environment began to pose threats to health and the quality-of-life (Persányi 1992:80–81). This branch of environmental civil society had its origins in the convergence of, on the one hand, local concerns about health problems and environmental destruction with, on the other, the emergence of opposition to the grandiose projects of the old regime, such as the Gabçikovo-Nagymaros hydroelectric system. It also became a place of political "refuge" for activists from the independent peace groups in Hungary, who were routinely harassed by the party and state. Indeed, even today the independent environmental sector, in contrast to conservationist groups, tends to see itself as more concerned about the effects of industrialism on people, although this distinction seems to have more to do with political beliefs than issues.

As mentioned earlier, in the late 1970s and early 1980s, in an effort to broaden the parameters of internal debate, the National Patriotic Front (NPF) decided to extend its social hegemony by making nature conservation a party-controlled issue area and limiting nature-related activities to party-sanctioned youth organizations and trade unions (Persány 1990:41; 1992:81). Conservationist groups were basically told to join and enjoy the advantages of official "protection," or go out of business. For some, the choice was eased by offers of financial support. This tactic worked for a time, but it soon came under growing challenge from the independent groups and the Danube movement, and eventually it collapsed.

The party then tried again: in 1984, in response to the growing numbers and influence of the independent groups, the Young Communists League (YCL) set up a national Youth Council for Environmental Protection. This was one of a number of such councils established by the YCL to represent the interests of different social sectors as well as to play a political role by channelling upwardly-mobile individuals into the party itself (Míro Kiss 1994). The Youth Council, which was allowed to operate with some autonomy so that it could maintain its distance from the party, brought under its wing the local, mostly county-based conservation groups. It then invited the independents to join, too. This strategy of cooptation was, however, unsuccessful in terms of its primary goal: legitimating the party's role in environmental protection and activism, especially in the face of the growing Danube movement. Nonetheless, the Youth Council continued in its labors and, in 1989, transformed itself into the National Society of Conservationists, an association of locally-based groups that remains in existence today, claiming as many as 20,000 members (Schmuck 1992).[23]

In 1988, the NPF tried—for the final time, as it turned out—to take over the leading environmentalist role by establishing the National Environmental Protection Society (NEPS), focused primarily around individual scientists and experts, with membership by invitation only. The Society was the first non-governmental environmental organization to gain legal recognition by the government under a law passed at the time. The law was not, however, meant for everyone: both the Danube Circle and the Society for Bird Protection asked to be legalized, but were refused. The leader of the Danube Circle, János Vargha, asked to join the Society, as well, but was turned down. As a result, the NEPS had almost no influence on or in environmental civil society in Hungary.

The most significant element of global civil society to emerge during the 1980s was the Danube Circle (*Duna Kör*), sparked by the 1977 agreement among Hungary, Czechoslovakia, and Austrian financiers to build a series of dams, barrages, and channels on the Danube, between Gabçikovo and Nagymaros. These were intended to generate hydroelectricity while maintaining the navigability of the river.

The system was first proposed in the late 1940s, when Stalin ordered the construction of an all-weather canal, on the Slovak side of the river, to enable a freshwater flotilla access to points farther west in the event of war

(Berényi 1994; Erdélyi 1994a, 1994b). That particular version of the project was never realized, but by 1977 the availability of Austrian financing, to be repaid by electricity revenues, appeared to make the project economically feasible. The interest of hydrological and construction interests in all three countries made it politically feasible (Berényi 1994; Erdélyi 1994a, 1994b). The project was not, however, universally supported, even within the HSWP and academe.

In 1979, the Hungarian Academy of Sciences was presented with a critical assessment of the project by several of its members. The report was rejected, but it was information supplied by contributors to this study that was later used by biologist-turned-journalist János Vargha who, beginning in 1981, attacked the hydroelectric project in a series of widely-read articles. The entire episode has been fairly well-documented in a number of places (Schapiro 1990; Vásárhelyi 1991; Feffer 1992:151–56; Fleischer 1993; Sibl 1993; Galambos 1993). Suffice it here to say that professional critiques of the project, publicly-limited but nonetheless widely-disseminated, provided a scientific (and political) basis for opposing the project.

The issue was taken up, first, by those concerned about its ecological effects and, later, by those more interested in a political issue around which to rally in opposition to the regime. As Tamás Fleischer, an associate of Vargha in ISTER (East European Environmental Research) put it, "The barrage, the monster made of concrete, was the unintended symbol of political power running rampant over everything. It signified the model of totalitarian party rule" (Fleischer 1993:441). To condemn the dam, consequently, was to condemn the regime. By 1988, the Danube Circle was able to turn out 40,000 people to protest before the Parliament Building in Budapest. Not long after, the organization was able to hand to the government the signatures of 140,000 people against the project. This groundswell of opposition was not, by itself, enough to halt the project, although it was threatening enough that the petitions disappeared, apparently stolen by regime insiders. Moreover, while it is generally agreed that the demonstration and petitions were important in the eventual decision by party and Parliament to oppose the project in 1989, most believe that it was the political/technical struggle within the Hungarian Academy of Sciences that ultimately determined the project's fate (Vasárhelyi 1991: 213; Fleischer 1993; Pál 1995).[24] A few observers have given the movement credit for bringing down the regime (Schapiro 1990), although others note that the party structure was already tottering in 1988 when János Kádár, head of the party since 1956, was removed and replaced, first, by Károly Grósz and, later, by Miklós Németh (Schöpflin, Tőkés, & Völgyes 1988; Varkonyi 1989; Fleischer 1993).

In retrospect, it is clear that the Danube movement was concerned with much more than the Danube. Throughout the 1980s, the movement's high visibility sparked a growing national interest in environmental issues, and stimulated the emergence of both the oft-threatened independent groups and growing numbers of university- and school-based ecology clubs. Many found themselves in trouble with the regime, which, as noted above, more-or-less refused to accord them official status so long as they were not under the wing of the party. Hence, most operated informally until 1988–89, when it finally became possible to organize legally. Today, these groups continue to operate independently of one another, for historical as well as structural reasons.

During the 1980s, autonomy from party and state was a valuable currency—and distrust of the government remains strong, even today—for oppositional as well as tactical reasons.[25] Many groups, as well, crystallized around strong individuals who still remain reluctant to see their groups institutionalized and their individual influence submerged in a larger organization run on the basis of bureaucratic operating procedures. Independence and autonomy are strengths, as well as weaknesses, in global civil society. On the one hand, they provide groups with a distinct identity and their leaders with visibility, and they minimize institutional constraints on policy and practice; on the other, they can make collective action difficult. The structure bequeathed to this particular civil society, makes it more difficult for these groups to make their own history. This historical baggage is not something that will be overcome easily.

1989 was a watershed year for the environmental sector as well as for East and Central Europe as a whole (Jancar 1992, 1993). For environmental civil society in Hungary, it was a year of collapse. In the transition to political pluralism, many members of the Danube movement and other groups now saw their chance to practice "real" politics, within an institutionalized system of political parties. As parties were established, these individuals set up green fractions within each, pushing for the inclusion of environmental planks in the party platforms. Where environmental matters were concerned, the "greens" in each party could agree with their former comrades in other parties, but they saw eye-to-eye on few other issues (Pál 1995). A Green Party was organized in late 1989 to run candidates in the first post-Communist elections in 1990; almost immediately, it fell victim to internal schism, as members from groups formerly affiliated with or protected by the HSWP clashed with members of independent groups. The latter were ejected and went on to form a second green party (Béres 1992a, 1992b; Míro Kiss 1994). Other parties, such as the Federation of Young Democrats (FIDESZ) and the Alliance of Free Democrats, were seen as more able to take on environmental issues under the new system, further draining support for the green parties. In the event, the environment did not become a major election issue, contrary to what many had expected.

The green parties, unable to put up enough candidates to meet the exacting entry requirements of the Hungarian electoral system, failed to capture a single seat in Parliament.[26]

Following the 1990 election, environmentalists debated at length about how to revitalize the movement. Was it better to reorganize the Green Party, to build a Green coalition to run in 1994, or stay out of politics entirely? Many of the conservationist groups had then and continue now to have a low opinion of national politics and politicians. They saw such participation as a waste of time. Nonetheless, a core group of several hundred felt that a Green Party was necessary, and in 1992, a process of reorganization was initiated. What happened, however, was quite unexpected. In early 1993, at an extraordinary Congress of the party, the then vice-chair packed the meeting with outsiders, took control, and expelled all those old members who disagreed with his platform. These views combined some ideas usually attributed to environmentalists, along with elements of nationalism, racism, anti-semitism, and eugenics, among other things. Those expelled from the "Hungarian Green Party," in turn, established the "Green Alternative." Given the shortage of time and money, the Green Alternative was unable to mount much of a campaign. Given public confusion between the two parties, the Green Alternative had difficulty establishing its own identity. Given the situation, neither party did very well in the 1994 vote (Csuja 1994; Stekler & Medvetsky 1994).

The period since 1990 is, therefore, best viewed as one during which environmental civil society has had to rebuild and relocate itself within the politics and society of Hungary. Gaining access to financial resources, in particular, has become a key goal because of the loss of governmental support after 1989 and the generally low degree of financial assistance now available through Parliament. For some former activists, the economic transformation (Kornai 1994) has meant that jobs which once provided a living wage *and* the time to do volunteer work for their groups (Sik 1994) no longer do so. Membership numbers have dropped off, too, as economic conditions have worsened. At the same time, while many groups are engaged in local conservation, restoration, and education projects, they do so without a larger strategy in mind; ironically, perhaps, the only groups in environmental civil society that *are* thinking strategically, and addressing the problem of rebuilding the environmental movement, are those seeking to participate in institutionalized politics.

As we shall see, these various activities are not bounded by the country's borders, and support has been provided from outside of Hungary. The Green Alternative has received advice and assistance from other Green Parties throughout Europe as well as those in the European Parliament. Environmental organizations and private foundations in the United States, the United

Kingdom, Japan, the Netherlands, France, and Scandinavia, among others, have provided resources of various sorts to groups in Hungary. And throughout Eastern and Central Europe, various environmental programs have been established and supported by governmental agencies in the West. These have all contributed to the revitalization of global civil society, although not to its coherence as a movement with a strategy.

History as structure, history as politics

Environmental civil society today

History and political economy are thus crucial to understanding the current condition of environmental organization in Hungary, especially where activism, practice, and the role of knowledge are concerned. While individual groups are quite active in their particular locales, the overall political effectiveness of the movement is constrained by three *internal* structural features growing out of the country's political, economic, and social history. This division is then reflected in the discourse of these fragments which, in turn, have considerable influence on local-global relations and tactics.

First, as noted earlier, the divide between conservationists and environmentalists continued to be strongly felt, reflecting, in part, the distinction made by participants between scientific and political approaches to Nature. In Hungary—by contrast with California—conservationists tend to see Nature protection as a primary value; we might call them "biocentric." Environmentalists tend to see human welfare as a primary value; they are more "anthropocentric" although they generally argue that welfare is enhanced only through some degree of harmony with Nature (Oelschlaeger 1991: ch.9). "Conservationism" in the Hungarian context resembles contemporary American "preservationism," in that it implies protection of Nature from further inroads by society. By contrast, "environmentalism" in the Hungarian context implies changes in existing political, social, and economic arrangements and is therefore not quite the same as its Western counterpart. To the outside observer, this may appear a somewhat fragile distinction, but in the Hungarian context it is quite important. It reflects the divide between the protected and independent groups, as discussed above, and suggests somewhat differing understandings of what constitutes politics.

The second reason for fragmentation is related to the first, and has to do with whether a particular group cooperated with the party or tried to maintain its independence under Communist rule. Those who cooperated tend to include some of the more conservationist organizations, and their members are sometimes derided as "watermelons"—green on the outside, red on the inside—by those who did not cooperate (although, to be sure, many conservationists do not fall into this category, just as not all "environmentalists" have clean records in this respect).[27] Resentments run deep, and some hold strong grudges. Evidence of this tension is seen most clearly with respect to the activities of the National Society of Conservationists (MTS) which, despite a record of collaboration with the old regime by its current president, continued until very recently to have good access to financial and other resources provided by the government and international organizations. Until 1994, the MTS had taken responsibility for organizing and running the annual national meetings of Hungarian environmental groups. Virtually all group leaders attend these meetings, although some complained that they would rather be organized by one of the independent groups, which is what finally happened in 1994.[28]

The third cause of fragmentation is what might be called the "charisma" problem, that is, the effect of strong individual leaders. This feature is often characteristic of organizations in civil society, no matter what the country. It is especially true of those that take an oppositional stance with respect to society and politics.[29] As I noted earlier, many of the nature conservation and ornithological groups established in the 1970s began informally, as students and teachers with similar values and interests went "out to Nature," as Hungarians often put it. These groups had no infrastructure, no membership as such, and no staff. To survive they depended on strong personal ties and charismatic leadership. Most chose to affiliate either with the party-sponsored umbrella organization or the MME but, even so, they remained fairly isolated from one another. The independent groups often came into being in a similar way. Once again, survival required one or two strong individuals who were both entrepreneurial and willing to continue their activities in spite of the threat of official harassment or repression. But the change of regime in 1989 did not result in the internal reorganization of these groups. As there was no tradition of civil associations, not to mention any experience with the institutionalization of civil groups, organizational dependence on strong leaders did not disappear along with the old regime.

As a result, many of the Hungarian groups are still dominated by the same forceful individuals that founded them. These people are well-known at home and abroad. They retain a sufficiently lofty reputation to be able to channel funding and control the flow of resources, the imagination to dream up projects and direct them, and the lion's share of the influence when it comes to effecting changes in their groups. Organizational independence is zealously guarded since, in what for the moment appears to be a zero-sum game, collaboration with others risks losing or having to share resources.[30] The dependence on strong individuals is further exacerbated by a tacit "turf" agreement, whereby groups in the cities and counties outside of Budapest agree not to organize projects or seek new members in a way that might intrude on the territory of others. Those umbrella organizations that do exist are specifically not intended to foster collaboration and are, in most respects, not much more than names under which others can gather.

One other feature of the country's socioeconomic landscape has had, and continues to have, influence over political, social, and economic life in the country, with concomitant effects on the fragmented nature of environmental civil society: structural centralization and peripheralization. For more than a century and a half—beginning even prior to the establishment of the Dual Monarchy in the 1860s—Budapest has been the center and focus of Hungarian life and culture. Its inhabitants routinely refer to anything outside of the metropolitan area as "the country." This core-periphery tension is further enhanced not only because there are no other cities in Hungary of a size comparable to Budapest, a consequence of the loss of two-thirds of the country's territory following World War I, but also the result of a century of state-sponsored efforts to exercise close control over the country's political and economic life as part of the program of nation-building. Centralization shapes not only material relationships within the country, but cognitive images and ideology, as well.[31] It has been instrumental in shaping the way the country functions and has had a commensurate effect on the Hungarian environmentalists.

During the second half of the nineteenth century, Budapest was developed as a counterweight to Vienna's dominance in the Austro-Hungarian Empire. Under the post-World War II communist regime, centralization was extended from infrastructure and politics to the country's "social infrastructure" of education, health and welfare, communications and economy. None of this has changed appreciably since 1989 (Fleischer, n.d.). Not only does the physical infrastructure continue to center on Budapest, the social infrastructure also remains dependent on the capital. In the absence of sweeping reforms, which are, so far, politically difficult to get through Parliament, social infrastructure, characterized by vested interests as well as institutional commitments, does not—indeed cannot—change quickly, at least not from the top.

Centralization as both physical and cognitive *structure* has consequences for everyone. For global civil society, the result is that most funds, expertise and external contacts flow through Budapest (there are, of course, some exceptions to this "rule," as we shall see below, but these are only developing slowly). Because Budapest is not only the capital but also the center of the life of political parties, all of whom have some commitment to "green" ideas, the parties continue to act as something of a "drain" on environmental groups there, in the sense that activities by Budapest-based groups are sometimes undertaken with the intent of influencing the parties.[32]

The structure of global civil society throughout the country more or less mimics the larger pattern of centralization. There are a disproportionately large number of environmental groups in Budapest. Many have more-or-less shared origins, having been established by one or more members of a core group of less than a dozen people. The same set of names shows up—and comes up in interviews—in a variety of combinations, as founders, staff and/or board members of the Regional Environmental Center for Eastern and Central Europe, the Independent Ecological Center, the ELTE Nature Club of Eötvös University, ISTER, Autonomia/Ökotárs, Green Circle, the Clean Air Action Group, the Green fraction of FIDESZ (Federation of Young Democrats), "Ecoservice" (an information clearinghouse) and others.[33] These individuals and groups tend to dominate environmental discourse in Budapest, and anyone looking for information about environmental conditions and activities in the country will, inevitably, be directed to them first.[34] Their dominance in the core means that they are approached first where the flow of funds and information into both the city and the "country" are concerned,[35] and this can have the effect of marginalizing groups that are newer, less prominent, or are out in the "country."[36]

While there are many organizations in Budapest, operating under a relatively clear division of labor, the pattern in smaller cities and towns is somewhat different. There, one tends to find a pattern of multiple, interlinked groups, each with a different local constituency. Each city usually has one or two prominent groups, associated via shared histories and overlapping memberships, but reflecting the "class" structure (such as it was) of the old system. Often, one group is oriented toward conservation and is the venture of technically- or scientifically-trained individuals—therefore deemed "professional"—while the other is more environmentalist, populist and grassroots. In Szeged, for example, a city in the southern part of the country, one found in 1993 five groups that, together, demonstrated a typical arrangement of this type: the Csongrád County Nature Conservation Society (affiliated with the National Society of Conservationists); the local branch of the Hungarian Ornithological Society; the Tisza Circle (somewhat more populist); the Southern Hungary section of the Green Party, and the Nature Conservation Club of the local university (Galle, et al. 1993). In the periphery of the "country"—that is, in the smaller towns and villages—one often finds single conservation/Nature-oriented groups established by school teachers and the local intelligentsia. These are even more marginalized than those in the smaller cities, although some are associated with one of the umbrella organizations based in Budapest.

Another consequence of over-centralization is a great deal of duplication and organizational inefficiency. While operating and project funds are available, they are, relatively speaking, scarce. With the high rate of inflation, they are growing scarcer.[37] There is, therefore, an incentive for environmental groups to seek international contacts, since these can provide an independent source of funds. Conversely, environmental organizations outside of Hungary and Eastern and Central Europe have an incentive to establish linkages with groups located inside the country. Not only does this enhance the credibility of both, it also contributes to the larger project of expanding environmental networks and socializing the Hungarian groups into the global system.[38] At the same time, these organizations are socializing the networks into Hungary, so to speak, since "indigenous knowledge" about the country can be thought of as a scarce resource from the external point of view. In other words, there are complementarities between the two, but these are also a source of tension and even conflict.

The core-periphery structure of global civil society in Hungary is beginning to change, however, as some aspects of government and production are decentralized. Some environmental protection functions have been transferred to the county- and municipal-level authorities, and control of enterprises that are privatized or become joint or foreign-owned ventures no longer rests with central planners. The owners of these factories are no longer as strongly subject to the whims of the center and must deal with local authorities over such issues as land use and air and water pollution (Szmirmai 1993). This means that environmental organizations in Budapest have lost some of the potential leverage over pollution problems in the "country," while the potential leverage of groups outside of the capital has increased, as they are often the only reliable source of technical information available to municipal and county authorities as well as the public. For example, in Nyíregyháza, in the northeastern part of the country, the city established a municipal environmental office in 1993 to provide itself with technical information as well as to support local environmental groups. The head of this office was also an active member of one of the major environmental groups in the county (Bélteki, Czsitu & Vass 1993).

From knowledge to practice

What are the political and social impacts of environmental civil society, as it exists today in Hungary? How do groups there organize, act and interact with each other and with "outsiders," both national and foreign? What are the sources of their knowledge and how do they put this knowledge into practice? And how does the history of environmentalism in Hungary, and its practice, fit into the larger arguments of this book? I focus on three important points here. First, the emergence of environmentalism and environmental civil society in Hungary during the 1970s and 1980s was largely an "indigenous" process, although it was informed by awareness of the rise of environmentalism as well as scientific work in ecology in the West. It is only in recent years, however, that foreign organizations began to make extensive contacts with groups within Hungary. Second, strategic and tactical alliances with environmental organizations outside of Hungary provide a mechanism for organizational survival, growth and effectiveness, as well as a means of challenging the centralizing tendencies of the new/old Hungarian state. Finally, environmental groups within Hungary appear, to date, more consequential for what they can accomplish in *local* contexts than what they are able to achieve together in *national* terms. Given the particular political and structural conditions that existed under the old regime, these points are not altogether surprising; that they continue to be apposite is, oddly enough, a reflection of the same state weakness evident in the case of California, as will be argued.

Global civil society as an indigenous formation

Earlier in this chapter, I indicated that many of the environmental groups to be found in Hungary today were established not as branches of international or even national organizations but, rather, as a result of the efforts of technically-trained intellectuals. In university towns—Szeged, Pécs, Mosonmagyaróvár, Debrecen, and others—faculty in the biological sciences were often the founders of these groups; in smaller towns, the groups formed around members of the intelligentsia, such as teachers. Some of these individuals had foreign contacts or had travelled abroad, but usually only in a scientific or educational capacity; travel for political networking purposes was not permitted. Others learned their ecology from scientific publications and books, which were relatively plentiful but generally accessible only to specialists. Not until the mid-1980s did foreign groups began to make occasional contact with groups in Hungary. In other words, Hungarian environmental groups were informed by what was going on elsewhere but were largely indigenous to Hungary.

Again, most of the early groups were largely conservationist (in the Hungarian sense) in orientation, dedicated to the appreciation and protection of Nature. Even though they were not overtly political, we can interpret their activities through the lens of resistance to the party-state, for several reasons. First, nature appreciation and conservation were not part of the official ideology of the state; if anything, "really-existing" socialism had a highly utilitarian view of Nature, seeing it primarily as an input to production.[39] Hence, Nature could be regarded as a realm that was not colonized by the official ideology, at least not in an evident fashion.[40]

Second, Nature can be understood as a cultural arena, one that, in fact, had its roots in the emergence of the Hungarian nation and state in the 1800s. As was the case in many European countries, identification between national character and Nature was an element in the development processes of the nineteenth century. In the Hungarian case, this was centered on the management of water and the romanticism associated with the *Pusta* (Great Plain). It was also an element later given voice through organizations such as the Scouts.[41] Beyond this, the Carpathian Basin—historical Hungary—defined the limits of the nation as well as the Nature within which it dwelled. In the context of the post-war settlement, which fixed boundaries between socialist states, Nature appreciation became a form of expressing the "true" Hungarian character.[42] One now sees this phenomenon re-emerging in the nationalism of the extreme right, although it seems to have limited resonance with most of the public.[43]

Finally, the attempts of the state, operating through the NPF and YCL, to capture and colonize the conservation groups—for ideological as well as international reasons—had the somewhat paradoxical effect of *legitimating* environmental discourse and ecological principles not only within but also outside of the authorized political system. The party, however, continued to see environmental protection as a narrowly-defined technical issue of concern to a limited social stratum, and failed to recognize the political implications of such a move. This opening was grasped by the independent groups and put to good use. In this schema, culture, Nature, history, and action became irrevocably intertwined, a phenomenon described by John Walton, who writes that "On the ground people construct their lives in consciously meaningful ways that cannot be read from state-centered directives any more than they can be deduced from modes of economic production" (1992:288).

The purpose and functioning of transnational alliances

In Hungary, we find an archetypical example of transnational networking within global civil society. That many of the environmental groups in Hungary have sought to establish connections of one sort or another with organizations in other countries is not in question; rather, it is the *character* of these connections that is of interest. My investigation of these linkages has focused largely on those between the United States and Hungary, although European organizations and agencies are also quite active. At first glance, the transfer of knowledge and practices through these linkages is largely about the technical-instrumental, concerned about the "how?" of doing things. At a second level, the "why?"—that is, the ideology or worldview associated with environmentalism and technology transfer—is also apparent.[44] Teasing out this second level is much more difficult than mapping the first and requires, in some instances, reading "between the lines" of interviews and literatures. To make this point concrete, I will focus, first, on the nature of U.S.-based assistance to environmental groups in Hungary and, second, on the alliances developed by three organizations focused on local river restoration.[45]

Since 1989, there have been growing efforts by foreign groups and governments to influence and assist environmentalists in Hungary. This has been a curious process, inasmuch as the goals of external actors are often not the same as those of the Hungarian groups themselves. Here, the local-global nexus comes into sharp focus, and the tensions between global civil society and the state system are most obvious. To illustrate these points clearly, it helps to understand the nature of some of these alliances. Funds, technical training, technology transfer, and volunteer assistance have been provided by a variety of environmental groups based in the United States and Europe, as well as agencies of the United States government and the European Community.

For example, several programs have been supported by U.S. government funds channelled through the U.S. Agency for International Development (U.S. AID). These have also involved as subcontractors other government agencies, including the U.S. Environmental Protection Agency (U.S. EPA) and the Peace Corps, and American environmental organizations, such as the World Wildlife Fund-USA, the Institute for Sustainable Communities in Vermont, and the Institute for Conservation Leadership in Washington (U.S. General Accounting Office 1994). The Peace Corps has sent "environmental" volunteers to the region, in addition to the usual English teachers and business advisors (Braus 1991). The German Marshall Fund, through a consortium of foundations and donors that includes the Rockefeller Brothers Fund and the Sasakawa Peace Foundation of Japan, has been engaged in similar activities. Finally, a number of private, non-profit groups, such as the River Watch Network in Vermont, the Global Rivers Environmental Education Network in Michigan, and the National River Watch in Great Britain have been collaborating with Hungarian groups in setting up stream and river restoration projects.

Why has this assistance been offered? The general rationale has been the propagation and maintenance of democracy, as put forth in the "Support for Eastern European Democracy Act" (SEED Act) of 1989, largely the brainchild of then-U.S. President Bush.[46] The SEED Act clearly articulates an ideology of political and economic liberalism. Environmental groups are seen as having been instrumental in the collapse of the old regimes in the region (although, of course, the logic does not exactly follow if one considers the cases of Romania or Bulgaria). Thus, U.S. AID, according to its literature, has applied "Freedom, fresh air, and free enterprise" to the region's environmental ills:

> Solving these [environmental] problems will require significant policy changes, more efficient environmental investments in both the public and private sectors, and more effective institutions. It will also demand increased government accountability and public participation in environmental management (U.S. AID 1992).

The U.S. EPA has been somewhat more explicit on this point:

> The US has made institution building a key part of its environmental assistance to the emerging democracies in Central and Eastern Europe. As a result of extensive discussions with government officials and knowledgeable NGOs in these countries, it has become clear that the meaningful integration of environmental protection and economic revitalization requires the establishment of effective environmental management organizations and adequately trained staff to manage and operate them (U.S. EPA 1992a:1).

The U.S. EPA's programs have included seed funding for the Regional Environmental Center for Central and Eastern Europe (in Budapest) and "institution building," as well as "direct technical assistance and demonstration projects" and "regional projects to focus on transboundary pollution or environmental problems common to the region." Much of this transfer has taken the shape of so-called training modules, intended to instruct individuals about the technical nuts and bolts of environmental management. The EPA has had a particular interest in establishing "environmental management training centers" to facilitate such instruction (U.S. EPA 1992a, 1992b).

The Peace Corps has pursued two environment-oriented strategies in Eastern and Central Europe. First, in keeping with its tradition of teaching English, there has been a growing trend toward "content-based" teaching, with a particular focus on environmental education. Second, the Peace Corps has been sending volunteers with some environmental "background" to work with national park services, municipal governments, schools, and NGOs. The last sometimes leads to odd situations, inasmuch as volunteers have been eager to show they are useful while the NGOs have not always had a clear idea of how best to utilize them (Shores 1993). Officially:

> The Peace Corps believes that environmental education can help people create an environmentally sustainable society that promotes economic success and social stability, as well as individual growth and empower-

> ment. Environmental education is a process designed to help people gain the awareness, knowledge, skills, motivation, and commitment to manage the earth's resources sustainably and to take responsibility for maintaining and improving environmental quality (U.S. Peace Corps 1992).

It is as much the ideology of liberal individualism that is alive and well here as any particular commitment to environmental protection or restoration.[47] Volunteers, however, do not go to Hungary with this ideology in mind; those with backgrounds in environmental science or activism aim to do good by doing well, and hope to teach their hosts the wisdom they have acquired back home. Unfortunately, their hosts often know more about the subject than do the volunteers. The Hungarian groups, moreover, have their own particular way of doing things, which is not part of the volunteers' training. As a result, volunteers have often found themselves writing or revising grant proposals in English or coming into conflict with their hosts over the "best" way to accomplish particular goals (more on this follows).

The Environmental Training Project for Central and Eastern Europe, run with funds from U.S. AID, has sought "to provide environmental management, pollution prevention and control and conflict management training" to the region,

> designed to help Central and Eastern Europe improve its indigenous capabilities to identify, assess, prioritize, and address environmental problems, taking into account the efficient use of natural resources and pollution reduction and prevention, while developing a competitive market economy (U.S. AID, n.d.).

Training programs are aimed at business and industry, NGOs, universities, and local and regional governments. The World Wildlife Fund-USA is undertaking the training of NGOs, with the goal of:

> empowering the public of Central and Eastern Europe, by strengthening environmental organizations and promoting the free flow of environmental information; enhancing environmental management in Central and Eastern Europe; promoting environmentally sound investment in Central and Eastern Europe; building domestic U.S. support and understanding of Central and East European environmental concerns (WWF 1992).

The activities of these U.S. government-sponsored efforts in the region might not, at first glance, seem to have much to do with the framework presented in chapter 3. Yet, it is telling, in my view, that these agencies have chosen to give environmental organizations and agencies such prominence in their programs. Indeed, some agency staffers seem to believe that the long-term effectiveness of U.S. environmental assistance to Eastern and Central Europe may come to depend more on NGOs than governments. Paradoxically, the place where such transfer seemed to be working best up to 1992, according to one AID staff member, was Bulgaria, where the regime in power at the time was composed largely of so-called ex-Communists. AID projects in Hungary were seen as being less successful because the government had not been very effective or cooperative; consequently, there was some thought being given to funnelling all AID money in Hungary through environmental groups (Freer 1993).[48]

Projects funded through private foundations and non-profit groups have similar objectives. The "Environmental Partnership for Central Europe," managed by the German Marshall Fund, provides funds, technical assistance, and administrative training to environmental organizations and local government agencies in Poland, the Czech Republic, Slovakia, and Hungary. The rationale for the program, according to the Partnership's literature, is as follows:

> Besides building environmental awareness and support, Partnership projects provide the first opportunity most people in formerly totalitarian countries have had to learn how to build consensus, make decisions together and experience other democratic practices, including speaking out and taking a stand (German Marshall Fund n.d.:16).[49]

The Partnership program has several components. First, through in-country representatives, the Partnership runs a competitive grants program for environmental groups. In Hungary, organizations affiliated with the Partnership have received grants for operating costs and salaries as well as funding for various projects. Second, the Partnership has established a program in "organizational development" and "leadership" training for staff of Central European non-governmental organizations. Group members are brought to the United States, where they receive two weeks of instruction in the care and feeding of NGOs. They are then placed for two weeks with organizations whose focus parallel their individual interests. Program managers expect that these individuals will carry what they have learned back to Central Europe.

The Partnership also sends American experts to Central Europe for the purposes of "transfer" of technology and organizational knowledge. It will also provide air and water monitoring equipment if it is used with the idea of having a "policy impact" (Kehoe 1993; Hunt 1993). It is this last objective that is proving most difficult in Hungary, at least from the American point of view, since the notion of influencing national environmental policy in a systematic fashion has been a somewhat unfamiliar one. Through its in-country office in Budapest, the Partnership has provided laptop computers and software to both organizations and individuals throughout Hungary, who comprise the members of an environmental computer network, *Zöld Pok* ("Green Spider"). The network, which became operational in mid-1993, is intended to facilitate communication and collaboration among environmental groups within Hungary, and it has become fairly active and lively.[50]

The experiences of the Partnership also highlight some of the difficulties associated with transferring knowledge and practice through global networks. The Partnership has not aimed, so far as I can tell, at "teaching" environmental groups in Central Europe about Ecology; it has been generally understood that there is already a great deal of expertise available with the Hungarian environmental community. Rather, the Partnership has attempted to transfer the *organizational culture* of U.S. civil society, in general, and the U.S. environmental community, in particular. This has included fostering a transition from a "charismatic" organizational structure to a more bureaucratized one (Foltanyi 1995), a move not always welcomed by group leaders, as previously noted.

The net effect of these U.S.-sponsored efforts has been a curious and not entirely successful one. What Hungarian groups have lacked, in particular, is money: Money with which to acquire the instrumentation that would allow them to determine just how "bad" various problems really are; money to run their organizations and projects; money to facilitate further fund-raising. What they have not lacked is scientific expertise. And, what they have not wanted is to be instructed in the environmental "problematique" by outsiders. What they have required, therefore, is the capability to write clear and compelling grant proposals that can be submitted to U.S- and Europe-based funding sources—and this might not be an activity that contributes most to the strengthening of civil society. Consequently, as noted, Peace Corps volunteers often have been pressed into writing grants, or revising already-written ones, or helping to reform or rationalize internal administrative and accounting procedures, rather than being utilized in a technical or educational capacity. Volunteers represent a source of essentially "free" labor that has enabled core group members to concentrate on their own projects and interests, and foreign funding has meant that NGOs are largely freed of the need to develop domestic sources of support for their work.

This particular contradiction has been less-evident in collaborative efforts focused on the treatment of specific environmental resources, such as the streams and rivers that run through most towns and villages. As we shall see, U.S. and European non-governmental organizations have become fairly active in providing various types of assistance—technical and organizational—to Hungarian groups. Political ideology—that is, liberalism—has been less of a concern in these instances, although politics—and a high degree of idealism—remain at the core of such efforts. Thus, as the Global Rivers Environmental Education Network (GREEN) puts it,

> [GREEN] seeks to improve the quality of watershed and rivers, and thereby the lives of people. GREEN uses watersheds as a unifying theme to link people within and between watersheds . . . Each watershed project is unique, and how it develops depends upon the goals and situation of the local community. . . . As they share cultural perspectives, students, teachers, citizens and professionals from diverse parts of the world are linked by a common bond of interest in and concern for water quality issues (GREEN n.d.).

GREEN has programs of this type in 136 countries.

The River Watch Network (RWN), based in Vermont, is more focused on the linkages between technological and scientific competence and political action, without much reference to larger goals. As RWN's materials put it, "We can help you clean up your river."

> River pollution . . . is generated by all of us and its solution requires active citizen participation. Federal, state and local governments are frequently unable to tackle these water quality problems because their resources for river monitoring are severely limited. . . . Gathering and interpreting scientifically credible water quality data underlies every River Watch effort. . . . RWN will never just send you a kit with a page of instructions for water sampling. . . . Each River Watch program is individually designed to meet the particular needs of its community and the conditions of its river. . . . RWN staff are river experts *and* community organizers (River Watch, n.d.; emphasis in original).

A third organization, Ecologia, is based in Pennsylvania, and has provided monitoring equipment to groups throughout Eastern and Central Europe to enable them to test local water sources for various types of pollution. Ecologia provides a training course in the United States in the use of the equipment, and groups are required to send periodic reports on their activities. The data are generally used for local purposes, to inform and influence municipal and county authorities (Majer 1995; Pannon Ecologists' Club 1994). In all three of these efforts, the focus is on adaptation of an organizational approach to *local* conditions, rather than the more general attempt of the programs described above to transplant organizational culture. The local approach does not necessarily guarantee greater success in the Hungarian context, but it does seem to generate greater commitment within the Hungarian organizations.

Acting locally, networking transnationally

In global terms, one of the most common forms of environmental conservation, protection, and restoration seems to involve water, via creek and river watersheds, lakes, wetlands and coastal waters. Perhaps this is because water, in concert with hills and valleys is so evocative of place, and the intimacy with place that some believe essential to human health and well-being (a point to which I return in chapter 7). Perhaps it is the operationalization of a bioregionalist paradigm focused on watershed, as discussed in chapter 4. Perhaps it is simply a concern with water quality. Whatever the reason, the numbers of groups dedicated to the protection and restoration of creek and river watersheds are myriad. The same seems to be the case in Hungary, where the Danube River, roughly bisecting the country, is seen as the "heart" of Hungary, both physically and emotionally (Figure 5.2).

The Danube River's watershed constitutes the core of the Carpathian Basin, which encompasses, more or less, Hungary as it was prior to the Treaty of Trianon. Thus, the Danube has historical resonance, too.[51] Lest such symbolism seem too pat, the river has also fulfilled a variety of mundane utilitarian functions, as a municipal and rural water source, a commercial waterway and a sewer for the eight countries through which it passes. It is no coincidence, therefore, that many groups engaged in local conservation, restoration, and education projects have focused on the Danube, Tisza, and Dráva rivers, and their tributaries. One survey identified approximately two hundred such projects within Hungary alone (Nagy 1994).

Around this theme, a number of alliances have been established between Hungarian environmental organizations and foreign ones, which provide an important conduit for the transfer of knowledge and practice, in addition to technical and financial resources. Some of these associations were initiated by the foreign groups; others by the Hungarian ones. Some of the Hungarian programs predated 1989; others have been established since then. The extent of these networks can best be seen through a description of the activities of three groups involved in river-related activities. The first, *Zöld Szív*, is an elementary school-based environmental education group; the second, the *Göncöl Alapítvány*, is a long-established community group that is engaged in education, restoration, lobbying, and legislative advising; and the third, the *Ormánság Alapítvány* mentioned earlier, is a regional development group working with community authorities. These groups, and numerous others not mentioned here, are all engaged in projects having to do with monitoring, restoration, and networking around Hungarian rivers and creeks.

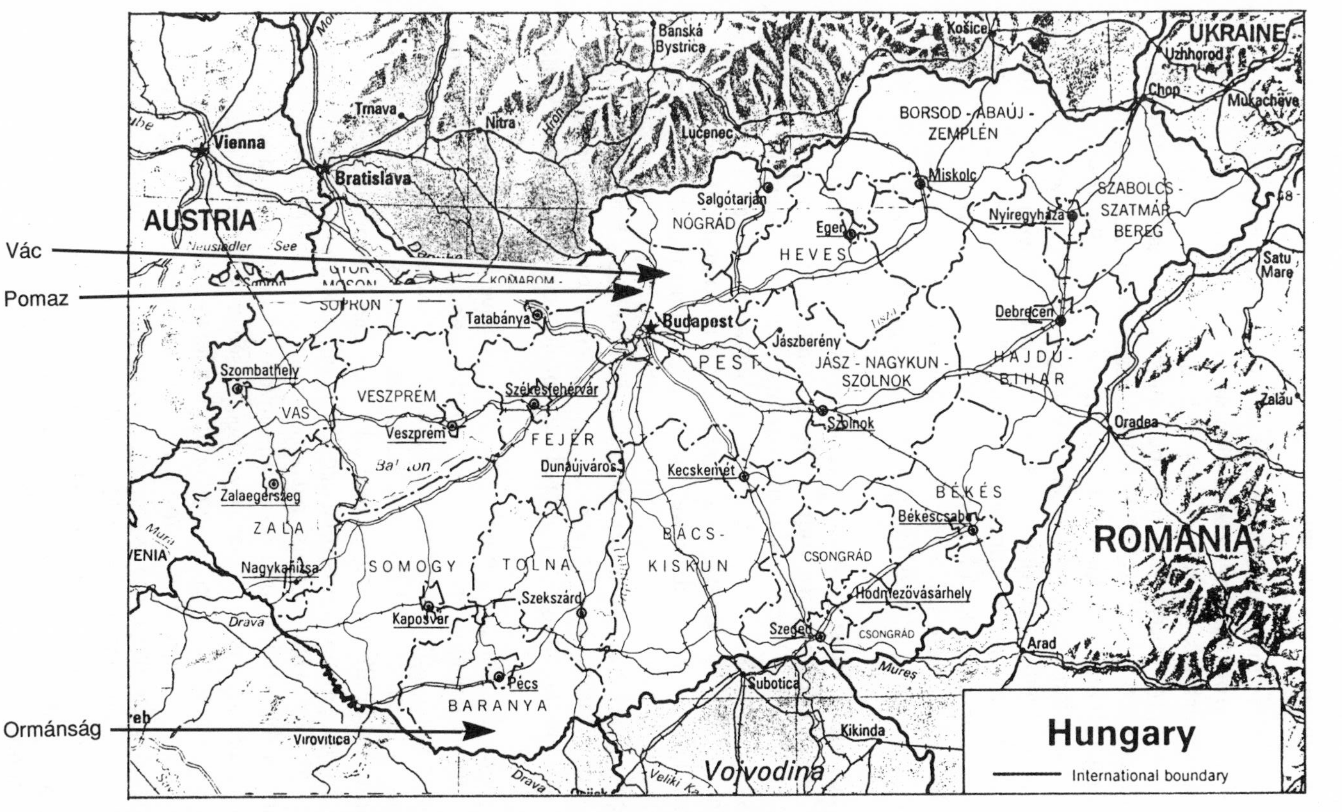

Figure 5.2. Source: U.S. Central Intelligence Agency, Base 802213 (R01145) 11–94.

Zöld Szív *("Greenheart")*

This environmental education program describes itself as a "youth movement for nature conservation," although it also numbers adults among its members. Founded in 1989 by Anikó Orgoványi, a primary school teacher in Pomáz, a town just north of Budapest on the eastern bank of the Danube, it claims more than three thousand members—mostly children eight to sixteen years old—in one hundred and fifty Hungarian cities and towns, and seven foreign countries (including the United States, Russia, the Netherlands, Germany, and the Czech Republic). As *Zöld Szív*'s literature puts it, the organization's aim is to:

> [L]ove the natural world and to appreciate and to protect its values. The practical task of our members is to explore, observe, take care of and protect natural value in the environment. That can be surface water, a plant or an animal or its habitat (Orgoványi 1991:5).

Zöld Szív is a member of national groups, such as the Danube Circle and the *Zöld Pok* and GreenNet computer networks, and has collaborated on projects with foreign organizations such as Greenpeace, River Watch, GREEN, and the National River Watch based in England. It operates a project for monitoring water quality along the Danube, with twenty-eight member groups from Germany to ex-Yugoslav republics (with the goal of extending the project "from the Black Forest to the Black Sea"). In Pomáz, members of *Zöld Szív* also monitor and try to maintain water quality in a creek that runs through the town and drains into the Danube. One of their more notable successes has been negotiating the installation of water treatment equipment in a local textile factory (Orgoványi 1992; Orgoványi & Houston 1993; *Zöld Szív* 1993).

By now, the organization's leaders have been socialized into Ecology. How did this happen? According to Orgoványi, there is no clear process to which she can point. By reading, acting, and collaborating, it seems, she and the members of her organization have come to an Ecological "sensibility." But the global view does not dominate the local; as she puts it, she places *Zöld Szív*'s work in a global context, but tells her students to focus on their local environment. Through having each of her students take responsibility for monitoring a specific stretch of the river, and acting if something needs to be done, the importance of Nature at the local level is brought home to them (Orgoványi 1992; Orgoványi & Houston 1993).

All of this is not to suggest that the organization's activities have led to major changes in environmental practices or quality around Pomáz. The state of the economy, in particular, makes it difficult to get authorities to act on behalf of environmental protection. Still, as an example of a locally-based NGO that has reached out to establish both national and transnational linkages, *Zöld Szív* is one example of the extent of the networks of global civil society. *Zöld Szív* is similar to many other environmental groups in Hungary, especially in terms of its primary focus on environmental education. Almost all groups have, in addition to a number of other projects, an environmental education effort focused at the primary and secondary levels. Virtually all of the larger groups have international contacts. These serve, on the one hand, to channel various kinds of resources into and local knowledge out of the country. They are also, as previously suggested, a mechanism for building national credibility and validating the legitimacy of the external contacts.

Göncöl Alapítvány *(Göncöl—the "Big Dipper"—Foundation)*[52]

This organization is located in Vác, also north of Budapest on the western bank of the Danube. *Göncöl* is an "independent," "full-service" organization, described in its literature as an "alliance of legal bodies, NGOs, volunteers and experts oriented to create and preserve nature and social and human values while remaining independent of any political and commercial values" (*Göncöl*, 1992). The group was first established in 1973 as a "youth science club," with a specific focus on astronomy. The group's founder, Vilmos Kiszel, had a science background, as did many of the older members. School-age children were also members, and a number of these individuals now work for the organization in a professional capacity. Over the next few years following its founding, the club extended its activities to other "cultural areas," including nature photography and observation, computers, and geology. In 1978, because it was considered non-political by the state, *Göncöl* was allowed to register as an independent association.

Throughout these early years, the group operated with environmental concerns in mind, but without explicit efforts directed toward environmental protection or conservation. Several times after 1978, the government offered to provide financial and other support to *Göncöl*; each time the group's leaders refused, and the organization was forced to shift its focus. Eventually, the group was able to acquire some degree of protection from the municipality of Vác, which allowed it to operate independently of state sponsorship. Only since 1989, however, has it been able to function without interference. Since then, it has acquired a national reputation for expertise and competence, engaging in science, education, lobbying, and technical assistance to the Parliament. Indeed, Kiszel has been deeply involved in working with various groups and committees in drafting the new environmental law (although there are some who are not impressed by this version). *Göncöl* has a staff of close to thirty, plus many more volunteers, publishes a monthly magazine, *Sűni*, for children aged eight to sixteen, operates environmental summer camps, and runs a "cultural" house in Vác (*Göncöl* 1992; Regional Environmental Center 1992; Kiszel & Czippan 1993).

Göncöl's transnational networking is extensive, with a particular focus on habitat maintenance and restoration and on water quality monitoring. The group's local riverine projects include monitoring of water quality in the Danube and habitat restoration of Gombas Creek, which runs through Vác. The former project is operated in cooperation with the River Watch Network, which has provided technical training and assistance to members of *Göncöl*. The group has also set up a cooperative program with organizations working on protection and restoration of the Hudson River in New York.

In 1992, the GAIA subgroup of *Göncöl* established the "Please Adopt a Stream" project to monitor water conditions in streams elsewhere in Hungary and to encourage local groups to involve municipal authorities, civil groups, and individuals in their projects. The program originally included only Hungarian groups—of which there are about forty—but, in recent years has grown to include Romanian and Slovakian organizations, as well. So far, the project has been more successful in "consciousness raising" than getting authorities to act. In Vác, for example, the municipal government and local water management authorities refuse to accept the water quality data collected by *Göncöl*, even though the authorities have collected no data at all (Nagy 1993, 1994; Rozgonyi 1994). This suggests that, until such projects acquire legitimation through the state, monitoring groups will have difficulty in convincing polluters to modify or cease their activities.

Ormánság Alapítvány

In contrast to *Zöld Szív* and *Göncöl*, which are based in more urban areas, the *Ormánság Alapítvány* is rural and focused on regional development. The organization is based in Drávafok, a small village southwest of Pécs, and not far north of the Dráva River.[53] The Ormánság is an ethnically-mixed area, including not only ethnic Hungarians but Croatians, Germans, and Gypsies, as well. In recent decades, the proximity of the area to the border with Yugoslavia (now Croatia), whose relations with Warsaw Pact countries were rather poor, kept it peripheral, and "underdeveloped." Today, this is both an advantage and disadvantage. On the one hand, it means that the region has been less affected by the "hyper-industrialization" that occurred in other parts of the country, although it has undergone ecological alteration dating back to the mid-nineteenth century, as a result of water-diversion projects. On the other hand, it has made the region a "territory of poor people and Gipsies [sic]," with mono-cultural, chemical-intensive agriculture, industrial-style animal husbandry, and deteriorating soil and environment (*Ormánság* 1992, 1993:1–2; Lantos 1993, 1994).

The central figure in the *Ormánság* Foundation is Tamás Lantos, trained as an agronomist, and employed during the 1980s as an ecological researcher in the biological research institute of the Hungarian Academy of Sciences (once again, we see the importance of individuals in such organizations). He became interested in combining sociology and ecology, and left the institute to establish the organization. With funding from several ministries of the Hungarian government and in-country sources (the latter supported by the European Union and the German Marshall Fund of the United States), as well as foundations in the United Kingdom and the Netherlands, the Ormánság Foundation became involved in developing a regionalized "rural sustainable development programme." The goals of the Foundation, according to its literature, are to contribute:

> to the growth of territorial independence of the Ormánság, its development as a whole integrated system
>
> to the long-term preservation (preventing deterioration and depletion of resources in the Ormánság)
>
> to the development of a habitat, appropriate and enjoyable for the inhabitants
>
> to the development of a culture and lifestyle corresponding with [sic] the sustainable state (*Ormánság* 1993:2).

To this end, the Foundation has established nine separate projects. These include: an "ecological culture" school in a building donated by the village of Drávafok to the Foundation, which is rehabilitating it; an organic demonstration farm and collaboration with local farming units to implement organic farming techniques; a project to ensure "basic subsistence for gypsies without depletion of local resources" through farming, animal husbandry, and industrial-handicraft workshops; a landscape preservation project for the benefit of the region's inhabitants as well as "eco-tourists"; a "living" floodplain museum dedicated to illustrating the region's "water culture" through demonstration projects; and an "organizing project" to foster the creation of local grassroots groups and to establish a framework for providing management advice and helping in regional fundraising. In this last category, the Foundation has also helped to establish groups such as the Ormánság Development Association, which includes twenty-five local governments, private enterprises, associations and foundations, and is oriented toward raising funds for the improvement of local infrastructure (*Ormánság* 1993:4–7; Lantos 1994, 1995).

The *Ormánság* Foundation is notable for its clearly-defined regional focus and its attempts to integrate Nature with livelihood and culture, which is unusual in Hungary. Lantos is interested in fostering what he calls "capital conservation": retaining as much of the natural capital stock as possible in the region, and exporting services, such as ecotourism, instead. There are fewer contacts between the *Ormánság*—both Foundation and region—and organizations and agencies outside of the country than is true of many other groups in Hungary's environmental civil society. Yet, it is clear from the Foundation's programs and plans that it, too, is linked to global civil society through its practices and sources of knowledge.

As is true of most, if not all, of the work being undertaken by environmental groups and organizations in Hungary, the projects of the *Ormánság Alapítvány* are still in the early stages of development and, so, their ultimate success is by no means assured. More than most, the Foundation is using the cultural-historical aspects of the region—its focus around land and water—as the basis for a larger vision of what it could become. Although neither Lantos nor the Foundation's written materials ever mention the term "bioregionalism," the projects are clearly conceived of in such terms. More to the point, they treat the *Ormánság* "bioregion" as not simply an ecological zone but one whose form was, and will be, shaped by political economy and history. In this respect, too, it is similar to some of the experiments underway in California, which seek to sustain both the resource base and the political economies of the communities dependent on it.

These three groups are only a few of a large number engaged in river-related activities in Hungary, and so they are examples and not archetypes. Still, three questions necessarily follow. First, are any of these activities having an effect on environmental quality in the country? Second, do such activities resemble the common-pool property resource regimes discussed in chapter 3? And, third, do these groups, and their activities, actually constitute a part of "global civil society? " At this time, one cannot say that environmental organizations in Hungary are having more than a marginal impact on the condition of the creeks and rivers there. They lack both the personnel and resources to do very much.

Still, we should not forget that the national government has devolved a great deal of environmental regulatory authority to the county and municipal level. More often than not, the local groups, in association with university faculty, constitute the only source of technical and scientific expertise available. To date, much of the data accumulated from the various monitoring and restoration projects has been used only to alert officials and the public of problems. Until such time as the government acquires the capacity to monitor in a rigorous fashion and enforce environmental regulations, local efforts will represent a substantial portion of all environmental monitoring, if not protection, in the country. Thus, any attempts to regulate and monitor discharges of effluents into local waterways may come to depend on the capacities of these groups. Such capacities, in turn, will depend on the availability of resources from both domestic and foreign sources, civil as well as governmental.

At face value, these widely-scattered projects do not resemble anything like common–pool property resource regimes. They do, however, communicate to group members and the public the notion of shared resources that must be cared for rather than abused. Prior to 1989, rivers were seen largely in utilitarian terms and were, therefore, treated rather badly. Today, they are still polluted, but there is a growing recognition not only of the economic importance of water quality, but of the significance of rivers in biological as well as cultural terms. Under current economic and political circumstances, it is too much to expect a mass movement to coalesce around protection of rivers, as one did under rather different circumstances during the 1980s. In the future, we might expect to see a growing appreciation for these rivers and creeks, and a much greater sense of shared responsibility for their protection.

Finally, the activities described here represent only a small part of all of the environmental practices under way in Hungary. Global civil society in Hungary is establishing many associations with groups in other parts of the world, setting up strategic and tactical alliances with them and, in some cases, using these alliances to acquire resources for domestic purposes. While most of the conservationist and environmentalist organizations have local origins, their transnational alliances are bolstering local capacities while integrating groups into the global networks of knowledge and practice. This is not to say that environmental civil society is being absorbed into some sort of global environmental culture; its members resist becoming the colonies or satellites of "foreign powers."[54] Local projects are central. Place, and a sense of it, is important to them, as it is to environmental groups in the civil societies of all countries. Global civil society is global, not universal.

Conclusion

Environmentalism in one country? This question could be answered in several different ways. Can we point to a particularly Hungarian form of environmentalism that differs, in some fundamental sense, from forms of belief and practice found elsewhere? In Hungary, as in California, we see a pattern of environmental politics and practice that is, to no small degree, the result of the confluence of particular historical circumstances and structures—a political economy in transformation yet still possessing many characteristics acquired during several *anciens regimes*; the transfer of knowledge and practice, within the country and across political boundaries; and the permissive conditions, established by the state, that lend themselves to particular types of symbolic discourse and action in preference to others. Global civil society in Hungary is influential not because it has its hands on the levers of political or economic power, but because it draws on both material and symbolic concerns of the country's people. While environmental groups are not in the business of providing services eliminated by the state's social welfare system, they can serve a local social welfare function in terms of finding and protecting endangered habitats (e.g., in Szeged and Vác), evaluating the seriousness and health implications of toxic waste dumps (e.g., in Miskolc), designing and lobbying for plans to improve municipal air quality (e.g., in Budapest), providing environmental education curricula at the elementary and secondary levels and public education about conservation and protection (almost everywhere), and so on. Indeed, in terms of local and county-wide monitoring, evaluation, and conservation capacities, these groups are often all that exist. As economic pressures on authorities and industries to cut corners, ignore regulations, and disregard hazards increase, the environmental sector could come to play an increasingly important watchdog role.

In terms of symbols, environmental civil society has, in the past, drawn on some particularly potent ones. Clearly, just as the Danube Circle drew on certain Hungarian themata in its campaign against the Gabçikovo-Nagymaros system, so do the groups currently active around environmental issues draw, to some degree, on the uniqueness of the Hungarian environment and its centrality to the Carpathian Basin. As is evident, in particular, in the *Ormánság*, the many "meanings" of Nature, both old and new, stand as a reservoir to be tapped during renegotiation of the terms of specific resource regimes. Rivers are not just rivers; streams are not just streams. They are a signifier of place and a source of identity, both large and small.

The question posed above could also be turned on its head: Given the globalization of environmental problems, does environmentalism in one country make any sense? As the Hungarian environmental sector becomes linked to and integrated with global networks of environmentalism and adopts the cosmopolitan ideologies and practices of transnational organizations such as the World Wildlife Fund and Greenpeace, it could lose its national characteristics. The evidence suggests however that, while

Hungarian groups are adopting some of these practices and beliefs, they are by no means ready to lose their identity in order to join the global networks. The tension between the local and the global remains, and each has something to offer to the other. The networks of environmental civil society are, indeed, global but increasingly tied to place, a point returned to in chapter 7.

CHAPTER 6

Environmental Organizing in Indonesia: The Search for a Newer Order

Judith Mayer

"Unity in Diversity"[1] is Indonesia's state motto, an ambitious creed for the world's fourth most-populous nation spanning a three thousand mile archipelago (Figure 6.1). The significance of such a concept of nationhood is striking as one travels through the country's diverse landscapes and cultures. Jakarta, Indonesia's capital, bursts with over eight million people, spreading industrial estates, housing developments, golf courses, and squatter settlements into western Java's micro-managed village rice terraces, gardens, hilltop forests, and artisanal fisheries. The bulldozers of massive logging and mining operations knock muddy roads and ore pits into the rainforests of Sumatra, Borneo, and New Guinea. They superimpose new landscapes of global capital onto the forests, watersheds and indigenous land use systems of hundreds of regional cultures and ethnic communities.

Indonesia's overall economic growth reached six to seven percent annually in the early 1990s (Shenon 1994a), with industrial growth rates leaping well above that (Ford 1994). The government claimed that dire poverty had been isolated in manageable "pockets" ("*Peta Kemiskinan*" 1993; Majelis 1993) where the state could focus development attention following the economic "take-off"[2] anticipated by President Suharto's[3] "New Order." Indonesia's "New Order"[4] regime has defined its success, and staked its legitimacy in the eyes of the Indonesian people, in terms of this economic growth. The regime's proponents insist that the dramatic improvements in living standards for much of the nation's population have depended on the regime's unprecedented political stability.

The environmental consequences of the economic boom are also unprecedented, if not in type, then certainly in their scale and rapid extension throughout the nation. Indonesians' reactions to alarming increases in pollution, degradation of forest and marine ecosystems, and state-backed expropriation of land and resources on which community life depends, have become increasingly politicized since the mid-1980s. Environmental organizing by non-governmental groups is fundamentally redefining "development" in an

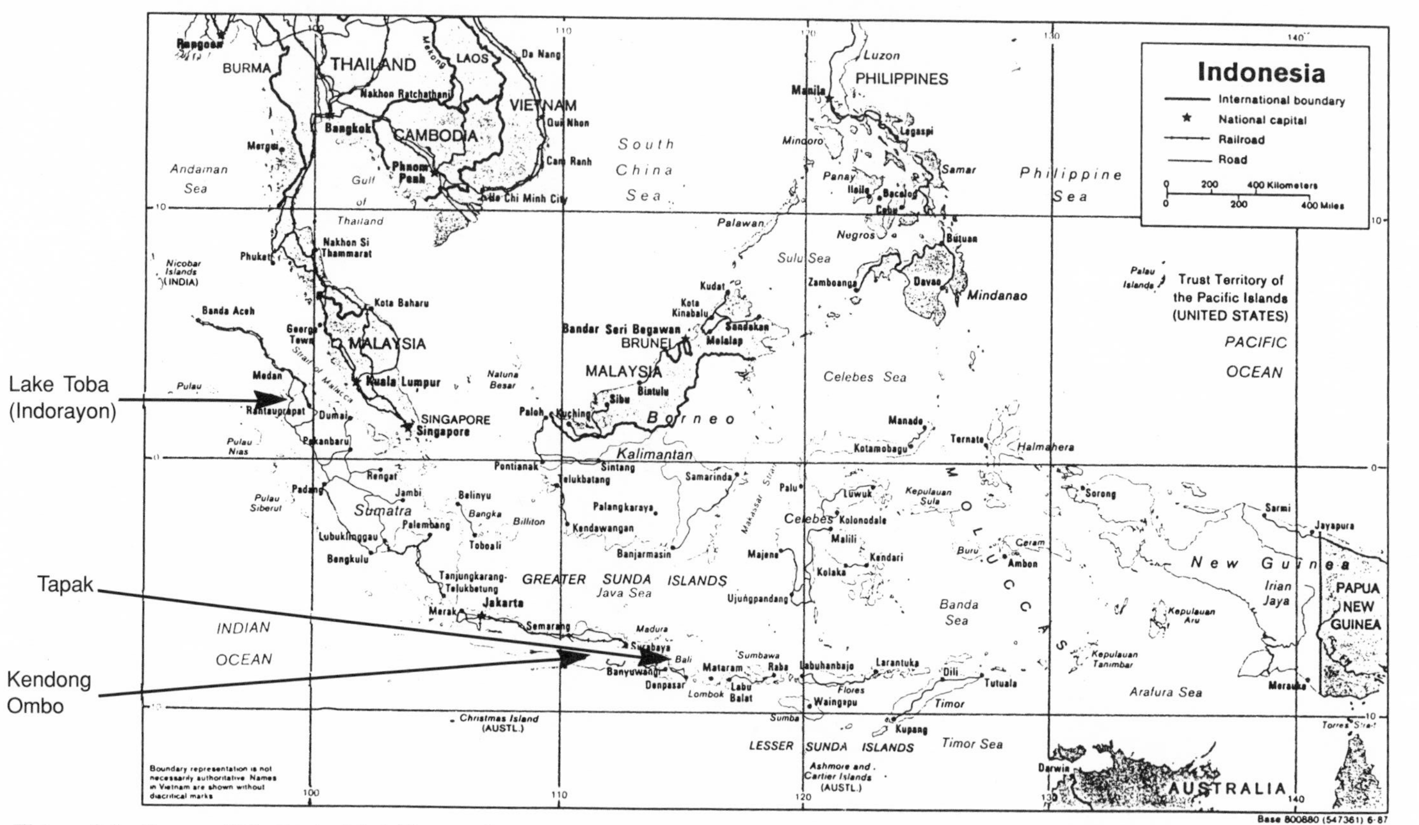

Figure 6.1. Source: U.S. Central Intelligence Agency.

Indonesian context. Environmental activists' alternative visions of Indonesia's future challenge many of the forms of authority wielded by President Suharto's New Order. Their insistence on a broader definition of "development" also challenges the very bases of the New Order's legitimacy.

Environmental organizations have played a crucial role in more general political change in Indonesia during the late 1980s and early 1990s. Since the mid-1980s, environmental groups have originated from or fostered many of the most significant challenges to the regime's authoritarian style, as well as to the New Order's links with the Indonesian military and global capital. They are a leading edge in the emergence of a civil society counterpoised against the New Order's attempts to monopolize political discourse and action. The political scope of environmental groups' activities challenges most New Order leaders' concepts of the narrow range of acceptable activities within civil society. Indonesian environmental groups' most common vision of civil society is not focused on the creation of a national culture (Anderson 1993) or support of depoliticized religious or social welfare activity. All of these occupy fairly comfortable places within the narrow space that Suharto's state provides for collective action beyond state-supported institutions. Environmental groups' orientations are not dominated by class, ethnic, or religious identities, all of which have ignited political sparks with the New Order. Indonesia's contemporary environmental movement is defined by its insistence on highlighting multi-stranded links among local and global phenomena—ecological, economic, and political. As state development policies ensure that "globalization" of Indonesia's economy and culture reaches even the archipelago's most remote regions, environmental activists are creating parallel, shadow networks of influence among "friends" throughout the country and abroad. These networks support new forms of collective action based on emerging understandings of global linkages, and their impacts on the "nature" and natural resources which are the foundations of both livelihood and community life.

This chapter explores the significance of environmental organizing in Indonesia from several perspectives. How do Indonesian environmentalists see the significance of their actions with regard to specific, immediate objectives of protecting or restoring environmental quality and ensuring communities' access to natural resources? How do they see their roles with regard to broader, longer-range political change? How have struggles to protect environmental quality become so closely linked with struggles by disempowered communities to retain or regain control over local resources? How does environmental organizing relate to various aspects of state activity and power? How has the environmental movement changed Indonesian political discourse around the future of the New Order's "developmental state"[5] and the reassertion of civil society? How do distinctive Indonesian national, regional, and "indigenous" formulations of environmental issues, priorities, styles of organizing and of communication interact with those of environmental groups beyond Indonesia's borders, and with those of foreign governments?

In answering these questions, this chapter considers how non-governmental organizations frame concerns about environmental quality in Indonesia as issues of both physical and cultural survival, and which call for action outside the exclusive sphere of state activity or authority. It also examines how non-governmental environmental groups have demanded that the state assume new roles and responsibilities to protect both the "environment" and the best interests of Indonesia's "little people." It discusses how these organizations' approaches are rooted in several streams of Indonesian intellectual and political tradition, as well as in increasingly global frames of reference regarding paths toward "sustainable development."

Finally, this chapter shows how tensions among Indonesian environmental groups' divergent ways of framing environmental problems, and different styles of action, affect their forms and strategies of organizing. Much of this tension among approaches relates to the multiple scales at which organizations portray causes and effects of environmental change, and their decisions about which aspects to emphasize. These span the extremely localized to the global. In some cases, strategies emphasize apolitical or highly technical analyses of issues such as climate change or biological diversity. In others, they portray environmental transformation in terms of political-economic conflict, exploitation, and expropriation. Some approaches have relied on ethically-neutral policy analyses or simple political expediency. Others inflame moral outrage to focus on ethical issues and basic human rights.

The tensions among organizing styles and orientations have reflected fluid divisions between those efforts whose primary focus is on a local community issue and those aimed at national policy; and between approaches that begin with technical problem definitions and those that define problems politically. As Indonesian environmental organizations have become more skillful in framing and presenting issues before the public, they have used this attention to galvanize significant changes in state policy, common practice and both style and substance of public discourse. Environmental organizers have also become more adept at combining approaches, and more willing to do so for strategic reasons.

National organizations increasingly use local controversies to highlight policy deficiencies, and to expose both social injustices and the devaluation of nature and natural resources that underlay them. "Technical" problems are revealed to embody questions of social justice, political empowerment, or basic needs of future generations—in short, fundamental questions of political authority and human rights. The ability to raise such issues in the extremely limited "political space" in which the Suharto regime tolerates criticism of its actions has put Indonesia's environmental movement into the forefront of forces for political change in the mid-1990s. In fact, the environmental movement's ability to introduce its concerns and construct its positions in global scientific terms, rather than value-laden and threatening political terms, has provided it with broader political space than other social movements have achieved. As Ann Hawkins explains,

> . . . environmental issues of global scope provide an opening through which formerly excluded participants within nation-states can express discontent for past development decisions, call for new voices to be heard, and articulate new visions to be encouraged. And, in situations where neither discontentedness nor new visions can be openly named and legitimately discussed, scientific and technical debates can also serve as proxies, providing a shield behind which other ideas may be advanced or explored . . . (Hawkins 1993:224).

The Global and the Local

In contemporary Indonesia, where a centralized state seeks to consolidate control over both environmental resources and the means by which to exploit, conserve, or manage them, environmental organizations often promote their perspectives and activities by appealing to sources of legitimacy outside the state. They remind government authorities of the state's explicitly proclaimed legal and development doctrines, though providing their own interpretations for these official positions. Many national groups pursue remedies for environmental degradation and resource expropriation based on complaints by members of specific local communities, and then use these local issues in appeals at a level of national principle.

Environmental organizations' prescriptions often refer to the need to recognize local knowledge about ecological and social conditions, and demand the state's recognition of local systems of property rights and resource management. They demand that the state restrain itself and the corporations it licenses from overriding longstanding local prerogatives. Environmental groups appeal to both political and ethical orientations that transcend Indonesia's borders. These concern conflicts that involve multinational corporations or foreign aid, rights of the people of a Southern, less-industrialized nation against the industrial North (and, increasingly, against East Asia's industrial "tigers"), and universal civil rights against the excesses of the state.

On issues important at both the local and global levels, Indonesian environmental groups often differentiate their positions relative to the government's within the Indonesian internal political context from their positions on similar issues in international fora. Within Indonesia, they act as critics of government policies that affect Indonesia's own environment and people. Yet on many issues, in international arenas they have lent their support to the government's positions vis-à-vis those of foreign governments, and some of the more extreme demands of international environmental conservation groups. Yet, to the extent that Indonesian environmental organizations' positions diverge from the government's approach to "global" issues within Indonesia, New Order leaders have portrayed environmental organizations' simultaneous appeals toward both the local and the global as threats to national development, and contrary to the Suharto regime's interpretation of the official national ideology, *Pancasila*.[6]

Closely allied to the mainstream of Indonesia's human rights movement, environmental activists have often defined their roles in terms of marrying local and global perspectives in an Indonesian style of environmentalism. This two-directional appeal, toward the local and the global, has enabled environmental organizations and the more amorphous movement they embody to gain support and credibility largely by bypassing the state. Environmental organizations challenge the New Order state to re-evaluate its policies not only in terms of its own tests of legitimacy (economic growth and political stability) but by defining "sustainable development" as a field of political action with a new set of standards in civil society.

The two-directional approach taken by Indonesian environmental organizations, looking to both the local and the global, has allowed Indonesian environmentalists' positions relative to some state policies to remain quite fluid through much of the 1980s and early 1990s. In an international forum such as the 1992 "Earth Summit" (UNCED) and the preparatory meetings leading up to it, representatives of several of Indonesia's most influential environmental groups took stands that were largely compatible with official Indonesian positions. With solicitously-negotiated support from major non-governmental environmental groups, Indonesia joined neighboring Malaysia and India in representing a Southern block at UNCED on issues ranging from biodiversity and intellectual property rights (Affif 1992a; *Environesia* 1992, 1993a) to climate change (Singh 1992; Sari 1992a).

Environmental groups' international face of acquiescence in 1992 was largely informed by a sense of social justice at a global scale rather than by any strong nationalist focus. It did not reflect confidence in the New Order's honest dedication to re-evaluating its prevailing model of development at home along lines that the environmental organizations hoped would emerge from UNCED. The usually-critical groups' expedient cooperation with government agencies in formulating national positions for UNCED enabled Indonesia's environmental "umbrella" organizations to broaden the overall range of issues about which the New Order would tolerate "constructive criticism." This convergence was not merely a matter of strategic expediency on the part of the non-governmental organizations. The major environmental groups actually had considerable influence on the official positions. NGO activists participated in task forces establishing national positions for the UNCED preparatory conferences, and in informal networks among technically-oriented environmentalists and technocrats in key ministries (Sari 1995). Yet only two years after UNCED, the door was slammed shut in mid-1994 by a crackdown on political dissent and the press freedoms that had gradually expanded during the early 1990s (Human Rights Watch 1994; Shenon 1994b).

Leading Indonesian environmental organizations backed the government's insistence that the Earth Summit recognize national sovereignty in designing means to protect biological diversity within national territory. Yet at home these same groups, led by the largest environmental "umbrella" organization, WALHI (the Indonesian Environmental Forum) insisted that misguided *national* development priorities were the culprits in undermining the relatively sustainable indigenous resource use systems and locally-adapted technologies that have allowed Indonesia to remain one of the earth's "mega-diversity" regions (Affif 1992b).

Similarly, while Indonesian environmental organizations wholeheartedly endorsed the government's Southern-block determination to place clear blame for global warming on over-consumption by the industrialized nations, they also pointed to extreme and growing inequalities in energy consumption within Indonesia itself on an order of magnitude equivalent to the "North/South" split. These gaps continue to widen between rural and urban Indonesia, and between politically dominant Java and the Outer Islands (*Environesia* 1988b; Sari 1992b; WALHI & LBH 1993). A similar position emerged with regard to intellectual property rights, another contentious issue at UNCED and, more generally, between Indonesia and potential foreign investors in pharmaceutical development and "biotechnology." While Indonesia's official position insisted on a national right to claim intellectual property rights for Indonesian-origin genetic material with commercial value to foreign companies, Indonesian environmental groups pointed out that the phenomenal diversity of locally-adapted varieties of indigenous cultivars is not the technical heritage of the Indonesian nation, but of the communities that nurtured, adapted, and bred them over hundreds of years and dozens of generations (Affif 1992a, 1992b; *Nekabija*, 1992, 1993). Indonesian environmental organizations' bitter disappointment in UNCED's seriously weakened resolutions confirmed their dedication to redefining development, both at home and globally, in terms that would not continue to mis-equate human or ecological welfare with economic growth alone, or any simple aggregate version of national development (Pranomo & Sari 1992).

A historical vocabulary of Indonesian social and political thought supplies the contemporary environmental movement with much of its rhetorical repertoire. Several historical definitions of "development" have been rediscovered by practical theorists wishing to legitimate home-grown Indonesian alternatives to the New Order's growth-oriented, authoritarian, technocratic development models. In a sort of archaeology of political culture, the environmental movement is rediscovering the pre-independence nationalist movement's organic images of development as "flowering" or unfolding from within (*pengembangan*) as opposed to the New Order's dominant mechanistic engineering image of development as construction (*pembangunan*; Heryanto 1988).

Combining the populist nationalism of the early independence movement with the prestige of international science also shields environmentalists to some degree against accusations that their focus on local prerogatives promotes subversive regional secessionism, or that their advocacy for disempowered communities and political-economic analyses of environmental problems are informed by treacherous Communism.[7] Indonesian environmental groups welcome environmentalists from abroad—both non-governmental activists and aid organizations—to join them in campaigns of common interest as equals. However, they have become increasingly selective in seeking and accepting technical, financial, and moral support for projects proffered by international "friends," foreign diplomatic missions, and multilateral aid agencies in which the Indonesian organizations' own agendas are of only secondary importance.[8]

The attention of environmental and human rights networks abroad has helped Indonesian environmentalists protect hard-won freedom to speak and act in the face of New Order disapproval and harassment. This has been facilitated by rapid improvements in telecommunications—accessible international telephone service, telefax, electronic mail and newslists—which environmental organizations have enthusiastically adopted. Non-governmental organizations abroad and some bilateral aid agencies have also funded activists' increasingly frequent travel to international meetings, as well as a steady stream of international volunteers helping out for short periods in the Indonesian groups' offices and on their projects.

Indonesia's environmental organizations have played crucial roles in more general political change, demanding an Indonesian version of *perestroika* in the late 1980s and early 1990s. Environmental activists have voiced outrage and idealism—often combined with patriotism—in both spontaneous and carefully-orchestrated protests and direct actions, discretely-phrased research, defiant journalism, and a skeptical willingness to cooperate with government agencies in pursuit of new approaches to "sustainable development."[9]

The expedient bargain of the late 1980s and early 1990s allowed a new generation of technocrats with some environmental ideals to call on non-governmental groups to help them build up their own constituencies within specific state bureaucracies,[10] and for environmental protection within the government as a whole. As state rhetoric in the early 1990s began to adopt a global language of "sustainable development," self-consciously "moderate" environmentalists prodded government agencies to fulfill the new environmental promises loudly espoused by state policies meant for public consumption.

By early 1994, environmental groups' critiques were self-censored less than ever by fear of harassment and arrest. Yet, the political "breathing room" that their expedient cooperation with the government had earned them during the period leading up to the 1992 Earth Summit collapsed in mid-1994. In response to investigative reporting about several expensive and unpopular decisions made by Minister for Science and Technology Habibie[11] (most notably, Indonesia's purchase of much of the former East Germany's naval fleet) the government banned Indonesia's three most widely-circulated news magazines (Shenon 1994b). In the midst of a general crackdown on civil liberties in Jakarta, six environmental organizations filed an unprecedented lawsuit against President Suharto, demanding reversal of a Presidential decree that authorized a substantial interest-free loan from the national "reforestation fund"—a stumpage tax fund reserved to support reforestation activities—to provide capital for an aircraft factory partly-owned by Minister Habibie.[12] Demands that the government take its own environmental rhetoric seriously came to a head in the environmentalists' lawsuit. Even before that, both national and local environmental organizations had been straining against the state's limits on freedom of expression. Environmental media referred openly to corruption, collusion between officials at all levels and business interests, "development" projects that impoverish or displace local communities, and the debt-financing and industrial conglomerate systems that destroy rather than protect Indonesia's natural wealth.

The state has found it difficult to either suppress or counter these criticisms when they have been expressed in terms of environmental science or economics ("rational" environmentalism), rather than the more familiar language of social justice (more politically dangerous in Indonesia). It is especially significant that this direct challenge to the President originated from the environmental movement, rather than one of Indonesia's emerging opposition political parties, the developing labor movement, or the mainstream of the human rights movement. Their statement reminded Indonesians of the President's self-proclaimed role as protector of the environment after the Earth Summit, rather than as raider of the coffers of Indonesia's relatively weak "environmental" programs. Environmental organizers were able to legitimate their challenge with the state's own rhetoric and ideals of conduct. Despite annoying increases in surveillance, harassment, and thinly-veiled threats of more serious retribution, many environmentalists were actually relieved to shed the conciliatory masks they had donned in the early 1990s. Leading environmental organizations were once again clearly identified as agents of protest and political change (Anonymous 1994).

Indonesian organizations' working relationships with counterparts abroad have played a significant part in this recent boldness. They have helped frame issues of community survival and planetary crisis in terms of "little people's" defense against greed, megalomania, sheer carelessness, and models of development that serve the powerful. Indonesian environmental groups' cultivation of international links has been motivated by a belief that, since demands made on Indonesia's resources and people by commercial, growth-oriented development have gone international, action to counter these demands must also draw on international networks for information, money, and strategic political support. The government counterattacked by casting the environmental groups' global orientations in suspect light, and banning them from receiving any foreign funds from either government or non-state sources, thereby cutting off a major source of their operating expenses (*Republika* 1994; *Media Indonesia* 1994).[13] Yet Indonesia's ability to meet the government's own development goals increasingly depends on complying with international environmental standards, many of them overseen by non-governmental organizations. A prime example is the government's interest in eco-labeling of Indonesian export products. The state's promise that all Indonesian wood product exports will be certified as coming from "sustainable" sources by the year 2000, in line with recommendations from the International Tropical Timber Organization (ITTO) (*Jakarta Post* 1993; *Bisnis Indonesia* 1992).

A History of Indonesian Environmental Management: State Perspectives

The types of issues that have engaged Indonesian environmental activists' efforts are as varied as Indonesia's natural and cultural environments themselves. However, Indonesian environmental organizations overwhelmingly focus their attention on controversies generated by threats to the livelihoods of marginalized, disempowered communities. Thus, the "environment" of the Indonesian environmental movement is emphatically defined in terms of access to and control over *resources*,[14] and political-economic issues of production and reproduction, rather than in terms of protecting a less anthropocentrically defined "nature."[15] Some impassioned campaigns do focus on conserving "natural" areas and habitats, including national parks or nature preserves. However, Indonesia's leading environmental organizations and consortia portray the "nature" to be protected by politicized action as landscapes and resources that have been formed through a history of social practices, customary institutions, and creative adaptation by local communities, past and present.[16]

These principles have profound implications for how Indonesian organizers approach a wide range of environmental issues, from the establishment of nature preserves to commercial logging and timber plantation development; from regional watershed and fisheries management to conservation research design and intellectual property rights; from family planning to state-sponsored resettlement ("transmigration") programs. In many cases, this orientation toward human *use* of nature gives Indonesian conservationists more in common with the state's development imperatives than with the preservationist orientations of many "Western" environmentalists. "Biocentric" concerns about whether trees have intrinsic value, or whether members of non-human species have rights, are rarely heard in discussions by Indonesian environmentalists. Likewise, the idea of preserving "wilderness" beyond all human use and habitation makes little sense to an environmental movement that is also trying to ensure respect and legal protection for the resource use rights of Indonesian citizens in remote areas. Many environmentalists argue that in a nation of landscapes formed by centuries of human habitation, the entire concept of "wilderness" hardly makes sense. Yet cultural traditions in which forests, relatively unaffected by human occupation and management, have important historical and even spiritual value also play important roles in Indonesian environmentalist thought.

In a populist legal tradition, Indonesian environmentalists often begin arguments to goad the state into enforcing anti-pollution laws, or arguments against both state and private expropriations of community resources, by citing Article 33 of the Indonesian Constitution of 1945. Article 33 states emphatically that the land and waters of Indonesia belong to the nation, and shall be used for the benefit of the people.[17] The ambiguity of this provision affords the New Order an extremely broad interpretation of state prerogatives, placing national interests or "national development" ahead of the rights of local populations. Environmentalists' and indigenous peoples' advocates usually interpret Article 33 much more narrowly, asserting that it actually directs the state to protect indigenous customary rights against outside private or commercial interests as well as the overzealousness of the state itself.[18] They claim that only this interpretation agrees with *Pancasila*'s social justice principle.

In 1980, eight years after the 1972 United Nations Conference on the Human Environment in Stockholm, Indonesia had yet to implement even a skeleton of laws explicitly aimed at environmental protection. Yet other laws had set the stage for the environmental controversies of the 1980s and 1990s. Indonesia's Basic Agrarian Law,[19] which mandated a large-scale land reform and land titling program, was enacted in 1960 under President Soekarno. It set the stage for many of the land rights altercations in which environmentalists and rural community activists later became embroiled with the government. In the Outer Islands,[20] the 1960 law set up apparatus for the state to recognize private and community holdings established under local customary law, above and beyond Constitutional provisions.[21] Other late-1960s laws, including the Basic Mining Act and Basic Forestry Law, both of 1967, provided for central government grants of commercial resource exploitation concessions to political friends of the new regime. Both measures were enacted in tandem with the New Order's foreign investment laws to encourage foreign investment in resource extraction. These laws asserted the rights of central government bureaucracies over land, forests and minerals, and reallocated rights from individuals and communities—many of whom claimed land and resource use rights under local customary law—to private companies, both Indonesian and foreign-owned, and to government-owned corporations.[22] The resource exploitation laws of the late 1960s also ensured that resource royalties would flow to the central government's coffers. From there, they could be invested in development programs throughout the nation, rather than remaining in the logging and mining provinces of the outer islands. This also gave government leaders resources for political favors, rather than allowing revenues from resource exploitation to remain in the localities that experienced the brunt of impacts from logging and mining.

While the resource laws, and regulations drafted to implement them, contained minimal provisions for mitigation of logging and mining impacts, even these mild "environmental" provisos were rarely enforced during Indonesia's petroleum and timber booms of the late 1970s and early 1980s. At the same time, urban and industrial pollution had reached crisis levels. By the late 1970s the chemical excesses of Java's "green revolution" had begun to backfire on the region's agriculture.[23]

Jakarta's progressive technocrats finally responded to worsening pollution, impelled both by pressure from fledgling environmental and consumer groups, and by examples of the industrialized countries. Several of them provided assistance for drafting and implementing environmental regulations, and gave ambitious students and mid-level civil servants opportunities for technical studies abroad. The Ministry of Population and Environment (known as KLH, an abbreviation for *Kependudukan dan Lingkungan Hidup*) was established in 1978, inspired by charismatic intellectuals including Dr. Otto Soemarwoto[24] and Dr. Emil Salim.[25] In 1982, under advice from the new ministry (with Dutch legal assistance[26] and Canadian technical assistance[27]), the Basic Environmental Management Act (Act 4 of 1982) established a clean and healthy environment as a right of all Indonesians. Environmentalists' populist challenges to the state also often cite Indonesia's Basic Environmental Act Number 4 of 1982, which proclaims that "... each person has the right to a good and healthy environment ..." and is obliged to prevent the problem of its destruction and pollution (Article 5, Paragraphs (1) and (2), Law Number 4 of 1982).

The 1982 law also enabled subsequent environmental regulation in areas which, until then, had been covered only by such maladapted provisions as business licensing and construction laws (designed to direct profitable investment not to prevent environmental depredation), and Indonesia's vague nuisance regulations (inherited from Dutch colonial laws of the 1920s; Tarrant, et al. 1987; *Environesia* 1990c:12). Both of these approaches put discretion for approving projects expected to have environmental impacts into the hands of local officials.[28] Yet these rules specified no consistent guidelines, little public accountability for decisions, no monitoring of actual impacts, and no provisions to establish liability for harm to people, property, or the natural environment. Under pressure from relatively new environmental and consumer groups in Jakarta, the 1982 law incorporated the government's first explicit legal recognition of legitimate roles of environmental non-governmental organizations and their right to participate in the state's environmental management decisions.[29] Much of the impetus behind the government's final agreement to these provisions came from examples of the roles of non-governmental groups that were written into environmental regulations of the industrialized countries that provided technical assistance for drafting the regulations. The risk that these provisions would feed criticism of government actions was softened, somewhat, by the same rules' emphasis on negotiation and consensus processes over litigation. The rules did little to provide an "even playing field" in negotiations between non-governmental groups and economically powerful businesses, not to mention the government itself.

Soon after 1982, the Ministry for Population and Environment (KLH) drafted regulations that required environmental impact analyses for specific types of large projects,[30] whether the projects were carried out by the government or private developers. These were passed in 1986 (Government

Regulation No. 29 of 1986, on Analysis of Impacts on the Environment) with implementing guidelines issued in 1987 that required environmental impact analysis studies, plans, mitigation, and monitoring (EMDI 1988). During the 1980s, regulation of polluting activities and issuance of permits for industrial facilities had been left to the Provincial and sub-provincial levels. It was only in 1990 that a Presidential instruction established an executive environmental impact management agency, BAPEDAL, to administer the new web of national environmental impact analysis and pollution control requirements (Arimbi 1993; *Environesia* 1990c; MacAndrews 1994).

Beginning in the late 1980s, spurred by the regulations of 1986 and 1987, community and environmental groups used their rapidly improving advocacy skills in this still-experimental legal framework to goad the government into taking environmental protection more seriously. In a far-sighted constituency-building move, the academically-rooted leadership and advisors of KLH—including Otto Soemarwoto, later head of the Ecology Institute at Padjadjaran University in Bandung; Koesnadi Hardjasoemantri, Rector of Gadjah Mada University in Yogyakarta, and Emil Salim, associated with Universitas Indonesia in Jakarta—planted newly-required environmental impact analysis processes within Indonesian academic life as well as the bureaucracy by establishing Environmental Study Centers in most provincial universities.[31] These centers were intended to organize consulting teams that could be hired by either government agencies or private enterprises to conduct the environmental impact analyses required for a wide variety of development projects. By providing a university locus for environmental discourse that was sanctioned—in fact, required—by the government, and ensuring that the centers had access to their own financial resources separate from the universities' general funds, the campus environmental study centers also helped extend ecological consciousness within the universities. The universities, more than any other institutions in Indonesia, represented a contested bridge between the state and civil society.[32]

Natural and social scientists—and their students—were drawn to the Environmental Study Centers not only for the intellectual content of the work they generated, but also for the lucrative consulting and travel opportunities they could provide.[33] Trying to balance state development imperatives with their own intellectual integrity, many academics involved in early environmental impact analyses were painfully aware of conflicts of interest between their roles as impartial investigators and as government employees assessing government-sponsored projects. Many were also uncomfortable with the tight political control of their findings, and of how these findings could later be used.[34]

The implications of this state control were not lost on those members of the "intelligentsia" who were less constrained by Indonesian academic controls—idealistic students who would leave the university, many to join the ranks of activists in the blossoming of non-governmental organizations in the

1980s.[35] Led by the universities' Environmental Study Centers, training workshops in environmental impact analysis mushroomed in the late 1980s, targeting academics and mid-level bureaucrats, as well as a new domestic consulting industry. During the late 1980s and early 1990s, non-governmental environmental organizations also organized environmental impact assessment training workshops, often with assistance from foreign experts and volunteers drawn from non-governmental environmental groups abroad. In some areas, community workshops nurtured "barefoot" analytical expertise based on local community members' knowledge of their own environment, and experiences, expectations, and senses of justice. One group in Manado, North Sulawesi, even produced a "Barefoot AMDAL" manual for use by community groups faced with impacts from government and commercial projects.

Questions and controversies about how to use the new anti-pollution laws and requirements led to policy splits within several government agencies, and schisms among environmental activists. The issues were both strategic and cultural. Should the movement allow implementation of the new environmental laws to rely on the consultative, consensus-based negotiations encouraged by the corporatist, "family-like" and often secretive management styles replicated throughout New Order political institutions? As these concerns were articulated during the 1980s, it became increasingly clear that the "playing field" would never be level for such negotiations in environmental conflicts in Indonesia. Consensus-based negotiation between the state, big business, and the "little people" of marginalized communities were inherently skewed toward the powerful. But how could environmental groups continue to emphasize political-economic and social justice aspects of environmental issues in Indonesia while still retaining a "place at the table" in negotiations with state agencies? To what extent should they embrace confrontation and demands for openness—quite the opposite of Indonesian styles of quiet "consultation and consensus"—and try to use the Indonesian judicial system to develop litigation-based public interest law? How appropriate were strategies like those American environmental organizations used to help implement and clarify new environmental regulations during the 1970s and 1980s? Would both of these approaches increase risks that the Indonesian environmental movement might simply fall into the government's agendas, rather than set its own course?

Emergence of Non-Governmental Environmental Organizations[36]

During the 1980s, two longstanding branches of Indonesian social movements coalesced into several overlapping networks of environmental organizations. One emerged from a technocratic orientation that focused on sound environmental management as a cornerstone of sound development.

This branch largely accepted the adoption of environmental management as a responsibility of state bureaucracies. Since the early 1980s, technocratic environmental management has been encouraged and orchestrated by leadership in academia and KLH, as well as more progressive pockets in the Ministry of Forestry, initially including several chapters of the urban-based "Green Indonesia Foundation."[37]

The second branch grew out of a long Indonesian history of social justice activism in both rural and urban areas, primarily in Java, and became aligned with indigenous land rights groups in the Outer Islands during the early 1980s. In contrast with the trust in technical and administrative approaches taken by "technocratic" environmentalists, these groups began with political-economic critiques of prevailing development patterns. Their environmental perspective on both local controversies and national policies focused on the land side of the old Indonesian Left's two pillars of "land and labor." While all organizations meticulously avoided any reference whatsoever to Marxist theory (in fact, by the 1980s, young activists who had not studied abroad had no direct exposure to Marxist thought at all), these groups traced both environmental degradation and community impoverishment to patterns of investment, particularly to the trail of big capital—whether or not they associated it with misguided state policies.[38] By the mid-1980s, activists in many politicized, environmentally-oriented organizations were wary of being labeled "watermelons"—*buah semangka,* in Indonesian—green on the outside, but red within. Older activists, in particular, were alert to the dangers of such a label, still vividly remembering the bloody anti-Communist campaigns during the New Order regime's early years. A generation of younger activists, however, had come of age during a time when political-economic critiques of state policies were not explicitly framed by Marxist rhetoric or ideology, and when Indonesia's Communist Party, which was brutally suppressed when the Suharto regime came to power, had become more political myth than daily reality.[39]

Grassroots organizers in small communities were, certainly, conspicuous targets for harassment, but many were focusing on clearly practical, down-to-earth projects, rather than work defined as explicitly political in an Indonesian context. Community and environmental activists of the late-1970s and 1980s focused their attention on small-scale, locally-controlled projects such as village clean water supplies, adult literacy, non-formal education, fuel-saving household technologies, renewable village energy sources, agroforestry nurseries, organic gardens, artisanal fishery improvement, and village credit unions.[40] Indonesian field workers with church-sponsored groups, including lay workers with Catholic organizations in the Outer Islands, were often treated with a great deal of respect, as missionaries pursuing spiritual callings by working with poor local communities.[41]

All of these practical activists were also in excellent positions to observe and document local abuses of power and disastrous local effects of environmental problems. They put members of the communities where they were working in touch with urban-based, more openly critical and politicized organizations.

Young organizations focused on environmental issues—often in combination with other community orientations (such as agricultural development, community health, or land rights) continue to emerge as student organizations mature. People active or loosely associated with these young organizations are more likely to refer to each other simply as "friends" rather than members. Not only do such designations provide an egalitarian public face, they also disguise fluid organizational structures and lines of responsibility to outsiders. The hope is that, as "small fish," (despite their large, often influential networks of associates) government authorities might see such educated non-governmental organizers as relatively harmless and controllable, working out youthful idealism through community safety valves with possible practical benefits.

Since the mid-1970s, young groups that specialize in assembling and disseminating information through small-circulation, cheaply-printed or photocopied newsletters, often publish unattributed or anonymous articles, and organize themselves as collectives with unobtrusive leadership and ambiguous, amorphous membership.[42] Many of these organizations began as idealistic student groups. In the late 1970s, after the government's crackdown on campus-based political criticism, activists in many of these groups, who often came from privileged backgrounds, turned their youthful idealism into "practical" work with poor communities. By the late 1980s and early 1990s, many of these people had established a great deal of credibility for the non-governmental groups they had organized, and had gained confidence in criticizing state development policies from a firm footing in appropriate technology and practical experience gained through grassroots organizing.[43]

Local organizations that come together to protest specific environmental injustices in their own communities are in an entirely different position, however, especially in rural areas where the New Order relies on the principle of the depoliticized "floating mass" to keep rural communities quiet, and prevent opposition political organizing from gaining a foothold.[44] "Activists" are often peasant community leaders who have little experience in dealing with state officials or commercial company managers, let alone standing their ground in acrimonious confrontations. While their analyses of the origins and consequences of environmental threats to their health, livelihoods, or communities may be sharply critical of specific state policies or abuses of economic and political power, such community leaders are accustomed to addressing government authorities with deference and "refined" respect.[45] Even in the mid-1990s, litigation to assign liability, assess damages, or issue injunctions is rarely used to settle community grievances in Indonesia. The emphasis on negotiations, consensus, and in extremely difficult cases, mediation, is even built into most of the country's environmental laws (*Kompas* 1993). Only after highly centralized government authorities have failed to respond to community complaints, and "traditional" consensus-based dispute resolution processes have failed to provide solutions acceptable to aggrieved communities, have villages mounted demonstrations, blockades, and sabotage (see Pangastudi, 1989). Civil and military forces have met these with arrests and, in some cases, violent forms of intimidation.[46] Several provincial environmental organizations, largely composed of students, began as "solidarity groups" that came together to provide moral, political, and material support for the actions of rural protesters in nearby areas.[47]

As early as 1980, it appeared that many of the non-government organizations working on environmental issues throughout Indonesia had a great deal in common with each other. These groups had enough informal contact—whether operating at local, regional, or national levels, and whether on rural or urban issues—for leaders of several organizations to form a consortium aimed at facilitating communication and sharing of resources, interacting with government decision-makers in Jakarta in a credible, professional manner, and helping to mobilize financial and technical resources available from both non-governmental international organizations, and from foreign aid agencies in Indonesia. In early 1980, ten Jakarta-based environmental, consumer, and human rights organizations established the Indonesian Environmental Forum (WALHI). Later in 1980, a national meeting of environmental and developmental organizations attracted seventy-nine groups, who formed an active network to promote environmental awareness and action. This network was led by consumer activist Erna Witoelar until 1986, and was instrumental in ensuring that the 1982 Basic Environmental Law recognized legal roles for non-governmental environmental organizations.[48]

Under the subsequent leadership of Abdul Hakim Nusantara, a lawyer who later became head of the Indonesia's Legal Aid Institute (LBH), WALHI built up its environmental advocacy capabilities, lobbying government agencies and, eventually, suing them. Establishing legal precedents for environmental organizations to have standing in legal processes, and as representatives of the public and the environment in deliberations on environmentally important state measures, has been a major focus of mainstream environmental groups' work in Jakarta. Yet by the late 1980s, especially after the enactment of the 1986 environmental assessment law and its implementation regulations in 1987, there was a strong sense among some of WALHI's member organizations that the umbrella group was over-extended. The Jakarta-based, increasingly professional organization had begun to pre-empt the local work of its member groups. Activists outside of Java felt that WALHI focused too much attention on its own organizational development, rather than assisting member groups in developing their own capabilities. Under the leadership of Agus Purnomo and M.S. Zulkarnaen, in the late 1980s and early 1990s, WALHI's network continued to grow by leaps and bounds. By the early 1990s, WALHI represented over three hundred organizations in all of Indonesia's twenty-seven provinces through *"forda"* or *forum daerah*.

WALHI also addressed the problem of over-extending both the central office staff's energy and its expertise by "spinning off" several specialized groups. Many of these became nodes or umbrellas for national action in particular fields, and for international action in the Southeast Asian region. They include specialized networks of organizations concerned with forest conservation (SKEPHI[49]), pesticides (KRAPP[50]) and marine issues. These were later followed by research and education groups, such as those focusing on climate change and sustainable development policy (Pelangi[51]), biological diversity (YABSHI[52]), as well as research and education on ecology and indigenous cultures throughout Indonesia (Konphalindo; LATIN; Sejati[53]). Dozens of regional and provincial community action organizations with strong orientations toward local environmental issues and education also sprang up during the 1980s, and many joined WALHI's network.[54]

WALHI also underwent a series of transformations in organizational structure, as the number and scope of its member organizations multiplied during the 1980s. After consolidating decision-making and campaign work in its Jakarta secretariat office during its initial years, in the early 1990s WALHI attempted to decentralize its decision-making and campaign work. This was intended to make WALHI a multi-level federation. This would increase the effectiveness of its member organizations, whose concerns were supposed to be brought to WALHI's attention through a regional forum in every province. WALHI leaders in Jakarta, and their provincial critics, intended this change to help focus attention on the concerns of groups beyond Jakarta and outside of Java, despite the concentrations of both expertise and financial resources in the capital. On WALHI's tenth anniversary in 1990, the network's first leader, Erna Witoelar, explained both the necessity of some centralization within the organization, and its dangers:

> WALHI's loose, non-threatening structure is a mixed blessing, causing both easy and wide acceptability as well as considerable confusion among

> government agencies, donors and NGOs who often find it difficult to measure the organisation's success. . . . The increasing merging of economic and political power in Indonesia more than ever exposes the need for a buildup of NGO power. But should this buildup mirror the other side's pattern of centralisation? Should NGOs develop a strong center, exposing themselves to threats of cooptation or, in the worst case, of severance? (*Environesia* 1990a)

The emphasis on WALHI's role as a loose network also ensures a great deal of leeway for the enormously varied organizational styles and strategies among its member organizations. The history of differences between WALHI and its earliest spin-off network, SKEPHI, is instructive. Even while WALHI sued several state agencies for breaking the government's own environmental impact analysis laws, WALHI insisted that its secretariat staff present an obliging front to government agencies willing to involve non-governmental environmental organizations in their policy-making processes.

SKEPHI's approach was generally less compromising. SKEPHI deliberately sacrificed opportunities for dialogue with state agencies in favor of the freedom to criticize their policies and actions in stronger, unequivocal terms. While many of the differences between WALHI and SKEPHI are matters of style as much as substance, and are largely of historical rather than current interest, the contrast remains emblematic of the multiple streams that have emerged in an increasingly fluid and complex environmental movement.

In one example of these differing styles of action, WALHI leaders took seriously the risk that its network would be co-opted by a late-1980s decision to continue participating in the Indonesian Forestry Action Plan process undertaken by the Ministry of Forestry in response to the international Tropical Forestry Action Plan.[55] There was early evidence that the national policy would be formulated with only token participation by any citizens' environmental organization, and that non-governmental environmental groups would not even be given access to crucial documents in a timely manner. Yet WALHI's national leadership decided to continue participating in the process and adopt an accommodating tone.

By contrast, SKEPHI activists openly blasted the process as a farce after initial meetings, noting the Ministry of Forestry's cynical approach to fostering participation by non-government groups (Jhamtani 1992). WALHI's leadership as a whole acknowledged that the danger of co-optation through offers to "participate" in any unbalanced, skewed-power policy forum could tear Indonesia's uneasy environmental "community" apart. Yet WALHI leaders decided not to repudiate TFAP, after having joined the planning process, despite its disappointing results:

> The criticisms of TFAP are felt intensely by the Indonesian environmental community. WALHI sees that by rejecting TFAP, it will be cut off from the only process in the forestry sector in which NGOs, at least on paper, are included. Indonesian NGOs want to change the mistakes made by other national action plans by influencing donors as well as those involved in the NFAP to pay attention to the real needs of the people of Indonesia.
>
> WALHI and the Indonesian members of INGI (International NGO Forum on Indonesia[56]) will try their best to work within the TFAP process as equal partners and aim their efforts at reorienting the forestry sector and steering the NFAP towards the real problems of deforestation (*Environesia* 1990d).

Yet this statement was also a tacit agreement that SKEPHI's stance was a necessary component of a viable "movement." In fact, the WALHI/SKEPHI split on TFAP may have been, in part, conscious strategy by both groups to allow the movement as a whole to "keep its foot in the door" with the Ministry of Forestry, while reserving the right for some segments of the movement to criticize more openly.[57]

Beginning in the late 1980s, SKEPHI activists tended to sustain a consistently confrontational approach not only to private timber companies, but to government forest policies and agencies, international aid agencies involved in forest management (such as FAO, which has had a major technical assistance presence in Indonesian forestry since the early 1970s) and multilateral development banks (the Asian Development Bank and the World Bank). They often extended their critiques to international nongovernmental environmental groups trying to affect Indonesian forest management, including the Worldwide Fund for Nature (WWF), which has assisted the Ministry of Forestry in developing National Park and nature preserve management plans throughout Indonesia. Until the 1994 crackdown, WALHI's publications tended to take a position that tried not to eliminate any possibility for dialogue with state agencies. WALHI also tried to develop alternative approaches to environmental management, as examples to put before the government.

By contrast, in the late 1980s and early 1990s, SKEPHI was more clearly dedicated to preserving the purity of its protest mode of operation. It challenged the New Order in its focus on the structures of capitalist exploitation of Indonesia's forests and forcible alienation of the people who depend on them. Yet, in its statements for mainstream publications and venues of discussion, SKEPHI generally focused on government abuses, conflicts of interest, negligent policies, and simple greed. Both SKEPHI approaches pushed against the limits of government tolerance for the network's continued existence. Its side-effect made WALHI, as a whole, look like raging moderates.

While WALHI clearly identified poverty and lack of legal protection for land rights of poor peasants in Java and indigenous communities in the Outer Islands as consequences of environmental degradation, issues of social justice were often subsumed in WALHI's broader programs of environmental protection and sound management. By contrast, social justice and injustice were always at the forefront of SKEPHI's agenda. Ironically, the unconditional priority of this overarching orientation allowed SKEPHI (whether or not speaking for its member organizations) to combine its social justice struggles with a relatively biocentric philosophical position in a much clearer, less ambivalent way than WALHI.[58] A 1990 SKEPHI pamphlet explained its orientation toward "people as part of nature conservation":

> "There can be no nature conservation without people; and no people without nature conservation," is a basic SKEPHI philosophy. Contained within this, is the paradigm that places forest and environment in a dialectic position with human beings. That is to say that humans are part of nature.
>
> It is SKEPHI's belief that nature destruction was and is caused by the alienation of humans from the ecosystem. Thus the problems of ecosystem cannot be separated from the problems of the community system (social, economic, political and cultural). Therefore, SKEPHI tries to introduce the term Biosphere Transformation.
>
> Biosphere is a unit in which the ecosystem and the social system exist side by side. Biosphere transformation denotes a process of change from the present unjust, exploited biosphere to a just and sustained biosphere. That is to say that the present system supports biosphere destruction and unjust distribution of resources. The situation has to be transformed to ensure sustained production of the biosphere itself and to ensure social justice (SKEPHI 1990).

By the mid-1980s, SKEPHI had established principles that would guide its style of action as well as the substantive issues the Secretariat would tackle. They emphasized the importance of social transformation for forest conservation. Although SKEPHI's Jakarta organizers came from mainly urban backgrounds, SKEPHI's wider network included several of Indonesia's more daring rural community groups. Aspirations for SKEPHI's future—not to mention the future of Indonesia's forests—drew on concepts that reflected SKEPHI organizers' familiarity with both a long history of rural organizing in Indonesia,[59] and principles of rural resistance movements in areas as distant as India, West Africa, and Brazil.[60] All addressed the need to overcome the paralyzing effects of marginalization by unlocking inherent strengths within communities themselves. SKEPHI's rhetoric emphasized raising consciousness about the soundness of community members' own experiences and skills, as well as recognizing locally-based traditions of action and organization—key components of the "local knowledge" so crucial to place-based civil society.

These internationally-recognized organizing tenets were combined with some distinctive Indonesian principles that had become prominent in New Order doctrine, such as the use of "social control" toward just forest use and conservation. In an Indonesian context "social control" indicates the use of peer pressure and, in some cases, the threat of public shaming to prevent corruption among low-level officials and community leaders. Other principles that most non-governmental groups dutifully embraced in the late 1980s were, however, conspicuously absent from SKEPHI's public face, which became associated with confrontation rather than conciliation[61]. SKEPHI explicitly modeled itself as a "pressure group" at a time when this term had not yet re-entered the New Order's political lexicon.

Divergent organizational structures and cultures between various kinds of non-governmental networks, and a multiplicity of political roles evolving in Indonesia's emerging civil society, complicated matters. As WALHI grew during the early 1990s, its role as the nation's most visible environmentalist force became highly problematic. Work of paid staff at the Jakarta secretariat began to take on a life of its own, above and beyond representing WALHI's member organizations. WALHI staff sought contact with state agencies, explaining environmental concerns to agency functionaries, responding to government invitations to participate in policy workshops or task forces, and tapping financial, technical, or political resources of international environmental organizations and official aid agencies. Yet resentment against the WALHI secretariat by activists in local organizations, particularly those outside Java, focused on an arrogant "Jakarta attitude" and increasing orientation toward the government rather than "the people," as well as on WALHI's control of funds from international sources.[62] This coincided with a development assistance milieu in which aid agencies sought to use national non-governmental organizations, such as WALHI, as "wholesalers" of their program assistance funds, expecting these groups to distribute funds to organizations under their umbrella, and to oversee their use. With the growing resources of its Jakarta organization, WALHI was at risk of losing its credibility with the web of local environmental groups based in Indonesia's regions.[63]

Much of the problem was due to WALHI's position as a rapidly growing, increasingly professional, and well-funded (by Indonesian standards) organization with a highly visible presence in the capital. Many of the Jakarta Secretariat staff, increasingly skilled in policy analysis, lobbying, press campaigns, and international networking, had little of the experience in grassroots community development work that continued to be the main focus of many of WALHI's non-Jakarta affiliates. At its 1992 national meeting, consequently, WALHI recognized a turning point in its role as a catalyst for both environmental protection and more general political change in Indonesia. WALHI transformed itself from a loose network into a federation of member organizations, focusing increased attention on creating a "regional forum" structure where organizations in each province could most easily share skills, join forces, and work flexibly together on priorities appropriate to their region.[64]

WALHI's Jakarta Secretariat would continue as a national clearinghouse for research, information dissemination, attempts to influence national government and international institutions, and policy-making. The Secretariat would generally take the lead in coordinating international lobbying campaigns with environmental groups abroad, consumer boycotts, or other multi-country activities. WALHI and its spin-off networks would also assemble delegations to represent Indonesia's non-governmental environmental community at international meetings, as it had for UNCED.

SKEPHI responded very differently to issues of growth, accountability, the threat of political co-optation, and the problem of balancing links with local grassroots work against the pull of international environmental networking. SKEPHI took much of the credit for pressuring American-based multinational Scott Paper Corporation to pull out of a joint-venture scheme with P.T. Astra, one of Indonesia's mega-conglomerates. The proposed eight-hundred-and-fifty-thousand hectare eucalyptus plantation and pulp mill located in a remote area of Irian Jaya (Indonesian West New Guinea) would have been the most extensive in Indonesian history, as well as one of Indonesia's most costly foreign investment projects. Indonesian environmentalists, including both SKEPHI and WALHI, threatened to pull their global networks into an international boycott of all Scott products if the project continued.[65] WALHI, SKEPHI, and organizations in Irian Jaya criticized the companies' inadequate, hastily-prepared environmental impact assessment of the planned venture's inevitable impacts on livelihood and cultures of an estimated twenty-thousand indigenous hunter-gatherers in the project area, in an area larger than the entire island of Bali (*Setiakawan* 1989; *Environesia* 1989a; *Down to Earth* in 1989, 1990).

WALHI as a whole had decided that, because it was inevitable that *some* company would target Irian Jaya's lowland forests for massive logging and/or a pulp mill in the future, Indonesian environmental groups would risk losing credibility as a constructive force if their strident position cornered them into pulling out of negotiations too soon. As WALHI's apologetic by an Irian Jaya organizer explained, "... the NGOs decided they could have greater influence on the outcome of this project and future projects if they played an integral role in the policy making process," as requested by KLH (representing the government) and Astra/Scott (*Environesia* 1989a).[66] Despite support of Irian Jaya groups for this more moderate stance, many activists at SKEPHI in Jakarta chafed at such a conciliatory position. Simple communication problems contributed to misunderstandings as well. Telecommunications between Irian Jaya and Jakarta remained difficult in the 1980s, not to mention those with rainforest activists outside of Indonesia. With a gradual change in leadership in the early 1990s,[67] SKEPHI refocused its network activities from serving as an information and action node for affiliated *organizations* to working more with like-minded individuals and directly with communities embattled in land-rights disputes with private companies or the government (Tjahyono 1992).

The early 1990s leadership at SKEPHI were veterans of late-1970s student protests, and wanted to build an organization that would be immune to the "middle-class syndrome." They eschewed expediencies of a newly-respectable and well-heeled environmental movement that hesitated to create disturbances for which there would be retributions "from above."[68] The post-Scott SKEPHI anticipated that consequences of their less-compromising positions might include bans of their publications, difficulties in fundraising, personal harassment, or even imprisonment (Tjahyono 1992; Hibani 1992; Abdullah 1992).[69]

While WALHI was widely circulating economic analyses of the absurdly low rates of economic rent (e.g., royalties and taxes) the government had captured from two decades of Indonesian timber exploitation—arguments designed to grab the attention of bureaucrats in the Finance and Forestry Ministries—SKEPHI was reinforcing its ties with unabashedly radical dissident human rights groups such as INFIGHT,[70] with which it shared an office and administrative staff. While WALHI struggled with the dilemma of whether to accept proffered funding from the new World Bank-administered Global Environmental Facility (GEF) following UNCED in 1992, SKEPHI burned its bridges even with the Ford Foundation, which had previously funded SKEPHI work.

A landmark court case[71] confirmed non-governmental organizations' standing to sue state agencies and private companies on behalf of the environment (and people harmed by pollution or deforestation). WALHI struggled with how the Jakarta Secretariat and local or Provincial organizations would coordinate efforts, including joint actions with national and Provincial offices of the Legal Aid Foundation (LBH), which was experiencing similar regional/national dilemmas in the late 1980s. While WALHI and LBH were contemplating whom to sue next, after having established their standing to sue on behalf of the environment in the North Sumatra Indorayon case (Sayadi & Quick 1992; WALHI & LBH 1993), SKEPHI had largely given up on the effectiveness of environmental or land rights litigation within a judiciary system that systematically silenced the voices of marginalized people (Tjahyono 1992). Yet, these historical differences between the two organizations do not necessarily indicate conflicting goals or factionalism within the environmental movement so much as a diversification of niches, pluralism of styles, and a conscious division of labor within a maturing environmental movement (Sari 1995).

In summary, a large segment of Indonesia's environmental movement is committed to getting the government to take seriously its new role as protector of the environment by introducing liberal political institutions—a bureaucratic regulatory framework, and recognition of local and indigenous property rights, with an independent judiciary—into Indonesia's corporatist developmental state, and in so doing, reconstituting at least a significant corner of the basis of state legitimacy.

More radical groups, and the local resistance movements of marginalized communities with whom they make common cause, define their actions in immediate terms of livelihood and survival, fighting to retain locally-based land and property rights—and the place-based ecological management systems in which they are embedded. Their tools are locally-initiated protests, stubborn refusal to be "resettled" by the state to accommodate highly capitalized "development" projects, and blockades. As a last resort, they have reclaimed resources that have been taken from them through actions of symbolic resistance—more conventionally recognized as sabotage.

The following section describes some representative cases of the environmental controversies of the late-1980s and early-1990s. These stories illustrate the increasing complexity of Indonesian environmental organizations' approaches and strategies, and the increasing importance of local environmental struggles' roles in and links with global civil society.

Tapak

In early 1991, several environmental organizations in Central Java, supported by WALHI and national consumers' groups, called for a boycott of products made by companies discharging toxic wastewater that poisoned wells and rice paddies, and wiped out artisanal fish ponds in the village of Tapak, near Java's north coast city of Semarang. Since the mid-1970s, during the north coast's industrial boom, pollution had gotten gradually worse in Tapak, and villagers had exhausted bureaucratic means to get the Central Java government to order the offending factories to stop polluting (Arimbi 1993; *Environesia*, 1991 articles). The call for a consumer boycott was meant to hurt the polluting companies' profits but, more important, was also intended to operate at a symbolic level. It challenged both consumers and the state to look behind glistening modern images of the soap, soy sauce, and Coca Cola ingredients of the manufacturers polluting Tapak. They noted that the deadly consequences of pollution in the village were direct results of state policies that encouraged industrialization at breakneck speed, at the expense of rural life and livelihood. The boycott campaign also served notice, via the sympathetic mainstream press, that neither negligent bureaucrats nor greedy industrialists would succeed in setting Indonesia's growing urban middle class consumer tastes against the livelihoods of either Tapak's residents or workers at the polluting factories. The populist boycott explicitly linked, rather than divided, the self-interests of Indonesian industrial workers, peasants, and consumers.

The Central Java government finally suspended six factories' production licenses. When the factories fired hundreds of workers in response, Indonesia's Zero Population Growth organization (acting as a workers' advocacy group, under New Order labor laws that prohibited independent labor unions) lobbied the Ministry of Labor to negotiate to require the companies to continue paying their displaced workers. Nabiel Makarim, head of Indonesia's new environmental protection agency, BAPEDAL, demanded that factory owners stop using threats to lay off workers as a way to blackmail the government into not enforcing new anti-pollution laws (quoted in Aditjondro 1991:4). The factories eventually resumed production, but only after they had agreed to negotiate with Tapak villagers, mediated by government officials (*Environesia* 1992).

Activist George Aditjondro[72] pointed out the futility of companies' attempts to pit factory workers against consumers and villagers. While Indonesia has its own tradition of consumer boycotts, Aditjondro traced the Tapak boycott rationale through American United Farmworkers' President Cesar Chavez' study of the Gandhian boycott of British textiles, and Gandhi's explanation of the need for solidarity with British textile mill workers. Indonesian boycott organizers also pointed out that several of the companies polluting Tapak's waters were subsidiaries or licensees of multinational corporations, whose products had displaced workers from local Indonesian enterprises.

The mainstream press also played a crucial role in the Tapak boycott, led by progressive newspaper *Suara Pembaruan.*[73] As Tapak became an experiment in complex mediated negotiations, which the new environmental laws recommend to avoid litigation (in keeping with Indonesia's tradition of "consultation and consensus"), press coverage sympathetic to the villagers helped balance the clout of the industries. This press coverage also helped turn government participants in the process from villains to heroes. Officials at KLH and BAPEDAL were grateful, since such positive press both helped to build these agencies' constituencies in support of environmental rules, and encouraged agency staff to deal candidly with the press and public.

Kedung Ombo Dam

In 1988 and 1989, reactions in Indonesia and abroad to the forced dislocation of almost thirty-thousand people in Central Java from villages behind the Kedong Ombo Dam were part of a growing international movement against big dam construction.[74] Opposition to Kedung Ombo, a thirty-megawatt hydropower project, illustrated two critical points to the Indonesian public-at-large. First, rural communities are victimized by state decisions on how to meet Java's rapidly-growing urban and industrial energy demands. Second, the nation as a whole is victimized by an international financial system that funds mega-projects through a vicious cycle of mega-loans from multi-lateral development banks—in this case, US $283 million from the World Bank and Asian Development Bank. NGOs pointed out that these loans must be serviced with revenues generated from industrial exports or the unsustainable extraction of petroleum and timber products which, in turn, aggravate environmental degradation and community dislocation. In the meantime, profits from dam construction fill the pockets of construction contractors and their political friends.

When the waters began to rise behind Kedung Ombo in early 1989, villagers in the flooded area did not depart quietly. As some moved to higher ground at the edges of the rising lake, or to higher ground that became islands in the middle, others responded to military eviction orders by simply walking into their homes and shutting the doors. Their resistance was extensively covered in the mainstream Indonesian press as well as newsletters of the local and national environmental and human rights groups that provided them with legal, political, and material support.[75] By early 1989, special police and army troops had closed off the Kedung Ombo Dam area and much of its upper watershed to people who did not live there, leaving about seven-thousand remaining residents living on new islands in a virtual state of siege. Students from the surrounding area, led by Indonesian Catholic priest Romo Mangun, held marches and vigils in solidarity with the members of the inundated communities. Boats they had hauled up for use by people on the new islands were confiscated by local authorities.

Indonesians were enraged not only by the inadequate compensation and resettlement arrangements that residents of the flooded area had been offered, but also by the arbitrary and secretive process by which these terms had been thrust on the affected communities, rather than openly negotiated (Pangestuti 1989). Even the few economic benefits to rural people remaining in the dam area were revealed as subsidies to corporate interests.[76]

The Indonesian press presented the dam project, villagers' resistance to forced relocation, and authorities' reactions to student environmentalists' support for Kedong Ombo victims as both ecological and human rights disasters. Intellectuals in Indonesia's progressive movements debated over whether Kedong Ombo was, in fact, a victory or a defeat—and about what it meant for the future of civil society and democracy in Indonesia, either way (Aditjondro 1990 and 1991; Budiman 1990; Tirtosudarmo 1991).

Newly savvy Indonesian environmental advocates with international friends documented the extent to which the dam was not only bad public relations for the government,[77] but bad engineering and bad economics. They pointed out parallels between planning fiascoes, secrecy, and repression surrounding the Kedong Ombo project and similar situations in other countries. They were guided in part by the arguments and tactics that Indian communities and environmentalists were using at the same time to protest the huge Narmada Sagar and Sardar Sarovar dams (also funded by World Bank loans).[78] Contact between Indonesian and Indian opponents to the Narmada dams was facilitated by the Asia-Pacific Peoples Environmental Network (APPEN, with its Secretariat in Penang, Malaysia), by the Environmental Defense Fund (working out of Washington, D.C. and Oakland, California), and by the California-based International Rivers Network.

Indonesian environmentalists analyzed the actual impacts of Kedung Ombo not only in terms of ecological destruction and social misery, which they refused to quantify in monetary terms, but also in terms of the extremely high total economic costs of the electricity the dam would eventually generate (assuming the dam would have a usable life shorter than its designers anticipated). These they counted not only as government mismanagement, but as forced subsidies to urban industrialists and middle class consumption by marginalized communities. Environmentalists carefully traced social and environmental costs of the dam: villagers' livelihoods and communities; production of their flooded land; the protected forests many displaced people moved to, and the responsibility future Indonesian generations would bear to repay Kedung Ombo loans.[79]

While waters in Lake Kedung Ombo rose to over 80 meters in the early 1990s, local resistance and environmentalist campaigns against the dam and its forced relocations profoundly affected energy and river-basin policymaking in Jakarta and throughout Indonesia. Environmental organizations in Indonesia hardly count the Kedung Ombo campaign itself as a victory.[80] Yet they note that government plans for most other large hydro-electric dams have been quietly shelved, after the distribution of actual costs and benefits were recalculated.

Indorayon: Pulp and Expulsion, Pollution and Plantations

During the late 1980s, Indonesia's environmental movement began to assemble one of its most complex cases. The Indorayon case brought together passionate popular resistance to land expropriation and pollution, environmental groups' extended analysis of regional impacts and global business practices, and judicial fireworks. The environmental movement portrayed the ecological and social ravaging of North Sumatra's Lake Toba region as an integrated process—*and fought it on that basis*.

P.T. Inti Indorayon Utama (IIU) opened its pulp mill on the Asahan River in 1989. Owned by the Raja Garuda Mas timber conglomerate, the company was assembled by entrepreneur Sukanto Tanoto (also director of Indonesia's joint plywood marketing board, which oversees Indonesia's majority share in the global hardwood plywood trade). The IIU mill was planned as Indonesia's largest pulpmill—a multi-line complex, eventually to produce bleached kraft pulp and rayon fibers at costs the company anticipated to be among the world's lowest (WALHI & LBH 1992). Financial capital, equipment, and technical expertise were all obtained from foreign sources, in international capital markets and as foreign aid.[81] In the early 1990s, the mill obtained raw materials—a million tons of wood annually, between 1989 and 1993—from a variety of sources in the mountainous Lake Toba region, home to the Toba Batak ethnic group. Wood sources for the mill included pine stands planted during the colonial period. Later the area was designated a protection forest to preserve the water catchment area that drains into North Sumatra's most productive wet-rice growing area. Indorayon also planned to use mixed hardwoods from the company's nearby selective logging concession, and from a former watershed protection area (recently redesignated) in older natural forest. In the early 1990s, IIU also clearcut part of its timber concession to establish a Eucalyptus plantation for future feedstock to its mill.

Characteristic of multiple claims on forest land throughout Outer Island Indonesia, the state had designated this land as "national forest." Much of it is also subject to Batak customary rights, and before 1989 was used by Batak communities to graze livestock and collect forest produce. IIU enlisted the aid of local military, civilian and forest police units to prevent local populations from continuing their traditional uses of the forest land which the company claimed for its own exclusive use, especially the areas that the company intended to convert to pulpwood plantations. IIU offered only minimal compensation to members of affected communities. Moreover, Batak opposition to IIU noted that the customary Batak "*pago-pago*" processes for land transfer, which requires unanimous agreement of adult male community members, were not properly carried out. Instead, customary procedures were "managed" by corrupt local officials who had no customary standing to conduct such transactions. The economic and cultural insult of the company's enclosure of customary land was added to the injury of erosion and landslides caused by IIU's logging and land clearing. One landslide destroyed a village, covered ricefields, and killed several people in 1989 (WALHI & LBH 1992:45).

Between 1986 (when mill construction began) and 1989 (when the mill began full-scale operations), several local officials and Indonesia's Minister of Population and Environment joined non-governmental groups to petition North Sumatra's Governor and the region's District Head not to approve either the investment permit for the mill or the highly irregular timber concession permits to log protected forest land without a full environmental impact investigation.[82] Provincial officials approved the permits anyway, the plant was built, IIU began logging and land clearing to support the mill and its future plantations.

Several regional environmental organizations, North Sumatra's Legal Aid Foundation, and WALHI decided to make IIU a test-case of Indonesia's new environmental laws, especially the 1986 environmental impact assessment law (*Environesia* 1988a:1,12). In 1988, WALHI and the other organizations filed the first of several connected lawsuits in North Sumatra. They accused several government agencies of failing to require that Indorayon conduct an adequate environmental impact assessment before beginning operations, and demanding that the company take financial responsibility for environmental damages it caused (*Environesia* 1989f:8–9).

The court case was widely covered in the Indonesian press, but the mainstream press used it more to illustrate the need for an independent judiciary than to focus on the ecological and social justice issues of the case. The trial took on an almost circus-like atmosphere on several occasions, when judges refused to admit evidence from local officials and village residents, but accepted evidence from the company. Judges even rejected expert testimony about the environmental impact of the IIU mill's construction-in-progress, and about environmental impacts of operations at similar mills. WALHI and LBH lost their suit on a technicality—the environmental impact assessment law had not yet been enacted when IIU got its initial investment permit in 1984. However, the trial helped establish non-governmental organizations' right to sue on behalf of the environment, and to get the government to implement or enforce its own laws—a landmark decision that set the groundwork for public interest environmental law in Indonesia.

Despite the company's claims in 1995 that it had installed adequate pollution control technology in the plant, IIU's mill was also still seriously polluting the Asahan River and adding an old-fashioned pulpmill stink to the region's air, creating an environmental mess reminiscent of North American and Scandinavian pulp regions in the 1930s.[83] Though non-governmental groups had collected their own spotty measurements of water pollution problems, the government had yet to effectively enforce North Sumatra's recently-upgraded pollution control standards.

Meanwhile, in a separate suit, rice farmers sued IIU for logging damage to the formerly-protected watershed that had supplied their irrigation water, while farmers in the same area blockaded IIU logging roads. Villagers living across the river from the pulp mill sued IIU for polluting the Asahan River, but dropped the suit before it went to trial under pressure from officials, claiming that they had been intimidated. At the same time, several student support groups had been formed in North Sumatra, petitioning provincial representatives, and staging marches from their Medan campus to the IIU plant on World Environment Day in 1989 (*Environesia* 1989d:8). The case gained international attention as well, through the Indonesian environmental organizations' newsletters and action alerts circulated to groups in Europe, North America, and especially Japan—the expected destination for much of IIU's pulp.[84]

The frustration of village people from Sugapa Village, located in the IIU plantation area, exploded in April 1989, just before the WALHI/LBH verdict in July. After villagers rescued a woman from an attempted rape by two plantation employees, villagers ripped out over sixteen-thousand Eucalyptus seedlings from IIU's plantation. Although both men and women were involved, police arrested only the ten women—an act which fed into the Indonesian and international environmental movements' tendency to identify peasant women as protectors of nature, even as they are disempowered in their own communities. The company claimed that, because women do not own land according to Batak customary law and that the village's men had ceded their land to the company, the Sugapa women were trespassing on Indorayon's land! The North Sumatra court fined the women for the cost of the seedlings they had ripped up, and sentenced them to six months in prison.

The women refused to accept the decision, defending their action with song and poetry, and appealing to Indonesia's Supreme Court. The prospect of another circus-like trial in Jakarta, and a petition with six-hundred signatures, convinced the judge to reduce the sentence if the women agreed to replant the seedlings. They did not. Instead, the women demanded compensation from IIU for their loss of income during the trial. Embarrassed by the whole business, IIU finally offered to settle out of court by *renting* the land in question from the villagers—a crucial precedent for other problematic timber plantations. The village of Sugapa was split on whether to accept or reject IIU's offer and, as of 1994, the matter remained unresolved. The North Sumatran environmental group that assisted the Sugapa women during the incident was banned for six months by the government, and was only allowed to resume activities after agreeing to abandon its legal aid program.[85] Indorayon's cynical manipulation of the sexual politics of Batak property rights in the 1990 trial made the Sugapa women instant national environmental heroes.

The complexity of this kind of multi-faceted environmental controversy, environmental and community organizations' multi-level approach to it appears to herald the future of environmental organizing in Indonesia. It combines analysis of regional ecological and social impacts, dynamics of multinational capital, ambiguities in Indonesian environmental and forestry law, support for indigenous land rights and resource management systems, local cultural symbolism and gender politics. The attention of an increasingly sophisticated and independent Indonesian press (despite the 1994 press bans) is a major tool in these campaigns. A new generation of Indonesian politicians and civil servants, and especially of an increasingly sympathetic Indonesian public, is ready to consider the centrality of environmental issues in sustaining Indonesia's future.

Environmental Organizing, Development, and Cultural Politics in Kalimantan

During the early 1990s, emerging trends in environmental organizing in the four Indonesian provinces of Kalimantan (on the island of Borneo; Figure 6.2) illustrate the ways in which the Indonesian environmental movement approaches increasingly complex combinations of material and symbolic issues, and relates them to goals of "sustainable development." More than in any other region of Indonesia, environmental organizations' activities in Kalimantan explicitly link efforts to sustain a multiplicity of indigenous cultures, and to defend and legitimate indigenous communities' locally-adapted resource use and environmental management systems. Material and symbolic aspects of Kalimantan's environmental and Dayak[86] rights movements are inextricably intertwined.

Since the late 1980s, two main streams of activity and concern have come together in Kalimantan's environmental organizing, aimed at protecting both the island's forests and the rights of Dayak communities to continue "traditional" forms of forest-based livelihood. The first stream involves demands to eliminate or reduce the impacts of large-scale state-licensed logging, mining, and plantation activities in Dayak communities' forests and customary territories. The second stream focuses on efforts to promote development models that legitimate and adapt, or at least are compatible with, indigenous resource use practices and institutions.

Dayak activists insist that massive logging and land clearing in the Kalimantan interior destroy not only their means of subsistence, but also generations of invested time and skill in sustainably managing the forests. Both of these effects threaten their cultural integrity and survival. Dayak rights advocates argue that, in addition to serving the interests of

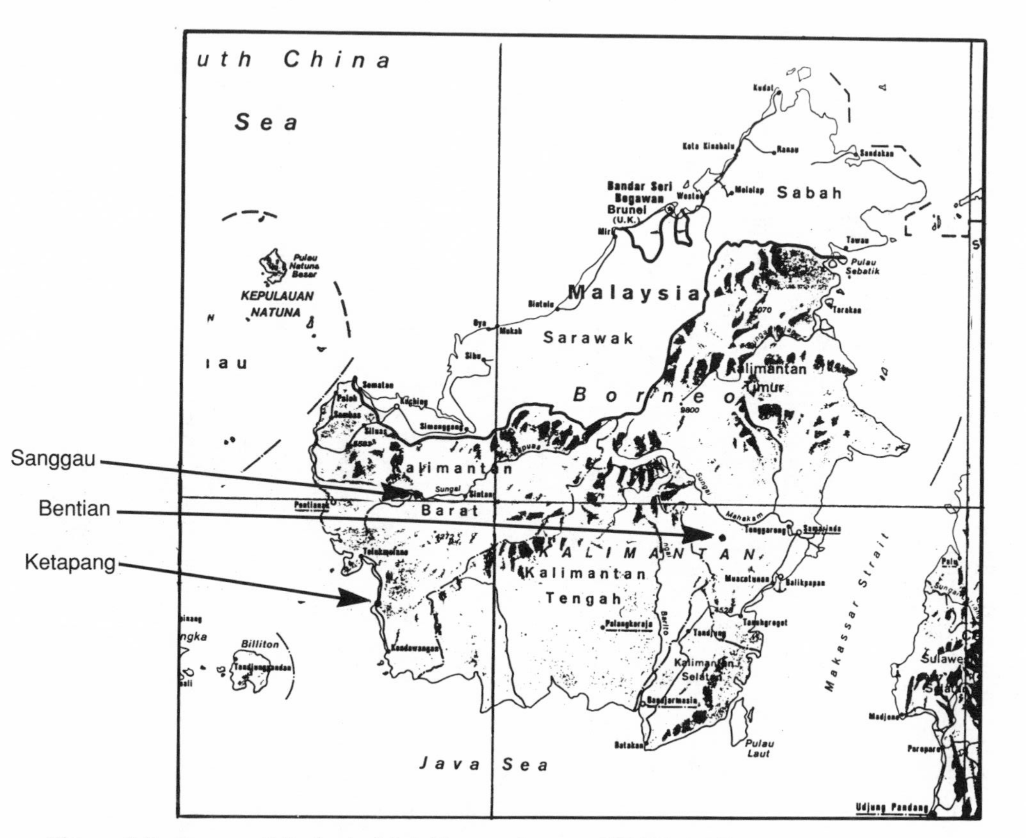

Figure 6.2. Source: U.S. Central Intelligence Agency (500869 9-72).

politically-powerful timber concession-holders, state expropriation of village customary land rights and forests for logging and plantation projects embodies a vision of national unity that reinforces the dominance of Java's ethnic groups over indigenous peoples of Kalimantan.

This combination of political-economic and ethnic issues is generally "taboo" in public discussion under the New Order regime. Community organizing based on such a discourse, and conducted without the state's imprimatur, also risks accusations of subversion, due to the regime's efforts to depoliticize the "floating mass" of rural people. Dayak rights and environmental groups' opposition to the expansion of the government's "transmigration" program is in part related to such ethnic considerations.[87]

During the early 1990s, a dual approach of environmental and Dayak rights movements in Kalimantan focused on both ecology and culture, on efforts to transform dominant Indonesian images of Dayak people, livelihood, ways of life, and of "nature" in Kalimantan's forests themselves. Nongovernmental organizations' documentation projects show the wealth of Dayak communities' ethnobotanical and ecological knowledge, which could also be used to prevent environmental degradation, or to rehabilitate already degraded lands. Projects that emphasize local environmental knowledge have also attempted to show how state recognition of Dayak communities' customary land rights and tree tenure systems will promote longer-term thinking and planning by community members themselves, and can contribute to more sustainable government forest management efforts as well.

Official policies of the highly centralized, timber-oriented forestry bureaucracy have passionately blamed shifting cultivators as the major culprits in forest destruction in Kalimantan.[88] Official Forestry Ministry and Agricultural Ministry policies continue to insist that the persistence of Dayak shifting cultivation indicates that its practitioners are backward and ignorant, in need of "guidance" to transform their means of subsistence. By contrast, Kalimantan's non-governmental environmental organizers portray Dayak communities not as primitive despoilers of the forest but as sophisticated managers of Kalimantan's land and tropical forest heritage, and as guardians of Kalimantan's biological diversity. Only since the early 1990s has official attention focused on the consequences of deforestation by massive commercial logging and state-sponsored land clearing, and to a series of catastrophic forest fires following a long drought in 1982/1983.

In seeking emotional reactions to the latest logging, mining, land expropriation, or socially generated "natural" disaster[89] in Kalimantan, environmental organizers are not averse to portraying Dayak ways of life to "outsiders" (in Indonesia and abroad) using timeless, romantic images of traditional tribal communities living in isolated harmony with the rainforest.

Yet these organizers have also mounted sustained efforts to develop detailed, accurate information about the enormous variety of actual local resource use and management systems, and how they are being affected by logging, government-backed land development schemes, and other outside pressures (Florus, et al., n.d.).

With the rapid pace of logging and subsequent forest clearing for plantation projects,[90] the stakes have risen for Dayak rights activists to show that their communities are at least as capable of managing their own territories in a sustainable manner as the state-approved schemes would be. Dayak rights advocates frame their arguments, and choose their organizing targets, to support claims that their communities' forms of environmental management can support both healthier forests *and* more prosperous communities than the state and corporate-dominated alternatives of commercial logging and plantations.

Dayak rights organizers concerned with sustainable forest use have begun to contribute to a rapidly growing international body of literature concerning indigenous environmental management and agroforestry systems, the roles of local knowledge in environmental management, and the cultural constructions of indigenous community (as opposed to state-based) systems of property and resource use rights.[91] For Dayak organizations, one of the most useful results of these lines of research has been new evidence of the similarities between many village-managed forests in Kalimantan and "natural" forests in terms of forest architecture and species composition (Padoch & Peluso 1996; de Jong 1993; Peters 1994; Seibert 1989). This supports the argument that indigenous forest management systems are relatively benign in their effects on forest health, and effective as *in situ* conservation of biological diversity. Dayak groups contrast their demands to enhance and adapt "traditional" agroforestry techniques with both conventional timber-oriented forest management, and with forest conservation strategies that attempt to eliminate "human disturbance" altogether. State policies based on either of these extremes would prohibit the most familiar means of livelihood for Dayak communities.

The uses of ecological and social sciences in Kalimantan's combined environmental and cultural campaigns are extremely important factors in the Dayak rights/environmental movement's construction of issues. The combined movement insists that recognition and adaptation of indigenous resource use systems are crucial steps toward achieving sustainable development in Kalimantan. The roles of both basic ecological and applied social research, and the importance of community-based forestry projects based on indigenous resource management and property rights systems, have also been key pathways for linking Dayak rights and environmental organizing in Kalimantan with international environmental movements.

High school and university-educated Dayak activists have sought work with both Indonesian and foreign-sponsored research and conservation projects. The environmental and Dayak rights groups themselves have encouraged foreign academic researchers, in particular, to work in communities where their organizations have been or would like to become active. They hope that resulting research will support arguments in favor of the sustainability of specific Dayak resource use practices. Likewise, urban-based Kalimantan groups have used their connections with sympathetic foreign researchers as "introductions" for community organizers to enter rural areas where the groups wish to promote organizational objectives. In some cases, they offer standard community development initiatives such as rural credit unions or clean water supplies. In others, they support village opposition to timber operations or plantation schemes. Contact with these regional organizers has helped embolden village-based, grassroots leadership in negotiations with timber and plantation companies and government officers. Village "movers and shakers" have also forged links between their rural action (whether protests or negotiations galvanized by particular local controversies, or community infrastructure projects) and the urban-based groups organized by a Dayak intelligentsia whose members, for the most part, also grew up in rural communities before leaving to pursue high school or university education.

These relationships between urban-based organizations and rural communities have lent legitimacy to the urban-based organizations' claims to represent the interests of indigenous forest-dependent communities in a national or global context. They have, in many cases, provided village activists with both material and moral support for understanding their rights under Indonesian law in negotiations with government officials and timber or plantation companies. The urban-based Dayak rights groups have also assisted with legal defense following demonstrations, accusations of sabotage, or other situations that have led to arrest or harassment of rural activists. These links provide village activists with opportunities to be heard in national and international debates on environmental and development issues that affect rural Kalimantan, and to be influenced by the directions of these broader discourses.[92] Dayak organizers have both contributed to and gained important rhetorical tools from emerging "global" worldviews that recognize both the social justice and ecological logic of supporting local communities' rights over local resources. The international movement provides them with tools that help legitimate experiential environmental knowledge based on place-specific traditional practice. Stories of the local movements' determination to sustain forests for community life rather than corporate timber production, or replacing them with single-commodity plantations, both inspire and echo the dedication of local movements elsewhere, whose activists could hardly even locate Borneo on a world map.

Local opposition to the establishment of timber plantations on Dayak communities' customary lands, goes to the heart of the congruence between environmental and indigenous rights advocacy in Kalimantan. The original forms of government-subsidized timber plantations were intended to plant both fast-growing and indigenous tree species on forest lands that had been very seriously degraded by logging, by shifting cultivation, or by wildfire. Healthy forest stands, and areas being intensively managed by village populations, were in principle off-limits for timber plantation development.

However, in establishing plantations in conjunction with transmigration projects,[93] forests that are actually integral parts of indigenous communities' extensive agroforestry production systems have been designated for plantation development. Government officials invite communities living in and around the plantation concession to give up their customary claims on land and forests, and join the new transmigration settlements as part of a compensation package. Yet many see this choice as a trap, intended not only to deprive them of their forest homes and their traditional forest-based livelihood, but also to destroy their customary communities and customary law, turning them into casual laborers completely dependent on the timber company that promises to employ them.

Conflicts between timber plantation developers and local communities have flared into national attention in both the Bentian region of East Kalimantan and the Ketapang area of West Kalimantan, among others. In the wake of the North Sumatra Indorayon cases, the Bentian and Ketapang incidents between 1992 and 1994 tested whether government officials and company managers had learned to take seriously regional advocacy organizations' power to embarrass them and communities' abilities to obstruct plantation work through demonstrations and blockades, moral suasion over plantation workers, or sabotage.

In each case, when communities asked for legal and negotiating assistance from regional Dayak rights, legal aid, and environmental advocacy organizations, these groups made clear that they intended to raise the visibility of the issues involved to a broader audience through their national networks. Companies and regional government officials would be portrayed as unreasonable within the areas where they operated. Indonesia's international insistence that its timber industry could be made sustainable and open to global scrutiny would also be brought into question on both environmental and human rights grounds.

In each case, regional activists in Kalimantan used their national and international networks to keep distant "friends" informed of the latest developments, and poised to bring to bear whatever pressure they could at a moment's notice. This included international lobbying of foreign human rights and trade commissions during periods when the Indonesian government was especially sensitive to international criticism on its environmental and human rights records.[94] In several cases, it appears that the threat of negative attention spurred officials in Jakarta to commission task forces to go to the troubled areas, investigate, and facilitate negotiations with local communities. With land expropriations largely halted, serious violence averted, lines of communication opened, and many regional officials forewarned to avoid confrontations elsewhere, the regional advocacy organizations cautiously count these cases among their success stories.

Yet, Indonesian organizers, particularly in the Outer Islands, increasingly recognize the risks of pulling international networks into campaigns on local or regional issues. They discourage international attention that is not carefully coordinated with local initiatives. Appeals to government officials from "friends" abroad can easily backfire if news items or "action alerts" in foreign environmental media confuse details of a case, present them with little understanding of the broader climate and sensitivities of the Indonesian political situation, or result in inappropriately timed or embarrassing international protests. Such uncoordinated efforts risk slamming shut painstakingly opened lines of dialogue and possibilities for negotiation. Misguided appeals from foreign environmentalists, especially with regard to complex issues in remote regions, open Indonesian communities and Indonesian activists supporting them to accusations that they have been led astray by un-Indonesian influences. Some Indonesian environmentalists, familiar with foreign organizations' membership and fundraising strategies, are concerned that the imperative for international "friends" to appear to be doing *something*—as well as the lucrativeness of foreign groups' "action alerts" for their own fund-raising—makes these foreign organizations insensitive to the potential that their efforts will backfire in Indonesia.

In many state and corporate trade association responses to environmental criticism from abroad, the international appeals themselves are cast as environmental imperialism. Campaigns by Indonesian timber product trade associations portray North Americans' concerns about tropical rainforest conservation and cultural survival of Outer Islands peoples as subtle propaganda by Indonesia's competitors—North American timber companies.[95] Yet many activists candidly admit that sustained international pressure, extreme conservation demands from abroad, and the unpredictability of international responses to half-hearted official "environmental" initiatives make the Indonesian groups' better-grounded proposals sound quite moderate, reasonable, and based in Indonesian realities. So, the "uncaptured" international critiques remain useful to Indonesian environmentalists, if inconvenient.

Environmental and indigenous rights advocates have played important roles in supporting recent "participatory forest management" initiatives in Kalimantan. They have also helped to keep Indonesian and foreign project professionals honest about the degree to which their "collaborative" forestry initiatives really reflect aspirations and contributions of village participants.[96] Dayak rights and environmental groups have been particularly critical of project management styles in which "community" decisions are too tightly orchestrated by project planners, and in which village people had no real voice in designing project decision-making processes in the first place (PLASMA n.d.). Yet, activists in these organizations have appreciated the "political space" that internationally-supported participatory forest management projects have provided for their own village organizing. These high-profile projects, all of which have some role for regional non-governmental organizations, have also helped build bridges between the Dayak rights/environmental organizations and regional government agencies concerned with forests, agriculture, and regional development planning.

Collaborative forest management efforts have recently become an important feature of nature preserve and national park planning in Kalimantan. While communities around the preserves are far from equal partners in these overall planning processes, presided over by a branch of the Forestry Department, collaborative projects give communities considerable leverage in negotiations. Planners understand that failure to get communities' active cooperation will compromise the preserves' potential to protect important habitats. Moreover, in views consistent with recent developments in conservation biology (Noss and Cooperrider, 1994), scientists have supported several Dayak communities' claims that their resource use practices do not destroy "nature," but actually *produce* the "natural" ecological characteristics and biological diversity of the landscapes and habitats which park planners wish to preserve.[97]

Nature preserve and national park planners at several sites in Kalimantan now accept the need to allow particular subsistence and extractive activities by long-standing local communities in designated zones within preserve borders. The precise lines of division between "nature" and "culture" in these cases become central to the success of "collaborative management," along with decisions about who has the right to draw them, and by what process and criteria they are drawn.[98] In Kalimantan, proponents of ideas about the social construction of "nature" have been remarkably direct in addressing normative issues of how longstanding a "local" community's presence and extractive activities should be, and at what intensity, for them to be considered part of the "desirable" landscape to be protected.[99]

The apparent congruence of environmental and Dayak rights interests has, on several occasions, collapsed over such issues, since endorsing the continuation of *all* current prerogatives of Dayak communities living in and near nature preserves may seriously compromise the preserves' habitat protection goals. Collaborative planning efforts have attempted to develop benchmarks of sustainability to resolve such issues and promote consensus among all parties. Yet addressing instances in which local community prerogatives would be detrimental to goals of environmental conservation have strained the sometimes shaky coalition between environmental and Dayak rights advocates. In resolving to focus on community prerogatives, rather than dwelling on their long-term ecological consequences, organizations with the dual focus have at times deliberately obscured contradictions between the two, or insisted that the *only* real problems with retaining all indigenous community prerogatives arise when outside commercial pressures and government projects compete with local communities for resources.[100]

Because of this, the representation of landscapes and environmental management systems of the communities that live in and manage these areas has become an extremely important issue in both environmental activism and collaborative forest management efforts in Kalimantan. Recently, the simple, universally-accessible ideas used in the sketch mapping exercises of "participatory rural appraisal" have been supplemented by high technology approaches using aerial photographs, satellite-aided geopositioning equipment, and computerized geographic information system databases (Fox 1990; Sirait 1992; Peluso 1995). Some indigenous forest management advocates use digitized maps discursively, to illustrate how Dayak village resource management systems can help conserve desirable aspects of the landscape as effectively as—and in some cases better than—management based on Forestry Department plans.

Disagreements among Kalimantan's environmental activists and indigenous rights advocates about the implications of using these new mapping technologies are indicative of varying worldviews, if not of potential splits, within the movement. On one side are people with an "environmental management" orientation, who tend to favor ensuring that Dayak communities and environmental groups have the most accurate and complete data possible to support their positions in disputes with state authorities. They point out that any mapping of community territorial and resource use boundaries should be at least as accurate as those produced by state agencies—especially those responsible for any decisions that could lead to expropriation of village resources. These high-tech activists are willing to invest the time and become beholden to international donors—and the state agencies that they must often cooperate with or appease—in order to support their arguments with technically impressive data.

On the other side are people who tend to take a stronger cultural and symbolic stand toward the representation of indigenous environments. They tend to disapprove of putting too much energy into mastering mapping technologies in which the state will always, ultimately, have an advantage, and which will produce representations of indigenous environments that most members of local communities will never really understand or "own." They fear that the emphasis on extreme accuracy could drag the non-governmental advocacy groups into quibbling over minutiae, rather than focusing on fundamental issues of understanding and empowerment. The "low-tech" advocates are concerned that although Dayak village people may be involved in generating data for sophisticated mapping, they would not be trained to manipulate these data to express their own sense of environmental concerns or values. They argue that while the high-tech mapping tools could be used by visiting "experts" and highly educated activists of the NGOs themselves to advocate community rights, the information such maps would convey does not remain readily available in community members' own "toolbox." Several Kalimantan environmental groups have turned down offers of computerized mapping equipment and training for these reasons. They argue that even if high-tech maps are more "accurate," the authenticity of maps made with higher proportions of villagers' knowledge, and lower proportions of expensive technology, could still help empower ordinary people through democratic village planning and decision-making about forest management practices. Even simple sketch maps are convincing in constructive protest to document the extent to which land expropriation could affect village access to resources, and community well-being.

Promotion of participatory, collaborative forest management processes in Kalimantan—by both non-governmental organizations and state-sponsored projects—has set into motion social learning processes that are fundamentally changing both government and community participants' ideas about the potential of development models that incorporate many of the environmental values of indigenous communities' resource use practices. Perhaps even more important from a political standpoint, however, are the lessons learned about broader-based participatory decision-making that involve both project representatives and village people. Lessons about participatory community problem assessment and decision-making processes run in several directions, involving the regional environmental and indigenous rights organizations, the state-sponsored participatory forest management projects, and even private timber company and plantation management.

The "ecological" worldviews that are important components of participatory forestry projects have also begun to be absorbed within the government forestry bureaucracies to a much greater extent than the limited scope of the projects themselves would lead one to expect. For example, in areas where prestigious participatory forestry projects have been active, government foresters rarely make blanket condemnations of shifting cultivation and Dayak forest use in ways still so common elsewhere in the bureaucracy. In collaborative project areas, government foresters begin to appreciate the logic and place-by-place uniqueness of indigenous styles of forest management.[101] This "spill-over" effect also benefits relationships between government officials and environmental or Dayak rights organizations, portraying their work in less suspicious light.

Broad audiences absorb the "ethos" of participatory management through project-sponsored workshops, seminars, exhibits, and training courses. The mutual influence between Dayak rights/environmental organizations and recent state-sanctioned collaborative forest management projects is extended. Both types of activities draw on the same relatively small pools of local and regional expertise on customary institutions and forests, and on the same pools of idealistic, relatively well-educated, and often highly politicized indigenous youth concerned with environmental and cultural survival issues. This cross-over facilitates some non-governmental organizations' efforts to present a cooperative face to the government. As official priority in Indonesia's sixth national development plan has shifted toward poverty alleviation (MPR 1993), non-governmental organizations throughout Kalimantan have been able to portray their positions and village activities as congruent with the anti-poverty priorities of the state (*Akcaya* 1993). Many of the older leaders, in particular, come from well-known families in the region, and have developed extensive social networks among provincial elites. Both their long-term stakes in being taken seriously, and their own social and professional connections above and beyond their work with the relatively new non-governmental groups, tend to keep possibilities open for at least informal discussion with regional political leaders. Non-Dayak activists in organizations with both environmental and ethnic foci—let alone relative newcomers to Kalimantan—have had to learn sensitivity to the complex personal and political ramifications of their associates' choices about which issues to tackle, which to avoid, and the timing and tone of action.

Several of the Kalimantan organizations engaged in both environmental conservation and indigenous rights issues now face a crossroads. As large-scale logging continues to deplete ancient forests, state-endorsed projects continue to demand land within village territories, and Kalimantan's environmental and Dayak rights groups gain political credibility, organizers must choose the most effective arenas for action. Some have opted for low-profile roles as educators and providers of technical assistance to practical rural projects. Yet increasingly, some groups have found niches as both advocates and mediators in conflicts between indigenous communities, private resource exploitation companies, and the state. Their abilities to help transmit and interpret community views to government bodies and through the press have helped resolve environmental conflicts among communities, commercial interests, and state agencies in a relatively tension-reducing manner. Their congenial urging to negotiate is, nonetheless, backed by the threat that they will use both their cordial links with angry villagers and their extensive national and international networks to embarrass public officials, and direct broad public attention to abuses of power in environmental conflicts in remote regions.

Conclusion

As we have seen in California and Hungary, one of the more effective means of protecting Nature is the combination of political alliances with an appeal to the legitimacy of local resource regimes. The same thing is taking place in Indonesia. It is precisely this combination of local and global connections that makes the environmental movement a significant force for political change in Indonesia.

Unique among Indonesian political actors, the environmental movement is both engaged in local issues, and able to make sense of them to the Indonesian public in terms of global relationships. In this process, environmental organizers have been able to tap into global networks that provide technical, financial, and political support, and to use Indonesia's unique regional histories and cultures, manifested through localized resource regimes, to legitimate their activities. Thus, Indonesia's re-emerging civil society taps into a sentiment critical of the current government's policies on the environment, regional development, and human rights, while remaining connected to the mainstream of national politics—and significantly affects both the tone and agenda of political change in Indonesia.

Still, the environmental movement has found that it must also build alliances with the state, since the political terrain for open criticism remains limited. The Suharto regime bases much of its claim to legitimacy on its ability to mobilize the wealth that can be extracted from Indonesia's natural resources, and the capital that finances such extraction originates, quite often, from foreign sources aligned with Indonesia's own politically powerful conglomerates.

Criticism of Indonesia's political economy has brought state power down on the heads of activists in many groups in civil society, and has threatened their abilities to organize at all. Prudence dictates avoiding direct attacks on the government and instead appropriating the regime's own symbols and ideology for critical purposes. If the wealth of the land belongs to the Nation, individuals' accumulation of disproportionate shares in their own bulging pockets becomes a violation of the Nation's purpose. Likewise, if Indonesia's richest heritage is the diversity of its cultures and Nature itself, then destruction of that diversity is an increasingly unviable platform on which the regime can stand.

As the three case study chapters suggest, civil society is both global and local. It is global in that far-reaching networks of knowledge and practice inform its activities. It is local in the extent to which no generalized science or ideology is sufficient to achieve its goals, especially where environmental protection and restoration become priorities. In California, Hungary, and Indonesia, environmental groups and alliances, all part of global civil society, have led the way in showing how people, places, and political economy must be included in the environmental protection policy process. This cannot be accomplished without a detailed knowledge of place. The final two chapters of this book turn to the importance of place in a politics of the environment, and the role of place in global environmental governance.

PART III

What Can Be Thy Place?

CHAPTER 7

Who Are We? Why Are We Here?
Identity, Place and Global Environmental Sustainability

> *[The view from an airplane], and the impersonality it provides, encourages the delusion that the globe is 'manageable,' after all, it is 'so small' in the 'vastness' of space. Furthermore, it is convenient that certain things like national boundaries are invisible. The world appears as a great and complex inkblot, encouraging the most free ranging imagination for how we would like it to be. . . . [T]he difference between the view from an airplane and the planetary view from space is that human things . . . do not appear at all. The 'whole earth' image celebrates a planet from which human life is entirely absent. All that touches us on a daily basis, the world we really live in, is missing*
>
> (Rubin 1993:37–38).

So far in this book, I have focused on two central themes. First, I have argued that the global environment is not, as the conventional wisdom would have it, a "natural" phenomenon but, rather, a social one, constructed through politics, economics, and culture. It is constructed, moreover, not as a single social space but as the aggregation of many such spaces that culminate in something we call "global" (Ruggie 1989). Second, I have suggested that environmental sustainability—by which I mean preservation and restoration of Nature at all scales—will ultimately depend not on "managing Planet Earth" through some enormously complex, centralized panopticon but, rather, on the knowledge and practices of thousands, if not millions, of renegotiated local and regional resource regimes that begin to look something like common–pool property resource systems.[1] These renegotiated resource regimes are appearing in more and more places around the world as a result of the activities of global civil society, and through the networks that connect the subjects of global civil society. What the end result of these activities will resemble is anybody's guess; whether it will be successful in global terms (whatever "success" means in this context) is highly uncertain; success might even be unlikely.[2] It is a Project—or many projects—still "in progress."

In this chapter, I place these projects in a spatial and historical context and argue that more is taking place here than people or groups simply "sustaining" the global environment (not that this is a simple task) or responding to global or local environmental change. The environmentalist component of global civil society is, in this context, a consequence not only of environmental "change"—pollution, deforestation, toxics—but also a result of the social transformation of Nature and, more generally, processes of change in global politics and economics. This involves, on the one hand, alteration in the meanings that Nature has for human beings, who never exist in a vacuum but are, in large part, the offspring of their individual and collective histories and political economies.

On the other hand, changes in political and economic structures and activities are also responsible for the growing prominence of this global civil society. As such, the social transformation of Nature can best be understood as involving individual and collective identities, and the literal *place* of conscious individuals within an increasingly globalized world, where older identities are being transformed or "disappeared." It is these particular, and particularistic, characteristics that differentiate "environmentalism" from many other forms of post-modern identity politics; paradoxically, it is this particular, and place-based facet of environmentalism that makes it a relative—albeit a distant one—to sometimes-virulent ethnic movements (see Rubin 1994; Robertson 1992: ch.6). The connection to place reminds us, as well, of the Romanticism that informed some of the nationalist catastrophes of the twentieth century, and warns us to be cautious (Bramwell 1989). All of this is not to say, as some might, that a Nazi "blood and earth" lies just beyond Earth First! It is, however, to recognize that social and political behavior, while not wholly determined by history, can be mightily influenced by it.

This chapter begins with a discussion about notions of identity. I argue that the generalized search for identity at the end of the twentieth century is driven not so much by a dissatisfaction with the practices of politics or the distribution of resources as by the dissolution of the bonds of nation and community under the pressures of economic globalization. I then turn to a discussion of how identities constructed around environmentalism and Ecology are linked to specific places, rather than more abstract "space," a connection that might help to foster the creation of common–pool property resource systems as well as new forms of political practice. Finally, I speculate on this implications of this relocation of identity for the prospects for global environmental sustainability.

Where are we? What are we doing here?

Environmentalism is, more often than not, characterized as a "new social movement" (NSM), one that has emerged only over the past three decades. Scholars of NSMs have tended to look at them either as an expressions of frustration with institutionalized politics (Tarrow 1988; Offe 1990; Melucci 1989) or as a manifestation of "post-industrial" identity politics (Hall 1991; Harvey 1990, 1991). My particular interest here is with the latter, inasmuch as the former are often somewhat ahistorical. Those who are "post" in their epistemological orientation tend to argue that we need to be more historically-materialist in analyzing NSMs and to look at changes in global modes of production and consumption, which create conditions whereby former identities are diminished or undermined. Thus, Stuart Hall writes:

> 'Post-Fordism' is . . . associated with broader social and cultural changes. For example, [among these are] greater fragmentation and pluralism, the weakening of older collective solidarities and block identities and the emergence of new identities associated with greater work flexibility, the maximization of individual choices through personal consumption.... In part, it is *us* who are being 're-made' . . . The 'self' is experienced as more fragmented and incomplete, composed of multiple 'selves' or identities in relation to the difference social worlds we inhabit . . . (1991:58).

David Harvey puts this problematic in a slightly different form:

> [T]he shifting social construction of time and space as a result of the restless search for profit creates severe problems of identity: To what space do I as an individual belong? Do I express my idea of citizenship in my neighborhood, city, region, nation, or world (1991:77)?

Out of this "maelstrom" of modernity, according to such arguments, there emerge the post-modern identities of gender, culture, race, ecology, and so on. Or, as Hall puts it, we see an "enormous expansion of `civil society,' caused by the diversification of the different social worlds in which men and women can operate . . . " (1991:63).

So far as I know, however, no academics considering the phenomenon of NSMs have given much thought to the importance of place, as opposed to the reconfiguration of space, in their emergence. Resource mobilization theorists take space as given by the political context within which social movements emerge; they tend to regard place as parochial, especially as NSMs reach across national borders to create global alliances. Somewhat paradoxically, post-modernists tend to celebrate the global connections engendered by social movements' *resistance* to the forces of economic globalism. Conversely, bioregionalists focus on place, and the connection between identity and specific places, but largely see themselves as resisting the depredations of contemporary capitalism and seeking a way back to a simpler, less-destructive life, rather than being a product of that system.

As suggested in chapter 2, and as is increasingly being argued in a number of literatures, identity cannot be constituted without reference to place, to the "conditions of existence" that help to define "who we are" and "what we are doing here" (Keith & Pile 1993b:28). If we look at the cases presented in chapters 4, 5, and 6, we find that the meanings that animate the environmental politics and practices of global civil society are less-than-clear signifiers outside of the specific contexts within which they take place. This does not mean that there are no environmental politics outside of specific places; rather, that the meanings informing such environmental politics are quite different from each other.[3]

Thus, for example, while there may be rivers and creeks all over Europe and the United States, and groups dedicated to restoration of creeks and rivers in many of those places, one does not find these organizations dedicating themselves to some universalized creek or river.[4] It is the specific river or creek in one's community, and the symbolic significance of that creek or river to the community, that is important. That significance can have economic content, of course, but it is also as likely to be a constitutive element of the community—a reason for its founding, the literal lifeblood of the original settlement, a point of connection to other places—even when such notions are not wholly-accurate. These reasons, rooted in the history and political economy of specific places, may be almost forgotten, leaving behind only a symbol. Such symbols are, by definition, location-specific (Gold & Gujar 1989). While all rivers are alike in some respects—which makes conferences on watershed restoration feasible—each is different from the other in terms of meaning. It is the possibility of a reconstitution of community, around specific places, that is central to the environmental politics of global civil society discussed in this volume.

The notion that economic forces have dissolved the bonds of community is not, of course, a new one; it can be traced back as far as Marx, if not farther (Berman 1982). For those working within the marxian tradition, however, such bonds were rooted in feudalism and the restriction of labor to place. Their dissolution was a prerequisite to the rise of capitalism and the formation of classes. Ultimately, the working class would become a transnational force, "for itself"—although, with the withering of the state, "transnational" would cease to have any meaning. This same logic is inherent in the globalization of capitalism, although it is capital that has become transnational and strives to eliminate borders (Ohmae 1990).

While capitalism's global success depends on the *economic* differences that give rise to an international division of labor, it also relies, to some degree, on the homogenization of specific *cultures*, which standardizes the preferences of all within certain categories who consume.[5] Thus, mass production—Fordism—addresses a whole stratum of increasingly-transnational, lower-income consumers—while flexible production—post-Fordism—is aimed at those who have more discretionary income and prefer to "customize" what they consume (Crook, Pakulski & Waters 1992: ch. 2). Mass-produced goods can, of course, be modified or adapted to specific national or cultural preferences (Reiff 1991) but, at some point, addressing such differences eats into profits.

The community as something characterized by social relations as well as relations of production consequently comes to be absorbed into a larger system characterized by relations of *consumption*. Almost literally, "you are where you eat," although the *where* need not be—indeed, cannot be—a fixed place. That one can travel to many of the world's great and not-so-great cities and, almost everywhere, eat all of one's meals either at McDonald's or, increasingly, in one of a panoply of seventy kinds of ethnic restaurants, is an admittedly puerile illustration of this phenomenon.[6] But the constitution of identity in terms of relations of consumption is sustainable only so long as those modes of consumption can be sustained. And modes of consumption depend, in turn, on modes of production. If the latter are undermined, the former collapse. To put this another way, "You don't work, you don't eat." What then?

This experience of "what then?" is an increasingly common one. As capital depletes the factors of production on which it depends for profits—be those trees, cheap labor, or the skills of symbolic analysts of one type or another—it searches out new supplies, new people, new places. Left behind are growing numbers of those who, having been downsized or depleted out of a job or function, have also been stripped of important components of their individual identities. They are brought to earth, so to speak, with a sudden and very hard impact. It is at that point that place, and place-based community, begins to acquire its importance, inasmuch as it can be invested with a meaning that begins to re-establish frayed social relations and, perhaps, new relations of production. The specific character of the restoration of community is, of course, context-dependent. This means that, in some places, this process fosters particularistic identities with the potential for great virulence and even violence.[7] In others, however, the community pulls together to navigate beyond the shoals of hard times and economic disruption.

Central to this reconstruction of identity, then, is the refashioning of the story of place and its role in the reconstitution of the self and the community (Duncan & Ley 1993:17). Ontologically, this means fashioning a new account of why one finds oneself in a particular place which, in turn, speaks to who one is. Lest this all seem unnecessarily abstract, consider the notion of "Guardians of the Forest," so casually tossed off in a conversation that occurred in the northern California town of Hayfork (see chapter 4).[8] To guard means to protect, but protect from whom? Others who would, presumably, destroy the forest and, in so doing, irrevocably destroy the community whose former identity was constituted around timber and the well-being it generated? Under the conditions of an extractive mode of production, one was a "logger" who cut down trees. Under the newly-imagined conditions of a sustainable mode of production—whose major products include those forest products (often non-timber) seeking niche markets as well as the experiencing of Nature through ecotourism—one is a "guardian" who sustains the forest. Under the earlier mode, an "environmentalist" was one who would deny access to the forest; under an idealization of this new mode, guardian and environmentalist might be almost indistinguishable.

Note, however, that new meanings and new roles do not necessarily mean new values: This is not an argument about "ecology and the human spirit" (Gore 1993). As noted in earlier chapters, the reconstruction of resource regimes—and the new roles these regimes engender—seems to crystallize around well-defined shared interests in specific places. Or, rather, interests are reconfigured in such a way that "communities of place" supplant "communities of interest." New institutional roles help to constitute new or redefined identities. These identities, in turn, allow people whom heretofore might have been in frequent and almost-violent confrontation with each other to find themselves in pursuit of similar, if not identical, goals. Values are eliminated from—or at least downplayed in—the equation. This does not mean that they have disappeared, but that in the reconfigured context, they no longer define opposing roles in political conflict.[9] In their description of conflict in Amazonia, Marianne Schmink and Charles H. Wood describe such a reconfiguration in the following way:

> [T]he preferences, interests, and ideas that define individuals—and that become the basis for collective action—are formed or constituted in the process of actions that engage participants in a dispute. From this perspective, people act not merely to meet preexisting ends but also to constitute themselves as persons and groups with particular and desired attributes. Because the interests that characterize different social groups are as much formed as they are revealed in the contexts in which people are engaged, they are mutable and subject to continual definition (1992:17).

Notwithstanding what I have intimated above, a politics and identity linked to place need not be parochial (Strassoldo 1992). This is most evident in the networks of indigenous peoples that have emerged over the past two decades to play a growing role in global politics (Wilmer 1993; Brysk 1996; Maiguashca 1994). Indigenous peoples are, by definition, linked to and constituted by the place that they claim as their own. Their legitimacy as actors is buttressed by the special knowledge they possess by virtue of those claims, as well as by their experiences and histories.[10] This knowledge is inseparable from ontology, inasmuch as it is often expressed in terms of myths or explanations that link the existence of Nature's goods—in a specific place—to a beneficent creator. Finally, it is this knowledge that, closing the circle, validates the claim to place and provides the key to localized sustainability.[11] As suggested below, the same sorts of claims are being made, increasingly, by self-identified groups who are not "indigenous" (or autochthonous) in the sense offered above, but who are, nonetheless, indigenous in terms of their identification with a specific locale.

What is this place? The social (re)construction of locale

We all live in places. How do we define them? How do we fit into them? What, if any, is our attachment to them? In the fall of 1993, as I worked on an early version of this chapter, vast areas of southern California were being consumed by the wildfires ordinarily associated with the particular chaparral indigenous to that region and its Mediterranean climate. This episode—hardly an unusual one—was the focus of extended and often tedious TV coverage. Television brings us the dramas associated with such events in real time, offering to us a mode of consumption peculiar to the late-twentieth century: The viewing of "natural" disasters.[12] The format is fairly predictable: The camera pans over scenes of devastation, caused by fire, water, earth, or air; someone is asked how s/he feels about the event; s/he responds that all has been lost—ten, twenty, fifty years of life and memories—and everyone on the street/in the canyon knew everyone else. Clearly, home is identity; without it, one is cast adrift. But why make one's home in this place, so apparently prone to burning? As Mark Reisner writes "A lot of Californians love nature but don't understand it in the least" (1993). Few inhabitants seem to recognize the dysfunctional relationship between human actions and locale-specific Nature as the reason for their individual and collective tragedies; instead, they blame fire departments. No indigenous peoples here.

It is difficult to be attached to and to identify with a place. Places of great beauty inspire the viewer, but they are consumed in a peculiarly passive way. Tourism becomes watching without participating; "production" is left to those who package the views. Urban places become the domain of sports teams, and the acquisition of a major sports franchise promises new life to collective identities. As fans of the New York Giants and the Brooklyn Dodgers will tell you now, almost forty years after the fact, when those baseball teams went West, an important element of community dissolved.[13] This mobility of meanings suggests that identities tied to urban places are very fragile; when factories move or close, those left behind are hard put to find new roles. Sometimes they must pick up and move. Just as "there are no atheists in foxholes," there are no indigenous peoples in cities (at least, not in the sense that we generally use the term).

Yet, there are many city dwellers who are passionately concerned about and committed to Nature (no doubt many of the southern California fire victims were themselves committed environmentalists). While their commitment may extend to specific places—parks, rivers, mountains, forests, seashores—for many, it does not extend to identification *with* those places. Their participation remains largely linked to modes of consumption: Experiencing place without giving something to it. Like as not, they are members of the new cosmopolitan class, who think nothing of travelling thousands of miles in order to experience Nature, those who think nothing of touring the Amazon but who never think about exploring their backyards (thus giving new meaning to the term "NIMBY"). The wealth that allows them to live in beautiful places has nothing to do with those beautiful places. The depth of environmental commitment is more easily measured when ecology comes into conflict with property, particularly of the private kind. Those who are burned out usually rebuild, often more heedlessly than the first time, in an effort to restake their claim. After the next fire, they will rebuild again; the property is, after all, theirs. Or is it?[14]

To a growing degree, the politics of ecology and place are also about the politics of ownership: Who has the right to determine what will be done with, or to, a particular place? The explosive potential of the transformation implicit in this question is evident, for example, with respect to the reauthorization of the U.S. Endangered Species Act. In 1993, Representative Billy Tauzin (then D-Louisiana, later R) warned that there would be a "real war in this chamber [the House of Representatives] over what kind of balance we want to strike between environmental protection and the *protection of human beings on their property*" (Stevens 1993b:B5; my emphasis). Yet, commitments to "ecosystem management," "coordinated resource management plans," or even bioregionalism all imply a property rights system that is different from those that have developed during five hundred years of European and colonial history. In this respect, Tauzin is right. Dominant systems of property rights are anthropocentric, in the fullest sense of the word, allowing human beings free reign over Nature. Virtually all of these property systems—public, private, common–pool, open access—assume an unlimited right to appropriate the product of place. These products include not only what can be extracted from Nature, either directly or via agriculture, but also the use of place for various types of pollution of and imposition on Nature. It follows, therefore, that a commitment to the environmental sustainability of place requires some alteration in these systems of property rights.

Students and scholars of environmental ethics have taken note of the problematic relationship between human beings and Nature, but have tended to restrict their analyses to the "appropriateness" of this relationship, given various utilitarian and moral views and frameworks (Stone 1993: ch. 10). What they have not done, for the most part, is to consider how notions of property and ownership, generally encoded in the law of the land, reflect a society's ethical framework and provide a signpost to human-Nature relationships in a particular society. Indeed, in a historical context, the notion of fully-private ownership might even be a minority view, inasmuch as appropriation for subsistence or limited access to portions of Nature have been much more common (Ostrom 1990: ch. 1). What differs between these two approaches to property has much to do with the dominant mode of production in a specific place.

Capitalism, which involves the extraction of surplus value and its conversion into mobile capital, tends to utilize property as a site at which, or from which, such extraction can occur. Once this has happened, property no longer has value *unless* it can be commodified as, or used to commodify, something else. Hence, forested land is, first, a source of capital via extraction and, then, a source of capital through "development" or eco-tourism of one sort or another. While the capital appropriated from a particular place might be reinvested in that place—especially were the place the actual property of those who live there—investment is more often made with an eye to the generation of additional capital that can be repatriated to locales where the return will be higher. Other modes of production—subsistence or small-scale exchange systems—are much more oriented toward the sustainable generation of "interest" out of a capital "stock."[15] Property, in these modes (such as they are), is subject to various constraints on use that are intended to ensure the reproducibility of the mode over time, and the continued generation of an interest stream.[16] Inasmuch as microeconomics is not much understood by the participants in these systems, other systems of meaning are utilized to justify these constraints. Generally speaking, these meanings seem to draw on or be linked to religion, culture, community, kinship or other kinds of institutional forms. Possession of and access to a resource is granted as part of a "trust" endowed on the user or user group in exchange for the protection and maintenance of the resource, which takes place in the context of a narrative of history and meaning (Gold & Gujar 1989). Such narratives do not necessarily make the system of access and use an equitable one—issues of power and wealth remain important—but they do have historical weight and are the basis of customary practices and habits, which gives them a certain degree of social legitimacy that externally-imposed systems do not possess. My point here is not to idealize or reify these forms of practice or make unrealistic claims on their behalf; only to point out the importance of socially-constructed and validated meanings in the maintenance of Nature.

Such constraints are not unknown within market-dominated societies, although in recent centuries they have lost much of their moral force. In *Social Limits to Growth*, Fred Hirsch points out that, historically, "[M]arket capitalism has been conditioned, confined, and supplemented by social controls of a variety of kinds" (1976:120; see also Polanyi 1957). According to Hirsch, these social controls—religious and ethical—have fulfilled a number of functions. In particular:

> [I]nformal social controls in the form of socialized norms of behavior are needed to allow the market process itself to operate. These range from personal standards such as telling the truth to acceptance of the legitimacy of commercial contracts as a basis for transactions. An important aspect is implicit agreement on the sphere of market behavior: on what can be bought and sold, what interests may be pursued individually and collectively. These matters are recognized as of crucial importance in the establishment of a market economy, but as an underpinning for existing market practices they have been neglected in modern economic analysis. The social prerequisites of markets have been studied by sociologists rather than by economists, who have been generally content to leave it so (1976:121).

Hirsch offers some interesting ideas on this point, proposing that we must look back to what he calls the "functional economic role for religious belief" in order to re-establish this fusion in practice, if not in principle (1976:138). He suggests that even Adam Smith, considered the father of modern capitalism and free markets, recognized the role of religion in acting as a restraint on the unfettered desires and self-interests of individuals. On this, Hirsch cites A.W. Coats, an economic historian who has written on Smith:

> [Men and women] could be safely trusted to pursue their own self-interest without undue harm to the community not only because of the restrictions imposed by the law, but also *because they were subject to built-in*

> *restraint derived from morals, religion, custom, and education* (Coats 1971:9, cited in Hirsch 1976:137; my emphasis).

Others have expressed this point somewhat differently. Mark Sagoff, for instance, speaks of the distinction, derived from Madison and the Federalists, as well as Rousseau, between *private* and *public* interests, where the latter have to do with the well-being of the *community* rather than the self (1988:10–11).

Thus, Hirsch proposes altruistic and socially-conscious behavior as a means of generating socially-responsible activities in the market, arguing that: "[R]estraints on individual behavior imposed in the collective interest can be enforced most effectively *when the sense of obligation is internalized* (1976:139; my emphasis). The problem with getting such an approach to work is that:

> [L]iberal market society has become accustomed to a different emphasis. Internalizing ad hoc *incentives* for people with privately oriented norms so that they direct their self-regarding actions in a socially desirable way is easier and more practicable than attempting to internalize social norms of behavior. In this approach, taxes, subsidies, and legal restrictions are imposed to supply the necessary incentives. The carrot and the fine get a more reliable response than the sermon (1976:140).

Hirsch argues that a different approach is possible: it is sufficient for people to behave *as if they were altruistic* in order to achieve the desired behavior. What is required is "[A] change in human convention or instinct or attitude of the same order as the shifts in social conventions or moral standards that have gone along with major changes in economic conditions in the past" (1976:146). Hirsch is looking at market societies as a whole; the argument formulated here is oriented toward spatially-limited portions of those societies. By vesting places with new meanings, and embedding new relationships between human beings and Nature in those meanings, one is, in effect, altering the ideational basis of society and setting the stage for deliberate changes in patterns of exploitation of the material base.

These new patterns may or may not be more sustainable than old ones, of course. Consider, for example, the transformation of the Monterey Bay along the California coast from one dominated by fisheries to one highly dependent on ecotourism, on the one hand, and as a site for the "production" of marine science and biodiversity, on the other. The indigenous Monterey Bay fisheries were mostly exhausted decades ago (McEvoy 1986); what remain are rockfish—some of which are now beginning to disappear—and anadramous fish that migrate into the bay seasonally from more-northerly coastal regions (MacCall 1995). The designation of the bay and adjacent areas as a federal marine sanctuary—ultimately with the intent of managing future extractive production—turns it into a recreational and scientific "resource" as well as an ecological one. But ecotourism is dependent upon outsiders, and the attempt to attract ever larger numbers of such visitors could well become, in the long-term, as unsustainable as the sardine fishery once was (Martin 1995c). As an ecological resource, the sanctuary is not only a site for scientific research but also an extension of the communities around it and, in this way, an expression of a Nature-society linkage. The first, ecotourist meaning remains rooted in the standard consumptive practices of late-twentiethth century capitalism; the second, ecological frame is, I would argue, more productive of a specific place and meaning.[17] Whether these two new "meanings" are compatible remains to be seen.

Constructing meanings for places as the basis for the social reconstruction of resource regimes creates vested "communities of place" among those who participate in this exercise, as I have suggested above. Such meanings help to transform a locale or resource from one fragmented into multiple private and public tracts to one "held in trust" by a newly-sensitized community. Within this new structure of meaning, the community acquires and expresses a stake in the place and, to some degree, becomes dependent on the protection and maintenance of place. Community and place become mutually constitutive, rather than locked in a relationship of extractive exploitation and heedless degradation. In this process, a subtle transformation of property rights has taken place, even though formal ownership may not have changed at all. A form of common–pool property resource has been created, in which the community as a whole is granted a say in how that place is to be used.[18] It is important to note, once again, that this transformation of meaning is neither a conflict-free process nor a process that ends conflict within a community. Changes in meanings do not automatically lead to immediate changes in the ownership or utilization of property. The process of renegotiation is—indeed, it must be—an ongoing one (Mitchell 1993:112–13).

More to the point, struggles over meanings are also struggles about power. In "stabilized" political economies, roles are defined in terms of power and legitimated through the hegemony of those who hold power: A logging community is, to a large degree, a static product of the capitalist commodification of trees. But that community does not exist in a vacuum; as we see with the arrival of the "counter-culture" in northern California, the cultural currents of the larger social context periodically cascade through, leaving a layer of cultural "silt" that fertilizes—for better or worse—what is already there. Inasmuch as the process of negotiation and renegotiation is ongoing and dynamic, meanings are never completely fixed, and it is this fluidity that, in the final analysis, makes management so difficult. Management, in this context, can be seen as an effort to *fix* points of reference, so that causality can be established and instructions issued to direct restabilization. But stability is a dream of power rather than a reflection of everyday life.

Place, Space, and Environmental Sustainability

What are the implications of "place" for the possibilities of "managing Planet Earth?" What does this process of the renegotiation of meaning, with its material consequences, look like in practice? And what does this mean for environmental sustainability as a concept or a practice? I have argued throughout this book that the complexities of the human-Nature relationship make the prospects of international environmental management difficult to imagine, much less put into practice. In chapter 2, I pointed out that environmental degradation was, in many instances, a product of long chains of economic and social activities, running through global "space," whose beginnings and endings were by no means clearly delineable. I also argued there that the commodities we often consume are directly implicated in many of the problems often blamed on nameless and numberless individuals "elsewhere." If we take these chains seriously, it becomes clear that we, too, are implicated in that degradation.

To take this point further, these are, in other words, the chains of free trade and comparative advantage—in both senses of the word—at work. The meaning conjured up by something as simple as a banana has nothing to do with the actual political and social conditions of its production—just as the consumption of beauty in California is often a consequence of wealth generated elsewhere. My point is, rather, that by associating it with such ideals as health and an imaginary jungle environment, the meaning of a banana is produced as part of the effort to encourage its consumption.[19] In idealizing it, we diminish, if not banish, the local consequences of banana plantations at the site of production. So long as such meanings are detached from place—and from these very real conditions of power and powerlessness—the illusion of global management will remain an attractive one. After all, if it is possible for "markets" to bring commodities ten thousand miles with nary a (visible) hitch, it should be similarly possible to send back the signals that will alter those behaviors thought to be degrading the global environment. There is, however, a hitch: The elimination or internalization of a cause of environmental damage at one point in the chain is quite likely to create new forms of damage elsewhere in the chain.

The environmental (and social) impacts of these long chains are obviously manifested in very specific locations and affect specific groups of people. They happen in *places,* in other words. A river might be polluted by a factory whose products—already in the midst of a long chain of production—are consumed on the other side of the world. The pollution, however, is experienced locally, in terms of human health and welfare and in the destruction of Nature. As a resource, water can be cleaned up or trucked in or obtained from deep wells. In terms of meanings, it is the river as something that, on the one hand, is specific to a place and, on the other, links places together. (Perhaps this is why creek and river restoration have become such widespread activities in many places around the world.) Whether the river is really critical in utilitarian terms is not important. It is the socially-constructed meaning of the river that is important to a specific group of people, and it is this meaning that provides the impetus to action.

Exploring the meanings of Nature provides the opportunity to better understand one's location in those long chains of economy; indeed, it can illuminate political economy in a way that abstract concerns about deforestation and habitat destruction in Amazonia never can. Once a community has come to understand that, for example, the closure of a lumber mill is a direct consequence not of a shortage of logs or a surplus of environmentalists, but of automation and foreign demand for whole logs—processes that augment capital accumulation elsewhere—the expendable role of the community in that chain becomes clear. By looking at alternative roles for Nature—in this example, forests as a means of buttressing community integrity—new forms of political economy can emerge, in which place acquires central importance. None of this means that "free trade" is blocked or that autarky is implied; rather, it provides new power to those at various points of what is now a more visible chain of linkages.

What does this all look like in practice? The Mattole River watershed organizations provide a useful example. To repeat the story told earlier, the objective of these groups has been the restoration of the salmon fishery, not only because it has utilitarian value, in terms of sport fishing and trawling at the river's mouth, but also because it is a symbol of significant meaning on which most of the valley's inhabitants seem to agree. Even if they do not hold actual title, the fishery has become a shared "property" of the watershed's residents, in which everyone has a stake, and which comes to define, in part, the identity of the place and those who live there. Restoration of the fishery implies not only restoration of various parts of the river but also self-enforced monitoring of activities that might affect the fishery, such as logging, ranching, and road-building. This monitoring and control arises not out of a precise assessment of costs and benefits—although such assessments are clearly not unimportant to the decision of an individual party to participate in the project—but out of the expectation of future interactions among participants on a host of other issues. Success is not, of course guaranteed, but it is more likely than it would be under an externally-mandated regime imposed by state agencies.

The state of California has tried to replicate—or bypass—the Mattole watershed project through "Coordinated Resource Management Planning" (CRIMP) and its Biodiversity project. There are something like sixty CRIMPS in place, and the Biodiversity project is continuing, with varying rates of success and conditions of autonomy, in different communities. Most of the CRIMPS deal with watershed maintenance and restoration, although a few involve management of rangelands and forests. Stakeholders generally include state and federal agencies with land holdings, local landowners, Indian tribes, rural conservation districts and, sometimes, environmental organizations and sport fishing or hunting associations. By and large, however, these projects are not the result of an extended process of negotiation among stakeholders, although they must be approved by all stakeholders in order to be implemented. Inasmuch as these are models for the type of "ecosystem management" championed by the Clinton administration, and several have been in place for more than a decade, their long-term progress will provide useful experience and data.[20]

Nevertheless, the CRIMP process suffers from several serious shortcomings. First, the CRIMP option is offered as an alternative to active intervention in ecosystems by authorized agencies: a landowner is, in essence, threatened with onerous regulation if he or she does not agree to the process.[21] Second, there is no attempt in this process to work out the "structural" position of a particular ecosystem within the larger economy and to determine what adjustments in that relationship might be necessary to ensure success. Ranchers, retirees and other stakeholders, however isolated they imagine themselves to be, are nonetheless participants in the larger economic system. At the same time, they constitute among themselves a unique "community" and are part, as well, of an ecological "community," neither of which seems to be incorporated into the process. Finally, the establishment of a CRIMP has little or nothing to do with Nature's meanings: it is a strictly utilitarian effort driven by agency imperatives and the desire to discover paths of least resistance to regulation. This is not, in short, a cultural project.

Why, in the final analysis, do these shortcomings matter? Or, to paraphrase Fred Hirsch, if people act as if they are sustaining an ecological community, why does it matter what their motives might be? I think it does. To return to the issues of identity and place discussed in the first part of this chapter, the importance of place is that it is a critical constitutive element of identity. As John Agnew—a cultural geographer—summarizes the literature:

> [P]lace is more than an 'object'. Concrete everyday practices give rise to a cultural mediation or 'structure of feeling' . . . or 'felt sense of the quality of life at a particular place and time'. This sense of place reinforces the social-spatial definition of place from *inside*, so to speak. The identification with place that *can* follow contributes yet another aspect to the meaning of place: only place or 'territory' in its differentiation from other places can become an 'object' of identity for a 'subject' (1993:263; emphasis in original).

By the same token, it seems to me, a degraded place is reflected in the injured or absent identities that one finds in environmentally-damaged parts of the world, both urban and rural.[22]

The sense of political powerlessness that people often feel in such settings arises not from the lack of power, per se, but because, as Agnew puts it, "They are *located* according to the demands of a spatially extensive division of labour, the global system of material production and distribution, and variable patterns of political authority and control" (1993:262). Structure—the historical structures of Braudel, Giddens, Cox and others—helps to put people in their place, but this does not mean that they are left without choices. John Walton argues this point as follows:

> The constitution of local society...is far more than an imposition or small-scale reflection of the national state. On the contrary, it is the evolving product of multiple influences—the people, the economy, natural resource, intermediate levels of state authority, local accommodation to some broader designs, determined resistance to others and, perhaps above all, *collective action founded on cultural meaning*. Action takes place within social structures that forcibly shape experience, yet people live in local societies where particular customs, exigencies, and choices mediate structural constraints. On the ground people construct their lives in consciously meaningful ways that cannot be read from state-centered directives any more than they can be deduced from modes of economic production (1992:287).

What this suggests is that place and identity, as sources of and motivators to collective action, are mutually constituted and created. The viability and sustainability of each comes to depend on the other. Together, they *are* what we call "Nature."

Sustaining the earth, sustaining ourselves

This "thing" that we call the "global environment" is, in many ways, a mosaic rather than a seamless picture. The mosaic adds up to a whole, but the whole is not dependent on every single piece of the mosaic being in place. The overall picture, so to speak, continues to remain apparent even when some of the pieces are missing (so the appropriate metaphor is, perhaps, "hologram" rather than mosaic). In saying this, I do not mean to suggest that some pieces of the whole are thoughtlessly expendable; rather, it is an acknowledgement that not all of the pieces of the whole can necessarily be saved or sustained. More than this, it is a recognition that there is no one place from which the pieces can be sustained: the responsibility lies, instead, with those who are able to find their "place" in each individual piece, and turn it into Nature.

Given this metaphor—for that is what it is, of course—the role of global civil society in environmental sustainability starts to become clearer. What is needed for global environmental sustainability is, on the one hand, a common project with, on the other, a recognition that the efforts in each piece of the mosaic must be sensitive to Nature (and society) in each piece of the mosaic. Governments are important, but most of them are not in a position to see these manifold projects through. Even county and municipal governments, as local as they are, are not in a position to manage environmental restoration. The responsibility, ultimately, will have to rest on social institutions, such as common-pool property resource systems or bioregions or restoration projects, developed and run by groups of stakeholders based in the "civil societies" of these many places. As the empirical chapters in this book illustrate, moreover, while these groups are in specific places, they are not isolated from one another. The networks of knowledge and practice are extensive and dense. To the extent, therefore, that this local civil society emerges in many different parts of the world, and makes material contact with its counterparts in other places in the world, it comes to represent a "global" civil society with a concern for both local and global environment. The apparent paradox—a global civil society rooted in a highly particularistic Nature and place—is not as paradoxical as it might seem at first glance. This last point is explored in the final chapter.

CHAPTER 8

Closing the Circle: Global Civil Society and Global Environmental Governance

Even though there is desperate need for worldwide change, limited by the knowledge my place makes possible, I hesitate to legislate the law of other places.... To act in the world and make it better you have to be someone, be somewhere, tied to institutions, related to people. And be limited by that body, place, and time. You have to have a place, a home

(Sikorski 1993:28)

What are the implications of the (re)construction of place and meanings for addressing the multiple aspects of environmental "change" that face us, both locally and globally? In chapter 2, I argued that "management" of the global environment presupposes a degree of control over human behavior, both individual and collective, that is quite unrealistic, if not politically improbable. I also suggested that the "local," however we might define the concept, can be a place of resistance to the efforts of resource managers and agencies to control what goes on there. Whether this resistance is, a priori, "good" or "bad" for Nature is not self-evident: under some circumstances, the calculus of high discount rates makes more sense than that of careful stewardship. But, by the same token, such a calculus of rapid exploitation seems likely to undermine and doom both the material and the ideational basis of a community embedded in a particular place. Both the global and the local can consume the seed corn; the trick is to find ways of not having to eat it.

By now, there is little need to reiterate the self-evident about this point: one avoids consuming the seed corn by, somehow, ensuring that production is sufficient to maintain reproduction, as it were. But reproduction at what level? At what level of affluence and poverty, of fenced-off wilderness and fenced-in cities? Few in the developed world propose a return to the subsistence levels of even a century or two ago, limited to what a household could produce from the land, even though for many in the developing world such affluence might far exceed that to which they now have access. Most who think about the seed corn question focus on increasing production: higher productivity, more inputs, greater capital-intensiveness. Thus, *Our Common Future*, the 1987 product of the hearings and deliberations of the Brundtland Commission (the World Commission on Environment and Development), envisions a five to tenfold increase in the size of the world's economic output over the course of the coming half-century. This, the commission avers, is absolutely necessary to eliminate "poverty," the fundamental cause of environmental damage (1987: ch.2).

Whether such growth is possible, let alone environmentally-acceptable, is not very obvious. Even imagining such a path depends on heroic assumptions about the accumulation of capital in both North and South, its investment in environmentally-protective ways, and the consuming proclivities of a global middle class that, while growing in absolute terms, already comprises a shrinking fraction of the world's population. In a world awash in surplus capacity of various sorts, both material and intellectual, demand-driven growth—especially of the environmentally-friendly sort—seems a faint hope on which to base a strategy for sustainable development. And governments, under pressure to reduce budgetary expenditures and deficits in order to provide more attractive conditions for capital, are unlikely, or unable, to provide the domestic funds required to reinforce the domestic political and economic stability that is also necessary to attract capital.[1] The mostly likely scenario for the future is, therefore, more business-as-usual: more people born into poverty, more inequitable consumption, more environmental degradation.

Lest this seem a too pessimistic way to end a hopeful book, such a future is not predetermined. But alternatives cannot grow out of indiscriminately-increasing production, in the hope that, as individual countries reach the $5,000 per capita GDP income level—equivalent, it should be noted, to an aggregate global GDP approaching $100 trillion when all countries are included—the necessary demands for and commitments to environmental protection and restoration will be made.[2] This overlooks the damage that will already have been done by that time and probably overestimates the ability of technology to compensate for or ameliorate that damage. What, then, are the alternatives? In this book, I have tried to sketch out some of them, drawing on the experiences and practices of people and groups "in the field" and in their communities. Conventionally, we categorize these actors under the rubric "environmental movement" or "environmental NGOs," all the while knowing that this does not begin to cover the broad range of purposes and practices in which these actors engage. I have used the term "global civil society" in preference, even though this, too, may be something of a misnomer.

Whereas "movement" has generally been used to connote protest against existing institutions—something in which environmentalists are certainly engaged—it does not encompass notions of *governance*, which I have addressed throughout this book. And it is governance that is critical to our future: Who rules? Whose rules? What rules? What kind of rules? At what level? In what form? Who decides? On what basis? *Who will make decisions regarding environmental conservation, protection and restoration, and on whose behalf?*

For the moment, capital seems to be in charge and, although there is an expectation that capital will find it in its best interests to shift its practices in a more "environmentally-friendly" direction, capital is unlikely to get into the business of governance, except indirectly (Smith 1994). To be sure, national governments and international regimes will not be irrelevant to this process, either, but the most they can hope to do is impose some regulatory constraints on the producers of environmental externalities, or legislate some incentives to encourage these producers to internalize those impacts. What governments and regimes cannot do—and will not do—is to challenge the constitutive basis of the present-day global system by asking: Who are we? Why are we here? And how can we decide what we want?

This final chapter looks more closely at this question of governance, inasmuch as I believe it is central to our future, and not only in environmental terms. I begin with a discussion of a much-noted phenomenon: economic integration accompanied by political fragmentation, and its political and social implications. If, indeed, there is a causal, or even dialectical, relation between the two, governance becomes a quite different proposition than "global management."[3] Next, I consider what global civil society can and cannot do where Nature and environment are concerned: it cannot change the big structures or systems that drive much of the environmental destruction and degradation of which we are so aware—at least, not in the short term. At the same time, however, individuals working together can act, which means that alternatives are not foreclosed.

I then return to the central question raised in chapter 2: *Where* must people act, and under what conditions, in order to begin a process of changing practices that affect the environment on a larger scale? Here I consider the ways in which the menu of possibilities in any given place is constrained by those big structures, but not fully determined by them. To paraphrase others: Women and men can make history, so long as they are aware of the conditions established by those who have come before. Finally, I conclude with a discussion of governance and the problem of, as Donald

Chisholm has put it, "coordination without hierarchy" (1989). Governance is about the creation of institutions where they do not already exist or their transformation where they do, and institutions are about rules and rule, as Nicholas Onuf might argue (1989).

My hunch is that the practices of global civil society are more about the creation or transformation of systems of rule and rules than about the reform, per se, of big institutions and structures. If this is so, the policy implications are rather different from what scholars of international relations and regimes have been telling us for some time: that transborder environmental problems borders can only be solved by states. Does this presage the spread of small-scale, potentially democratic *poli*? I am skeptical. Does it suggest a diffusion of power, authority and legitimacy beyond what we have already seen in many parts of the world? Probably. Does order or chaos follow? Good question.

W(h)ither the Global Polity: Growing Together or Coming Apart?

Back in 1990—in what now seems like ancient times—the Public Broadcasting System televised a mini-series entitled *After the Warming*. With James Burke as writer/commentator/guide, the program provided graphic illustrations of an imagined 2050, looking back upon a chaotic past disrupted by global warming. The impacts were, of course, widespread and horrific: how else to illustrate the premise of the show? But the proffered solution was somewhat hubristic: a "Planetary Management Authority" run, "of course" (as Burke put it), by Japan. The PMA—housed in a futuristic building that, even today, looks woefully modern and anachronistic—would be a "large technical system"—people are nowhere mentioned—consisting of a formidable system of computers and sensing devices. Utilizing a complex climatic model, the system could assess the impacts on global climate of human activities all over the planet. As necessary, the PMA would then issue appropriate directives to mitigate or ameliorate the climatic consequences: a global panopticon, in other words (but in a prison in which the inmates would be free to run riot). Not a world state, but a world manager, with complete authority and power (and, perhaps, black helicopters?)

Such a centralized management system is quite improbable. It flies in the face not only of logic but also a contemporary global politics that is characterized as much by fragmentation within existing polities as by global economic integration among them (Gill 1994; Sakamoto 1994). Indeed, it is probable that these two processes—integration and fragmentation—are intimately related to each other (Robertson 1992: ch.6), a point to which I will return. If this is so, it suggests that the "global management" problem will be even more difficult than has been so far imagined, inasmuch as the number of sovereign or "semi-sovereign" entities participating in world politics could well increase over the coming decades from the fewer than two hundred we now have to many more. That is not the only complication: many of these entities may not even exercise effective political control over their own juridical territories, much as is presently the case in various "failed" states around the world consumed by various types of wars.[4]

Why are integration and fragmentation linked? Global economic integration is a condition whose origins are to be found in the mid-nineteenth century, with the Industrial Revolution, the rise of English liberalism and the institutionalization of free trade as propogated by the Manchester School (Crook, Pakulski & Waters 1992). With fits, starts, and retreats, such integration has reached into more and more places in the world, creating myriad webs of material linkages. The fact that such integration has become so widespread does not, of course, mean that all places in the world share in the resulting benefits. It is uneven development that makes capitalism so dynamic and the constant search for new combinations of factors that drives innovation; the fact that there are multiple economic "systems" present in any one location simply adds to the dynamism of the process.[5] Today's comparative advantage may, consequently, be tomorrow's competitive drag.[6]

The political implications of such a process have not been given serious thought. Comparative advantage is no longer a feature of states as a whole—which it has never really been, in any event—but of regions and locales, where the combination of material, technological and intellectual is, perhaps only momentarily, fortuitous (Noponen, Graham & Markusen 1993; also Jacobs 1984). The specific advantages of a place such as Silicon Valley—in many ways, a historical accident as much as the result of deliberate policy[7]—have only limited spillover in terms of the country as a whole. These conditions, moreover, seem not to be easily reproduced in the short term.[8] The competition among places to attract investment and jobs thus becomes more of a zero-sum game than a positive sum one, and this point is not lost, for example, on U.S. states and cities who have established foreign trade offices and regularly send trade missions abroad, as well (Shuman 1992, 1994).

Capital has its choice of locations in which to invest; by contrast, cities, communities, places—and to a certain degree, labor—have a limited set of tactics through which they can attract capital. As a January 1995 article in the *San Francisco Examiner* describing the activities of a consulting firm providing city and regional marketing programs for economic development put it, they resemble those

> of an international arms dealer—selling weapons to one ruler and then making a pitch to the neighboring potentate based on the new threat. Part of the pitch for these [economic development] programs is that a region needs its own program to survive against the rival programs of other areas (Trager 1995).

Such competition can become the cause of considerable political antagonism, against both the neighbors who win and the authorities who have contributed to these conditions of competitive struggle in the first place.[9]

How such antagonisms play themselves out is contextual and contingent, of course, and often depends on pre-existing social, political, and even geographic "fault lines" that fracture under the pressures of real, potential, or imagined competition. In some places, these fault lines were intended to be administrative, but were drawn up in ethnic or national terms; in other places, the fault lines are linguistic, religious, clan-based, "tribal," or even vaguely cultural (Derlugian 1995). It goes without saying that those places in which people have fallen to killing each other have nothing to offer global capital—they have, quite literally, fallen out of "history"—but those places able to break away from the political grip of larger polities, as Slovenia escaped the competitive drag of Serbia, will be well-placed to participate in the global economy. Inevitably, this process of political fracturing and fragmentation will lead to a much more complex global system, which our modern concepts of state and power will hardly begin to describe.[10]

Some have suggested that we confront a "new medievalism"; others have proposed as organizing principles "heteronomy" or "heterarchy."[11] Ole Wæver writes, for instance, that

> For some four centuries, political space was organized through the principle of territorially defined units with exclusive rights inside, and a special kind of relations on the outside: International relations, foreign policy, without any superior authority. There is no longer one level that is clearly *the* most important to refer to but, rather, a set of overlapping authorities (1995: n. 61).

What is important here is the concept of "authority," rather than "government" or "power." As John Ruggie points out, in a political system—even a relatively unsocialized one—*who* has "the right to act as a power" (or authority) is at least as important as the *capability* of actors to force others to do their bidding (1989:28). In the emerging "heteronomy," authority will be fragmented among many centers, often on the basis of specific issues.

In a way, this is a form of functionalism (really, functional differentiation), inasmuch as different authorities will deal with different problems. Older theories of functionalism envisioned political integration as the outcome of international functional coordination. Thus, for example, there was an expectation that the emergence of international agencies, dedicated to specific issue-linked tasks, would bring states together in non-political fora, thereby dampening and eliminating historical antagonisms. These agencies would, in turn, form the basis of a worldwide bureaucracy that would evolve into world government (Haas 1964; Mitrany 1966). This has not happened, although it may yet, inasmuch as the entire process might take many decades, rather than the few originally envisioned. The type of functionalism I propose here, however, is something quite different, because it does not suppose political integration as a likely outcome; rather, it is instrumental and limited.

In the present instance, functionalism is a consequence of rapid *innovation*, of the generation of new scientific-technical and social knowledge(s) required to address different types of issues and problems.[12] Inasmuch as there is too much knowledge for any one actor, whether individual or organization, to assimilate, it becomes necessary to establish knowledge-based alliances and coalitions, whose logic is only partly-based on space. In other words, "local" knowledge is spatially-limited, while "organizational" knowledge is spaceless. When combined, the two become instrumental to technical and social innovation.[13]

Access to these new knowledges also leads to new forms and venues of authority, in that only those with access can act successfully and authoritatively, and thereby acquire legitimacy. In some sense, the "management" function finds itself located at that level of social organization at which the appropriate combination of "local" and "global" knowledges come together; these levels are most likely to be local and regional. Or, as Richard Gordon put it,

> Regions and networks . . . constitute interdependent poles within the new spatial mosaic of global innovation. Globalization in this context involves not the leavening impact of universal processes but, on the contrary, the calculated synthesis of cultural diversity in the form of differentiated regional innovation logics and capabilities. . . . The effectiveness of local resources and the ability to achieve genuine forms of cooperation with global networks must be developed from within the region itself . . . (1995:196, 199).

Such functionalist regionalization points back toward the political fragmentation discussed above: lines must be drawn somewhere, whether by reference to Nature, power, culture, innovation or some other logic. From the perspective of political organization, these lines may be as "fictional" as those which currently separate one country from its neighbor. Still, they are unlikely to be "illogical," inasmuch as they will probably map in some fashion onto already-existing patterns of social and economic activity. Obviously, such a vision of the future reiterates those questions raised above: "who rules," "whose rules" and "which rules?" I will return to this point below.

The Agency-Structure Question Redux

Where, in all of this emerging structure, is there a space for agency, for organized political action? At its core, the agent-structure debate is more than just an obscure discussion among academics (Wendt 1987; Dessler 1989). It is really about the possibilities of political action in a world where, to repeat what John Agnew has written, "[People] are *located* according to the demands of a spatially extensive division of labour, the global system of material production and distribution, and variable patterns of political authority and control [and, one might add, nature]" (1993:262). This is not to say that people's lives are determined by these patterns; only that their choices must be made within the constraints imposed by those patterns.

The image of the (usually) Great Man making history or, at least, making change, remains a potent one, yet it is the rare Great Man or Woman who is actually in a position to do so (short of pushing the button that would destroy both humanity *and* Nature). It is only in times of real, verifiable crisis that large-scale opportunities to engineer real ideational and material change make themselves felt. Even then, it is the courageous and, perhaps, foolhardy individual who is willing to exercise such opportunities. As Mikhail Gorbachev discovered, the best of intentions, sometimes, "cannot hold" the center together. And, sometimes, the "stickiness" of structures and the institutions that accompany these patterns defy all efforts to change them as illustrated by current conditions in Russia (Rosenau 1986).

What and where, then, are the possibilities for action, if they are not to be found at the macrolevel? I argued in chapter 7 that historical structures help to put people in their place, but this does not mean that they are then left without choices. To reiterate what John Walton says about this point (quoted in full in chapter 7), "Action takes place within social structures that forcibly shape experience, yet people live in local societies where particular customs, exigencies, and choices mediate structural constraints" (1992:287–88). Beyond this, I would argue, there are historical junctures at which the "menu of choices" expands, so to speak, offering alternative paths that might not, at other times, be available.[14] Agency is, thus, a matter of becoming aware of alternatives and helping to foster conditions under which meaningful choices can be made.

Crises occur, of course, at all different levels and spatial scales. The death throes of a formerly-stable community may hardly be noticed by those outside of it; indeed, a community's complete disappearance may hardly cause a ripple in the larger society. To those who are members of that community, however, the ripple is a tidal wave. But, to carry the metaphor a bit farther, such a wave washes away old mental constraints as well as old modes of production: What might have seemed anathema before is now a matter of necessity. Structures still matter, but less than they might have mattered at another time; choices about the future are now possible. As Ruggie puts it,

> Periods of fundamental political transition—of transformation—are characterized by a generalized loss of predictability and control among social actors. The reestablishment of an effective system of rule once again fixes parametric conditions" (1989:28).

Crises of one sort or another, at these scales, are not that uncommon; they are a "deviation" from the structures of everyday life, as Braudel might have put it, had he been asked.

Environmental change often takes the form of such microlevel crises: When the trees or fish give out, when the air or water become unbearably polluted, when toxic wastes bubble up in backyards, the individuals living in a place, a community, are faced with the disruption of their accustomed way of life. To them, such a situation *is* a crisis; they *must* respond. The first—and sometimes the only—impulse is to attack those individuals or institutions held responsible for the crisis; the second impulse is often to organize politically in order to seek redress or rectification; the third is to make sure the crisis does not happen again. Love Canal—whether it was a health hazard or not (Rubin 1994:219; Cable & Cable 1994:75–84)—was notable not because it was a toxic waste dump but, rather, because it became the locus of political agency in the face of big and mostly immovable institutions and structures. Moreover, the lessons learned from Love Canal were transmitted, through a variety of means, to other individuals and communities facing similar circumstances. One local crisis crystallized a whole realm of innovative social and political action, a newly-emergent element of civil society (Szasz 1994). This pattern has been, and is being, repeated in a myriad of places around the world, as a result of people in one place hearing about the actions of people in another, becoming globalized in the process.

Such agency should be distinguished from the form more common to contemporary or modernizing societies, consumer preference, choice or autonomy—often called "green consumerism"—which is not agency at all. Rather, it is a response to particular profit-seeking strategies pursued by capital. After all, the "green" consumer can only choose from what is offered on the supermarket shelf or in the catalogue printed on forty-percent "post-consumer" paper (but not, itself, recyclable). Many choices are, presumably, throttled in labs, boardrooms, and accounting offices before they ever see the market.

Beyond this, if a green product does not offer the desired rate of return, it is likely to be pulled from the shelf by its maker, thereby denying the consumer even that small choice. Choice then simply becomes a range of alternatives offered within a highly-structured set of constraints (the market).[15] Using the market, therefore, to influence or motivate behavior runs the risk of eliciting very different outcomes from those anticipated or hoped for. As was observed in the 1970s, when U.S. consumers chose to purchase more fuel-efficient automobiles as gasoline prices rose, they ended up driving farther than before, since the cost per mile of travel had dropped![16] It is not my intention to dismiss environmentally-driven consumer behavior as irrelevant; only to point out that it is subject to very real constraints imposed by others. And, although environmental protection mediated via markets can improve various types of environmental quality, these do not (and cannot) alter fundamental institutional structures and practices.[17] What, then, can do this?

Making Choices, Taking Action

History does count. Any social situation in which people, both individually and collectively, find themselves is a product of history, as Marx pointed out; to this, we might add, it is both the history of people and the history of places, *made by people*. To understand how one has arrived at a particular time and place, therefore, one has to know what has come before. In the language of economics, the present is a product of path dependency, and one needs to know how and why that path was chosen. This history, in turn, says something about the menu of choices for the future available at any given time.[18] While such statements might seem self-evident, and perhaps even simplistic, they are neither: most of our routine behaviors are the result of habit, of repetition, of unquestioned circumstances, of *institutions and associated practices*. This is the environment within which we make ordinary choices; indeed, it is the realm of the rational actor, with exogenous preferences, so loved by microeconomists (Stone 1988). But there are constraints on choices: not all that might be imagined is necessarily possible (Long 1992b:24–25). As John Thompson has put it

> As constellations of social relations and reservoirs of natural resources, specific institutions form a relatively stable framework for action and

> interaction; they do not determine action but *generate* it in the sense of establishing, loosely and tentatively, the parameters of permissible conduct (1984:135; emphasis in original).

Sometimes, however, social constraints make what is a necessary choice very difficult, if not almost impossible. It is at this point that human agency becomes important, as the individual actor struggles to move away from habit-driven action, which simply reproduces the status quo.

Individual choice and action are not, however, sufficient to effect changes in habit-driven behaviors characteristic of people in particular social and political contexts. As Norman Long points out:

> Effective agency . . . requires organizing capacities; it is not simply the result of possessing certain persuasive powers or forms of charisma. . . . *[A]gency (and power) depend crucially upon the emergence of a network of actors who become partially, though hardly ever completely, enrolled in the "project" of some other person or persons.* . . . It becomes essential, therefore, for social actors to win the struggles that take place over the attribution of specific social meanings to particular events, actions and ideas (1992b:23-24).

These struggles over the "attribution of specific social meanings" are not about science or data or cost-benefit ratios or, indeed, about any of the things that are quantifiable. Rather, they are, as suggested in chapter 7, about ontologies and epistemologies of place, life, and history, within which the methods and findings of science and economics are tools, or means, to an end. Again, not all social meanings are available—the repertoire is limited by history, political economy, and culture—but successful agency is possible when a context can be explained in terms of one or more of the meanings in the repertoire. What is central, therefore, to effective social action is the ability to recognize the relationship between choices and meanings. Indeed, such an ability is central to politics, inasmuch as the articulation of the relationship is essential for successfully "enrolling" people in a "project" (Stone 1988:309; Schurmann 1974:33–39).

It now becomes apparent how and why, at the international level, "projects" are so problematic. Consider the question of climate change, which is ordinarily described in terms of highly uncertain impacts that are difficult to quantify (e.g., a two to three degree centigrade *average* rise in global temperature as a result of a doubling of greenhouse gas levels in the atmosphere). Implicit in these numbers is the notion that everyone will be affected to his or her detriment. Consequently, echoing Dr. Pangloss, the present—the *status quo ante* to the future—is the "best of possible worlds." The intended result, as Deborah Stone points out, is the creation of a "natural community" (1988:135)—residents of the Blue Planet, whether animal, vegetable, or mineral—with a shared interest—*Our Common Future*, as the Brundtland Commission put it. In this case, the interest lies in preventing or minimizing global environmental change, even though the actual result of global environmental change may be quite different from the implied outcome, depending on who you are and where you live. This common interest requires the construction of a shared, albeit artificial, history and culture around the process of both change and response, which allows a group of actors to negotiate a treaty (or "text") on which they can all agree. The treaty, in turn, tells a story with a specific social meaning.

Thus, for example, in the preamble to the Framework Convention on Climate Change, the parties "acknowledge that"

> [T]he global nature of climate change calls for the widest possible cooperation by all countries and their participation in an effective and appropriate international response, in accordance with their common but differentiated responsibilities and respective capabilities and their social and economic conditions . . . (International Negotiating Committee n.d.:2).

As posed in the document, this is a story about a problem and the conditions deemed necessary, by the signatories, to its resolution. What is not told here—or, for that matter, anywhere in the convention itself—are the actual social meanings that the parties and the members of their societies bring to the negotiations. These meanings can be read in the controversies that litter the growing literature and debates on the potential political, economic, and social impacts of climate change.[19] Conversely, the collective social meanings embedded in the convention by the delegates have little or no significance to the members of their societies who must, ultimately, implement the terms of the document.[20] It is questionable, therefore, whether these individuals will "enroll" in this project.

In other words, to be successfully implemented, the Framework Convention on Climate Change must have many different social meanings, each of which is context dependent, but each of which may be "essentially contested" by other parties to the convention. Certainly, reports from the International Negotiating Committee meetings directed to prepare for the first Conference of the Parties in March 1995, and that meeting itself, suggest that numerous different social meanings still stalk the meeting halls.[21] If this is so, then which meaning(s) are accepted as legitimate, and how their legitimacy is established, becomes central to the exercise. International relations realists would simply argue that power is what determines meaning—if they thought meaning had any importance at all (Mearsheimer 1995). A closer look at the climate example suggests otherwise.

To illustrate this point, let us return to the question implied earlier: What is to be measured? If the numbers tell a story, which numbers tell which story? Who decides which numbers are "right?" And who is privileged to tell one story as opposed to another? This is, quite evidently, not just a matter of science or policy. Consider, for example, the problem of methane, which is a much more potent greenhouse gas than carbon dioxide (by a factor of twenty-one; chlorofluorocarbons are almost six thousand times as potent as CO_2; WRI 1992a:207). Methane concentrations in the atmosphere are increasing even more rapidly than carbon dioxide: between 1965 and 1992, CO_2 concentrations grew by eleven percent, while methane concentrations increased by twenty-five percent (WRI 1994:366). Yet, if we look at the major sources of methane emissions—solid waste, coal mining, oil and gas production, wet rice agriculture, and livestock—we find that rice and cattle account for almost sixty percent. Moreover, as we might further expect, the vast majority of methane emissions associated with rice production (ninety-three percent) originates in Asia (WRI 1994:364).

This raises the question of how to rank one type of emissions source against another in terms of social or chemical importance, thereby somehow arriving at a shared valuation or metric of the different uses. But who is to say how wet rice cultivation is to be compared to oil and gas production. Is the metric to be in dollars and cents? In caloric value? In terms of subsistence values to rural communities? In terms of symbolic meanings?[22] My intention here is not to offer a way to parse this particular problem; indeed, I am not sure there *is* any way to quantitatively resolve the inherent conflicts in this all-too-real example. Rather, I mean to emphasize that the resolution of such a question will mostly depend on how the story is told, on whose social meaning is more compelling and able to garner more "votes."[23]

In the midst of struggles over meaning, then, history counts not only in terms of explaining how one has arrived at a particular place, but also how convincing is the story to be told. This, in turn, has much to do with being able to make choices under constrained conditions, inasmuch as the ways in which a story is told will generate different projects and programs. To illustrate this point more clearly, let us consider, for one final time, the case of the Mattole River watershed and the efforts there to re-establish the salmon run. Several different stories could be told about this "bioregion." One has to do with the erosive effects of logging and ranching along the river's watershed, and the resulting obstructions to salmon seeking their spawning grounds (Stevens 1994:B7; Martin 1994b:A1).[24] A second has to do with depletion of the river's salmon population by sport and commercial fishers, who are engaged in what appears to be a Hardinesque "tragedy of the commons" (McEvoy 1986). Yet a third would suggest that the decline of the salmon is a result of a number of complex, interacting factors, and that responsibility cannot be placed on any one activity or group of actors. Each of these stories suggests different projects, with different outcomes. The third, which is most inclusive, is also the most open-ended, inasmuch as it establishes no single blame and suggests a shared effort to address the causes.[25]

This, then, is the basis for the possibilities open to agency and action. What is central is the ability to place historically a given context, to make strategic decisions about how that history is to be told, and to understand how the confluence of structures provides openings for different futures. Of course, no choices are final, although they can and do foreclose other choices, both in the present and in the future. And, as much of this book suggests, such choices may be best made at the most localized level at which they could help to address a spatially-delimited problem and still make practical and political sense. If we accept the notion, presented in chapter 2 and further explicated in chapter 7, that decisions made at the supra-local level cannot be very sensitive to local conditions and might, in fact, engender local resistance that undermines the decision, it becomes clear that, somehow, localized agency is a necessary, albeit not a sufficient, element of environmental governance.[26] The key question, which I address in the following section, is whether it is possible to nurture a governance system that privileges local choice and, at the same time, takes into account the global complexities and connections raised in chapter 2.

Who rules? Whose rules? From global environmental management to global environmental governance

In order to understand the relationship between locally-based civil society (as I have described it in this book) and global governance, something can be learned by examining governance at the local level. In his study of the century-long struggle against Los Angeles by the residents of the Owens Valley in eastern California, for example, John Walton (1992) argues that groups or social movements engaged in resistance to the state can, sometimes, find ways of allying with other parts of the state in the pursuit of certain goals. In the Owens Valley, an emergent environmental movement was able to draw on the expanding authority of the federal state, and its legitimation of various environmental strategies, to pressure the city to alter its patterns of water removal from the Valley. To Walton, this suggests that the concept of the state—and, I would argue, governance—is too limited. The state is not restricted to discrete levels of governance, although many administrative functions and bureaucracies are; it is more than that. As Theda Skocpol points out:

> On the one hand, states may be viewed as organizations through which official collectivities may pursue collective goals, realizing them more or less effectively given available state resources in relation to social settings. On the other hand, states may be viewed more macroscopically as configurations of organizations and action that influence the meanings and methods of politics for all groups and classes in society (1985:20).

In other words, states and (in this instance) civil society interact dialectically, recreating and legitimating each other over and over. The state is engaged in government; civil society, in governance.[27]

What, then, do I mean by the term "governance?" According to James Rosenau

> Governance . . . is a more encompassing phenomenon than government. It embraces governmental institutions, but it also subsumes informal, non-governmental mechanisms whereby those persons and organizations within its purview more ahead, satisfy their needs, and fulfill their wants. . . . Governance is thus a system of rule that is as dependent on intersubjective meanings as on formally sanctioned constitutions and charters. . . . [I]t is possible to conceive of governance without government—of regulatory mechanisms in a sphere of activity which function effectively even though they are not endowed with formal authority (1992:4-5).

Ernst-Otto Czempiel offers a somewhat more straightforward definition of governance as the "capacity to get things done without the legal competence to command that they be done" (1992:250). Most of the contributors to the volume from which these quotes are taken hold the view that the state, and the state-system, are being eroded in a number of ways by the processes of globalization and the emergence of "powerful people" (Rosenau 1990). Their focus is, therefore, on the emergence of various transnational processes that have erosive effects on the power and authority of states (mostly powerful ones).

This particular focus overlooks, I suggest, the growth of institutions of governance at *all* levels of analysis, with concomitant implications for state and system.[28] Indeed, even though we recognize that there is no *world government,* as such, there is *global governance.* Subsumed within this system of governance are both institutionalized regulatory arrangements—some of which we call "regimes"—and less formalized norms, rules, and procedures that pattern behavior without the presence of written constitutions or material power.[29] This is not the state, as we commonly understand the term, but it is *state-like*, in Skocpol's second sense. Indeed, we can see emerging patterns of behavior in global politics very much like those described by Walton in the case of the Owens Valley: alliances between coalitions in global civil society and the international governance arrangements associated with the UN system (Wilmer 1993; Wapner 1996).

To further illuminate this argument, let us return, for a moment, to what scholars of international environmental policy and politics regard as the *sine qua non* of their research: the fact, as it is often put, that environmental degradation respects no borders. This feature automatically thrusts many environmental problems into the international realm where, we are reminded, there is no government and no way to regulate the activities of sovereign states. From this follows the need for international cooperation to internalize transboundary effects, a need that leads logically to the creation of international environmental regimes. Such regimes, it is often noted, are the creation of states, and scholars continue to argue about the conditions necessary for their establishment and maintenance (Litfin 1993). Whether they undermine the sovereignty of states or are, in themselves, a form of state-building is, as yet unclear (Deudney 1993:286–89; Thompson 1992); what is less well-recognized or acknowledged is that some regimes are merely the "tip of the iceberg," so to speak, or they will be, if they reach fruition. Much of the implementation and regulation inherent in regimes, such as the emerging one addressing climate change, will take place at the regional and local levels, in the places where people live, not where their laws are made. If this climate regime is successful—whatever "success" means in such a context (Young 1994b; Sand 1994)—it will, for all practical purposes, function as a global institution of governance with elements at the local, regional, provincial, national, and international levels. It will, in effect, transfer some of the jurisdictional responsibilities now in the hands of the "state" both upwards and downwards to other entities, enhancing political authority at the global as well as the local levels.

But the politics of this, and other, similar regimes, will make domestic politics simple, by comparison. Rather than two- or even three-level games,[30] what we see are "n" level games, in which intermediate levels are squeezed or strong-armed by those above and below. This is commonly discussed in terms of coalitional strategies between grassroots social movement organizations and international institutions but, in fact, these coalitions are much more complex. They often link multiple levels as well as multi-level actors, and shift and change, as a situation demands. Thus, for example, the campaign to "save the Amazon rainforest" includes indigenous groups, rubber tappers and, in some instances, *garimpieros*, regional research organizations, social movements in Brazilian cities, international environmental organizations based in the United States and Europe, industrialized country governments, and international organizations. Arrayed in opposition are the Brazilian government and military, organizations of ranchers and landowners, Brazilian state governments, other industrialized country governments and, in all likelihood, national and international corporate actors (Hecht & Cockburn 1990; Schmink & Wood 1992; Oliveira Filho 1988; Cleary 1993; Hecht 1993). Each of these actors has, in one way or another, staked out or acquired a certain amount of "governance authority" within a poorly-specified political, economic and/or social realm. Each of these actors, at one time or another, finds it useful to ally with others, at other levels, so as to put pressure on yet other actors, at still other levels. The result might look more like a battlefield than a negotiation—and, indeed, violence is an all-too-real component of this particular campaign—but, while there is no definitive ruler, the process is not entirely without rules.[31]

And what is this process ultimately about? It involves negotiating over the terms of the story that will prove most compelling as a "project"—and whether that story is a local, regional, national, or global one. Of course, such stories are never finalized; to reiterate Charles Lipson's remark (see chapter 2) in a different context, the outcomes of social negotiations "do not have fixed meanings or decontextualized significance. Rather, they are continually reproduced and redefined in the dispute process as the actors use or resist existing standards" (1985:2). Or, according to Marianne Schmink and Charles Wood,

> Ideological positions (and repositioning) such as these are not mere reflections of material interests. Nor are they static features of people's consciousness. To the contrary, we treat ideologies as part of the arsenal of weapons the contestants actively forge and mobilize in the contest over boundaries and the content of accepted discourse. In the process, they alter the definitions of themselves and their understanding of the world around them. Social action therefore has a *constitutive* property. By this we mean that the preferences, interests, and ideas that define individuals—and that become the basis for collective action—are formed or constituted in the process of actions that engage participants in a dispute. From this perspective, people act not merely to meet preexisting ends but also to constitute themselves as persons and groups with particular and desired attributes. Because the interests that characterize different social groups are as much formed as they are revealed in the contests in which people are engaged, they are mutable and subject to continual redefinition (1992:17–18).

What should we call such a process? Clearly, it is governance but not government (although it does contain elements of government). At the same time, it does not mark the end or disintegration of the state as an institutionalized form of politics (although it might, of course, mark the end of *particular* states).[32] And, while it does suggest the proliferation of all kinds of local political institutions, of varying power and authority, it does not mean that, inevitably, the world faces the "coming anarchy," as Robert Kaplan has put it (1994). Governance is and will continue to be uneven, there will be both rule and rules, there will be "tame zones" and "wild zones," places where life is orderly and places where life is not ordered (that is, disorderly or not ordered by external power). In some of the latter instances, environmental governance will hardly be a priority; in the former, it will likely be important, if not central.[33] One role of "global civil society" in such situations is, therefore, the creation and legitimation of the institutions and practices of global and local environmental governance.

The function of global civil society in global environmental governance is best understood in comparison with that of civil society within states, especially democratic ones.[34] As I pointed out earlier, within many states, civil society and state are mutually constitutive. Each is necessary for the functioning of the other, and each serves to legitimate the other. At times, moreover, civil society fulfills a regulatory function in place of the state, as is the case with, for example, the medical and legal professional associations found within the United States as well as other countries (Meister 1994). These associations not only provide credentials to practitioners, through certification of practitioner's knowledge, they also provide a set of rules and norms that a practitioner must adhere to, at the risk of losing her or his license to practice.[35] While these rules and norms have a moral quality to them—as, for example, in the Hippocratic Oath—there is clearly the element of self-interest about them, too.

But this is true of most, if not all, of the associations of civil society. Not everyone observes *all* of the norms and rules to which they have subscribed *all* of the time, but the adherence rate is generally pretty good.[36] More to the point, the members of these associations internalize these rules and norms and follow them, whether the element of self-interest is evident or not (which returns us to the argument made by Fred Hirsch, discussed in chapter 7). Rules, in other words, take the place of explicit rule; governance replaces government; informal networks of coordination replace formal structures of command.

Such a system need not necessarily be a second-best one, either. There is reason to think that a governance system composed of collective actors at multiple levels, with overlapping authority, linked through various kinds of networks, might be as functionally-efficient as a highly-centralized one.[37] Such a decentralized system of governance has a number of advantages over a real or imagined hierarchical counterpart. As Donald Chisholm points out

> [F]ormal systems often create a gap between the formal authority to make decisions and the capacity to make them, owing to a failure to recognize the necessity for a great deal of technical information for effective coordination. Ad hoc coordinating committees staffed by personnel with the requisite professional skills appear far more effective than permanent central coordinating committees run by professional coordinators (1989:11).

He goes on to argue that a formal system works so long as appropriate information, necessary to the system's function and achievement of its goals, is available. The problem is that

> Strict reliance on formal channels compounds the problem [of trying to prevent public awareness of bureaucratic failure]: reliable information will not be supplied, and the failure will not be uncovered until it is too late to compensate for it. Informal channels, by their typically clandestine nature and foundation on *reciprocity and mutual trust*, provide appropriate means for surmounting problems associated with formal channels of communication (1989:32; my emphasis).

Compare this observation with Richard Gordon's discussion of the organizational logic of innovation:

> While strategic alliances involve agreements between autonomous firms, and are oriented towards strengthening the competitive position of the network and its members, inter-firm relations *within* the alliance itself tend to push beyond traditional market relations. Permanently contingent relationships mediated by strict organizational independence and market transactions—the arms-length exchange structure of traditional short-term linkages—are replaced by long-term relations intended to endure and which are mediated by highly personalized and detailed interaction. . . . *Cooperative trust, shared norms and mutual advocacy overcome antagonistic independence and isolation* (1995:183–184; first emphasis in original; second emphasis added).

Relations such as those suggested here develop when the costs of acquiring information through "normal" channels becomes too great. Both bear a remarkable resemblance to transactions and economies oriented around kinship relations, in which "trust" and "membership" function in place of formal hierarchies and markets.[38] As suggested in chapter 3, the phenomenon of "networking" also resembles the form of organization described here, a form that is characteristic of relations within global civil society. It is a form of organization that is "local," in the sense that it is largely unique to either place or social formation. It is a form that best lends itself to cooperation without centralization, without "global management."

One Earth, Many Worlds

At the beginning of the Atomic Age, the World Federalists became notorious for arguing "One World or None." Forty years later, the Brundtland Commission observed, as though the question were not in doubt, "The Earth is one but the world is not" (1987:28). From both perspectives, a world then divided among states—fewer than 80 in 1945; 165 in 1987 and, less than a decade later, 185, as the energies of secession have been loosed—was doomed to endless squabbling, conflict, war, and misery. For better or worse, "one world" is no more forthcoming today than it was fifty years ago; it is not much more likely to have emerged fifty years hence, either.

Indeed, a paradox—post-modern perhaps—emerges: *One Earth, many worlds*. Perhaps the problem is not that our political institutions are too small or not encompassing enough; perhaps they are too big. Perhaps the terms "big" and "small" just don't mean anything in this context. Perhaps there is no logical or optimal size or number for them; rather, it all depends. It depends on the problem, it depends on the culture, it depends on history and political economy, it depends on the time and place. We cannot command that boundaries be redrawn on the basis of some sort of "objective" science or quantifiable indicators and expect it to be so. *For human societies, even ecosystemic boundaries are no more "natural" than political ones*. Growing numbers of observers suggest that human beings *construct* their landscapes as well as Nature around them—and these are only some of the many social institutions that we inhabit. If so, we can hardly say that there are any boundaries, or even limits to the numbers of possible "worlds," except, perhaps, those handed down to us or reconstructed by us. And even those boundaries, reified as they are, are constantly shifting, as we change our individual and collective identities, and as our identities are changed for us.

How, then, are we to proceed? I suspect that it is governance through some form of non-state-based social relations, rather than hierarchy or markets, that is most likely to protect Nature. Such governance seems to be one feature—but not the only one—of an emerging global political economy characterized by economic integration and political fragmentation. This form of governance will help to protect Nature because the agents within these social formations may, through a process of negotiating "projects," find a shared interest, even as they are ideologically disparate. These formations will not—cannot—be fixed or stable; they will change with exigencies and contingencies.

The fundamental units of governance will, in this system, be defined by both *function* and *social meanings*, anchored to particular places but linked globally through networks of knowledge-based relations. Coordination will occur not only because each unit fulfills a functional role where it is located but also because the stakeholders in functional units share goals with their counterparts in other functional units. They also share a set of norms and epistemologies associated, in this instance, with what I have called "Ecology" (in contrast to "ecology"; see Sachs 1992:26–37). The localization of practice makes social difference acceptable; the globalization of knowledge makes shared goals practical; the boundaries are everywhere and the connections go everywhere. In analytical as well as policy terms, this is not a very satisfying or parsimonious framework. It does not provide an entry for either easy explanation or manipulation. It relies on the possibly heroic assumption that people can and will help to create social choice mechanisms, in their collective self-interest, that will also help to protect Nature. And, it is most decidedly not "international relations," as we conventionally understand them.

All of which raises one last question: Where, ultimately, in this Green World *is* our place? Our place, it would seem, is where our social relations are most dense, most complex, that is, the place that has the most meaning for each of us. This is not to argue that we must be bound to the land (or landscape) where we live, as were medieval serfs. It is, however, to propose that only by knowing the places in which we live—and the people(s) who live in those places—can we begin to talk, with some degree of meaning and serious intent, of protecting those places. In saying this, I do not posit a need or inevitability for some sort of global consciousness-raising or heightened spirituality as the *sine qua non* for environmental sustainability; that will follow from action in the material world. Place is a material, as well as a mental, construct. The tools are in hand; let us begin.

Notes

Chapter 1

1. For some thoughts on the nature of global "space," see Ruggie (1989:31).

2. I distinguish here between *government* and *governance*, the latter involving the regulation of human activities through non-formalized mechanisms (Rosenau & Czempiel 1992; and chapter 8, below). Those familiar with the international relations literature will recognize in this language—rules, principles, norms, and practices—the definition of an international regime (Krasner 1983).

3. The very notion of "modern" civilization is a problematic one since what we really see is something that ranges from the "post-industrial" all the way to near-feudal. For a discussion of uneven development set in the context of international relations, see Buzan (1995).

4. As suggested in chapter 2, the entire venture of making policy at the global level is fraught with difficulties. Deborah A. Stone's work (1988) has more-or-less confirmed for me many of the doubts I have had regarding the potential for making effective policy.

5. I do not mean to suggest here that states have not played a role in resource conservation. But the state's role has, to date, largely taken the form of the Conservationist notion of rational use to promote economic efficiency; see, e.g., Hays (1980).

6. I make this claim even though there are recent analyses that suggest trains to have been much less important to economic development than has long been supposed. The point I wish to make here is less about material transformation than shifts in worldviews.

7. It is interesting, in this context, to note that *tracks* were not preordained for *trains*; see the discussion of steam carriages in Beasely (1988). I am indebted to Glenn Church for bringing this point to my attention.

8. The impact of trains in this way is graphically illustrated by William Cronon in *Nature's Metropolis* (1991). See, especially, chapters 2 and 7.

9. A theoretical explanation of how such change might sometimes take place abruptly, in the absence of catastrophes such as war, can be found in Thompson (1979).

10. This is an argument originally made by Antonio Gramsci; see the discussion in Brian Ford (1994).

11. An application of discourse analysis to the construction of an international environmental regime can be found in Litfin (1994).

12. In this sense, therefore, the distinction between "environment" and "development" is vanishingly small. The question is better asked: "Who determines the relationship between society and Nature, and to what end?"

13. The attentive reader will, of course, recall the association of David Brower with each of these organizations; that, it seems to me, says something about the role of human agency in a phenomenon that is presented here in terms heavily weighted toward the structural.

14. Ecologists, anthropologists, and rural sociologists, among others, are coming to recognize that there is no such thing as a "natural" ecosystem, in the sense of one being untouched by human intervention. What distinguishes landscapes that we ordinarily think of as "natural" from those we think of as degraded has more to do with the presence or absence of identifiably human artifacts, such as buildings, highways, and rubbish dumps. See, e.g., Smith (1990) and Peluso (1992).

15. More generally, the term "ecosystem management" is being utilized to describe this approach.

16. This is not to say that such an approach has never been proposed, or even implemented, elsewhere. See, e.g., Feldman (1991: esp. ch. 9).

17. How one is to describe these areas is somewhat problematic on two counts. First, there are few, if any, groups of people who have not had some contact with "outsiders." Second, the notion of "underdeveloped" is meaningful, if then, only in relation to some degree of industrialization. In fact, as will be seen in chapter 6, many of these remote societies possess very sophisticated methods for managing and exploiting local resources.

18. It might be added here that these organizations do not shirk from adopting tactically-appropriate positions on issues depending on whether they are confronting the Indonesian government at home or are participating in international fora such as the 1992 UNCED meeting in Brazil.

19. During the summer of 1994, for example, the Indonesian government cracked down on environmental activists and organizations, arresting some and forcing others to shift their *modi operandi* (Shenon 1994a, 1994b). In order to protect the identities and safety of individuals and groups, therefore, the descriptions in chapter 6 are necessarily more vague than in chapters 4 and 5.

Chapter 2

1. I use the term "Nature" in this chapter and book to describe that within which human social arrangements are embedded (akin to the notion of "second nature"). This is in contrast to that which refers to biological and geophysical systems ("first nature"; see Smith 1990).

2. What I am describing here is quite similar to the notion of Gramscian hegemony; see, for example, Augelli & Murphy (1988: ch. 1) and Gill (1993).

3. The term "global environmental change" here refers to that set of alterations in environmental resources arising from externalities produced by industrialization and economic growth, as well as those resulting from poverty and overuse of subsistence resources (see, e.g., W. Clark 1989). These alterations may cumulate in a variety of ways, as discussed below. In using the general term "environmental problems" later in this chapter, it glosses over the vast differences among those phenomena that are commonly placed in this category. Global climate change and soil erosion, although both fitting under this umbrella, have very different technical, social, and political characteristics, and they are connected to the "world system" in different ways (Blakie 1985). This is a point that has not been explored in depth, although a recent effort in this direction can be found in the work of Mary Clark (1989).

4. In other words, I dismiss the role of environmental determinism in explaining or responding to environmental change, whether local or global. See Joni Seager's (1993:2–3) comments on the agency-structure problem as applied to environmental problems.

5. For trenchant critiques of the global management paradigm, see Chatterjee & Finger (1992, 1994); Hawkins (1993); and Seager (1993).

6. As Deborah Stone (1988: ch. 9,15) points out, all politics are about drawing boundaries between categories and interests. For an interesting discussion of the politics of "boundary-drawing" in the early United States, see Deudney (1995a:210–214).

7. Of course, as indicated by the Basel Convention on the Control of Transboundary Movements of Hazardous Wastes and Their Disposal, the management of toxic wastes is, increasingly, being addressed at the international level. The Convention only addresses the transfer of toxics *between* countries and says nothing about their generation and management *within* countries.

8. Lest this seem like splitting hairs, consider the social consequences of living with or without air conditioning in the southern regions of the United States.

9. This is not meant to imply that agency does not meet structure at the global level. For reasons that will become clear below, however, we need to recognize the importance of the micro-level. For a useful discussion of the agent-structure problem, see Dessler (1989) and Marx (1990).

10. The concept of "complexity" as I use it here is derived from a comparable concept in ecology; I do not, however, make any assumptions about relationships between the complexity and stability of social systems. See May (1974) and Woodley, Kay & Francis (1993).

11. This point is one that has long been recognized in anthropology, geography, and rural sociology; see, e.g., Blakie (1985).

12. These systems are generally thought to be economic, although as Brazil's efforts to construct the *Calha Norte*, or "Northern Trench," in Amazonia demonstrate, the systems can be strategic, as well (Oliveira Filho 1990).

13. The whole issue of boundaries and borders is problematic, to say the least. Nature "draws" few, if any, sharp or clear boundaries; instead, one finds zones of transition, or "ecotones" (Holland, Risser & Naiman 1991). By contrast, the history of human institutions is largely about drawing lines, although the notion of "borderlands," which is finding growing support in fields such as geography and cultural studies, corresponds much more closely to what we find in Nature. See, e.g., Massey (1993) and Tsing (1993).

14. An "open access" commons is one which is open to all on a "first-come, first-served" basis, and to which no property rights have been assigned, by contrast with a common–pool resource, to which property rights are shared among members of a user group (Libecap 1989; Bromley 1992).

15. This notion of networks is drawn from economic geography, which looks at nodes of production at large scale, rather than treating with political actors as the appropriate unit of analysis, as is the case with most of the international relations and much of the international political economy literature. An interesting application of this idea can be found in Alger (1990); see also various chapters in Peet & Thrift (1989).

16. The notion of "resource regimes" as I use it here is adapted from Young (1982). Further discussion of this idea follows.

17. The growing literature on environmental regimes is almost entirely focused at this level; see, for example, Young & Osherenko (1993); Haas, Keohane & Levy (1993); Susskind (1994).

18. Although the terms *conservation*, *preservation*, *protection* and *restoration* are often used interchangeably, they are not the same. Traditionally, *conservation* implied the rational use of natural resources on some sort of sustained yield basis; today it is more commonly used to denote *preservation* of Nature from further exploitation by humans. Environmental *protection* is generally used to refer to the cleanup of pollutants from human activities or the maintenance of environmental quality through assorted regulations, market incentives and technologies. Environmental *restoration* indicates an effort or program to return a ecosystem or component of Nature to some *status quo ante*.

19. I omit here any discussion of the "collective action" problem in its more classical sense. See Olson (1971) and Hardin (1982). A discussion of its application to global climate change can be found in Lipschutz (1991a). For a discussion of cooperation under anarchy, see Axelrod (1984).

20. Cogent critiques of Hardin's "tragedy" can be found in Herring (1990); Wade (1988); Ostrom (1990); and Stone (1988).

21. See Litfin (1994: 191–94) for a discussion about the political and social differences between ozone depletion and global warming, and Lipschutz (1994) for a critique of this FCCC process.

22. International agreements are often institutionalized in terms of an "international regime," which may have some administrative and technical capacities for encouraging implementation, but which rarely possess the means to threaten the imposition of sanctions against defectors (Young 1994, 1989; Young & Osherenko 1993; Litfin 1993). The ozone agreements commit signatories to reduce the use of certain substances by particular dates; a protocol to the Framework Convention on Climate Change (FCCC) will probably include such commitments as well. The ozone agreements do not, however, specify how these reductions are to be accomplished; that is largely left up to the individual states to decide, and the same will be true for the protocol to the FCCC. There are, however, restrictions on trade in ozone-depleting substances with non-signatories (see, e.g., German Bundestag 1989: 260–66). This will be much more difficult to accomplish with respect to global warming.

23. For my definition of the "state," I turn to Alfred Stepan who characterizes it as:

> [T]he continuous administrative, legal, bureaucratic and coercive systems that attempt not only to structure relationships *between* civil society and public authority in a polity but also to structure many crucial relationships within civil society as well (1978: xii; emphasis in original).

24. "Political will" is a notoriously difficult quantity to pin down; it is generally used when an analyst is unsure of what domestic politics consists. An insightful critique of the notion of "political willpower" can be found in Kennedy (1990). And this says nothing, moreover, about the problem of so-called two-level games (Putnam, 1988; Evans, Jacobson & Putnam, 1993; Leatherman, Pagnucco & Smith, 1994).

25. The notion of "resource-rich" has to do with access to capital and global markets and not national factor endowments.

26. The notion of environmental *externalities* in the form of pollution, for example, is well-known; the economist's answer is to internalize the costs of such activities through taxes, regulations, etc (Pearce & Turner 1990). As suggested below, my use of the term here is somewhat different.

27. In fact, the "second" or "black" economy can, in some situations, come to represents a not-inconsiderable faction of total economic activity, but the structure

of such economies place them entirely outside the realm of any sort of accurate measurement, let alone regulation (Wheelock 1992; Sik 1994).

28. Herring points out that "Historical work on actual common-property systems in the [Indian] subcontinent suggests that local institutions became marginalized or criminalized as the state centralized control and removed local authority through novel proprietary claims" (1990).

29. This is a notion that is also the subject of much speculation and academic conflict: W(h)ither the state? See chapter 8 below and Held (1991); Crook, Pakulski & Waters (1992); Held & McGrew (1994); and Gill (1994). For a contrary view, see Thompson & Krasner (1989).

30. This phenomenon is already evident in national economic policymaking where uniform policies such as an energy tax are claimed to discriminate against areas where distances are such that private transportation dominates over public.

31. The literature on local-state organizational and management relations is extensive and growing. See, e.g., Maniates (1990a, 1990b). Studies linking local, state, and international levels remain rare; a recent effort in this direction is Rose (1993).

32. Oran Young (1982) has used this term in an international context; I have adopted it here in recognition of the existence of resource-using social institutions at the local and national levels.

33. I should note that, on the one hand, Young's models of regime formation are not wholly accepted by many regime theorists working more closely with economic models and rational choice theories (e.g., Krasner, Keohane, Gilpin). On the other hand, his models are widely accepted, albeit often in a different language, among those working in an institutional or anthropological perspective. See Ostrom (1990) and Dryzek (1987). A somewhat different view of regimes can be found in Keeley (1990).

34. The assumption of international "anarchy" is not necessarily a valid one, at least not as it is conventionally stated; see Onuf (1989) and Bergesen (1990).

35. This does not mean that they are not "negotiated" in the sense of being dynamic and flexible; only that there are no formal negotiations involved. See Tsing (1993) for a discussion of this concept of negotiation.

36. Indeed, if one adopts some of the approaches of recent sociological research, the "encounters" between groups such as environmentalists and loggers or ranchers bear a striking resemblance to "'interface' situations [in the developing world] where the different life-worlds interact and penetrate" and in which "actors' interpretations and strategies . . . interlock through processes of negotiation and accommodation" (Long 1992a:5–6).

37. According to Darryl Cherney: "Earth First! is the civil rights movement for Mother Earth" (Earth First! organized Redwood Summer; Franke, 1990:16). There

has been discussion about the possibility of granting legal "rights" and "standing" in courts to elements of nature, to be accomplished by some sort of legal ruling or legislation; see Stone (1987) and the critique of such ideas in Rubin (1994).

38. John Dryzek uses the term *social choice mechanisms* to denote the more general case: "A social choice mechanism is a means through which a society . . . determines collective outcomes . . . in a given domain" (1987:7).

39. In point of fact, that Redwood Summer did not result in the immediate emergence of a new social choice structure does not mean that such a process is not taking place; indeed, there is a great deal of accumulating evidence to suggest that it is happening, albeit at the level of "historical structures," as Robert Cox might put it (1987).

40. Tim Ingold, quoting M. Godelier, writes that: "[I]n all societies *the holding of property constitutes a relation between persons*, so that forms of ownership of territory function as social relations of production" (Godelier 1979, in Ingold 1986:136; my emphasis).

41. Regulative rules describe how one *plays* baseball; constitutive rules establish what *is* baseball. The original example is to be found in Rawls (1955:25) as cited in Ruggie (1989:33, fn. 6). See also Dessler (1989).

42. Note that for "open access" resources," there are, in effect, neither constitutive nor regulative rules: exploitation is open to whomever has the capability for taking. "Common property" and "private" resources are subject to both types of rules.

43. Obviously, a powerful actor can also redefine constitutive rules through coercion, but this still requires at least some cooperation from those being coerced.

44. The U.S. federal government has also been known to "create" commons outside of the normal legislative process, for example, using the Clean Water Act of 1972 to designate as marshlands what appear to be dry farmlands (Robbins 1990:A1). Such cases have led to efforts by the Bush and Clinton administrations and the Republican-dominated 104th Congress to override the legislation via regulatory amendment as well as regulatory repeal and new regulations.

45. A view often held of social movements; as Richard Darman, Director of the Office of Management and Budget in the Bush administration once observed, the label "environmentalist" is "a green mask under which different faces of politico-ideology can hide." It would be, he said, a "regrettable irony" if, just as American values have prevailed "in the East-West struggle, they were to be lost in what some environmentalists like to term the struggle for 'global management'" (quoted in Shabecoff 1990:1).

46. It should be noted, nonetheless, that such rules are often legitimated, crystallized, and offered "protection" through government coercion by legal action and sanctions.

47. The point is that institutional reforms, such as the Endangered Species Act, that ignore the histories and political economies of the communities affected by them, are almost certain to generate "resistance" (*The Economist* 1995a:21–22). Ironically, perhaps, such resistance is often viewed favorably when it occurs in developing countries, less favorably when it happens in industrialized ones.

48. After all, why was there so much Northern opposition to the "New International Economic Order?" Why did the United States refuse to ratify the UN Convention on the Law of the Sea in 1982? Why is there so much resistance by some countries to the provisions of the Framework Convention on Climate Change?

49. Indeed, international regimes are much more likely to reinforce the power and position of those already on top (Conca 1994).

50. The literature on the emergence of international regimes is divided on this point. Some realists see them as instruments of state power that emerge only at the behest of powerful or hegemonic states (Krasner 1983); others doubt whether they can have any effect at all on the conduct of international relations (Mearsheimer 1995). Liberal institutionalists are more optimistic on this point, and see possibilities for reform and maintenance (Keohane 1984). Clearly, regimes might not serve the interests of the powerful—as in the case of UNCLOS—but then their "effectiveness" is called into doubt (see Haas, Keohane & Levy 1993; Young 1994b).

51. To be sure, the maintenance of a common-pool property resource, which can be regarded as a localized resource regime, serves to reproduce structurally the internal social relations of that regime but, at least, these are relations that are more evident to participants. This is a point that needs to be further investigated. In particular, in view of Herring's point about the "nesting" of resource regimes, does a series of coordinated, hierarchically-linked set of regimes promise to be any better at conservation than what now exists?

52. Although there are longstanding arguments for the decentralization of administrative systems and functions in development planning, the argument presented here has its roots in the "sociology of knowledge" literature. For a discussion of problems with decentralization, see Karim (1991). For a good summary of the sociology of knowledge literature, see Haas (1992b:20–26).

53. This obviously begs the question of where to place jet-setting financiers who have no permanent base, produce no material goods, and contribute to environmental degradation via the exhaust fumes of planes and cars and the toxic wastes generated in the manufacture of cellular phones, laptop computers, and so on. It is paralleled in negotiations over implementation of the Framework Convention on Climate Change having to do with who gets debited for bunker and aviation fuel emissions on or over the high seas; see Lipschutz (1994).

54. I use the term "property rights" here in a rather broad sense to refer to all of those arrangements, either codified as law or less-formal arrangements, that "define or delimit the range of privileges granted to individuals [or organized collectivities] to specific assets" (Libecap, 1989:1). For my purposes, these assets refer

to environmental resources, including land, water, forests, species, etc., and include access, harvesting and other types of usage rights, as well as outright private or collective ownership. The reader should note that many analyses of property rights with regard to resources and environment tend to discount or disregard "informal" usage systems; this often leads, as Ronald Herring has pointed out (1990), to the marginalization or criminalization of such systems.

55. The political consequences of ignoring variability can be seen in a cases of water in shared river basins, where flows from high-water years are sometimes used to determine allocations among parties, with resulting conflicts during low-water years (Shiva 1991:121–70). Indeed, such variability seems to undermine many attempts to define "sustainable yields" (McEvoy 1986, 1988). This type of variability is somewhat different in the case of fossil fuels or minerals where the variations are mostly a function of strictly exogenous economic and political variables. For an argument that casts this latter case in terms of property rights, see Lipschutz (1989: ch. 2, 3).

56. This is an intuitively logical conclusion that has been discussed in some detail by Richard B. Norgaard, albeit in a slightly different form (1987). He makes the point that the economic homogenization resulting from social organization based on specialization and exchange has had the effect of wiping out the type of "local knowledge" essential to the maintenance of resources and biological diversity. A critique of the notion of "maximum sustainable yield" (as opposed to the much more difficult-to-define "optimum yield") can be found in Dorfman (1985).

57. This is not meant to reify such knowledge. "Indigenous peoples" have, at times, proved as hard on their environment as industrialized societies (Norgaard 1981, 1987; Peluso 1992; Orr 1992: 31–33).

58. This point was made with some emphasis in interviews with Jon Kennedy and Harley Greiman (1992), U.S. Forest Service and Vicki Campbell (1992), U.S. Bureau of Land Management. As we shall see in chapter 4, those often described by old timers as "new arrivals" may have lived in an area for more than twenty years. This brings to mind the somewhat apocryphal story of Norman Cousin's complaint that, after having lived for twenty or thirty years in New England, he was still not accepted as a "local" in his community, while only a few days after arriving in California, Governor Jerry Brown asked him to join the State Commission on the Arts.

59. While "indigenous knowledge" is a reasonably well-understood concept, the application of this concept to industrialized society is somewhat more problematic (Breyman 1993). I would argue that, in the latter case, the equivalent body of knowledge is a much more subtle and fragmented thing. Nonetheless, there are at least two ways in which what we "know" from our experiences within spatially-defined spheres of activity might fall into the realm of "indigenous" or local knowledge: (1) how various pieces of local society "work"; and (2) how the pieces are connected. Ulf Hannerz calls this type of knowledge "common sense" (1992: ch. 5; see also Lindblom & Cohen 1979:12–13).

60. Even multinational corporations have a "local" presence in small-scale political economies; their particular strength within such resource regimes lies both in the extent to which these presences are locally-dominant and in the possibility of their "defection" through abandoning a locality.

61. For a trenchant critique of the notion of "economic man," see Orr (1992: ch. 1).

62. Even patterns of resource use systems in industrialized countries are the result not of rationalized economic planning but of historically-contingent episodes and accretions. Liebcap's account of mineral rights contracting in California and Nevada nicely illustrates this last point (1989: ch. 3)

63. Witness, for example, the many recent claims by Native Americans demanding the restoration of historical property rights to resources such as salmon, and the reaction of others to these demands. What then, is the difference between "local" and "international" regimes if both are unjust and reproducers of inequitable power relations? This is a valid question for which I do not have an answer. In spite of the optimism and idealism of many proponents of local control, localism is not always a democratic force (Stone 1988:300–304); indeed, it was the federal government's use of its leverage against "states rights" that was responsible for the legislation of civil rights in the 1960s and 1970s.

64. Much of the data used to argue for limits on takings from the Mattole River fishery (on the northern California coast) was collected by the Mattole Watershed Salmon Support Group, a local group with some scientific expertise but little access to high-tech monitoring systems (Campbell 1992; see also chapter 4).

65. This argument obviously does not hold true for phenomena such as the stratospheric ozone hole or global warming, but I do not mean to assert that localized resource management systems are *sufficient* sources of technical data; flows through wide-ranging informational networks are important, as well. I do argue that, because types of "global" problems are aggregations of "local" practices, action must be taken at the latter level as well as the former. The relationship between scientific-technical and local knowledge is not one that has, to the best of my knowledge, been explored in a systematic sense. For some thoughts on the matter, see the special issue of *International Organization* edited by Peter Haas (1992a). For an analysis of the relationship between science and the "Green" movement, see Yearley (1991: ch. 4). For an exploration of the role of knowledge in social movements, see Breyman (1993).

66. "Path dependency" means that where you start strongly influences where you end up; the classic example is the QWERTY typewriter keyboard, which was originally designed to slow down typists. It is generally agreed to be an inefficient design, but the sunk costs of using it are, by now, much too high to write off. For a discussion of path dependency, see Krugman (1994).

Chapter 3

1. My use of the term "technology" thus extends beyond the hardware to include the beliefs, explanations, and practices critical to its dissemination. The automobile does not become a technology in this sense until the infrastructure—material and ideational—is in place to make it socially reproducible (Winner 1977).

2. What may be new is the sheer globalization of the NGO phenomenon; that NGOs themselves are not as new as we sometimes like to think can be seen in Dominick (1992: esp. ch. 2).

3. This particular term, or terms like it, seem to be coming into widespread use. See Lipschutz (1992/1996); Gill (1991); Booth (1991); Wapner (1995a; 1996); Ghils (1992); Falk (1992); Macdonald (1993); Tinker (1993); Rich (1993); and Walzer (1995).

4. See, e.g., Tarrow (1988). Claus Offe suggests that absorption of NSM ideologies by institutionalized politics is not straightforward, but that institutionalization is a commonplace outcome (1990).

5. A recent exploration of the difference between "international system" and "international society" can be found in Buzan (1993).

6. Indeed, Raymond Cohen has argued that, because of the spread of the state system beyond Europe, the notion of diplomatic culture is no longer very useful at all (1991).

7. I owe most of the content of this paragraph to consultations with J. Peter Euben and Robert Meister, but have also drawn on Wolfe (1991), Walzer (1992, 1995), and Cohen & Arato (1992).

8. This point was suggested to me by Alan Gilbert, and it is particularly evident in the movement to restore rights of sovereignty to indigenous peoples.

9. What follows is informed and inspired by Cox (1987), Gill (1991, 1993, 1994), Laferrière (1992), and the essays in Sakamoto (1994).

10. The rise of ethnic "nationalism" in the period since the end of the cold war suggests that, although the state as political form has come to occupy all available space on the planet, the number of states has not yet stabilized. By some estimates, there are several *thousand* potential ethnies in existence, based on various cultural differences.

11. As Harry Truman is purported to have said, the Truman Doctrine and Marshall Plan were "two halves of the same walnut" (cited in LaFeber 1993:62–63).

12. It is also much less parsimonious; Gill criticizes the "dominant neo-realist rational choice approaches to the study of IPE [international political economy] . . . [for] the tendency to extreme parsimony in explanation relative to the infinite complexity of its object of analysis" (1993:46).

13. This is the basis for the famous neo-classical argument that non-renewable resources are "inexhaustible." As Jessica Tuchman Mathews puts it: "As a nonrenewable resource becomes scarce and more expensive, demand falls, and substitutes and alternative technologies appear" (1989:164).

14. According to Kim Rodrigues, University of California Extension Forester in Eureka, California (1993), members of the Mattole Restoration Council, from the Mattole River valley in northern California, have travelled all the way to British Columbia acting as advisors to other watershed groups. See also the discussion of river restoration in chapter 5.

15. But note that urban stream and river restoration is also growing in popularity, for both aesthetic and economic reasons, and the consumer and environmental justice movements are also largely urban (Szasz 1994).

16. The notion of networks is briefly addressed by Tarrow (1988) and Sikkink (1993). See also Annis (1992), Frederick (1992), and below.

17. This statement is based on my attendance at three days of INC-9 in Geneva, Feb. 7–18, 1994, and discussions with Augus P. Sari, Climate Action Network and Professor W. Jackson Davis, UC-Santa Cruz and the Monterey Institute of International Studies.

18. See Stone on myths, metaphors, and numbers (1988: ch. 6, 7).

19. The literature on the sociology of knowledge as it applies to activist environmental movements is, so far, limited. There is a growing literature on the role of "epistemic communities" as advisors to governments; see, for example, P. Haas (1990, 1992a). What has not been investigated in any great detail is the role of such experts in environmental movements. For a study of this sort in other movements, see Hoffman (1989). For an analysis of this point, see Hannerz (1992: ch. 5). In addition, it should not be thought that specifying numbers and models are not themselves political acts; see Stone (1988).

20. As Arthur McEvoy puts it "[J]ust as people develop their views of the world through interaction with their social and material environments, so, too, do those views change as people continually make the world over in response to changing ways of understanding it" (1988:214). See also the essays in Gill (1993).

21. The change in American attitudes is, perhaps, best illustrated by the film *Flipper*, seen and reified by millions of children when I was growing up. In the film, the human hero's father, a fisherman, regards dolphins as pests that compete for fish and should therefore be killed. At the time, such attitudes were quite common; today, they are increasingly regarded as outmoded and somewhat barbaric.

22. This raises another meaning undergoing cultural transformation. Increasingly, biological and genetic diversity are being valued for their potential contribution to biotechnology and the discovery of new medicines, materials that promise a "better life." This brings to mind the alchemists' search for the "philosophers'

stone," which was reputed to be a mechanism not only for transforming lead into gold (material) but also a means of spiritual transformation.

23. I do not mean to reify or romanticize "locality," since it can also be a place of brutality, cruelty, insensitivity, indifference and poverty. See Berman (1982: esp. Part V) and the essays in Keith & Pile (1993).

24. A phenomenon discussed in chapter 4, and noted in Yaffee (1994), Walker (1992), and Brown (1995).

25. There are, for the most part, no regions in the United States to which loggers can migrate any longer en masse in the hope of finding employment in logging. Mobility is more likely to be downward.

26. Or, as David Harvey has put it: "While crises in the experience of space and time, in the financial system, or in the economy at large, may form a necessary condition for cultural and political changes, the sufficient conditions lie more deeply embedded in the internalized dialectics of thought and knowledge production. For it is ever the case that, as Marx (*Capital*, 3 vol., New York, 1967, p. 178) has it, 'we erect our structure in imagination before we erect in reality'" (1989:345).

27. For the moment, I will avoid the question of what "success" means. Centralized global management might achieve "success," but at high social and political cost. These are not irrelevant considerations and, to a growing degree, they are being recognized in the increasing resistance by local agents to centralized environmental management strategies. See Peluso (1992) and Hawkins (1993).

28. This raises the problem of how to regard social units. As suggested below, where the environment is concerned, organizations are one place to start. They are, however, embedded in something that is larger. And some form of social learning is also transmitted to society-at-large through educational and other processes that we do not yet understand very well.

29. This point is made, albeit in somewhat different language, by both Cohen (1991) and George (1993).

30. The concept of an "epistemic community" is, in my view, a problematic one; indeed, Peter Haas' conceptualization of the term has so expanded since he first described it that it now includes all who share a similar science-based understanding of particular phenomena or processes.

31. According to Jean-François Lyotard, scientific debate is about dissensus, not consensus (cited in Litfin 1994:26).

32. Vandana Shiva puts this problematic nicely, in speaking of the imposition of "technological solutions" on society: "[S]ince both nature and society have their own organisation, the superimposition of a new order does not necessarily take place perfectly and smoothly. There is often resistance from people and nature, a resistance which is externalised as 'unanticipated side effects'" (1991:21).

33. For example, human beings are social animals that form organized groups within which they communicate with a shared language, and so on. But the form of organization and the details of the language can differ among even very small groups living in close proximity to each other, as seen in the case of the highlands of Papua New Guinea.

34. This is one more form of the universalism-particularism dialectic. Holism is desirable but particularism may be necessary in order to see how the parts come to make the whole.

35. Indeed, Ernst Haas notes that "Consensual knowledge may originate as an ideology" (1990:21). I have argued elsewhere that "organizing principles," which "posit a relationship between individual action and ideal objectives," function as "soft constraints" on social action (Lipschutz 1989:26, 29; Thompson 1984:135).

36. Sachs again:

> The concept [of ecology] joins two different worlds. On the one side, protest movements all over the globe wage their battles for the conservation of nature, appealing to evidence allegedly offered by that scientific discipline which studies the relationships between organisms and their environment. On the other side, academic ecologists have seen with bewilderment how their hypotheses have both become a reservoir for political slogans and been elevated to principles for some post-industrial philosophy. The liaison between protest and science can hardly be called a happy one (1992b:30).

37. The intersubjective nature of the relationship between the ecologist and that which s/he studies becomes especially clear when s/he becomes engaged in bargaining to protect that object (Peterson 1992). The goal of maintenance in this instance should be compared with that of nuclear physicists, who destroy nuclei in order to better understand them.

38. More to the point, as ecosystemic principles—especially those involving biodiversity and habitat preservation—are raised in the context of particular social arrangements and institutions, the schemas under which Nature is exploited or preserved, owned or shared come into question. Since all societies have some such schema—which we ordinarily call "property rights"—it seems to me that Ecology implicitly or explicitly raises questions regarding those arrangements. This point is addressed in the California case study (chapter 4).

39. See also the discussion of functionalism, neofunctionalism, and epistemic communities in Litfin (1994:40–51).

40. For a case study in which such a shift has not happened, see Deudney (1995).

41. I cannot think of a term that captures this quality exactly. Environmental ethicists argue that Nature should have rights (e.g., trees should have standing, as argued in Stone 1987). This is generally regarded as a biocentric, rather than an-

thropocentric, perspective, although it should be recognized that this could also be seen as anthropomorphizing Nature. Those who favor the "wildness" of Nature are committed to a similar idea, albeit a more extensive one (Oelschlaeger 1991).

42. For better or worse, my ten-year-old daughter has not been taught the Pledge of Allegiance, but she knows all about food chains and predator-prey relationships.

43. We do not, of course, know under what conditions these small, plastic items are produced in the People's Republic of China. And their essential non-biodegradability is attested to by the fact that, years after the hamburgers have returned to nature, old Happy Meal toys keep resurfacing in my home.

44. And, I have glossed over the valid criticism that at least some of this social learning is virtually indistinguishable from what we once called "propaganda." Indeed, some measurable fraction of the American public regards environmentalism as exactly that (Rubin 1994).

45. Stephen J. Gould makes much the same point about life in general in *Wonderful Life: The Burgess Shale and the Nature of History* (1990). The difference is that in Gould's world, contingency is largely the result of random accidents; in social life, it is the consequence of agents, social forces, and historical tendencies (Long & Long 1992). An extended discussion of this point can be found in Wright (1992).

46. In the United States, the metaphor of the "Net"—derived from Internet, Bitnet, Econet, etc.—has been superseded, first, by the so-called information superhighway (which, for better or worse, lends itself to various kinds of satirical and cynical observations) and, more recently, by the "web" (after the "World Wide Web"). All of these are used to convey two debatable and ideology-ridden notions: "information is power" and "freedom of choice."

47. As we shall see, power and hierarchy are, inevitably, present in the networks of global civil society, but resistance helps somewhat to moderate differences of this sort.

48. By this definition, computer networks such as ECONET are only a small "hardware" part of global civil society, facilitating the exchange of news; for a critique of the notion of the power of computing in terms of generating information, see Winner (1986) and Lipschutz (1992/96).

49. In truth, organizations such as the World Wildlife Fund, World Resources Institute, and Greenpeace more closely resemble multinational corporations. They have annual budgets in excess of $100 million. They can be found in offices and projects around the world. Some even engage in "friendly" mergers and takeovers (WWF and the Conservation Foundation, WRI and the U.S. branch of the International Institute for Environment and Development). One could go so far as to suggest that some environmental organizations are engaged in "cultural capitalism," as they try to sell environmental goods and services, and develop relationships with multinational corporations such as General Motors, DuPont, and so on.

50. Judith Mayer has pointed out that vanguard status can go beyond the control of money, staff, and projects. One could also regard as "vanguards" those groups with the most intensive and transformative contacts with other organizations, local as well as national and global.

51. I am thinking, in particular, of one acquaintance in Hungary who was instrumental in the establishment of several environmental NGOs, served an abbreviated term as a junior minister in the government of Jozef Antall, was on the Board of the Regional Environmental Center for Eastern and Central Europe, was then employed by the European Community's "embassy" in Budapest, ran for the Hungarian Parliament as a candidate of the Young Democrats (FIDEZ) in 1994 (and was not elected), and in 1995 was a vice president of FIDEZ as well as director of a U.S. EPA environmental training project based in Budapest. The same story could be told about any number of individuals.

52. Bruce Rich suggests that in the developing countries, alone, there are hundreds of thousands of NGOs with more than 100 million members (1994:284, citing Alan During, "People Power and Development," *Foreign Policy* 76 (fall 1989):66).

53. The privatization of civil society is a fairly recent phenomenon; for one exploration of the shifts from private to public and back, see Hirschmann, (1982).

54. It may be that the role of NGOs lies primarily in their ability to channel local knowledge upward and global knowledge back down to the local level. This would be in keeping with Michael Maniates' analysis (1990a, 1990b).

Chapter 4

1. This is not to suggest that such distinctions are made, or even held, by those involved in these projects. "Management according to ecosystemic principles," sometimes offered as an alternative to the first concept, still assumes the existence of a "manager"—inevitably, a human one.

2. This process is being documented by a number of academics and graduate students throughout California, and detailed articles, books, and dissertations should begin to emerge in the near future.

3. Since the original signing of the MOU, eight more agencies have joined the effort. The original signatories included: the California Resources Agency, the U.S. Forest Service, U.S. Bureau of Land Management, California Department of Forestry, California Fish & Game, U.S. Fish & Wildlife Service, California Parks & Recreation Department, National Park Service, State Lands Commission, and University of California Agricultural & Natural Resources.

4. This has become something of a risky business, inasmuch as some landowners in rural areas have threatened to shoot resource agency staff who come onto their property.

5. See, for example, Kate Showers' (1994) interesting description of the disastrous impacts of American soil conservation practices transplanted to Lesotho by the British.

6. While the literature of the period is vast, the names most closely associated with the American environmental movement of the late 1960s and early 1970s include Paul Ehrlich, Barry Commoner and, to some extent, David Brower. Spokespersons for the conservation organizations were not as well known. One history of the American environmental movement is Hays (1987); there are a growing number of other histories, as well. For a thoughtful critique of the movement, see Rubin (1994).

7. As Chapman and Reiss put it, "The word *habitat* is used extensively in ecology when describing where an organism lives. Unfortunately, it is difficult to give a precise definition of the term habitat. The word is a Latin one and literally means 'it inhabits' or 'it dwells'" (1992:109).

8. Thus, central to the recent controversy over the condition of the Northern and California Spotted Owls was how many were to be found in the forests of northern California and the Pacific Northwest, and not whether their preferred habitat was disappearing. See, e.g., Diringer (1993).

9. Yaffee offers an insightful and informative discussion of the (non)-application of the ESA in the case of the Northern Spotted Owl (1994: ch. 1–5).

10. Thus, as is often noted, the ESA has no regard for "endangered" workers but neither can it be applied to the conditions of the habitat within which the endangered species is located. Still, as we shall see below, species cannot be easily preserved if their habitat is threatened and the political implications of this point are explosive.

11. For all practical purposes, this is a distinction without a difference, since some requisite number of males and females of a species, whether paired or not, must be present for reproduction to occur.

12. In other words, habitat, but habitat for the single species only.

13. See Stone (1988) for a discussion of the politics of facts and numbers.

14. This, in turn, has led to the local backlash most evident in the Wise Use movement.

15. There is a history of redwoods preservation in California dating from the early years of the twentieth century, which grew as much out of a perceived need to protect public water supplies as the trees themselves. Such protection has depended largely on the transfer of private lands into public hands, a process that, in recent years, has become increasingly expensive. For example, purchase of the 4,500 acre redwood Headwaters Forest in northern California—one of the last unlogged old growth redwood tracts in private hands—from Pacific Lumber, a subsidiary of the Maxxam corporation, might cost California as much as $500 million (Neumann & Sampson 1992:14).

16. Eventually, the federal government did step in; more on this follows.

17. It should be noted that, since many communities in the region are heavily dependent on logging, the full "trickle-down" impacts might be much greater.

18. Or, as Brock Adams, a vice president of the National Audubon Society described Option 9, "This is war. It's political science, not biological science" ("Forests Plan Attacked . . . " 1993).

19. It is worth noting here that the political and social implications of protecting habitat are culturally contingent, and vary from one country to the next. The creation of nature reserves in developing countries, for example, usually overrides the traditional property rights of those who live in the area. Ironically, perhaps, loggers and indigenous peoples often find themselves riding in the same boat; less ironically, indigenous peoples and commodity extractors find themselves whaling from the same boat, as well.

20. This is the position of the Pacific Legal Foundation and other organizations with a conservative and/or libertarian bent; see Wallace, Moles & Rodrigues (1993) and Schneider (1992).

21. The classic exposition of the difference between "strong" and "weak" states is to be found in Katzenstein (1978); see also Krasner (1978: ch. 3).

22. As I point out, CRIMP and "ecosystem management" are, for all practical purposes, the same.

23. The problem has something to do with economies of scale: if the "appropriate" scale is a watershed, which watershed? And, if it is a region comprising many "ecosystems," where are boundaries to be drawn? Again, the designation of the area to be covered is as much a social matter as a "natural" one.

24. In other words, lines must be drawn, via some social choice process, around not only natural systems but social ones, as well.

25. See Long and Long (1992) for a discussion of an "actor-oriented approach" to sociological field research that emphasizes the range of possibilities confronting individuals "embedded" in social institutions and other structures. Walton (1992) takes a similar approach.

26. The following discussion draws on the Ewing (1992) and Kennedy & Greiman (1992) interviews, although the stories told by others disagree on several important points.

27. As is often the case with "texts," the precise way in which this happened is disputed by participants in the process and outside observers.

28. The pitfall in such a scheme is that the reproduction rate of exploited species, such as fish, can fluctuate a great deal from one year to the next. Hence, what is "sustainable" one year might lead to a collapse the next (Woodley, Kay & Francis 1993; Stevens 1993c; Yoon 1994).

29. A certain confusion about the concept is, therefore, not entirely surprising. According to Al Wright, with the U.S. Bureau of Land Management, the bioregional focus of the Biodiversity Strategy is a result of "the need to move beyond technical experts, to concentrate on natural boundaries" (quoted in U.S. BLM 1993: 6).

30. Without detailed survey data, it is difficult to pinpoint just how widespread and influential this environmental rationality is; still, a number of offhand comments during various interviews with agency staff suggest that it is there. Yaffee (1994) makes note of this phenomenon as well.

31. For example, in a 1991 report on biological diversity, a task force of the Society of American Foresters proposed that "An ecological perspective of forest health recognizes that dead trees are as functionally and structurally important [to biological diversity] as live trees" (Petit 1991).

32. See, e.g., *Inner Voice* (1992), the association's newsletter, which addresses the Earth Summit in Rio and other forestry issues in a global context.

33. There is a very active North American bioregional association that holds periodic conferences, and bioregionalism has acquired more concrete standing through such international efforts as the setting aside of various biological and ecological reserves. Planet Drum sponsors an annual late-summer gathering of the northern California Shasta Bioregional Group. See Andruss, Plant, Plant & Wright (1990).

34. See, e.g., "Biogeography" in Chapman & Reiss (1992:228–42). As described in this text, biogeographic regions are generally continental in scope. See also Press (1995).

35. More to the point, even though bioregional provinces have standing in *natural* history, they are *ahistorical* from the perspective of human societies. This is only one among several problems with the concept as a political/social one (Lipschutz 1991c; Pepper 1993:185–94).

36. Indeed, a distaste for politics as practiced in "Sacramento" and beyond is evident even among the field representatives of the various state and federal resource agencies. The bioregionalists and environmentalists appeal to the determinism of Nature to legitimate their political and social claims; their opponents, some of whom belong to the "Wise Use" movement, appeal to God for legitimacy, while others invoke "natural right" and the frontier ethic (almost no one invokes "history" any longer). Sacramento and Washington, D.C. are, in this context, anathema. On the invocation of Nature for purposes of legitimating political stances, see Oelschlaeger (1991: ch. 9). For a critique of this as determinism, see Pepper (1984: ch. 6, 7; 1993) and Agnew & Corbridge (1995:56–65).

37. Again, potential problems here. Even in largely pristine ecosystems, populations of species can vary radically from one year to the next, in response to weather, predator populations, and so on. Without longitudinal data, it is difficult to say much about ecosystem dynamics in a specific region.

38. This statement ignores environmental planning, which is centered on the principle that science and politics *must* be integrated into growth management policies if environmental protection is to result. But such planning takes place largely at the local level, in cities and counties, and turf battles make it extremely difficult for the state to intervene in the growth management process.

39. The central issue here is one of social reproduction. Under conditions of stress and uncertainty, owls and murrelets will die; human beings will adapt, but they may adapt in ways that are destructive of the system of social reproduction. This type of behavior is seen most clearly with regard to fisheries; see, e.g., Miller & Fluharty (1992). Environmental managers would like to know, of course, how to intervene so as to sustain a eco-social system without radically altering the premises on which it is based.

40. A more concrete expression of this idea is to be found in Aldo Leopold's "land ethic" (1966); see also Oelschlaeger (1991: ch.7). For critiques of environmental legitimation by science and environmental determinism, see Pepper (1984; 1993).

41. There is also substantial evidence that many species' numbers vary in a stochastic and even chaotic fashion (Yoon 1994).

42. For example, at least one collective in the Trinity Alps, Trinity Alps Botanicals, has collected digger and other large pine cones for export to Japan, where they sell for the equivalent of $8–12 apiece (the collector receives about one dollar per cone; Curry 1993). A serious problem often pointed out for many developing countries is that the local "indigenous knowledge" now being commodified in tropical forest was largely eliminated decades ago; the same holds true in the Pacific Northwest. This means that ethnobotanists have to rely on comparative data to find potentially-valuable forest products, looking for analogue species and relying on laboratory testing.

43. The whole process of local resistance to and struggle against the industrialized state is not, to my knowledge, one that has been very well documented for those who are not "indigenous peoples" or ethnic or racial minorities, although see Walton (1992) and Gaventa (1980). For interesting parallel studies, see Peluso (1992) and Schmink & Wood (1992).

44. From an ecosystemic perspective, rehabilitating roads and clearing up litter might actually degrade the forest by removing nutrients.

45. For instance, messages on the Econet conference on Northwest and California forests were, to a large degree, hostile to the Clinton logging proposal presented as "Option 9" in 1993. Most of these messages came from urban environmental groups, although a few originated in rural areas.

46. This strategy has been discussed in the case of international negotiations by James Sebenius (1984, 1991).

47. One might formulate this process in negotiating strategy terms as, first, trying to change the terms of the game in order to establish a new contract zone

and, second, negotiations on where within the contract zone agreement best meets the demands of the parties. See Young (1994: ch.4).

48. For example, in the case cited above, the road rehabilitation and thinning work will be carried out by unemployed loggers, even though there might be others more qualified in terms of ecological science to do it. This is a political decision, not a technical one. (Indeed, the very notion of *roadwork* as an environmental protection tactic is a political one.)

49. Of course, some of the stakeholders *are* California and federal agencies, such as the BLM and U.S. Forest Service. As I noted previously, the field representatives of these agencies may find it more advantageous, for tactical reasons, to "go native," thereby helping to weaken the bureaucracy, rather than upholding agency positions and risk losing all authority within the local realm.

50. The reasons for this include overfishing, the degradation of watersheds, channelization, in some instances, and the construction of dams, which makes it difficult for the salmon to swim upstream to spawn. According to some, the problem is attributable to the replacement of small-scale hatcheries along individual streams and rivers by large-scale ones that raise "standard" fish which are, apparently, unable to "smell" their way to their home waters (Steelquist 1992). A record chinook salmon year in 1995 suggests this is not quite an accurate account of what is happening (Gaura 1995).

51. Indeed, prices for finished lumber have risen so rapidly and by so much in the mid-1990s that a growing number of new homes are now being built with steel framing.

52. The largest city in the province is Eureka, with 27,000 people. An informative discussion of the role of local elites in local politics can be found in Salisbury (1993).

53. In other rural parts of the state, such as the central and southern Sierra Nevada, a third "layer" of migrants from city suburbs has arrived in recent years, with yet another set of cultural sensibilities (Duane 1995).

54. The coast is "lost" because the coastal highway (State Highway 1 south of Leggett; US 101 north of Eureka) was never completed. Access is limited by the poor quality of roads, or their absence.

55. According to some calculations, marijuana cultivation is one of the largest agricultural crops in California, although there is no way to be sure of this. In any event, a major part of the California marijuana crop comes from the "Emerald Triangle" of Mendocino, Humboldt, and Trinity counties.

56. I attended the meeting in Ferndale, California (August 19, 1993) at which the idea was introduced. It received a very hostile response from landowners in the Bear River watershed. Their lawyer, in essence, warned all state and federal agencies to "keep out."

57. Paradoxically, in 1994 there was a season, and California-based stocks and catches were up, but the influx into regional markets of salmon caught off the coast of Alaska threatened to put California salmon trawlers out of business, once again. The 1995 chinook season was the best in many years, especially farther south, with the result that markets were glutted and the low prices received by fishers led them to go on strike. More of a threat to the industry is the imminent listing of the coho salmon as endangered, which is likely to affect the chinook fishery as well (Martin 1995a).

58. According to Jerry Moles (1993), University of California Extension, in 1992 the director of the Hayfork Economic Alliance was fired from his job for participating in such meetings.

59. Bailey has since moved to Redding because her husband was unable to find logging work around Hayfork (Martin 1995b).

60. This underlines a point to which I will return: the role of the state in legitimating new ethics and rationalities. As John Walton puts it: "[T]he state is extended and transformed when new powers are legitimately claimed by a progressive or welfare state as well as when citizens create organizations with a legitimate public mandate . . . or successfully represent their grievances (such as environmental degradation) as matters under state authority" (1992:300).

61. As noted earlier, Brock Adams, a vice president of the National Audubon Society said of Option 9, "This is war. It's political science, not biological science" ("Forests Plan Attacked . . . " 1993).

62. For example, the group spent a great deal of time discussing a proposal submitted by Joseph Bower, a Hayfork resident and "environmentalist," "which would involve creating firebreaks along highways by clearing litter and underbrush to a distance of 100 feet on either side." What was the basis for the 100 feet, some wanted to know? Wouldn't it make more sense to add "plus or minus," so that clearing could be adapted to the specific conditions of each location? Bower's choice of 100 feet was predicated on it being an easy distance to measure, one that would not require technical assessment and approval. The group seemed not altogether comfortable with this argument, and finally settled on 100 feet, but up to 150 as needed.

63. It should be noted that the generally anti-environmental and pro-business position of the Republican Party, which has been gradually acquiring power in the California legislature, could eventually overcome the deadlock and put an end to resource agency autonomy.

Chapter 5

1. Summaries in translation of materials and articles in Hungarian were provided by Rita Aronson, Zsuzsa Gille, and Ida Míro Kiss. This chapter could not have been written without their assistance.

2. This region is the focus of the monograph by Bertalan Andrásfalvy, *A Duna mente népénk ártéri gazdálkodáasa Tolna és Baranya megyében az ármentesítés befejezéséig* ("The flood-ecology of the communities living along the Danube, in particular the counties of Tolna and Baranya, until the end of the Flood Control Project") (1975, 1989); see also Bartos (n.d. 1) and Csaba (1993). Andrásfalvy, a professor of ethnography at the Janus Pannonius University in Pécs, is a member of the Board of Trustees of the Ormánság Foundation.

3. The construction of big dams is hardly unique to the old Soviet bloc, of course, and similar impacts can be found almost everywhere that such projects have been undertaken. See, for example, Reisner (1988); Ascher & Healy (1990: ch. 5 and 6); Shiva (1991: ch. 4); and Phinney & Torrice (1994).

4. Tamás Pál (1995) has pointed out to me that the Hungarian Socialist Workers Party was never monolithic. Rather, it was stratified, characterized by interest-based politics and split between Budapest and the "country." See also Seleny (1994).

5. In fact, the first Nature Conservation Act, dealing with forestry and birds, was passed during the nineteenth century.

6. At the current rate of exchange in 1996 ($1=150 ft), two billion forints equals approximately $13 million; at a time when urban bus fares were typically a couple of forints, it was a substantially larger sum, but still not overwhelming.

7. For recent assessments of political and economic conditions in Hungary, see Deák (1994); Viviano (1994a, 1994b); Bakos (1994); Hankiss (1994); Racz & Kukorelli (1995).

8. Persányi (1992:81) points out that, in Hungary, the Central Committee of the party never dealt with environmental issues or problems.

9. Groups lacking a clear leadership and organizational structure are especially frustrating to those in positions of power and authority, because there is no one with whom to "cut a deal"; see, e.g., Hamilton (1994:214).

10. The period was, in any case, one of emerging political opposition to the regime; see Bozóki, Körösényi & Schöpflin (1992).

11. That many of the founders of the various Hungarian environmental groups have been trained in biology, chemistry, or another one of the sciences helps to maintain this distinction.

12. This parallels a similar disdain for institutionalized politics among the residents of northern California and, more generally, amongst virtually all practitioners of local environmentalism.

13. As discussed in chapters 2–4, one of the key elements at the core of environmental conservation is property rights: who has the right to do what to or with a resource?

14. More to the point, because artifacts and science seem to emerge and operate of their own accord, the politics behind their emergence and operation often remain obscured.

15. For example, once the project to dam the Danube began to acquire political currency, the party organizations permitted members and academics to establish committees and meetings to consider the issue. Not only did these provide a controlled forum for discussions, it also helped to marginalize external critics as not being sufficiently "scientific."

16. All of this is doubly ironic, of course, insofar as "scientific Marxism" was propagated as the basis for politics and economy. This raises interesting questions about who believed what.

17. Somewhat ironically, one of the most ardent environmentalist advocates of "professionalization"—as expressed in my interview with her—was a leader of one of the two Green Parties running in the 1994 election and has become very active in lobbying in the Parliament (Schmuck 1992).

18. In particular, the interviews conducted in Indonesia by Judith Mayer seem to point to a similar process there; see chapter 6.

19. For example, how are we to regard U.S. Vice President Gore's *Earth in the Balance* (1992)? While it is clearly not in tune with the environmental policies of the Clinton administration, neither can it be dismissed as irrelevant to policymaking.

20. Thus, the officially-sanctioned auctioning and selling of "rights to pollute" represents the creation of new property rights within a classical economic discourse. Among the most ardent advocates of this process is the Environmental Defense Fund, an organization once considered much more radical than it actually is today.

21. This can be seen in the ongoing debate about the Northern spotted owl and old-growth forests in the Pacific Northwest. Is the scientific issue the absolute number of breeding pairs, or trends in the number that indicate something about long-term ecosystemic health? This question, in itself, obscures some very real political questions about the future of the region's political economy, as suggested in chapter 4. For another perspective on the technology-politics interface, see Hukkinen, Rose & Rochlin (1990).

22. At its peak, prior to 1989, the Hungarian Ornithological Society had about 16–18,000 members. As a result of the country's economic crisis, by 1993 membership had dropped to roughly 7,500 members (Kállay 1993).

23. Its membership is probably far smaller. In 1992, the Society's membership list included 60 groups and 73 individuals. It seems unlikely that each group had an average membership of 300.

24. The project, once thought irretrievably dead, has been resurrected by Slovakia. There are also some in Hungary—including former opponents of the

project—who now see in the dam's operation an expression of national sovereignty, not to mention a non-nuclear source of electricity.

25. This was evident in debates at the annual conference of Hungarian environmental groups, which I attended in Nyíregyháza on March 17–19, 1995.

26. The Hungarian electoral system is a particularly complex one. One hundred and seventy-six MPs are elected in individual constituencies; 152 on regional party lists in the countries and Budapest; and 58 on the national list (which are distributed after all votes have been tallied). In order to win a seat, therefore, a candidate not only must receive enough votes to finish among the winners in the district or region, the party must also receive at least four percent of the total *national* vote. Consequently, any party that does not run candidates in every constituency has little chance of getting into Parliament. For details, see Gabel (1995).

27. The records of particular individuals who remain prominent today in the environmental sector are still a source of some bitterness for others; more than one person described some of these individuals to me, in no uncertain terms, as unreformed Communists. See, especially, the articles by Zsuzsa Béres (1992a, 1992b).

28. The Environmental Ministry provided the bulk of the funding for the meetings through 1993, funnelling them through the National Society of Conservationists, testimony to the continuing importance of personal ties in Hungarian politics. The Society has since lost a significant share of its funding, resulting in a reduced role among environmental groups.

29. The life history of David Brower—John McPhee's "archdruid"—stands as a prominent example of this phenomenon. Brower was executive director of the Sierra Club, but was fired in the 1960s for acting in violation of the organization's bureaucratic strictures. He then founded and presided over Friends of the Earth, with which he had a similar falling out, for almost identical reasons, in the 1980s. Subsequently, Brower established, and is currently titular head of, Earth Island Institute, an organization whose early reputation was almost as dependent on Brower's stature as on its own activities. Meanwhile, he has also been welcomed back into the Sierra Club.

30. This does not mean that collaboration does not take place: for example, Levegö Munkacsoport—the Clean Air Action Group in Budapest—is a coalition of twenty-eight groups (including several outside of Budapest). But the success of this group relies, to a significant degree, on work and reputation of a single charismatic individual.

31. The image of modern Hungary as the core of the Carpathian Basin—which includes much of pre-World War I Hungary—continues to exercise a powerful hold in the political life of the country, including some parts of global civil society (see Figure 5.1).

32. Notwithstanding, few of the groups outside of the ones affiliated with parties (e.g., FIDESZ Green Fraction; Socialist Greens) have been effective lobbyists

of either parties or Parliament, although such skills have been more successfully applied at the municipal level and are now being developed at the national level.

33. This is, I think, a common feature of oppositional organizations in "civil society." Groups tend to form and splinter as dominant individuals disagree or seek greater autonomy. The splinters go off to establish new groups, which also eventually splinter, and so on. It is curious that those individuals who are so committed to collective action that they form groups, also have the greatest tendencies toward individualism and domination of whatever groups they have founded.

34. Marlise Simons (1994), for example, offers quotes from two of these same individuals.

35. This point is not meant as disparagement of the Budapest-based organizations; I only wish to illustrate how centralized the environmental movement remains. This phenomenon is quite common elsewhere, as well: funders want to be assured that they are not throwing away their money, so they go first to those individuals and organizations with "good" reputations. Smaller groups or groups in the periphery that have virtually no chance of tapping directly into these sources of assistance must work through more "reputable" intermediaries in the capital. Increasingly, however, these latter groups are establishing direct ties with funding sources in other countries. It should also be noted that there are no private foundations in Hungary of the sort that exist in the West, and few member-based organizations. As a result, funds come either from Parliament or external sources (usually American or European).

36. For example, in compiling a list of individuals for the purpose of conducting a survey, I was directed to the same group of prominent individuals, a number of whom I had already interviewed.

37. It should be noted, however, that a little money still goes a long way in Hungary. The MTS managed to run the 1993 national two-day conference, attended by about 250 people, on a budget of one million forints—approximately $12,500 at the then current rate of exchange.

38. More accurately, these collaborative efforts contribute to the project of "recolonizing" the East, by bringing it into the sphere of Western economic and political liberalism, a project that, throughout the former Soviet bloc, has more recently led to the return to power of ex-socialists and ex-communists (Frankland & Cox 1995).

39. Some have argued, of course, that the socialism practiced in the Soviet bloc had little to do with Marxism, which had a very different view of Nature. This point is addressed by Pepper (1984: esp. ch. 6).

40. Zsuzsa Gille (1994) argues that Nature did play a central role in the socialist ideology of production, by defining spaces with no utilitarian value as "wastelands."

41. The pre-World War II Scouts were succeeded by the Young Pioneers, who engaged in tree-planting and the cultivation of gardens. These, however, were seen as activities of production, not preservation.

42. This maps onto the rural-urban conflict that seems to be, or have been, a regular feature of the industrialization process. In this case, cosmopolitanism (identified with Jews and the party state) was in direct opposition to the qualities required of a "true" Hungarian.

43. For example, when respondents were asked in a public opinion poll whether Hungary should accept the transfer of Transylvania from Romania back to Hungary, the majority said no, citing the high economic costs of such a move (Kenez 1994).

44. The reader might be puzzled by my association between the "why" of the linkage with ideology and worldview, rather than simply the "goal" of a clean environment. No one denies that Nature has taken a beating throughout Eastern Europe, with concomitant effects on human health and welfare; this, alone, should be justification for technology transfer. Yet, not only science but also politics are involved here, and no politics is devoid of either ideology or worldview (Stone 1988; Haraway 1991).

45. The alliances established by these three groups only begin to describe the extent of the network-building that is taking place in Hungary; the whole task would require a separate volume.

46. This was also the basis for the establishment of the Regional Environmental Center for Central and Eastern Europe in Budapest (U.S. GAO 1994:54–57).

47. None of this should come as a surprise, of course. In his biography of John Foster Dulles, Townsend Hoopes ascribed to his subject the belief that "American economic and technical superiority rested in large part on the *moral* superiority of the free enterprise system. Only men [sic] operating in political freedom could achieve spectacular industrial progress. And as political freedom and economic progress were interdependent partners, it followed that emerging nations, given a choice, could not fail to choose allegiance with the West" (1973: 286; see also Packenham 1973).

48. Although I do not discuss it here, the European Union is also providing various types of support for environmental protection activities through its PHARE program.

49. As the history described earlier in the chapter suggests, the argument presented in this quote is not quite correct.

50. The efficacy of computer networks as a means of facilitating collaboration among users is, in my view, overrated. For example, in writing about human rights issue-networks in Latin America, Kathryn Sikkink (1993) never mentions computer networks. For optimistic views of computer-based communication and political networking, see Frederick (1992) and Annis (1992).

51. The potentially incendiary quality of rivers and watersheds should not be underestimated, especially in the context of nationalism in Hungary. According to an article in *Budapest Week* (Szendrei 1993:5) that reported on the activities of István Csurka, a right-wing member (since expelled) of the then-governing Hungarian Democratic Forum, "At the early February national meeting of the Magyar út [Hungarian Way Foundation] circles [established by Csurka], there was a map behind the rostrum which showed Hungary's rivers but not the national borders. . . . In the eyes of many observers, that map was yet another example for [sic] a drive to reconsider the peace treaties which had defined Hungary's borders." To this, Csurka replied, "Rather than calling it a map, I would say it was a symbolic manifestation of our desire to eliminate the borders, to make them fully penetrable. . . . On that illustration, there were no borders. There were rivers and ways. Hungarian ways."

52. An *alapítvány* is a not-for-profit organization and not a private foundation in the American sense.

53. As noted earlier, this region is the focus of the monograph by Andrásfalvy (1989).

54. To put it another way, Hungarians are indigenous people, too.

Chapter 6

1. In Indonesian, the term is *Bhinneka Tunggal Ika*, with roots in Sanskrit, like many Indonesian terms of statecraft.

2. President Suharto's regime launched its first five-year development plan in 1968, following a Rostowian modernization model. After a twenty-five-year approach, a "take-off" period during Indonesia's second long-term planning period to sustained economic growth was expected to bring Indonesia into the ranks of the world's prosperous industrial nations. See Hill (1990a; 1990b) and Robison (1986).

3. This chapter and notes use the post-1972 spelling of the Indonesian president's single name (Suharto). However, the pre-1972 spelling, with Dutch orthography, is still often used in Indonesia. References to "Soeharto" in citation titles are cited as such.

4. The "New Order," or *Orde Baru*—the technocratic, military-backed regime associated with the rule of Suharto, Indonesia's second president—is the term by which Indonesia's current developmental state has been known since shortly after President Suharto's regime overthrew the Soekarno government in 1966. The term also has roots in Mussolini's references to Italy's Fascist new order, although these origins are unknown to most Indonesians by the mid-1990s.

5. Indonesia's "New Order" is often referred to as a post-colonial "developmental state," in which the authoritarian regime justifies repressive policies based on the need to ensure political stability to foster economic growth. Whether or not

it is also defined in terms of redistributive justice, "development" becomes the basis of state legitimacy. Development and national integration are defined in terms of the state's consolidation of control over natural resources within Indonesian territory, and the New Order's interpretation of Article 33 of the 1945 Constitution (discussed later). See Barber (1989) and Hill (1989).

6. *Pancasila* (the Five Principles), named in Sanskrit as many revered Indonesian symbols, was adopted as a set of semi-official tenets during the Soekarno era. The Suharto regime has elevated Pancasila into a rigid state ideology, promoted through mandatory indoctrination of students and government employees. All registered social organizations are obliged to espouse Pancasila since the passage of the "Social Organizations Law" in the late 1980s. The five principles are: One supreme divinity; Just and civilized humanity; Indonesian unity; the People led by wise policies in consultation and representation; and Social justice for all Indonesian people.

7. Indonesia' post-independence history is full of regional political movements and their suppression. The New Order virtually prohibits publicly promoting "*sukuism*" (a derogatory expression equivalent to "tribalism" or "ethnicism") aside from the Javacentric orientation that is virtually taken for granted in national policies. Norms of political discourse that preclude discussion of ethnic discrimination, and even the mention of class conflict, serve as boundaries within which environmental organizations construct their "legitimate" critiques of government policy and the New Order itself.

8. Indonesian environmental organizations have been especially wary of accepting offers of financial assistance from the Global Environmental Facility (GEF, put into place pursuant to UNCED in 1992) administered by the World Bank, from the U.S. Agency for International Development (AID), and from quasi-independent programs that it bankrolls, such as the Biodiversity Support Program.

9. Sustainable development language as subsequently used in policy documents was strongly influenced by the late 1988 translation of *Our Common Future* into Indonesian, jointly distributed by the Ministry of Population and Environment and the Indonesian Environmental Forum (*Wahana Lingkungan Hidup*, or WALHI, Indonesia's best-known consortium of environmental organizations).

10. Particularly active in this regard have been the non-line agencies of the State Ministry for Population and the Environment, under the charismatic leadership of Minister Dr. Emil Salim during the 1980s and early 1990s, and technical support of Dr. Otto Soemarwoto, and the increasingly influential Social Forestry sections of the Ministry of Forestry.

11. Dr. Habibie's rise to influence in the early 1990 is indicative of a generational transition in New Order technocratic power. The older generation of military leaders who came to the fore during the New Order transition along with President Suharto, and the "Berkeley Mafia" of American-educated fiscally conservative economists began to lose influence in the early 1990s, replaced by "high technology" enthusiasts whose leaders were educated in a German engineering tradition.

12. The lawsuit, filed in August 1994, demanded cancellation of the loan. The administrative court dismissed the suit in October under a ruling that the President is answerable only to the National Assembly. (Letter to the Head of the Jakarta State Administrative Court, August 23, 1994, signed by representatives of WALHI (Indonesian Environmental Forum); LATIN (Indonesian Tropical Nature Foundation); FORSIKAL (Foundation Forum for Population and Environmental Study); PLASMA (Human Resource and Environmental Development Foundation); ICEL (Indonesian Center of Environmental Law Foundation; and Pelangi Indonesia Foundation (WALHI & others 1994). It is ironic that the "environmental" concerns cited in the lawsuit related to the reforestation program specifically—a program which the environmental movement had sharply condemned in the past. See WALHI & LBH (1993).

13. The 1994 ban on parties to the suit against the President from receiving funds from abroad echoed a previous ban on all Dutch aid to NGOs in the wake of the Netherlands' condemnation of the government's actions in the 1991 "Dili Massacre" in East Timor, and the subsequent Dutch decision to shift bilateral aid from government programs to NGOs.

14. Juan Martinez-Alier and Eric Herschberg (1992) summarize many of the recent discussions of this distinction emphasized in the political-ecology literature, and point out, following Ramachandra Guha and others, that this is a fundamental difference between the histories of the Northern preservation-based environmental movements and the Southern livelihood-based movements.

15. In most discussions of the "environment" by Indonesian environmental organizations, the term used is "*lingkungan*," which generally refers to an environment defined by a space around something, or a *place*, or "*lingkungan hidup*," the "living environment," with all of the ambiguity associated with the English term. By contrast, early government environmental documents, and those of relatively early government-sponsored environmental groups such as *Yayasan Indonesia Hijau* (the Green Indonesia Foundation) more frequently referred to "*alam*" or "nature." By contrast, in neighboring Malaysia (which shares much basic vocabulary with Indonesia, since *bahasa Malaysia* and *bahasa Indonesia* are rooted in the same Malay trading language), until very recently even environmentalists' favored term was "*alam sekitar*," or "natural surroundings." It is a subtle difference in interpretation, but sets a tone for many aspects of issue definitions.

16. Sandra Moniaga, one of Indonesia's leading environmental advocates, explains: "The maintenance of the present level of biodiversity of Indonesia's tropical forests results from indigenous communities' conservation and forest management practices" (quoted in *Environesia* 1993b).

17. This provision of the Indonesian Constitution has recently been subject to intense debate in discussions of the appropriate role of the state in land management and environmental protection. The government asserts that the state has a constitutional right to appropriate land and resources from individuals and communities to further the goal of development for the welfare of the nation, since the Constitution does not count either private or customary property as basic rights.

Private and customary land claims made under local customary law are recognized by the state, but only to the extent that they do not interfere with the state's own development programs. While laws and regulations set standard rates for compensating owners of some customary property (especially planted trees), the Constitution does not explicitly limit the state's power of eminent domain, or mandate just compensation for property taken by the state as a basic right.

18. This and related "narrow constructionist" interpretations have been advanced by noted jurists including Jacobus Frans, formerly West Kalimantan governor's advisor on customary law, and appointed Head of the regional government of Kapuas Hulu District in 1995. By contrast, dissident Adnon Buyung Nasution (head of Indonesia's Legal Aid Foundation, the country's leading human rights group, and a leader of the dissident "Petition of Fifty" group) insists that the unamended 1945 Constitution provides for a fundamentally authoritarian and state-heavy form of government.

19. This law led to significant land reform, especially in Java, although many of these initiatives were reversed during the bloody aftermath of the Suharto takeover.

20. Islands other than Java, Madura, Bali, and for some purposes Lombok. For a variety of historical reasons, customary law in several areas of West and South Sumatra is also more clearly recognized in Indonesian national law than most local law, because of the law's explicit use of the term "*hak ulayat*," which is in fact the local-language term used in these areas, in several hastily-drafted post-independence national laws (Lev 1973).

21. Law number 5 of 1960 (the Basic Agrarian Law) contains sections relating to customary law as unwritten laws that still continue to function in practice. Local customary law provisions most indisputably recognized in national law were the provisions that were in use as of 1960. Thus, the Basic Agrarian Law crystallized customary law, rather than acknowledging the dynamic "living law" of daily practice in most rural areas of Indonesia's Outer Islands. See Frans L. & S. Jacobus E. (1991) and Moniaga (1991).

22. The largest of these state-owned corporations is Pertamina, the state oil corporation. Many other corporations were actually joint ventures between Indonesian and foreign companies. The foreign company supplied working capital and management expertise, and the Indonesian partner received (and gave out) political favors. Particularly important from an environmental perspective were numerous logging companies that worked huge timber concessions that had been allocated as political favors to military friends of the Suharto regime. Lucrative timber concessions were given out to military figures as individuals, who then needed to link up with joint-venture partners to capitalize their logging business, or to entire military units, which used logging to generate their own revenues. See Robison (1986).

23. While the green revolution "package" of irrigation, insecticides, and herbicides did help Indonesia to become self-sufficient in rice by the early 1980s, the

price of such production included chemical poisoning of fisheries, and unprecedented pesticide resistance by insects such as the brown leaf hopper. This led to major regional crop failures by the late 1970s. In the mid-1980s, fertilizer subsidies were drastically cut, and experiments in "integrated pest management" set the stage for the government to ban fifty-seven commonly-used pesticides. The fact that these ecologically-sound decisions coincided with a foreign exchange crisis following the early-1980s drop in oil prices was not lost on environmentalists, who use these examples to show that sound environmental policy is often good economic policy as well.

24. See Soemarwoto (1989), Indonesia's most widely-read explanation of both the rationale for environmental impact analyses, and the law requiring them in Indonesia.

25. See Salim (1979), which explains links between the environment and development, especially in Indonesia, and was published immediately after the establishment of the Ministry of Population and Environment.

26. The basic structures of Indonesian law were adapted from Dutch colonial law after independence. Provisions of specific colonial laws not addressed directly in the Constitution are only gradually being superceded by Indonesian laws (Lev 1973).

27. Canadian technical assistance to the Ministry for Population and Environment was provided by the Canadian International Development Agency, CIDA, through a multi-university project on Environmental Management Development in Indonesia (EMDI).

28. At the *Kabupaten*, or district level (the sub-Provincial level of appointed regional government officials).

29. Article 19 of Act No. 4/1982 also defines these self-reliant community organizations, or "people's self-reliant institutions" (*Lembaga Swadaya Masyarakat*, in Indonesian abbreviated LSM) involved with the environment to include " . . . professional groups, which by the nature of their profession are concerned with and interested in handling environmental problems . . . hobby groups, which use individual motivation to preserve the environment, . . . [and] interest groups, whose special interests in development issues can contribute to the conservation and improvement of the environment, such as consumers groups, women's organizations, legal aid institutions, religious groups, community self-help promoters both in rural and urban areas, etc." (*Environesia* 1990b: 4).

30. There was initially quite a bit of confusion about the types of projects that required studies. Parts of the definitions triggered the need to do an assessment for projects with investments above a specified level. Others refer to specific development sectors, both in terms of projects for which analyses are required, and for which projects are exempted.

31. Both Soemarwoto and Koesnadi (author of Indonesia's most widely-read text on environmental legislation, 1989) founded such early centers at their respective institutions.

32. Indonesia's prestigious government universities, organized in tightly-controlled hierarchies of authority and with at least one campus in every province, are among the state's most effective institutions of "social control." Both faculty and students are indoctrinated in, and must publicly espouse, state development ideology and demonstrate familiarity with the government's interpretations of *Pancasila*. The depth of state (and even military) control of campus life has been the source of both quiet faculty outrage and the New Order period's most explosive incidents of student unrest. These included 1974 street protests triggered by Japanese premier Tanaka's visit to Jakarta, when students were dismayed by the government's encouragement of Japanese investment in Indonesia. In 1978, campus protests initially focused against rampant government corruption and its impact on "little people," and later exploded in reaction to violent military occupations of several campuses. Hundreds of students were arrested and an unverified number killed. Military takeovers of campuses resulted in the expulsion and in some cases long-term imprisonment of dozens of student protesters, particularly from two of Indonesia's most prestigious universitites, the Institute of Technology in Bandung and Gadjah Mada University in Yogyakarta. The political influence of student protesters was clearly demonstrated by the government's tolerant and even positive responses to 1993 protests (initiated by Moslem student groups) against the government lottery, and against a notorious state cover-up of the murder of Marsina, a young East Java labor organizer represented as a martyr by several of Indonesia's progressive social movements (see *Editor* 1994; Budiman 1994).

33. "Lucrative," that is, by Indonesian academic standards. To sustain middle class lifestyles on civil servant salaries, most university instructors balance their teaching requirements with other jobs or enterprises.

34. The ways in which faculty quietly directed their annoyance *within* the university system rather than blasting it to the outside have helped to strengthen the universities as nodes of ecological thought able to influence state decisions. While more confrontational environmental groups risk cutting off communications with the bureaucracies, campus-based environmentalists often express virtually the same substantive opinions in ways more acceptable to bureaucratic audiences (Djuangsih 1992).

35. Students active in university "nature-lover" social clubs that sponsored hiking, camping, or athletic adventure expeditions have often formed the cores of more politicized provincial environmental groups after they graduate, while maintaining connections with old campus friends who have joined local and regional bureaucracies. Many students expelled from prestigious universities after the 1974 and 1978 protests went on to organize both rural and urban community self-help groups, especially in Java. These supported local education, "alternative" development projects, and direct action protests on "environmental" issues, from urban scavenging to rural household fuel shortages; from pesticide poisoning to land expropriations.

36. Much of this history, and its relationships to environmental movements in other areas of Southeast Asia, is discussed in several recent works in English (see Belcher & Gennino 1993; Rush 1991; Hafild 1993; Riker 1992).

37. *Yayasan Indonesia Hijau* chapters provided good public relations support for KLH's work, in a respectful, moderate tone. When some of the local groups became increasingly critical of government policies, their permits to distribute pamphlets and other literature were withdrawn. Such was the fate of the Surabaya chapter in 1989. KLH continues to publish a magazine, *Serasi*, which promotes a technocratic management perspective.

38. Good examples of this mode of analysis are found in *LINK*, a periodic independent publication aimed at activists in a variety of non-governmental organizations, by the *Lembaga Informasi Kemasyarakatan* (Public Information Institute; see *LINK* 1988).

39. The Indonesian Communist Party (Partai Kommunis Indonesia, or PKI) was the world's largest outside of the Soviet Union in 1920, and continued to be a major political force throughout the post-Independence Soekarno period, until the group of generals led by Suharto used the threat of a Communist coup as the pretext to take power by military force in 1965. The Communist Party remains outlawed in Indonesia, and older Indonesians who survived the anti-Communist campaigns of the mid-1960s remain extremely reluctant to discuss any pro-Communist sympathies they may have held in the past.

40. Some of the best-known of these included "appropriate technology" groups such as *Dian Desa* (Village Light) in Central Java, and *Mandiri* (Standing on One's Own) in West Java.

41. Catholic lay activists, missionaries, and pastors in Indonesia of the 1980s were all influenced to some degree by the concepts of Liberation Theology that were energizing the Church in distant Latin America and neighboring Philippines. However, the Catholic hierarchy in Indonesia recognized that Liberation Theology's characteristic institutions—"Base Communities" as foci of social and political "conscientization"—would be seen as threats to the New Order's insistence on maintaining a depoliticized "floating mass," particularly in rural areas. While many local Catholic leaders were extremely sympathetic to local social justice movements, national Catholic leaders in the 1980s were painfully aware of the Church's precarious position—representing Indonesia's Catholic population with its high proportion of ethnic minorities, and initially the strongest opposition within Indonesia to the invasion of East Timor in 1975 and its subsequent annexation.

42. Such loose organizational structures are explicitly discouraged by Indonesian laws, which require all social organizations that hold meetings and distribute publications to register with the local government. All legally registered social organizations must designate responsible officers, and have hierarchical structures, to mirror the paternalistic leadership patterns promoted by the New Order state.

43. The "middle-aged" confidence of non-governmental organizers' critiques of state policies are exemplified by flamboyant figures such as Hariman Siregar, a physician-activist on health care issues (Subhan, Adi & Pujisriastuti 1993).

44. The "floating mass" principle refers to the New Order's idea that party politics should not affect rural populations, in effect, prohibiting opposition political organizing in rural areas. This gives a monopoly "voice" in rural areas to the New Order's "Functional Group" (GOLKAR, or *Golongan Karya*), a quasi-party in which virtually all civil servants are members. For relevance of the "floating mass" concept to rural environmental organizing, see Moniaga (1991).

45. "Refinement," in an Indonesian context, transcends aesthetic values and becomes the sign of a civilized, credible and respectable person. Approaching authority without proper refined courtesy ("*sopan santun*"), or expressing anger and distress in unambiguously defensive or aggressive terms ("*emosi*") makes any representative lose face and credibility as a leader. While this is emphatically the case in rural Java, it is also a characteristic of approaches to authority in the somewhat less formal interactions outside of Java.

46. It is difficult to know how often demonstrations or sabotage result from failure to resolve environmental complaints, especially in rural areas, because of relatively tight press control in Indonesia—mainly through self-censorship. With a loosening of self-censorship between about 1990 and mid-1994, however, press reports of local demonstrations, blockades, and sabotage became increasingly frequent. Environmentalists and muckraking journalists also documented systematic intimidation by local authorities of village leaders in environmental disputes (most notably in the North Sumatra Indorayon case, the Central Java Kedung Ombo Case, the East Kalimantan Bentian case, discussed below, and the Irian Jaya Freeport mine case).

47. Among these were the Study Group for the Development of Community Initiatives, in Siborong-borong, North Sumatra, which supported victims of the nearby Asahan Dam project (and later formed a core of people easily reactivated to support communities protesting abuses by the Indorayon Utama pulpmill and logging operations, further upstream), as well as a Solidarity Group for Kedung Ombo Victims, a Central Java student group with church ties, supporting protests by residents of communities forced to vacate the area flooded by the Kedong Ombo Dam.

48. Erma Witoelar had also been employed part-time by KLH during some of this early WALHI period. Clearly, the new ministery's leadership understood the need for non-governmental environmental organizations to build a public constituency for government environmental protection activities.

49. SKEPHI originally stood for the Joint Secretariat for Indonesian Forest Conservation (*Sekretariat Kerjasama Pelestarian Hutan Indonesia*), but the group now refers to itself as a network rather than a secretariat, or *Jaringan Kerja Pelestarian Hutan Indonesia*, the Indonesian Network for Forest Conservation.

50. KRAPP, the pesticides network, is also the Southeast Asian affiliate of the international Pesticides Action Network based in San Francisco.

51. Meaning "Rainbow", founded by former WALHI head Agus Purnomo and engineer Agus Sari, focusing mainly on policy research. It is also the secretariat for the Southeast Asia Climate Action Network.

52. *Yayasan Bina Sains Hayati Indonesia*, the Foundation for Indonesian Biological Science, headed by former WALHI staffer Hadi Pranomo.

53. Jakarta-based Konphalindo (the National Consortium for the Conservation of Indonesia's Environment) was founded in 1991 by Hira Jhamtani, formerly leader of SKEPHI. LATIN (*Lembaga Alam Tropika Indonesia*, or the Indonesian Tropical Nature Institute), was founded by young scientists formerly on WALHI's staff, and is active in research mainly in Western Indonesia, and environmental advocacy in Jakarta. Sejati (Institute for Environment and Culture) is a Jakarta-based organization dedicated to educating both the Indonesian and international publics about Indonesia's indigenous peoples through documentary films and exhibits.

54. Among the best known are those that have been involved in high-profile controversies, including several in Irian Jaya (Western New Guinea), Kalimantan (Indonesian Borneo), Sumatra, Bali and Lombok, as well as those in Java, many of which are among the oldest rural-based non-governmental organizations. A partial list of active regional environmental groups of the early-1990s can be found in Belcher & Gennino (1993).

55. The Tropical Forestry Action Plan was initiated in 1985 (and issued in 1987) by the World Resources Institute (WRI), the United Nations Development Program (UNDP), and the World Bank, and later carried on under the auspices of the Food and Agriculture Organization (FAO). Tropical forest nations participating in the process then followed with their own national action plans (WRI & FAO 1987).

56. INGI was the progressive non-governmental organizations' "shadow" of IGGI, the Inter-Governmental Group on Indonesia, made up in the late 1980s of official aid donor organizations, led by the Dutch government. IGGI was disbanded after the 1991 "Dili Massacre," when Indonesian troops opened fire on demonstrators in East Timor. The Netherlands protested and announced that its official aid in the future would be channeled entirely through non-governmental organizations, rather than to the Indonesian state. The Indonesian government responded by prohibiting non-governmental groups from accepting any financial assistance from the Netherlands, whether from the government or from private organizations. When IGGI disbanded, there was discussion about whether INGI should close down as well. Human rights and environmental organizations argued that since Indonesia's non-governmental organizations were increasingly important to Indonesia's future, the continuation of INGI was, perhaps, even more important as a pro-active progressive body than as a dissenting one. See several articles in the international newsletter on Indonesian environmental issues, *Down to Earth*, from early 1992.

57. This insight was provided by one anonymous reviewer of this chapter who was involved in the NGO responses to the TFAP process.

58. Of course, WALHI's emphasis on facilitating communication and development of an extremely heterogeneous membership makes many unambiguous philosophical positions difficult.

59. Much of the history of Indonesian rural organizing from both the colonial and the Soekarno periods has been suppressed by the New Order, especially if it harkened back to Communist Party influence. Even much of the language of Indonesian rural organizing was either suppressed by the New Order's version of acceptable political speech, or simply appropriated and redefined through New Order political doctrines.

60. Such as the transformative "activation" of passive communities (similar to West African "*animation rurale*") through ". . . development of awareness and cultivation [of] self reliance from within" (drawing on both Latin American concepts of "conscientization" and Gandhian concepts of self-reliance of almost a spiritual nature; SKEPHI 1990:12).

61. *Musyawarah* and *mufakat*, the joint pillars of the New Order image of appropriately de-politicized decision-making in villages and approved social organizations. In *Pancasila* indoctrinations, they are equated with patriarchal "family styles" of decision-making.

62. By 1993 WALHI received financial or technical assistance from several United Nations agencies (UNDP, UNEP, and UNICEF), bilateral development agencies or Jakarta embassies of the United States, Canada, Germany, Sweden, the Netherlands, United Kingdom, Switzerland, Belgium, France, Italy, Singapore, Malaysia, Thailand, the Philippines, Australia, New Zealand, Mexico, Norway and Finland (note Japan's conspicuous absence). It also received aid from the Ford and Asia Foundations, Friedrich Nauman and Friedrich Ebert Stiftung, CUSO, and Oxfam, and environmental groups including the World Resources Institute, Environmental Defense Fund, Greenpeace, Friends of the Earth, the Climate Action Network, World Conservation Union (IUCN), Institute for Development Research, and Volunteers in Asia, among others.

63. Many member groups actually threatened to boycott WALHI's national meeting in 1992 because of these issues, among others. (*Environesia* 1993a:7).

64. The 1992 national meeting also elected three executive co-directors, to facilitate the substantive work, administration, and financial accountability of the increasingly complex organization.

65. The incipient boycott, letter-writing campaign, and demonstrations clearly had an impact on Scott's public relations stance, even if it had yet to hit the corporation's "bottom line" by the time they decided to pull out of the Irian Jaya venture, as shown in elaborate project explanations and promotional material the U.S.-based company sent out in response to letters and petitions throughout 1989.

The boycott would have been modeled along lines similar to the international boycott of Nestle's products due to the company's unscrupulous promotions of its infant formula in Africa. The San Francisco-based Rainforest Action Network (RAN) and equivalent groups in Europe and Australia had already released a barrage of "Action Alerts" about the project through enormous mailing lists.

66. Most of the community organizations involved in environmental action in Irian Jaya have their roots in Catholic and Protestant church-based missionary and development groups, including both the American-based progressive Maryknolls, and the anti-military Mennonites.

67. SKEPHI's late-1980s positions were strongly molded by Hira Jhamtani, noted for her penetrating political-economic analyses of Indonesian forestry issues, and strong "Southern" voice in international environmental fora. She went on to found *Komphalindo,* with a focus on research and education.

68. Indro Tjahyono, SKEPHI's most frequent early-1990s spokesman, had been imprisoned for two years following the 1978 student demonstrations in Bandung; Saleh Abdullah was active in Moslem student and human rights groups, which were subject to increasing scrutiny and harassment in the early 1990s, especially following the "Tanjung Priok incident" in which the army violently suppressed demonstrations associated with charismatic Moslem preachers in north Jakarta.

69. By 1992 SKEPHI could no longer depend on the Indonesian postal service to carry clearly-marked domestic or international mailings of its publications, although their publications permits were never actually rescinded.

70. INFIGHT, the Indonesian Front for the Defense of Human Rights, circulated early 1990s statements explaining the group's "move away from the liberal human rights perspective based on notions of the individual to a more structural perspective based on the collective . . . to defend the interests of the oppressed class [nb: references to "class" as used in a marxist sense are absolutely taboo in the New Order lexicon]. INFIGHT's strategy statements explained that "INFIGHT's Human Rights Struggle cannot be caught up nor restrained by legal/formal rules and regulations as these legal boundaries are put up by a fascist state," though if necessary, INFIGHT would " . . . use the terminology of conventional human rights declarations to benefit INFIGHT's own vision/mission." INFIGHT also intended to employ a "network and a 'cell-system' model of communication" for clear communication with members and as a safety precaution. See photocopied pamphlet "INFIGHT" (1992).

71. See the brief account of the Inti Indorayon Utama case later in this chapter.

72. Aditjondro has been a community and human rights organizer in both Java and Irian Jaya (Indonesian West New Guinea), with a break for graduate study at Cornell University, from where he advised American environmental groups on formulating lobbying strategies regarding development aid to Indonesia. He is one of the leading intellectual voices in Indonesia's environmental and human rights movements. In 1994 he gained national fame by releasing names of over two-hundred-

and-seventy victims of the "Dili Massacre" in 1990, which the government claimed had taken no more than fifty lives. Since 1990 he has been a target of state harassment, as a spokesman of both the environmental and human rights movements.

73. *Suara Pembaruan* ("Voice of Renewal") is the most recent incarnation of the banned *Sinar Harapan* ("Ray of Hope"), and has a policy of publishing at least one environmental news story every day. The paper's guiding spirit, Aristides Katoppo, is also a WALHI advisor. Katoppo was ordered to divest himself of business interests in *Suara Pembaruan* by the government. After the mid-1994 crackdown on freedom of the press in Indonesia, Katoppo helped found the Indonesian Independent Journalists Association.

74. *International Rivers Review,* a newsletter published by the International Rivers Network, based in Berkeley, California, is devoted to pointing out the interlocked problems created by big dams. Canadian-based EnergyProbe has also helped organizations throughout North and South America, Asia, and Africa sort through the complex technical and political-economic issues involved in proposing alternatives to large energy projects, especially hydro-electric dams.

75. The story was told in numerous articles in national daily newspapers *Kompas* and *Suara Pembaruan* throughout 1988 and 1989; *"Jalan Keluar Kedung Ombo,"* (the issue's lead story and associated articles in the issue) *Tempo* 21:9; *Environesia* (1989b, 1989c); and SKEPHI & KSKPKO (1990).

76. This included a highly subsidized company that farms *tilapia* fish in Lake Kedung Ombo, which was supposed to provide employment for peasants whose farms had been inundated. Unfortunately, the fish provide few local jobs, and are too expensive for the Indonesian market. The company, which exports the fish to the United States, explains in a glossy pamphlet: "The Regal Springs . . . create and gather in lake Kedong Ombo, where twelve-thousand acres of open water with a visibility of 7 ft make our fish flourish. The lands surrounding the lake are uninhabited forest preserve guaranteeing a pollution free environment. PT Aquafarm Nusantara has received an exclusive lease to grow Tilapia in cages in this lake. The fish are fed a balanced diet of American grains and vitamins. The pristine environment combined with these high quality feeds are the first step towards a perfect product." ("Regal Springs Tilapia" 1993).

77. Heartbreaking press stories about Kedung Ombo victims have had the longest "legs" of virtually any single environmental issue in Indonesia.

78. See extensive critiques of these projects in *International Rivers Review* since the mid-1980s and general coverage in a documentary video by Phinney and Torrice (1994). See also the broad critique of World Bank development policies in Rich (1994).

79. See several WALHI and SKEPHI publications, 1988–1991, on the Kedung Ombo situation.

80. In fact, Kedung Ombo is conspicuously absent from WALHI's accounts of its achievements after thirteen years, in 1993 (*Environesia* 1993a: 4–5).

81. The mill was built with investment capital from a consortium of foreign banks, designed by Canadian consultants, equipped by a Finnish company with Finnish export investment credits; the Swiss Bank Corporation capitalized the rayon plant with convertible bonds, and an interest-free Finnish government loan covered costs of a research and training center (WALHI & LBH 1992: 43–44).

82. While investment location decisions on this scale tend to be controlled from Jakarta, District and Provincial level officials must also approve the final permits. While this is normally a "rubber stamp" process, since these regional officials are appointed in Indonesia's top-down system, Governors and District Heads (*Bupati*) have refused to approve controversial projects. The Asahan River region had already experienced a catalytic set of environmental controversies around the construction of the Asahan Dam and the dam-powered Inalum Aluminum smelter a few years earlier. The experience of both regional powerlessness and the temptation of lavish payoffs to regional and local officials had galvanized a core of regional civil servants, student and Protestant church groups, and progressive members of the Medan-based legal community to be wary of large-scale resource-intensive investments.

83. North Americans and Scandinavians have visited IIU's area frequently, as both IIU consultants and employees, and representing environmental organizations (WALHI & LBH 1992: 44, 46).

84. Ironically, Japanese investors in the Inalum aluminum smelter (powered by the Asahan Dam, downstream from the IIU plant), were among the parties most concerned about siltation from IIU logging operations settling behind Asahan Dam, and pollution from IIU's pulpmill corroding Asahan's concrete structures and turbines. If Asahan Dam's generating capacity is impaired, the aluminum smelter could also close down (see several reports in *Environesia* issues, 1988–1993.)

85. The group is KSPPM, for the Community Initiative Study and Development Group (WALHI & LBH 1993).

86. *Dayak* is a generic term that refers to virtually all of the indigenous non-Moslem ethnic groups that have historically practiced shifting cultivation in the Borneo interior.

87. The transmigration program has moved hundreds of thousands of people from the densely populated islands of Indonesia—especially Java and Madura—to new government-built settlements in rural Kalimantan in conjunction with the establishment of cash crop plantations. Since the mid-1980s, transmigration has also been used to relocate members Dayak communities whose customary lands and forests have been appropriated by the government for "development" by plantation companies.

88. Especially since the early 1970s, when the national government began to allocate logging concessions on land that the Ministry of Forestry had designated as state forest—much of which is also claimed under local customary rights by Dayak communities and forest-farming households.

89. The cause of massive forest fires in Kalimantan since the 1980s has been an issue of contention between environmental and Dayak rights activists and Indonesia's forestry bureaucracy. Dayak communities have traced devastating wildfires in their areas to logging debris and micro-climate changes associated with large-scale forest clearing and plantation development. Government foresters in Indonesia continue to attribute the worst conflagrations to escaped swidden fires from Dayak shifting cultivation. Recent research indicates that the worst periods of wildfire have multiple causes, exacerbated by periodic droughts caused by El Niño and other large-scale meteorological phenomena.

90. Many of them are approved by the Forestry Ministry as measures to "rehabilitate" lands still under shifting cultivation rotations,

91. Several Dayak rights and environmental organizations in Kalimantan publish newsletters and periodic journals. The *Kalimantan Review* is published in Pontianak by West Kalimantan's Institute for Dayakology Research and Development. *Gaharu* is published in Samarinda by East Kalimantan's Plasma Borneo.

92. For example, these urban-based organizations have invited and covered expenses for village activists to speak to governors and provincial assemblies, to address the national assembly and international aid organizations in Jakarta, and to international environmental and indigenous rights conferences. These organizations have also published information about particular local issues and stories in their newsletters, which are circulated among Dayak and environmental organizations throughout Kalimantan and elsewhere in Indonesia.

93. These projects are designated as Hutan Tanaman Industri/Transmigrasi projects, or HTI/Trans. The transmigration component was added to timber plantation planning in the early 1990s, when plantation developers found they could not recruit a sufficiently reliable, quiescent labor force from nearby indigenous communities in the Outer Islands for highly seasonal by labor-intensive plantation work.

94. These threats were particularly effective during 1993 and 1994, after the government had published its "eco-labeling" plans for forest product exports, and in conjunction with Indonesia's high-profile roles in meetings of the Nonaligned Movement, Asia Pacific Economic Council, and the World Trade Organization. Indonesia was also eager to protect its "most favored nation" trading status with the United States, which was already threatened by progressive Americans' criticism of Indonesia's actions in East Timor.

95. Both of these assertions formed the basis for expensive Indonesian and Malaysian international publicity campaigns responding to threats of an international boycott of their timber product exports.

96. Among the most notable of these initiatives are the Social Forestry Development Project in Sanggau, West Kalimantan (assisted by the German international aid agency) and participatory planning efforts in the Kayan-Mentarang region of East Kalimantan (assisted by the Worldwide Fund for Nature and the Ford Foundation). Virtually all of the regional environmental and Dayak rights organizations

have been involved in some participatory village forest management projects targeting specific types of resources or local management problems.

97. The Kayan-Mentarang "Culture and Conservation" project in East Kalimantan, and the Danau Sentarum and Bukit Baka planning projects in West Kalimantan are all sympathetic to this argument.

98. Because of the high profile and strong international attention given to park and preserve planning in Kalimantan, as one of the world's "mega-diversity" regions, recent developments in conservation biology thought take hold relatively quickly in Kalimantan's park and preserve planning processes.

99. The Worldwide Fund for Nature's (WWF) "Primary Environmental Care" initiative takes these assumptions as the starting point for both environmental education in the vicinity of proposed national parks and nature preserves in Indonesia, and in assisting members of local communities to participate in park planning and management processes (Diaz 1993).

100. This "fudge" is most commonly made with regard to issues of village logging for local use versus for commercial sale beyond the village, as well as over the question of whether shifting cultivation can be sustainable under conditions of rapid village population growth.

101. This observation is based on several years of the author's interactions with government foresters in Kalimantan, and observations of significant changes in basic attitudes toward local populations near project areas during that period.

Chapter 7

1. Two intriguing, if sometimes naïve, versions of this idea can be found in Orr (1992: ch.12) and Sachs (1992c:102–14).

2. See Oran Young (1994b) for a discussion about "effectiveness" (as opposed to "success").

3. Melucci argues that the "new conflicts develop in those areas of the system where both symbolic investments and pressures to conform are heaviest. . . . They are interwoven with the fabric of everyday life and individual experience" (1989:12). An informative discussion of NSMs and their role in institutionalized politics can be found in Jamie Anderson (1994:3–6).

4. There are, of course, organizations such as those discussed in chapter 5, which do operate in this mode. They depend, however, on the establishing links with *local* organizations working on rivers and creeks in *specific* places.

5. This is, admittedly, a simplistic statement, inasmuch as economic "globalization" is only one facet of the "global economy" (Gordon 1995).

6. The opportunity to "choose" between seventy or more ethnically-defined types of food is offered primarily to those with the discretionary income to make

such choices, although the appearance of "food courts" offering a smaller variety of "national" choices illustrates how even ethnic diversity can be marketed profitably (Reiff 1991).

7. I mean to suggest here that, depending on context, ethnic and sectarian identities are one way in which the process described here can play itself out. Many of those societies where these identities have emerged are "post-socialist," but it has been exposure to the capitalist world system that has undermined such relations of consumption as did exist there. This is, quite obviously, a point subject to vociferous dispute, but for a more extended exploration see, e.g., Derlugian (1993a).

8. What identity dominated before: "Exploiters of the Forest?" See also the discussion of the meaning of "whale" offered in chapter 3.

9. This is not to suggest that politics, somehow, magically disappears; only that it is redirected. Elinor Ostrom's analysis suggests that the politics in such situations are shifted from a focus on participation (or constitution) to a focus on distribution (or regulation; see 1990: ch. 6). See also chapter 2 in this volume.

10. This does raise an important point: such claims might be legitimate and yet not be historically "true." But, then, politics is not really about "truth" (Stone 1988: ch. 13).

11. It is not my intention here to analyze the validity of these knowledge claims; only to point out their attachment to place and group identity.

12. I put the term in quotes because, of course, none of these are "natural" in the sense of being Nature-caused. Arson was the cause of some of the Los Angeles fires but, more than this, such disasters arise from the dysfunctional relationship between human habitation and Nature. Fire is a regular part of the chaparral environment; human housing is not. Mark Reisner notes that the Indians of pre-Spanish times called the present-day Los Angeles Basin the "Valley of the Smokes" (1993).

13. Every year, Stephen Jay Gould writes a baseball article for the *New York Review of Books* (e.g., 1993, 1995). Without fail, he bemoans the day these two teams left New York, even though he remains a Yankees fan to this very day.

14. Public property is implicated here, as well; witness the response of mountain bikers and ORV operators to proposals to restrict access to park and wilderness lands in the interest of protecting fragile ecosystems (but see also Petit 1994)

15. This is, essentially, the model offered by Herman Daly's "steady-state economics" (1991: Part 1).

16. This is not meant to suggest complete self-sufficiency or autarky; only that, in the main, it is the local "property" base that is central to production and reproduction (see, e.g., Netting 1990).

17. To put this another way, ecotourists have the choice of many bays up and down the California coast—Bodega, Tomales, San Francisco, Monterey, Morro. There

is only one of each of these bays, however, and each is different, something that is meaningful only to those who come to "know" one.

18. Which is why the arrival of the state's resource agencies, whose staff's claim "I'm from the government and I'm here to help you," are regarded with such suspicion: the common interest rooted in a shared meaning has not been established. The Republican initiative in the 104th U.S. Congress to require compensation to owners for any environmentally-linked "taking" has been clearly designed to halt such transformations in property rights regimes.

19. Or, as Duncan and Ley put it: "On the one hand, a commodity is the outcome of a set of economic relations between people, and between people and nature. But no less is it a site of meanings, of values and valuing, a magical realm where materiality is infused with symbolic meaning" (1993:12). Cynthia Enloe provides an amusing account of the commodification of the banana in *Bananas, Beaches & Bases* (1990: ch. 6).

20. The entire process is, however, hostage to presidential politics. California Governor Pete Wilson, under whom the Biodiversity project was begun, might well disavow it as part of his future electoral plans.

21. As I observed at the 1993 meeting in Ferndale, on the Lost Coast, at which the merits of a CRIMP were described to the residents of the watershed adjacent to the Mattole. There is no reason to think that the majority of landowners in any "ecosystem" would not fear, more than anything, the unwanted intrusion of government agencies on their property.

22. For an interesting, albeit biologically-determinist exploration of this notion, see Stevens (1993a:B5) and the book he describes, *The Biophilia Hypothesis* (Wilson & Kellert 1993).

Chapter 8

1. The complexities of such a balancing act are well-illustrated by the "peso crisis" that hit Mexico in late 1994 and early 1995; see Kerr (1995).

2. For a discussion of the relationship between income levels and environmental protection, see Bailey (1993).

3. Already, in a world of 185 states, the prospect of getting all to act together is problematic; how much more difficult will this be in a world of 200 or 500 states (Davis 1994:A1)? Another indication of the potential multiplication of nations is the 1995 conference in the Hague of the "Unrepresented Nations and Peoples Organization" (Viviano 1995:A1).

4. A graphic, if sometimes inconsistent, description of such places can be found in Kaplan (1994).

5. By this I mean that in any one location, there are economic systems of local, regional, national, transnational and global extent as well as capital whose mobility is associated with these different levels. These systems are linked but not all of a single piece. Thus, for example, Silicon Valley is tightly integrated into the "global" economy, but some of its inhabitants are also participants in a service-based economy that, although coupled into global systems is largely directed toward meeting "local" demand. For further discussion of the notion of "multiple" economies, see Gordon (1995).

6. See the letter, responding to a review in *The New York Review of Books*, Oct. 20, 1994, by Benjamin Friedman. The writer suggests that, as with evolution, economic success may be highly contingent on specific temporal and spatial circumstances (Blume, Siegel & Rottenberg 1995:53).

7. The term for such historical contingency is "path dependency." See Krugman (1994: ch.9).

8. How intentional or fortuitous is, of course, the key question. Silicon Valley was hardly the product of chance; rather, it was the result of intentional mobilization of resources by the state in its pursuit of national security (Gordon 1995). The difficulty of maintaining such a development pole is illustrated by the relative collapse of the high tech center on Route 128 around Boston. Some of the difficulties facing policymakers who might like to repeat such mobilization are discussed in Crawford (1995).

9. In California, for example, such antagonisms have led Governor Pete Wilson to declare that "California is a proud and sovereign state, not a colony of the federal government" (Capps 1995:A1).

10. The point I am making here is not that "states" will disappear, but that power and legitimacy will become much more complex and problematic than they seem to have been for the past fifty to one hundred years. Just to take an example from the news of November 16, 1994: The U.S. Federal Reserve Board raised its basic interest rate by 3/4 of a percentage point, in order to moderate domestic economic growth and thereby stifle incipient inflation. This move pleased investors and distressed producers and consumers. And what were the impacts of this move on U.S. "power?" Or, as Bill Clinton is reputed to have said upon taking office, "you mean to tell me that the success of my [economic] program and my re-election hinges on the Federal Research and a bunch of [expletive] bond traders?" (quoted in Hayden 1994).

11. The best-known discussion of the "new medievalism" is to be found in Bull (1977:254–55, 264–76, 285–86, 291–94). The notion of "heteronomy" is found, among other places, in Ruggie (1983a:274, n. 30). The term "heterarchy" comes from Bartlett & Ghoshal (1990, cited in Gordon 1995:181).

12. The following paragraphs are based on Gordon (1995). He argues for the existence of three "logics" of world-economic organization: internationalization;

multi-/transnationalization; and globalization. The last is "heterarchical" and non-market and, as he puts it, involves "valorization of localized techno-economic capabilities and socio-institutional frameworks . . . [with] mutual reciprocity between regional innovation systems and global networks" ("Concurrent Processes of World-Economic Integration: A Preliminary Typology," handout in colloquium, Nov. 30, 1994, UC-Santa Cruz). Gordon is, essentially, making arguments about the organization and flows of knowledges, and his typology maps rather neatly (I think) onto my descriptions of the global networks of civil society.

13. Judith Mayer has almost convinced me that organizational knowledge is also mostly contextual, inasmuch as successful organization aimed at solving a localized functional problem must be based on a solid understanding of local social relations (personal communication, Jan. 26, 1995). See also the discussion of "tacit knowledge" in Hodgson (1992) and also Maniates (1990a, 1990b).

14. "Path dependency," in other words, proceeds from specifiable choice points; the trick is to recognize such points when they present themselves. For a discussion of path dependency, see Krugman (1994: ch. 9). This should not be confused with the chaos theory equivalent of the "butterfly's wings" creating hurricanes.

15. The notion that demand will create its own supply is true, even in highly flexible markets, only to the extent that someone sees a profit potential. If a "critical mass" of consumers is not to be found, neither will the product.

16. This point is briefly alluded to in Landsberg (1979: 133). It was certainly my experience: my 1971 Toyota Corolla got a now-picayune thirty miles to the gallon, but it only cost fifteen dollars to drive from Texas to New York. Even after gasoline prices doubled or tripled, the cost of gasoline for the trip, divided three ways, was still not much more than ten dollars.

17. See, e.g., Passell (1994:C1), which describes a swap of carbon dioxide credits for sulfur dioxide allowances.

18. Such a menu is best illustrated in a paper by Maria Todarova (1995) for a project on ethnic conflict and global security in which she shows how the collapse of the communist regime in Bulgaria left an underdetermined situation in which Muslims (not Turkish, but Bulgarian) have been presented with a choice of "identities," ranging from demands for economic improvement within Bulgaria to fusion with Turkey to conversion to Christianity to American patronage. Which will ultimately be chosen depends on the extent to which the agents of each choice are able to mobilize these people.

19. Compare, for example, Benedick (1991); Schneider (1990); Leggett (1990); Hawkins (1993); Shiva (1991); Seager (1993); and Chatterjee & Finger (1994).

20. Or, as T.H. Marshall once put it, "[W]e find that legislation, instead of being the decisive step that puts policy into immediate effect, acquires more and more the character of a declaration of policy that it is hoped to put into effect some day" (1950:59).

21. A short, but unpublished, description of one such meeting can be found in Ronnie D. Lipschutz, "Is It Warm in Here or Is It Just Me? A Report on Global Climate Negotiations" (1994), available on request from the author. Details about the meetings can be found in the *Earth Negotiations Bulletin* and *ECO*, both of which can be found on Econet on the World Wide Web.

22. Lest these questions seem ridiculous, as I noted earlier, one major point of controversy in the climate negotiations has to do with the accounting for carbon emissions from marine bunker fuels: Who gets the debit? A similar dispute has arisen over the allocation of greenhouse gas credits from joint implementation.

23. I do not use the term "vote" here in its literal sense, although it is for precisely such reasons that recorded votes are rarely held in such negotiations. The ideal is consensus, which means that the contestation over social meaning occurs mostly in small, informal groups that meet in the hallways or over coffee. A typically whiny American perspective on the entire voting process in such international fora can be found in Lind (1994) and has been echoed by Pat Buchanan, too.

24. The salmon fishery is actually more complicated than this. One needs to distinguish between chinook, which spawn in major river systems and which, in mid-1995, had reappeared in great number, and coho, which spawn in creeks and streams, and will probably be listed under the Endangered Species Act (Martin 1995a).

25. Actually, this case is a subset of a larger one having to do with the overall condition of the watershed. One could also tell stories about various chemicals leaching into the water supply, clear-cutting, overgrazing, or zealous environmentalists. These, however, would largely foreclose more inclusive choices.

26. More to the point, just as there was great resistance in the American South to the implementation of civil rights for blacks during the 1960s, there is no reason to think that local governance will, by its very nature, necessarily be "environmentally-friendly." Pursuing this parallel further, it is difficult to imagine governments sending national troops into communities in order to enforce the letter of environmental law, although there are a growing number of groups throughout the Western United States who seem to believe this could happen (Helveg 1995).

27. This is, essentially, that same view as that offered by Antonio Gramsci; see the discussion of this point below.

28. For one perspective on this phenomenon, see Leatherman, Pagnucco & Smith (1994:23–28).

29. This point is a heavily disputed one: To wit, is the international system so undersocialized as to make institutions only weakly-constraining on behavior, as Stephen Krasner (1993) might argue, or are the fetters of institutionalized practices sufficiently strong to modify behavior away from chaos and even anarchy, as Nicholas Onuf (1989) might put it? For a fully-doubtful view, see Mearsheimer (1995).

30. The notion of "two-level games," in which negotiators in international fora must "play" with other states as well as their domestic constituencies, was originally developed by Robert D. Putnam (1988); see also Evans, Jacobson & Putnam (1993). A brief discussion of "three-level" games can be found in Leatherman, Pagnucco & Smith (1994).

31. One might ask why these should not be treated as simple interest groups lobbying various institutions of governance at different levels? This perspective is correct, to some degree, but some non-governmental groups exercise governance jurisdiction in some arenas, while some governmental agencies find themselves lobbying in other arenas.

32. I have in mind here the notion that the negotiation of such stories—or the failure to renegotiate them—is, in a sense, behind the collapse of states such as Yugoslavia and Somalia, and the civil wars in places such as Rwanda and Chechnya. A detailed discussion of such stories and "storytelling" can be found in Derlugian (1995).

33. Actually, this raises an interesting question. If a system of global governance can tolerate the presence of non-territorialized political institutions not modelled on or subordinate to the state—for example, "tribes" and "clans," as opposed to cities and counties—there is no reason why tribes and clans could not also be involved in environmental governance, as is already partly the case in many projects underway throughout the world (Haddock 1994).

34. As Brian Ford puts it, if we look at the "functional system of governance associated with the particular level of civil society in question, whether it be on a global or regional level...[it is important to recognize that] this system of governance is a political formation that not only transcends both geographical borders and state jurisdictions, but as a matter of practice includes elements of the institutional machinery of various states" (1994:1).

35. Some economists argue that such regulation is simply a means of preventing entry to too many practitioners, and that, given the choice, people will choose more competent practitioners over less competent ones. This, however, begs the question of harm done to those who are first in line for an incompetent practitioner. The classic statement of the licensing problematic can be found in Frank Norris's *MacTeague* (1899/1964).

36. Which may be why we are so shocked when the rules of such professions are violated in a major way. Such associations provide a setting in which social constraints operate more strongly than in society at large. To violate the rules is to violate a trust, and this could lead to one being thrown out into the cold, cruel world (Hechter 1990).

37. Much of the following discussion is based on Chisholm (1989).

38. Another example of this phenomenon is the wholesale diamond trade in New York, Antwerp and Israel, which historically was based on trust in one's ethnic or religious "kin." For a discussion of clans, trust, and information, see Alvesson & Lindkvist (1993), Ouchi (1980), and Fukuyama (1995).

Bibliography

Interviews, conversations, talks, seminars, communications

Abdullah, Saleh. 1992. Staff at SKEPHI, Jakarta, personal communication, August.

Affif, Suraya. 1992a. Biodiversity Program manager, WALHI, Jakarta; International Consultative Group for the Global Biodiversity Strategy, personal communication, August.

Anonymous. 1994. Interviews with various Indonesian environmentalists in Jakarta and West Java, February and July/August.

Bélteki, Zoltán, Czilla Czsitu, and Imre Vass. 1993. Upper Tisza Foundation, Nyíregyháza, March 2, interview.

Berczes, Viktoria, and Attila Sántha. 1992. *Zöld Kor*, Pécs, Hungary, August 30, interview.

Berényi, György. 1994. Hungarian American Society, Budapest, June 29, interview.

Bower, Joseph, and Susan. 1994. Trinity Bioregion Group, Hayfork, California, September, conversation.

Campbell, Vicki. 1992. Arcata, California BLM, July 30, interview.

Childs, John Brown. 1992. "Rooted Cosmopolitanism: The Transnational Character of Indigenous Particularity," Stevenson Program on Global Security Colloquium, University of California, Santa Cruz, Oct. 19.

Csuja, László. 1994. Green Alternative Party, Budapest, June 21, interview.

Curry, Jim. 1993. Trinity Alps Botanicals, Hayfork, California, August 17, conversation.

Diaz, Gillian. 1993. Staff at Worldwide Fund for Nature, Jakarta, personal communication, June.

Djuangsih, Nani. 1992. Director of the Institute of Ecology, Padjadjaran University, Bandung, personal communication, July.

Dobson, Don. 1995. Santa Cruz fisherman, July 10, conversation.

Duane, Timothy P. 1995. City and Regional Planning, UC-Berkeley, August 30, conversation.

Erdélyi, Mihály. 1994a. Hydrogeologist, Budapest, July 1, interview.

Ewing, Robert. 1992. California Dept. of Forestry and Fire Protection, Sacramento, June 11, interview.

Foltanyi, Zsuzsa. 1995. Ökotárs Environmental Partnership Office, Budapest, March 21, interview.

Freer, Lori. 1993. U.S. AID Bureau for Europe, Washington, D.C., Feb. 5, interview.

Fülöp, Sándor. 1995. Environmental Management and Law Association, Budapest, March 21, interview.

Gallé, László, Gyula Molnár, Istvan Bogdan, and Elemér Szalme. 1993. Jate University, Szeged, March 4, interview.

Hibani, Hidayat. 1992. Staff at SKEPHI, Jakarta, personal communication, August.

House, Freeman. 1992a. Mattole Watershed Alliance, Arcata, California, July 30, interview.

Hunt, Irmgard. 1993. U.S. Project Director, Environmental Partnership for Central Europe, German Marshall Fund, Washington, D.C., Feb. 4, interview.

Illés, Zoltan. 1994. FIDESZ, Budapest, June 24, conversation.

Jhamtani, Hira. 1992. Founder of Konphalindo; former leader of SKEPHI, personal communication, August.

Jungwirth, Jim, and Lynn. 1993. Watershed Research and Training Center, Hayfork, California, August 17, conversation.

Kállay, György. 1993. Hungarian Ornithological Society, Mosonmagyarovar, March 5, talk.

Kehoe, Kieki. 1993. Consultant to the Institute for Conservation Leadership, Feb. 1, phone conversation.

Kelly, Dick. 1993. Executive Director, Shasta Alliance for Resources & Environment (SHARE), Redding, California, August 17, interview.

Kenez, Peter. 1994. March 10, personal communication.

Kennedy, Jon, and Harley Greiman. 1992. Forest Service-USDA, Sacramento, June 12, interview.

Kiszel, Vilmos, and Katalin Czippan. 1993. *Göncöl Alapítvány*, Mosonmagyarovar, March 7, conversation.

Lantos, Tamás. 1995. *Ormánság Alapítvány*, Pécs, Hungary, March 14, interview.

———. 1994. *Ormánság Alapítvány*, Drávafok, Hungary, June 25, interview.

Lucas, Gail. 1992. Little River, Mendocino, July 31, interview.

MacCall, Alec. 1995. National Marine Fisheries Service, Tiburon, California, July 14, phone conversation.

Majer, József. 1995. Dept. of Ecology & Zoogeography, Janus Pannonius University, Pécs, Hungary, March 15, interview.

Meister, Robert. 1994. Santa Cruz, conversation.

Miró Kiss, Ida. 1994. Green Alternative Party, Budapest, June 21, conversation.

Moles, Jerry. 1993. University of California Extension Service, August 3, phone conversation.

Nagy, Agoston. 1994. *Göncöl Alapítvány*, Vács, Hungary, June 28, conversation.

———. 1993. *Göncöl Alapítvány*, Vács, Hungary, March 1, interview.

Nasution, Adnon Buyung. 1994. Head of Indonesia's Legal Aid Foundation, leader of the dissident "Petition of Fifty" group, personal communication, March.

Orgoványi, Anikó. 1992. *Zöld Szív*, Pomáz, Aug. 28, interview.

———. and Mary Houston. 1993. *Zöld Szív*, Pomáz, March 8, interview.

Pál, Tamás. 1995. Social Conflicts Research Center, Hungarian Academy of Sciences, Budapest, March 14, 20, meeting.

Peters, Charles. 1994. New York Botanical Garden, personal communication and lecture on composition and succession of managed forests in West Kalimantan, Borneo Research Council Conference, Pontianak, July 10–14.

PLASMA (Samarinda) and Institute for Dayakology Research and Development (Pontianak) n.d., personal communication with members and staff.

Rodrigues, Kim. 1993. University of California Extension Forester, Eureka, California, August 18, interview.

Rozgonyi, Kata. 1994. "Adopt-a-Stream" administrator, *Göncöl Alapítvány*, Vács, Hungary, June 28, e-mail communication.

Sari, Augus P. 1995. Staff of Pelangi, Jakarta; Climate Action Network, Southeast Asia, personal communication, May.

Schmuck, Erzsébet. 1992. National Society of Conservationists, Budapest, August 25, interview.

Shores, John. 1993. Peace Corps, OATPS, Washington, D.C., Feb. 5, interview.

Spivy-Weber, Frances. 1992. Director, UNCED U.S. Citizens Working Group on Forests, Washington, D.C., March 7, conversation.

Stekler, Ottó, and Zoltan Medvetsky. 1994. Hungarian Green Party, Budapest, June 22, interview.

Stuart, Connie. 1993. North Coast Environmental Center, Arcata, California, August 18, interview.

Szirmai, Viktória. 1992. Social Conflicts Research Center, Hungarian Academy of Sciences, Sept. 1, interview.

Tjahyono, Indro. 1992. Leader of SKEPHI, Jakarta, personal communication, August.

Williams, Kelly. 1993. U.S. Bureau of Land Management, Redding, California, August 17, interview.

Zuckerman, Seth. 1992. Journalist and Mattole resident, San Francisco, June 24, interview.

Books, Journals, Newspapers

Acheson, James M. 1989. "Where Have All the Exploiters Gone? Co-management of the Maine Lobster Industry," pp. 199–217, in: Fikret Berkes, ed., *Common Property Resources—Ecology and community-based sustainable development* (London: Belhaven Press).

Aditjondro, George. 1991a. "Boycott Ethics," *Environesia* 5, #2: 4.

———. 1991b. *"Aksi Massa dan Pendidikan Masyarakat Hanyalah Dua Aspek Gerakan Kaum Terpelajar di Indonesia (Suatu tanggapan balik buat Arief Budiman),"* *Kritis* 5:3, 87–103.

———. 1990. *"Dampak Sistematik dan Kritik Kultural Yang Terlupakan: Suatu* Refleksi *Terhadap Kampanye Kedung Ombo Yang Lalu,"* *Kritis* 4:3, 44–51.

Affif, Suraya A. 1992b. "Biodiversity for Whom?" *Environesia* 6, #3: 5.

Agnew, John. 1993. "Representing Space—Space, scale and culture in social science," pp. 251–71, in: James Duncan and David Ley, eds., *Place/Culture/Representation* (London: Routledge).

——— and Stuart Corbridge. 1995. *Mastering Space: hegemony, territory and international political economy* (New York: Routledge).

Akcaya. 1993. *"LSM Tidak Hanya sebabai Pemrotes,"* September 24.

Alder, Emanuel. 1991. "Cognitive Evolution: A Dynamic Approach for the Study of International Relations and Their Progress, pp. 43–88, in: Emanuel Adler and Beverly Crawford, eds., *Progress in Postwar International Relations* (New York: Columbia University Press).

Alger, Chadwick F. 1990. "The World Relations of Cities: Closing the Gap Between Social Science Paradigms and Everyday Human Experience," *International Studies Quarterly* 34, #4 (December):492–518.

Alvesson, Mats, and Lars Lindkvist. 1993. "Transaction Costs, Clans, and Corporate Culture," *Journal of Management Studies* 30, #3 (May):427–52.

Anderson, Benedict. 1991. *Imagined Communities* (London/ New York: Verso, 2nd ed.).

Anderson, Jamie Jacobs. 1994. "Social Movements and Environmental Politics in Urban Brazil," paper prepared for delivery at the 1994 Annual Meeting of the American Political Science Association, New York, Sept. 1–4.

Anderson, Terry L., and Peter J. Hill, eds. 1994. *The Political Economy of the American West* (Lanham, Md.: Rowman & Littlefield).

Anderson, Terry, et al. 1991. *Free Market Environmentalism* (San Francisco: ICS Press).

Anderson, Walter Truett. 1990. *Reality Isn't What it Used to Be* (San Francisco: Harper & Row).

Andrásfalvy, Bertalan. 1989. "Die Traditionelle Bewirtschaftung der Überschwemmungsgebiete Ungarns" (Traditional Management of the Hungarian Floodplains), *Acta Ethnographica Acad. Sci. Hung.* 35, #1–2:39–88.

Andruss, Van, Christopher Plant, Judith Plant, and Eleanor Wright, eds. 1990. *Home! A Bioregional Reader* (Philadelphia: New Society Publishers).

Annis, Sheldon. 1992. "Evolving Connectedness Among Environmental Groups and Grassroots Organizations in Protected Areas of Central America," *World Development* 20, #4:587–95.

Arasu, K. T. 1994. "Soeharto Faces Funds Challenge," *Reuters Jakarta* Press Release, August 23.

Arimbi, H. P. 1993. "Problems in Enforcing Environmental Law in Indonesia: A Prediction," *Environesia* 7, #1: 13–14.

Ascher, William. 1995. *Communities and Sustainable Forestry in Developing Countries* (San Francisco: ICS Press).

——— and Robert Healy. 1990. *Natural Resource Policymaking in Developing Countries—Environment, Economic Growth and Income Distribution* (Durham, NC: Duke University Press).

Asimov, Isaac. 1983. *The Foundation Trilogy* (New York: Ballantine).

Assetto, V. J. 1993. "External Influence on Environmental Policy-Making in Hungary," paper presented at the 34th Annual Meeting of the International Studies Association, Acapulco, 23–27 March.

Associated Press (Jakarta, Anonymous). 1994. "Court Rejects Suharto Suit," December 12.

Augelli, Enrico, and Craig Murphy. 1988. *America's Quest for Supremacy and the Third World—A Gramscian Analysis* (London: Pinter).

Axelrod, Robert. 1984. *The Evolution of Cooperation* (New York: Basic).

Bailey, Norman A. 1993. "Foreign Direct Investment and Environmental Protection in the Third World," pp. 133–43, in Durwood Zaelke, Paul Orbuch, and Robert F. Houseman, eds., *Trade and the Environment—Law, Economics, and Policy* (Washington, D.C.: Island Press).

Bakos, Gabor. 1994. "Hungarian transition after three years," *Europe-Asia Studies* 46, #6 (Nov.):1189–1214.

Barber, Charles Victor. 1989. *The State, the Environment, and Development: the Genesis and Transformation of Social Forestry Policy in New Order Indonesia.* Ph.D. dissertation (Berkeley: University of California).

Bartlett, C., and S. Ghoshal. 1990. "Managing Innovation in the Transnational Corporation," pp. 215–55, in: C.Y. Doz and G. Hedlund, eds., *Managing the Global Firm* (London: Routledge).

Bartos, Tibor. n.d. 1, "Vízmüvelö Szabad Világ—Beszélgetés Andrásfalvy Bertalan müvelödésügyi miniszterrel" (The Free World of Water-Culture—An interview with Minister of Culture Bertalan Andrásfalvy), *Harmadik Part* #8, pp. 4–13.

———. n.d. 2, "Éló Vizet" (Live Water!), *Harmadik Part* #7, pp. 16–23.

Beasely, David. 1988. *The Suppression of the Automobile* (New York: Greenwood).

Belcher, Martha, and Engela Gennino, eds. 1993. *Southeast Asia Rainforests: A Resource Guide & Directory* (San Francisco: Rainforest Action Network, in cooperation with the World Rainforest Movement).

Benedick, Richard E. 1991. *Ozone Diplomacy—New Directions in Safeguarding the Planet* (Cambridge, Mass.: Harvard University Press).

Benford, Robert D., and Scott A. Hunt. 1992. "Dramaturgy and Social Movements: The Social Construction and Communication of Power," *Sociological Inquiry* 62, #1 (Feb.):36–55.

Béres, Zsuzsa. 1992a. "Divisions in the Green Party of Hungary," pp. 235–36, in: Mike Feinstein, *Sixteen Weeks with European Greens* (San Pedro, CA).

———. 1992b. "Hungary in Transition: The Ecological Issue, Part 2," pp. 238–39, in: Mike Feinstein, *Sixteen Weeks with European Greens* (San Pedro, CA).

Berger, John J. 1990. *Environmental Restoration: science and strategies for restoring the Earth* (Washington, D.C.: Island Press).

Bergesen, Albert. 1990. "Turning World-System Theory on Its Head," pp. 67–82, in: Mike Featherstone, ed., *Global Culture—Nationalism, Globalization, and Modernity* (London: Sage).

Berkes, Fikret, ed. 1989. *Common Property Resources—Ecology and community-based sustainable development* (London: Belhaven Press).

Berman, Marshall. 1982. *All That is Solid Melts Into Air* (New York: Simon & Schuster).

Bijker, Wiebe E., Thomas P. Hughes, and Trevor J. Pinch, eds. 1987. *The Social Construction of Technological Systems—New Directions in the Sociology and History of Technology* (Cambridge, Mass.: MIT Press).

Bisnis Indonesia. 1992. *"Dephut sekesaikan rencana induk pembangunan HTI,"* April 9.

Blakie, Piers. 1985. *The Political Economy of Soil Erosion* (London: Longman).

Block, Fred. 1990. *Postindustrial Possibilities: A critique of economic discourse* (Berkeley: University of California Press).

Blume, Marshall E., Jeremy J. Siegel, and Dan Rottenberg. 1995. "Technology's Lesson," *New York Review of Books*, Jan. 12, p. 53.

Bonner, Arthur. 1990. *Averting the Apocalypse—Social Movements in India Today* (Durham, N.C.: Duke University Press).

Booth, Douglas E. 1994. *Valuing Nature—The Decline and Preservation of Old-Growth Forests* (Lanham, Md.: Rowman & Littlefield).

Booth, Ken. 1991. "Security in Anarchy: Utopian Realism in Theory and Practice," *International Affairs* 67, #3 (July):527–45.

Bozóki, András, András Körösényi, and George Schöpflin, eds. 1992. *Post-Communist Transition—Emerging Pluralism in Hungary* (London & New York: Pinter & St. Martin's).

Bramwell, Anna. 1994. *The Fading of the Greens* (New Haven: Yale University Press).

———. 1989. *Ecology in the 20th Century—A History* (New Haven: Yale University Press).

Braus, Judy. 1991. "The Peace Corps joins in; can teaching English help the upper Tisza?" *EPA Journal* 17, #4 (Sept.–Oct.):53–54.

Breyman, Steven. 1993. "Knowledge as Power: Ecology Movements and Global Environmental Problems," pp. 124–57, in: Ronnie D. Lipschutz and Ken Conca, eds., *The State and Social Power in Global Environmental Politics* (New York: Columbia University Press).

Broad, Robin, and John Cavanagh. 1993. *Plundering Paradise: The Struggle for the Environment in the Philippines* (Berkeley: University of California Press).

Bromley, Daniel W., ed. 1992. *Making the Commons Work—Theory, Practice, and Policy* (San Francisco: ICS Press).

Brown, Beverly A. 1995. *In Timber Country: Working People's Stories of Environmental Conflict and Urban Flight* (Philadelphia: Temple University Press).

Brysk, Alison. 1996. "Turning Weakness into Strength: The Internationalization of Indian Rights," *Latin American Perspectives* 23, # 2 (spring): 38–57.

Buckley, R. 1994. "A Framework for Ecotourism," *Annals of Tourism Research* 21, #3:661–69.

Budiman, Arief. 1994. "People Power: *Proses yang Sedang Berjalan*" *Editor* 7, #15 (Jan.): 28–29.

———. 1990. *"Gerakan Mahasiswa dan LSM: Ke Arah Sebuah Reunifikasi (Catatan untuk G.J.A.),"* *Kritis* 4:3, 53–59.

Bull, Hedley. 1977. *The Anarchical Society—A Study of Order in World Politics* (New York: Columbia University Press).

Burawoy, Michael, and Pavel Krotov. 1992. "The Soviet Transition from Socialism to Capitalism: Worker Control and Economic Bargaining in the Wood Industry," *American Sociological Review* 57 (Feb.):18.

Burkey, Stan. 1993. *People First—A Guide to Self-Reliant, Participatory Rural Development* (London: Zed Books).

Buzan, Barry. 1995. "Security, the State, the 'New World Order,' and Beyond," pp. 187–211, in: Ronnie D. Lipschutz, ed., *On Security* (New York: Columbia University Press).

———. 1993. "From international system to international society: structural realism and regime theory meet the English school," *International Organization* 47, # 3 (summer): 327–352.

———. 1991. *People, States and Fear* (Boulder: Lynne Rienner, 2nd ed.).

Cable, Sherry, and Charles Cable. 1994. *Environmental Problems Grassroots Solution—The Politics of Grassroots Environmental Conflict* (New York: St. Martin's).

California Executive Council on Biological Diversity. 1994. "Imperiled Salmon Inspire Citizens to Restore Mattole River Watershed," *California Biodiversity News* 1, #5 (summer):1, 4–5, 8.

"California Coordinated Resource Management and Planning, Statewide Registry of CRMP Areas," circa 1993, photocopy, no date, no author.

California State Legislative Counsel's Digest. 1989. "Assembly Bill No. 1580, Chapter 1241," as approved October 1.

Capps, Steven A. 1995. "Wilson sworn in with a blast at feds," *San Francisco Examiner*, January 8, p. A1.

Carroll, Thomas F. 1992. *Intermediary NGOs—The Supporting Link in Grassroots Development* (West Hartford, Conn.: Kumarian Press).

Chapman, J.L., and M.J. Reiss. 1992. *Ecology—Principles and Applications* (Cambridge: Cambridge University Press).

Chatterjee, Pratap, and Matthias Finger. 1994. *The Earth Brokers—Power, Politics and World Development* (New York: Routledge).

———. 1992. "The same old order," *Ecocurrents* 2, #3 (Dec.).

Chisholm, Donald. 1989. *Coordination without Hierarchy—Informal Structures in Multiorganizational Systems* (Berkeley: University of California Press).

Clark, Mary E. 1989. *Ariadne's Thread—The Search for New Modes of Thinking* (New York: St. Martin's Press).

Clark, William C. 1989. "The human ecology of global change," *International Social Science Journal* 121, 315–46.

Cleary, David. 1993. "After the frontier: problems with political economy in the modern Brazilian Amazon," *Journal of Latin American Studies* 25, #2 (May):331–50.

Coats, A. W., ed. 1971. *The Classical Economists and Economic Policy* (London: Methuen).

Cohen, Jean L., and Andrew Arato. 1992. *Civil Society and Political Theory* (Cambridge, Mass.: MIT Press).

Cohen, Raymond. 1991. *Negotiating Across Cultures—Communication Obstacles in International Diplomacy* (Washington, D.C.: United States Institute of Peace Press).

Cole, Constance H. 1993. "Centers of Economic, Political and Social Decision Making in Central America and Central Europe," paper prepared for the 34th Annual Convention of the International Studies Association, Acapulco, 23–27 March.

Commoner, Barry. 1990. *Making Peace with the Planet* (New York: Pantheon).

Conca, Ken. 1994. "Environmental Protection, International Norms, and National Sovereignty: The Case of the Brazilian Amazon," in Gene Lyons and Michael Mastanduno, eds., *Beyond Westphalia? National Sovereignty and International Intervention* (Baltimore: Johns Hopkins University Press).

———. 1993. "Environmental Change and the Deep Structure of World Politics," pp. 306–26, in: Ronnie D. Lipschutz and Ken Conca, eds., *The State and Social Power in Global Environmental Politics* (New York: Columbia University Press).

Cox, Robert W. 1993. "Structural Issues of Global Governance: Implications for Europe," pp. 259–89, in: Stephen Gill, ed., *Gramsci, Historical Materialism and International Relations* (Cambridge: Cambridge University Press).

———. 1987. *Production, Power and World Order* (New York: Columbia University Press).

Crawford, Beverly. 1995. "Hawks, Doves, But no Owls: International Economic Interdependence and the Construction of the New Security Dilemma," in: Ronnie D. Lipschutz, ed., *On Security* (New York: Columbia University Press).

Cronon, William. 1992. "A Place for Stories: Nature, History, and Narrative," *Journal of American History* (March):1347–76.

———. 1991. *Nature's Metropolis—Chicago and the Great West* (New York: Norton).

———. 1983. *Changes in the Land: Indians, Colonists and the Ecology of New England* (New York: Hill & Wang).

Crook, Stephen, Jan Pakulski, and Malcolm Waters. 1992. *Postmodernization—Change in Advanced Society* (London: Sage).

Crosby, Alfred W. 1986. *Ecological Imperialism—The Biological Expansion of Europe, 900–1900* (Cambridge: Cambridge University Press).

Crowfoot, James E., and Julia M. Wondolleck. 1990. *Environmental Disputes: Community Involvement in Conflict Resolution* (Washington, D.C.: Island Press).

Cruikshank, Jeffrey. 1987. *Breaking the Impasse: Consensual Approaches to Resolving Public Disputes* (New York: Basic).

Csaba, Vass. 1993. "Olvasónapló a Dunáról" ("A Reader's Journal on the Danube"), *Ökotáj* #5 (autumn):62–71.

Czempiel, Ernst-Otto. 1992. "Governance and Democratization," pp. 250-71, in: James N. Rosenau and Ernst-Otto Czempiel, eds., *Governance without Government: Order and Change in World Politics* (Cambridge: Cambridge University Press).

Dalton, Russell J. 1994. *The Green Rainbow—Environmental Groups in Western Europe* (New Haven: Yale University Press).

Daly, Herman E. 1991. *Steady-State Economics* (Washington, D.C.: Island Press, 2nd ed. with new essays).

———, and John B. Cobb, Jr. 1989. *For the Common Good—Redirecting the Economy Toward Community, the Environment, and a Sustainable Future* (Boston: Beacon Press).

Davis, Bob. 1994. "Global Paradox: Growth of Trade Binds Nations, but it also can Spur Separatism," *Wall Street Journal*, June 20 (Western ed.), p. A1.

Deák, István. 1994. "Post-Post-Communist Hungary," *New York Review of Books*, August 11, pp. 33–38.

DeBardeleben, Joan. 1991. *To Breathe Free—Eastern Europe's Environmental Crisis* (Washington, D.C./Baltimore: Wilson Center Press/Johns Hopkins University Press, 1991).

——— and John Hannigan, eds. 1995. *Environmental Security and Quality after Communism—Eastern Europe and the Soviet Successor States* (Boulder: Westview).

Derlugian, Georgi M. 1995. "The Tale of Two Resorts—Abkhazia and Ajaria before and since the Soviet Collapse," Center for German & European Studies, University of California, Berkeley, Working Paper 6.2, March.

———. 1994. "There is Such a Party of Zhirinovksy! Towards the Ethics and Aesthetics of Russia's Eventual Dictatorship," December, draft.

———. 1993a. " 'Ethnic' Violence in the Post-Communist Periphery," *Studies in Political Economy* 41 (summer):45–81.

———. 1993b. "Power, Ethnicity and the Real Economy in the Ex-Soviet Southern Tier," paper presented at the Conference on "Reconfiguring State and Society: Social and Political Consequences of Liberalization in Comparative Perspective," UC-Berkeley, Berkeley, California, April 22-24.

Dessler, David. 1989. "What's at Stake in the Agent-Structure Debate?" *International Organization* 43, #3 (summer):441–74.

Deudney, Daniel. 1995a. "The Philadelphian system: sovereignty, arms control, and balance of power in the American states-union, circa 1787–1861," *International Organization* 49, #2 (spring):191–228.

———. 1995b. "Political Fission: State Structure, Civil Society, and Nuclear Weapons in the United States," pp. 87–123, in: Ronnie D. Lipschutz, ed., *On Security* (New York: Columbia University Press).

———. 1993. "Global Environmental Rescue and the Emergence of World Domestic Politics," pp. 281–305, in: Ronnie D. Lipschutz and Ken Conca, eds., *The State and Social Power in Global Environmental Politics* (New York: Columbia University Press).

Diringer, Elliot. 1993. "Timber Groups Wants State Owls Off List—Industry counts thousands in California's forests," *San Francisco Chronicle*, Oct. 7, p. A3.

Dominick, Raymond H., III. 1992. *The Environmental Movement in Germany* (Bloomington: Indiana University Press).

Dorfman, Robert. 1985. "An Economist's View of Natural Resource and Environmental Problems," pp. 67–96, in: Robert Repetto, ed., *The Global Possible—Resources, Development, and the New Century* (New Haven: Yale University Press).

Down to Earth is published in Britain by a consortium of environmental and human rights groups.

Drabek, Anne Gordon, ed. 1987. *Development Alternatives: The Challenge for NGOs*, supplement to *World Development* 15 (autumn).

Dryzek, John S. 1987. *Rational Ecology—Environment and Political Economy* (Oxford: Basil Blackwell).

Duncan, James, and David Ley. 1993. "Introduction: Representing the Place of Culture," pp. 1–21, in: James Duncan and David Ley, eds., *Place/Culture/Representation* (London: Routledge).

Durning, Alan B. 1989. *Action at the Grassroots: Fighting Poverty and Environmental Decline* (Washington, D.C.: Worldwatch Institute, January).

Earth Negotiations Bulletin. 1995. (NGO newsletter reporting on procedural aspects of UN Framework Convention on Climate Change negotiations.)

Easterbrook, Gregg. 1994. "The birds—the spotted owl: an environmental parable," *New Republic*, March 28, pp. 22–27.

ECO. 1995. (NGO newsletter reporting on UN Framework Convention on Climate Change negotiations.)

The Economist. 1995a. "When mining meets golf," July 1, pp. 21–22.

———. 1995b. "Survey of the Internet," July 1–7, special report.

———. 1993/94. "Biology meets the dismal science," Dec. 25–Jan. 7, pp. 93–95.

———. 1993. "Survey of Eastern Europe," special report.

———. 1991. "Tree-lover, spare the woodman," June 22, pp. 19–20, 23.

Editor. 1994. Vol. 7, #15, January (Issue with a series of articles focusing on 1993 protests).

Ekins, Paul. 1992. *A New World Order—Grassroots movements for global change* (London: Routledge).

——— and Manfred Max-Neef, eds. 1992. *Real-Life Economics—Understanding wealth creation* (London: Routledge).

Emil, Salim. 1979. *Lingkungan Hidup dan Pembangunan* (Jakarta: Mutiara).

Enloe, Cynthia 1990, *Bananas, Beaches & Bases—Making Feminist Sense of International Politics* (Berkeley: University of California Press).

Environesia. 1993a. "Peoples Participation in Sustainable Development," Vol. 7, #3.

———. 1993b. "CIFOR Establishment: Consistent with Conservation?" Vol. 7, #1.

———. 1992. Vol. 6, #1.

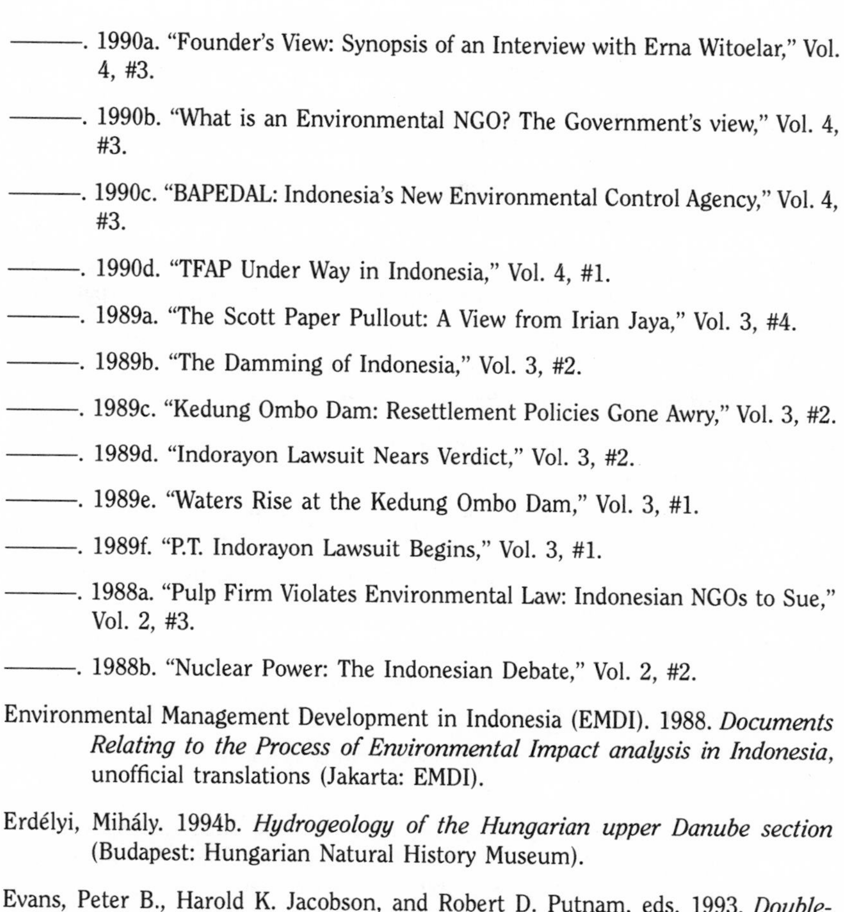

———. 1990a. "Founder's View: Synopsis of an Interview with Erna Witoelar," Vol. 4, #3.

———. 1990b. "What is an Environmental NGO? The Government's view," Vol. 4, #3.

———. 1990c. "BAPEDAL: Indonesia's New Environmental Control Agency," Vol. 4, #3.

———. 1990d. "TFAP Under Way in Indonesia," Vol. 4, #1.

———. 1989a. "The Scott Paper Pullout: A View from Irian Jaya," Vol. 3, #4.

———. 1989b. "The Damming of Indonesia," Vol. 3, #2.

———. 1989c. "Kedung Ombo Dam: Resettlement Policies Gone Awry," Vol. 3, #2.

———. 1989d. "Indorayon Lawsuit Nears Verdict," Vol. 3, #2.

———. 1989e. "Waters Rise at the Kedung Ombo Dam," Vol. 3, #1.

———. 1989f. "P.T. Indorayon Lawsuit Begins," Vol. 3, #1.

———. 1988a. "Pulp Firm Violates Environmental Law: Indonesian NGOs to Sue," Vol. 2, #3.

———. 1988b. "Nuclear Power: The Indonesian Debate," Vol. 2, #2.

Environmental Management Development in Indonesia (EMDI). 1988. *Documents Relating to the Process of Environmental Impact analysis in Indonesia*, unofficial translations (Jakarta: EMDI).

Erdélyi, Mihály. 1994b. *Hydrogeology of the Hungarian upper Danube section* (Budapest: Hungarian Natural History Museum).

Evans, Peter B., Harold K. Jacobson, and Robert D. Putnam, eds. 1993. *Double-Edged Diplomacy—International Bargaining and Domestic Politics* (Berkeley: University of California Press).

———, Dietrich Reuschemeyer, and Theda Skocpol. 1985. "On the Road toward a More Adequate Understanding of the State," pp. 347–56, in: Peter B. Evans, Dietrich Reuschemeyer, and Theda Skocpol, eds., *Bringing the State Back In* (Cambridge: Cambridge University Press).

Evernden, Neil. 1992. *The Social Creation of Nature* (Baltimore: Johns Hopkins University Press).

———. 1993. *The Natural Alien—Humankind and Environment* (Toronto: University of Toronto Press, 2nd. ed.).

Falk, Richard. 1992. *Explorations at the Edge of Time—The Prospects for World Order* (Philadelphia: Temple University Press).

Feffer, John. 1992. *Shock Waves—Eastern Europe after the Revolutions* (Boston: South End Press).

Feldman, David L. 1991. *Water Resources Management—In Search of an Environmental Ethic* (Baltimore: Johns Hopkins University Press).

Feshbach, Murray, and Alfred Friendly, Jr. 1992. *Ecocide in the USSR: Health and Nature Under Siege* (New York: Basic).

Fiedler, Peggy L., and Subodh K. Jain, eds., 1992. *Conservation Biology: The Theory and Practice of Nature Conservation* (New York: Chapman & Hall).

Finger, Matthias. 1994. "NGOs and Transformation: Beyond Social Movement Theory," in: Thomas Princen and Matthias Finger, eds., *Environmental NGOs in World Politics: Linking the Local and the Global* (London: Routledge).

Firor, John. 1990. *The Changing Atmosphere—A Global Challenge* (New Haven: Yale University Press).

Fisher, Duncan, Clare Davis, Alex Juras, and Vukasin Pavlovic eds. 1992. *Civil Society and the Environment in Central and Eastern Europe* (London, Bonn & Belgrade: Ecological Studies Institute, Institut für Europäische Umweltpolitik, & Eko-Center), May.

Fleischer, Tamás. 1993. "Jaws on the Danube: Water Management, Regime Change and the Movement Against the Middle Danube Hydroelectic Dam," *International Journal of Urban and Regional Research* 17, #3:429–52.

———. n.d. "Infrastructure and Networks in Hungary's Economic Development," Budapest: Fleischer Research Periphery.

Florus, Paulus, Stepanus Djuweng, John Bamba, and Nico Andasputra. n.d. *Kebudayaan Dayak: Aktualisasi dan Tranformasi* (Jakarta: Gramedia & Institute of Dayakology Research and Development).

Ford, Brian. 1994. "Trade, Transnational Civil Society and the Formation of Ethical Content in World and Regional Systems: Transcending the Posted Borders of the Modern System," paper presented at the American Political Science Association Conference, New York, 1–4 Sept.

Ford, Maggie. 1994. "Booming Indonesia Follows Tigers' Path," *Australian Financial Review*, January 13, p. 35.

"Forests Plan Attacked as Favoring Loggers." 1993. *San Francisco Chronicle*, June 18, p. A2 (*Washington Post* wire service).

Foster, John Bellamy. 1993. "The Limits of Environmentalism Without Class: Lessons from the Ancient Forest Struggle in the Pacific Northwest," *Capitalism, Nature, Socialism* 4, #1 (March):11–42.

Fox, Jefferson. 1990. "Diagnostic Tools for Social Forestry," pp. 119–33, in: Mark Poffenberger, ed., *Keepers of the Forest: Land Management Alternatives in Southeast Asia* (Manila: Ataneo de Manila University Press).

Franke, Catherine. 1990. "An Interview with Redwood Summer Organizer Darryl Cherney," *The Monthly Planet* (Santa Cruz), July.

Frankland, E.G., and R.H. Cox. 1995. "The legitimation problems of new democracies: postcommunist dilemmas in Czechoslovakia and Hungary," *Environment and Planning C: Government and Policy* 13:141–58.

Frans, S., and E. Jacobus. 1991. "*Hak milik adat atas tanah pada masyarakat suku bangsa Dayak Kenyah di Kecamatan Pujungan Kabupaten Bulungan Propinsi Kalimantan Timur*" (manuscript for the "Culture and Conservation" project, Kayan-Mentarang, from Ford Foundation, Jakarta).

Frederick, Howard H. 1992. (hfrederick @igc.apc.org), "Computer Communications in Cross-Border Coalition-Building North American NGO Networking Against NAFTA," Oct. 6, downloaded from Econet.

French, Hilary. 1990. *Clearing the Air: A Global Agenda* (Washington, D.C.: Worldwatch Institute, Jan., Worldwatch Paper 94).

Friedman, Jonathan. 1990. "Being in the World: Globalization and Localization," pp. 311–28, in: Mike Featherstone, ed., *Global Culture—Nationalism, Globalization, and Modernity* (London: Sage).

Fukuyama, Francis. 1995. "Social Capital and the Global Economy," *Foreign Affairs* 74, #5 (Sept./Oct.): 89–103.

"Future Economics: An interview with Chris Woods," 1992, pp. 138–41, in: Laura Walker, ed., *Mattolia—Visions of Our Grandchildren's World* (Petrolia, CA)

Gabel, Matthew J. 1995. "The Political Consequences of Electoral Laws in the 1990 Hungarian Elections," *Comparative Politics* 27, #2 (Jan.):205–14.

Gaharu is published by Plasma Borneo in Samarinda.

Galambos, Judit. 1993. "An International Environmental Conflict on the Danube: The Gabcikovo-Nagymaros Dams," pp. 176–226, in: Anna Vari and Pál Tamás, eds., *Environment and Democratic Transition—Policy and Politics in Central and Eastern Europe* (Dordrecht: Kluwer Academic).

Gallopin, Gilberto C., Pablo Gutman, and Hector Maletta. 1989. "Global impoverishment, sustainable development and the environment: a conceptual approach," *International Social Science Journal* 121 (Aug.): 375–98.

Gamman, John K. 1994. *Overcoming Obstacles in Environmental Policymaking—Creating Partnerships through Mediation* (Albany: SUNY Press).

———. 1991. "Creating an Open Decisionmaking Process to Improve Environmental Policy Implementation: Applying Negotiation Strategies to International Development," prepared for the U.S. Agency for International Development, October, photocopy.

Gaventa, John. 1980. *Power and Powerlessness: Quiescence and Rebellion in an Appalachian Valley* (Urbana: University of Illinois Press).

Gaura, Maria A. 1995. "Fisher strategies paying off," *San Francisco Chronicle*, July 19, 1995, p. A1.

George, Alexander L. 1993. *Bridging the Gap—Theory & Practice in Foreign Policy* (Washington, D.C.: United States Institute of Peace Press).

Gerlach, Luther. 1993. "Negotiating Ecological Interdependence Through Societal Debate: the 1988 Minnesota Drought," pp. 185–220, in: Ronnie D. Lipschutz and Ken Conca, eds., *The State and Social Power in Global Environmental Politics* (New York: Columbia University Press).

———. 1990. "Cultural Construction of the Global Commons," pp. 319–42, in: Robert H. Winthrop, ed., *Culture and the Anthropological Tradition—Essays in Honor of Robert F. Spencer* (Washington, D.C.: University Press of America).

German Bundestag, ed. 1989. *Protecting the Earth's Atmosphere—An International Challenge* (Bonn).

German Marshall Fund n.d., "On the Ground," *TransAtlantic Perspectives* 27.

Gerth, H. H. and C. W. Mills, eds. 1946. *From Max Weber: Essays in Sociology* (New York: Oxford University Press).

Ghai, Dharam and Jessica M. Vivian. 1992. *Grassroots Environmental Action—People's Participation in Sustainable Development* (London: Routledge).

Ghils, Paul. 1992. "International Civil Society: International Non-Governmental Organizations in the International System," *International Social Science Journal* 133 (August):417–29.

Gill, Stephen. 1994. "Structural change and global political economy: Globalizing élites and the emerging world order," pp. 169–199, in: Yoshikazu Sakamoto, ed., *Global transformation: Challenges to the state system* (Tokyo: United Nations University Press).

———. 1993. "Epistemology, Ontology and the 'Italian School'," pp. 21–48, in: Stephen Gill, ed., *Gramsci, Historical Materialism and International Relations* (Cambridge: Cambridge University Press).

———. 1991. "Reflections on Global Order and Sociohistorical Time," *Alternatives* 16: 275–314.

———, Robert Cox, and Kees Van Der Pijl. 1992. "Structural Change and Globalizing Elites—Political Economy Perspectives in the Emerging World Order," prepared for the International Conference on Changing World Order and the United Nations System, Yokahama, Japan, 24–27.

Gille, Zsuzsa. 1994. Field statement, Board of Studies in Sociology, UC-Santa Cruz, October.

———. 1992. "The Invisible Back-Scratching Hand of State Socialism—The Pattern of Nature Transformation and the Construction of the Environmental

Problem in Former Socialist Countries," Master's Thesis, Board of Studies in Sociology, University of California, Santa Cruz, Nov. 24.

Global Rivers Environmental Education Network (GREEN), n.d. informational brochure.

Godelier, M. 1979. "Territory and property in primitive society," in: M. von Cranach, K. Foppa, W. Lepenies, and D. Ploog, eds., *Human ethology* (Cambridge: Cambridge University Press).

Gold, Ann Grodzins and Bhoju Ram Gujar. 1989. "Of Gods, Trees and Boundaries: Divine Conservation in Rajasthan," *Asian Folklore Studies* 48:211–29.

Göncöl. 1992. "*Göncöl* Foundation for nature conservation, environmental protection, arts, education and culture and the encouragement of a value oriented society," (Vác, Hungary) brochure.

Gordon, Richard. 1995. "Globalization, New Production Systems and the Spatial Division of Labor," pp. 161–207, in: Wolfgang Litek and Tony Charles, eds., *The Division of Labor—Emerging Forms of World Organisation in International Perspective* (Berlin: Walter de Gruyter).

Gore, Albert. 1993. *Earth in the Balance—Ecology and the Human Spirit* (New York: Plume).

Gould, Peter C. 1988. *Early Green Politics—Back to Nature, Back to Land, and Socialism in Britain, 1880–1900* (Sussex/New York: Harvester/St. Martin's).

Gould, Stephen J. 1995. "Good sports & bad," *New York Review of Books*, March 2, pp. 20–24.

———. 1993. "Baseball: joys and lamentations," *New York Review of Books*, November 4, pp. 60–65.

———. 1990. *Wonderful Life: The Burgess Shale and the Nature of History* (New York: Norton).

Haas, Ernst B. 1964. *Beyond the Nation-State* (Stanford: Stanford University Press).

———. 1990. *When Knowledge is Power—Three Models of Change in International Organizations* (Berkeley: University of California Press).

Haas, Peter M., ed. 1992a. *Knowledge, Power, and International Policy Coordination, International Organization* 46, #1 (winter).

———. 1992b. "Introduction: Epistemic Communities and International Policy Coordination," *International Organization* 46, #1 (winter):1–36.

———. 1990. *Saving the Mediterranean—The Politics of International Environmental Cooperation* (New York: Columbia University Press).

———, Robert O. Keohane, and Marc A. Levy, eds. 1993. *Institutions for the Earth—Sources of Effective International Environmental Protection* (Cambridge, Mass.: MIT Press).

Hackman, Sandra. 1992. "After Rio—Our Forests, Ourselves," *Technology Review* 95, #7 (Oct.):33–40.

Haddock, David D. 1994. "Foreseeing Confiscation by the Sovereign: Lessons From the American West," pp. 129–46, in: Terry L. Anderson and Peter J. Hill, eds., *The Political Economy of the American West* (Lanham, Md.: Rowman & Littlefield).

Hafild, Emmy. 1993. "Indonesia: The Environmental Movement, the Politics and the Indigenous Rights," paper presented at a workshop on Environment, Human Rights, and NGO Political Activism in the Third World, University of California at Santa Cruz, January 16.

Hall, Stuart. 1991. "Brave New World," *Socialist Review* 21, #1 (Jan.-March):57–64.

Hamilton, Cynthia. 1994. "Concerned Citizens of South Central Los Angeles," pp. 207–33, in: Robert D. Bullard, ed., *Unequal Protection—Environmental Justice and Communities of Color* (San Francisco: Sierra Club Books).

Hankiss, Elemer. 1994. "Our recent pasts: recent developments in East Central Europe in the light of various social philosophies," *East European Politics and Societies* 8, #3 (fall):531–43.

Hannerz, Ulf. 1992. *Cultural Complexity—Studies in the Social Organization of Meaning* (New York: Columbia University Press).

———. 1990. "Cosmopolitans and Locals in World Culture," pp. 237–51, in: Mike Featherstone, ed., *Global Culture—Nationalism, Globalization, and Modernity* (London: Sage).

Haraway, Donna J. 1991. *Simians, Cyborgs, and Women—The Reinvention of Nature* (New York: Routledge).

Hardi, Peter. 1992. *Impediments on Environmental Policy-making and Implementation in Central and Eastern Europe* (Berkeley, Calif.: Institute of International Studies, University of California, Berkeley, Policy Paper No. 40).

Hardin, Garrett. 1968. "The Tragedy of the Commons," *Science* 162:1243–48.

Hardin, Russell. 1982. *Collective Action* (Baltimore: Johns Hopkins University Press).

Hardjasoemantri, Koesnadi. 1989. *Hukum Tata Lingkungan* (Yogyakarta: Gadjah Mada University Press, 4th ed.)

Harvey, David. 1991. "Flexibility: Threat or Opportunity," *Socialist Review* 21, #1 (Jan.-March):65–77.

———. 1990. *The Condition of Postmodernity* (Cambridge: Blackwell).

Hastings, Elizabeth Hann and Philip K. Hastings. 1994. *Index to International Public Opinion, 1992–1993* (Westport, Conn.: Greenwood Press).

Hawkins, Ann. 1993. "Contested Ground: International Environmentalism and Global Climate Change," pp. 221–45, in: Ronnie D. Lipschutz and Ken Conca, eds., *The State and Social Power in Global Environmental Politics* (New York: Columbia University Press).

Hayden, Tom. 1994. "Orange County Could Use Some Role Models," *San Francisco Chronicle*, Dec. 21, p. A23.

Hayfork Economic Alliance, n.d., informational materials (circa 1992).

Hays, Samuel P. 1987. *Beauty, Health, and Permanence: environmental politics in the United States, 1955–1985* (Cambridge: Cambridge University Press).

———. 1980. *Conservation and the Gospel of Efficiency—The Progressive Conservation Movement* (New York: Atheneum, 1980).

Healy, Melissa and Paul Richter. 1993. "Clinton's Extensive Plan for Forests," *San Francisco Chronicle*, July 1, p. A3 (*LA Times* wireservice).

Hecht, Susanna B. 1993. "The logic of livestock and deforestation in Amazonia," *BioScience* 43, #10 (Nov.): 687–96.

——— and Alexander Cockburn. 1990. *The Fate of the Forest—Developers, Destroyers and Defenders of the Amazon* (New York: HarperPerennial).

Hechter, Michael. 1990. "The Emergence of Cooperative Social Institutions," pp. 13–34, in: Michael Hechter, Karl-Dieter Opp, and Reinhard Wippler, eds., *Social Institutions—Their Emergence, Maintenance and Effects* (New York: Aldine de Gruyter).

———, Karl-Dieter Opp and Reinhard Wippler, eds., *Social Institutions—Their Emergence, Maintenance and Effects* (New York: Aldine de Gruyter).

Held, David and Anthony McGrew. 1994. "Globalization and the liberal democratic state," pp. 57–84, in: Yoshikazu Sakamoto, ed., *Global transformation: Challenges to the state system* (Tokyo: United Nations University Press).

———. 1991. "Democracy and Globalization," *Alternatives* 16:201–20.

Helvarg, David. 1995. "The Anti-environ Connection," *The Nation*, May 22, pp. 722–23.

Herring, Ronald. 1990. "Resurrecting the Commons—Collective action and ecology," *Items* (SSRC) 44, #4 (December).

Heryanto, Ariel. 1988. "The Development of 'Development'" (translated by Nancy Lutz), *Indonesia* 46:1–24.

Hill, Hal, ed. 1990a. "Indonesia's Industrial Transformation—Part I," *Bulletin of Indonesian Economic Studies* 26, #2 (August): 79–120.

———. 1990b. "Indonesia's Industrial Transformation—Part II," *Bulletin of Indonesian Economic Studies* 26, #3 (Dec.):75–110.

———, ed., 1989. *Unity and Diversity: Regional Economic Development in Indonesia since 1970* (New York: Oxford University Press).

Hinrichsen, Don and György Enyedi, eds. 1990. *State of the Hungarian Environment* (Budapest: Statistical Publishing House).

Hirsch, Fred. 1976. *Social Limits to Growth* (Cambridge: Harvard University Press).

Hirschmann, Albert O. 1982. *Shifting Involvements—Private Interest and Public Action* (Princeton: Princeton University Press).

Hoberg, George. 1993. "From Logroll to Logjam: Structure, Strategy, and Influence in the Old Growth Forest Conflict," paper prepared for delivery at the Annual Meeting of the American Political Science Association, Washington, D.C., Sept. 2–5.

Hodgson, Geoff. 1992. "Rationality and the influence of institutions," pp. 40–48, in: Paul Ekins and Manfred Max-Neef, eds., *Real-life economics—understanding wealth creation* (London: Routledge).

Hoffman, Lily M. 1989. *The Politics of Knowledge—Activist Movements in Medicine and Planning* (Albany: SUNY Press).

Holland, Marjorie M., Paul G. Risser, and Robert J. Naiman. 1991. *Ecotones: The Role of Landscape Boundaries in the Management and Restoration of Changing Environments* (New York: Chapman & Hall).

Hoopes, Townsend. 1973. *The Devil and John Foster Dulles* (Boston: Atlantic-Little, Brown).

Horváth, Agnes and Arpád Szakoczai. 1992. *The dissolution of communist power—The case of Hungary* (London: Routledge).

House, Freeman. 1992b. "Bioregional Approaches to Biodiversity," spoken at California Studies Conference IV, Sacramento, 6 Feb.

Hughes, Thomas P. 1987. "The Evolution of Large Technological Systems," pp. 51–82, in: Wiebe E. Bijker, Thomas P. Hughes, and Trevor J. Pinch, eds., *The Social Construction of Technological Systems—New Directions in the Sociology and History of Technology* (Cambridge, Mass.: MIT Press).

Hukkinen, Janne, Emery Rose, and Gene Rochlin. 1990. "A salt on the land: A narrative analysis of the controversy over irrigation-related salinity and toxicity in California's San Joaquin Valley," *Policy Sciences* 23:307–29.

Human Rights Watch. 1994. "Tightening Up In Indonesia before the APEC Summit," Vol. 6, #12 (October).

Hungarian Ministry for Environment and Regional Policy. 1991a. *A Glance at the Environmental Protection and Regional Development in Hungary* (Budapest).

———. 1991b. *Hungary's National Report to United Nations Conference on Environment and Development 1992* (Budapest, Dec.).

"Hungary: Environmental Pollution" 1990. *The Lancet* 335 (June 16):1450–51.

Hungerford, Andrea L. 1994. "Changing the management of public land forests: the role of the spotted owl injunctions," *Environmental Law* 24, #3 (July):1395–1434.

Hunter, Robert. 1979. *Warriors of the Rainbow: A Chronicle of the Greenpeace Movement* (New York: Holt, Rinehart and Winston).

Indonesian Government Regulation No. 29 of 1986, on Analysis of Impacts on the Environment.

Indonesian Law Number 4 of 1982.

Indonesian Law number 5 of 1960 (the Basic Agrarian Law).

INFIGHT 1992, "INFIGHT: Indonesian Front for the Defense of Human Rights" (Jakarta: INFIGHT).

Inglehart, Ronald. 1995. "Public Support for Environmental Protection: Objective Problems and Subjective Values in 43 Societies," *PS: Political Science & Politics* 28, #1 (March):57–72.

———. 1990. *Culture Shift in Advanced Industrial Society* (Princeton: Princeton University Press).

Ingold, Tim. 1986. *The appropriation of nature—Essays on human ecology and social relations* (Manchester: Manchester University Press).

Inner Voice. 1992. Vol. 4, #3, May/June.

In Our Hands—Directory of Non-governmental organizations accredited to the United Nations Conference on Environment and Development 1992, UNCED Secretariat.

International Negotiating Committee for a Framework Convention on Climate Change n.d., *United Nations Framework Convention on Climate Change* (Geneva: UNEP/WMO Information Unit on Climate Change).

International Rivers Review, published by International Rivers Network, Berkeley, CA.

Jacobs, Jane. 1984. *Cities and the Wealth of Nations—Principles of Economic Life* (New York: Random House).

Jakarta Post. 1993. "Poor Planning Causes Shortage of Wood Supplies," December 29.

Jancar, Barbara. 1992. "Chaos as an Explanation of the Role of Environmental Groups in East European Politics," pp. 156–84, in: Wolfgang Rüdig, ed., *Green Politics Two* (Edinburgh: Edinburgh University Press).

———. 1993. "The Environmental Attractor in the Former USSR: Ecology and Regional Changes," pp. 158–84, in: Ronnie D. Lipschutz and Ken Conca, eds., *The State and Social Power in Global Environmental Politics* (New York: Columbia University Press).

Jensen, Deborah B., Margaret S. Torn, and John Harte. 1993. *In Our Own Hands—A Strategy for Conserving California's Biological Diversity* (Berkeley: University of California Press).

Jones, E.L. 1981. *The European Miracle—Environments, economies, and geopolitics in the history of Europe and Asia* (Cambridge: Cambridge University Press).

de Jong, Wil. 1993. "Wise Use of Forest Resources in Kalimantan: A Potential for Development,"*Tropenbos Newsletter* 5, November, pp. 2–4.

Jungwirth, Lynn. 1994a. "Fire and You," message posted to Econet (ipc.apc.org) conference <env.klamath>, Sept. 1.

———. 1994b. Message posted to Econet (ipc.apc.org) conference <env.klamath>, July 18.

Kalimantan Review is published by West Kalimantan's Institute Dayakology Research and Development.

Kaplan, Robert D. 1994. "The Coming Anarchy," *The Atlantic Monthly*, February, pp. 44–76.

Karim, M. Bazlul. 1991. "Decentralization of Government in the Third World: A Fad or Panacea?" *International Studies Notes* 16, #2 (spring):50–54.

Katzenstein, Peter, ed. 1978. *Between Power and Plenty: Foreign Economic Policies of Advanced Industrial States* (Madison: University of Wisconsin Press).

Kay, Jane. 1990. "North Coast split over logging of old growth," *San Francisco Examiner*, Jan. 12, p. A1.

———. 1989. "Tree Wars," *Image* (*San Francisco Sunday Examiner*), Dec. 17, pp. 14, 16.

Keeley, James F. 1990. "Toward a Foucauldian Analysis of Regimes," *International Organization* 44, #1 (winter):83–105.

Keith, Michael and Steve Pile. 1993a, eds., *Place and the Politics of Identity* (London: Routledge)

———. 1993b. "The politics of place . . . ," pp. 1–21, in: Michael Keith and Steve Pile, eds., *Place and the Politics of Identity* (London: Routledge).

Kennedy, Paul. 1990. "Fin-de-Siècle America," *New York Review of Books*, June 28, pp. 31–40.

Keohane, Robert O. 1989. "Neoliberal Institutionalism: A Perspective on World Politics," pp. 1–20, in Robert O. Keohane, *International Institutions and State Power* (Boulder: Westview Press).

———. 1984. *After Hegemony: Cooperation and Discord in the World Political Economy* (Princeton: Princeton University Press).

Kerekes, Sandor. 1993. "Economics, Technology, and Environment in Hungary," *Technology in Society* 15, #1:137–47.

Kerr, Sarah. 1995. "Mexico: The Confidence Men," *New York Review of Books*, August 10, 1995, pp. 34–37.

Kessel, Frank. 1992. "On Culture, Health, and Human Development," *Items* (SSRC) 46, #4 (Dec.):65.

Kilényi, Géza. 1990. "Environmental Policy in Hungary—Environmental Legislation," pp. 35–40, in: Don Hinrichsen and György Enyedi, eds., *State of the Hungarian Environment* (Budapest: Statistical Publishing House).

"Klamath GIS Project," 1994, Hayfork, Calif., photocopied brochure.

Kompas. 1993. *"Mediasi dan Negosiasi, Alternatif Penyelesaian Sengkata Lingkungan,"* July 21, p. 8.

Kornai, János. 1994. "Transformational Recession: The Main Causes," *Journal of Comparative Economics* 19:39–63.

Korten, David. 1990. *Getting to the 21st Century—Voluntary Action and the Global Agenda* (West Hartford, Conn.: Kumarian Press).

———, ed. 1986. *Community Management—Asian Experience and Perspectives* (West Hartford, Conn.: Kumarian Press).

Krasner, Stephen D. 1993. "Westphalia and All That," in: Judith Goldstein and Robert O. Keohane, eds., *Ideas and Foreign Policy* (Ithaca: Cornell University Press).

———, ed. 1983. *International Regimes* (Ithaca: Cornell University Press).

———. 1978. *Defending the National Interest—Raw Materials Investments and U.S. Foreign Policy* (Princeton: Princeton University Press).

Krugman, Paul. 1994. *Peddling Prosperity—Economic Sense and Nonsense in the Age of Diminished Expectations* (New York: Norton).

LaFeber, Walter. 1993. *America, Russia and the Cold War—1945–1992* (New York: McGraw-Hill, 7th ed.).

Laferrière, Eric. 1992. "The Globalization of Politics: Environmental Degradation and North-South Relations," paper presented at the annual Conference of the Canadian Political Science Association, University of Prince Edward Island, Charlottetown, 31 May–2 June.

Landsberg, Hans H. (chairman). 1979. *Energy—The Next Twenty Years* (Cambridge, Mass.: Ballinger).

Larkins, Jeremy and Rick Fawn, eds. 1996. *International Society after the Cold War* (London: Macmillan).

Lavelle, Marianne. 1995. "Now Spotted Owl Flies to Pro-Business Congress," *National Law Journal* 17, #45 (July 10):B1.

Leatherman, Janie, Ron Pagnucco, and Jackie Smith. 1994. "International Institutions and Transnational Social Movement Organizations: Transforming Sovereignty, Anarchy, and Global Governance," Kroc Institute for International Peace Studies, University of Notre Dame, August, Working Paper 5:WP:3.

Leggett, Jeremy, ed. 1990. *Global Warming—The Greenpeace Report* (Oxford: Oxford University Press).

Leopold, Aldo. 1966. *A Sand County Almanac, with essays on Conservation from Round River* (Oxford: Oxford University Press).

Lev, Daniel S. 1973. "Judicial Unification in Post-Colonial Indonesia," *Indonesia* 16:1–37.

Libecap, Gary D. 1989. *Contracting for Property Rights* (Cambridge: Cambridge University Press).

Lind, Michael. 1994. "One Nation One Vote? That's Not Fair," *New York Times*, Nov. 23 (nat'l. ed.), p. A15.

Lindblom, Charles E. and David K. Cohen. 1979. *Usable Knowledge—Social Science and Social Problem Solving* (New Haven: Yale University Press).

LINK. 1988. *Lembaga Informasi Kemasyarakatan* (Public Information Institute), such as the 1988 special issue on Land in Capitalism (*Tanah Dalam Kapitalisme*), *LINK* 3.

Lipschutz, Ronnie D. 1992/96. "Reconstructing World Politics: The Emergence of Global Civil Society," *Millennium* 21, #3 (winter):389–420; reprinted in revised form in Jeremy Larkins and Rick Fawn, eds., *International Society after the Cold War* (London: Macmillan).

———. 1995. "Impacts of Climate Extremes and Variability in the Monterey Bay Region," proposal submitted to the National Oceanographic and Atmospheric Administration, U.S. Dept. of Commerce, August.

———. 1994. "Is It Warm in Here or Is It Just Me? A Report on Global Climate Negotiations, March, unpublished essay.

———. 1991a. "Bargaining Among Nations: Culture, History, and Perceptions in Regime Formation," *Evaluation Review* 15, #1 (Feb.):46–74.

———. 1991b. "From Here to Eternity: Environmental Time Frames & National Decisionmaking." Paper prepared for a Panel on "De-nationalizing" the State: The Transformation of Political Space, Social Time, and National Sovereignty, Conference of the International Studies Association, Vancouver, B.C., 19–23 March.

———. 1991c. "Wasn't the Future Wonderful? Resources, Environment, and the Emerging Myth of Global Sustainable Development," *Colorado Journal of International Environmental Policy and Law* 2, #1 (winter):35–54.

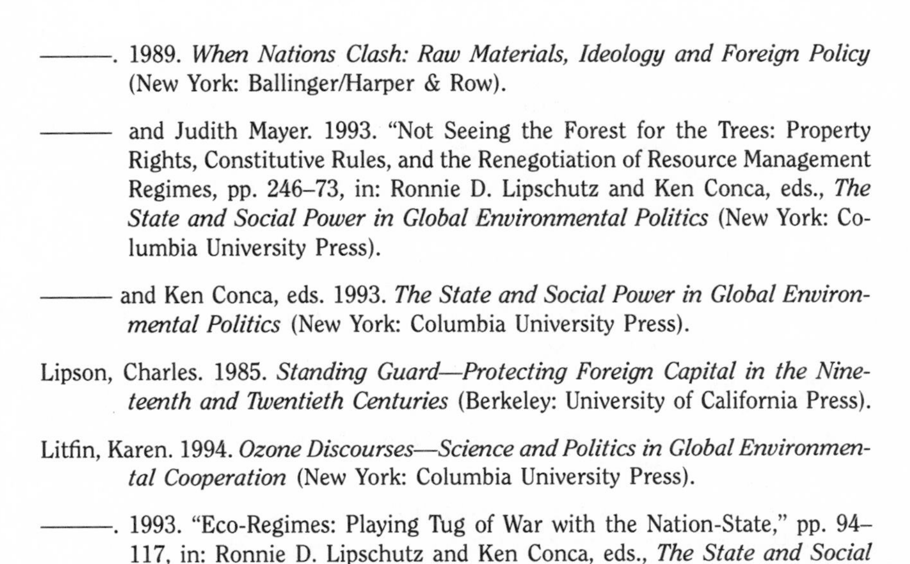

———. 1989. *When Nations Clash: Raw Materials, Ideology and Foreign Policy* (New York: Ballinger/Harper & Row).

——— and Judith Mayer. 1993. "Not Seeing the Forest for the Trees: Property Rights, Constitutive Rules, and the Renegotiation of Resource Management Regimes, pp. 246–73, in: Ronnie D. Lipschutz and Ken Conca, eds., *The State and Social Power in Global Environmental Politics* (New York: Columbia University Press).

——— and Ken Conca, eds. 1993. *The State and Social Power in Global Environmental Politics* (New York: Columbia University Press).

Lipson, Charles. 1985. *Standing Guard—Protecting Foreign Capital in the Nineteenth and Twentieth Centuries* (Berkeley: University of California Press).

Litfin, Karen. 1994. *Ozone Discourses—Science and Politics in Global Environmental Cooperation* (New York: Columbia University Press).

———. 1993. "Eco-Regimes: Playing Tug of War with the Nation-State," pp. 94–117, in: Ronnie D. Lipschutz and Ken Conca, eds., *The State and Social Power in Global Environmental Politics* (New York: Columbia University Press).

Long, Andrew. 1992. "Goods, knowledge and beer—The methodological significance of situational analysis and discourse," pp. 147-70, in: Norman Long and Ann Long, eds., *Battlefields of Knowledge—The Interlocking of Theory and Practice in Social Research and Development* (London: Routledge).

Long, Norman. 1992a. "Introduction, " pp. 3–15, in: Norman Long and Ann Long, eds., *Battlefields of Knowledge—The Interlocking of Theory and Practice in Social Research and Development* (London: Routledge).

———. 1992b. "From paradigm lost to paradigm regained? The case for an actor-oriented sociology of development," pp. 16–43, in: Norman Long and Ann Long, eds., *Battlefields of Knowledge—The Interlocking of Theory and Practice in Social Research and Development* (London: Routledge, 1992).

——— and Ann Long, eds. 1992. *Battlefields of Knowledge—The Interlocking of Theory and Practice in Social Research and Development* (London: Routledge).

Luke, Timothy W. 1993. "Green Consumerism: Ecology and the Ruse of Recycling," pp. 154–72, in: Jane Bennett and William Chaloupka, eds., *In the Nature of Things—Language, Politics, and the Environment* (Minneapolis: University of Minnesota Press).

MacAndrews, Colin. 1994. "The Indonesian Environmental Impact Management Agency (BAPEDAL)—Its Role, Development, and Future," *Bulletin of Indonesian Economic Studies* 30, #1 (April):85–103.

McCay, Bonnie J. and James M. Acheson, eds. 1987. *The Question of the Commons—The Culture and Ecology of Communal Resources* (Tucson: University of Arizona Press).

Macdonald, Laura. 1993. "Globalizing Civil Society: Interpreting International NGOs in Central America," paper presented at the International Studies Association annual meeting, Acapulco, March 24-27.

McEvoy, Arthur F. 1988. "Toward an Interactive Theory of Nature and Culture: Ecology, Production, and Cognition in the California Fishing Industry," pp. 211–29, in: Donald Worster, ed., *The Ends of the Earth* (Cambridge: Cambridge University Press).

———. 1986. *The Fisherman's Problem* (Cambridge: Cambridge University Press.)

McHugh, Paul. 1992. "Reinventing the Map," *This World* (*San Francisco Chronicle/Examiner*), Sept. 13.

McKay, Tim. 1992. "Scores of Fish Stocks in West are Deemed Dead or On Way Out," *Econews* (Northcoast Environmental Center), May, p. 3.

———. 1991. "Judge Gives a Hoot, Axes Timber Sales," *Econews* 21, #5, June, p. 1.

Magyar Természetvédők Szövetsége. 1992. "Kampány a Környezeti Jogokért," December.

Maiguashca, Bice. 1994. "The transnational indigenous movement in a changing world order," pp. 356–82, in: Yoshikazu Sakamoto, ed., *Global transformation: Challenges to the state system* (Tokyo: United Nations University Press).

Majelis Permusyawaratan Rakyat Indonesia (MPR). 1993. *Ketatapan-ketatapan MPR Republik Indonesia 1993 beserta GBHN 1993–1998* (Surabaya: Sinar Wijaya).

Maniates, Michael F. 1990a. "Organizational Designs for Achieving Sustainability: The Opportunities, Limitations, and Dangers of State-Local Collaboration for Common Property Management," paper prepared for presentation at the First Annual Meeting of the International Association for the Study of Common Property, 27–30 Sept., Durham, N.C.

———. 1990b. *Organizing for Rural Energy Development—Improved Cookstoves, Local Organizations, and the State in Gujurat, India* (Berkeley: Energy & Resources Group, UC-Berkeley, unpublished Ph.D. dissertation).

Markoff, John. 1993. "A Legal Thicket Amid the Redwoods," *New York Times*, June 4 (nat'l. ed.), p. C1.

Marsh, George Perkins. 1863/1875. *The Earth as Modified by Human Action* (New York: Scribner, Armstrong).

Marshall, T.H. 1950. *Citizenship and Social Class* (Cambridge: Cambridge University Press).

Martin, Glen. 1995a. "Proposal to List Coho Salmon as 'Threatened'," *San Francisco Chronicle*, July 20, p. A1.

———. 1995b. "Hayfork: Are the Good Times Really Over for Good? *San Francisco Chronicle Sunday*, Sept. 3, p. 4.

———. 1995c. "Trouble Waters," *San Francisco Chronicle Sunday*, March 26, p. 1

———. 1994a. "Rebuilding the North Coast Economy—Eureka, Arcata offer 2 solutions," *San Francisco Chronicle*, Oct. 8, p. A17.

———. 1994b. "Salmon Lose Struggle for Shasta River," *San Francisco Chronicle*, Aug. 22, p. A1.

———. 1993. "New Harmony in Timber Country," *San Francisco Chronicle*, July 8, p. A1.

Martinez-Alier, Juan and Eric Hershberg. 1992. "Environmentalism and the Poor: The Ecology of Survival," *Items* (SSRC) 46, #1, pp. 1–5.

Marx, Leo. 1990. "Post-Modernism and the environmental crisis," *Philosophy and Public Policy* 10, #3/4 (summer/fall).

———. 1964. *The Machine in the Garden: Technology and the Pastoral Ideal in America* (New York: Oxford University Press).

Massey, Doreen. 1993. "Power-geometry and a progressive sense of place," pp. 59–69, in: Jon Bird, Barry Curtis, Tim Putnam, George Robertson, and Lisa Tickner, eds., *Mapping the Futures—Local Cultures, Global Change* (London: Routledge).

Mathews, Jessica T. 1989. "Redefining Security," *Foreign Affairs* 68, #2 (spring):162–77.

Mattole Restoration Council. 1995. *Dynamics of Recovery—A Plan to Enhance the Mattole Esutary* (Petrolia, CA, February).

May, Robert M. 1974. *Stability and Complexity in Model Ecosystems* (Princeton: Princeton University Press, 2nd ed.).

Mayer, David. 1993. "Below, Beyond, Beside the State: Peace and Human Rights Movements and the End of the Cold War," pp. 267–95, in: David Skidmore and Valerie Hudson, eds., *The Limits of State Autonomy—Societal Groups and Foreign Policy Formulation* (Boulder: Westview).

Mearsheimer, John J. 1995. "The False Promise of International Institutions," *International Security* 19, #3 (winter):5–49.

Media Indonesia. 1994. "*Tim Penasihat Hukum Presiden Minta PTUN Tolak Gugatan Tujuh LSM*," November 1.

Melucci, Alberto. 1989. *Nomads of the Present—Social Movements and Individual Needs in Contemporary Society* (London: Hutchinson Radius, John Keane and Paul Mier, eds.).

Memorandum of Understanding. 1991. "California's Coordinated Regional Strategy to Conserve Biological Diversity," Sacramento, CA., September.

Memorandum of Understanding. 1990. "Coordinated Resource Management and Planning in California," Sacramento, CA., January 11.

Migdal, Joel S. 1988. *Strong Societies and Weak States—State-Society Relations and State Capabilities in the Third World* (Princeton: Princeton University Press).

Miller, Alan. 1991. *Gaia Connections—An Introduction to Ecology, Ecoethics, and Economics* (Savage, Maryland: Rowman & Littlefield).

Miller, David L. 1989. "The Evolution of Mexico's Spiny Lobster Fishery," pp. 185-98, in: Fikret Berkes, ed., *Common Property Resources—Ecology and community-based sustainable development* (London: Belhaven Press).

Miller, Kathleen A. and David L. Fluharty. 1992. "El Niño and variability in the northeastern Pacific salmon fishery: implications for coping with climate change," pp. 49-88, in: M.H. Glantz, ed., *Climate variability, climate change, and fisheries* (Cambridge: Cambridge University Press).

Miró Kiss, Ida. 1992. "Hungary," pp. 51-74, in: Duncan Fisher, Clare Davis, Alex Juras, and Vukasin Pavlovic, eds., *Civil Society and the Environment in Central and Eastern Europe* (London, Bonn & Belgrade: Ecological Studies Institute, Institut für Europäische Umweltpolitik, & Eko-Center, May).

Mitchell, Don. 1993. "Public Housing in Single-Industry Towns—Changing landscapes of paternalism," pp. 110–27, in: James Duncan and David Ley, eds., *Place/Culture/Representation* (London: Routledge).

Mitchell, John G. 1991a. "War in the Woods I: Swan Song," pp. 13–55, in: John G. Mitchell, *Dispatches from the Deep Woods* (Lincoln, Neb.: University of Nebraska Press).

———. 1991b. "War in the Woods II: West Side Story," pp. 56-99, in: John G. Mitchell, *Dispatches from the Deep Woods* (Lincoln, Neb.: University of Nebraska Press).

Mitrany, David. 1966. *A Working Peace System* (Chicago: Quadrangle Books).

Molnár, Géza. 1991. "Folyószbályozás régen és ma" (River Control Then and Now), *Öko* 2, #1 (March):17–29.

Moniaga, Sandra. 1991. "Towards Community-based Forestry and Recognition of Adat Property Rights in the Outer Islands of Indonesia: A Legal and Policy Analysis," presented at the Workshop on Legal Issues in Social Forestry, Environment and Policy Institute, East-West Center, Bali, November 4–6.

Moran, Emilio F., ed. 1990. *The Ecosystem Approach in Anthropology—From Concept to Practice* (Ann Arbor: University of Michigan Press).

Mott, Richard. 1993. "The GEF and the Conventions on Climate Change and Biological Diversity," *International Environmental Affairs* 5, #4 (fall):299–312.

Mulgan, Geoff and Helen Wilkinson. 1992. "The enabling (and disabling) state," pp. 340–52, in: Paul Ekins and Manfred Max-Neef, eds., *Real-Life Economics—Understanding wealth creation* (London: Routledge).

Nechodom, Mark. 1992. Ph.D. dissertation, History of Consciousness, University of California, Santa Cruz, ch. 2 draft, Oct. 27.

Nekabija, the magazine of WALHI's biodiversity program.

Nelson, J.G. 1994. "The Spread of Ecotourism—Some Planning Implications," *Environmental Conservation* 21, #3 (fall):248–55.

Netting, Robert McC. 1990. "Links and Boundaries: Reconsidering the Alpine Village as an Ecosystem," pp. 229–45, in: Emilio Moran, ed., *The Ecosystem Approach in Anthropology—From Concept to Practice* (Ann Arbor: University of Michigan Press).

Neumann, A. Lin and Gregory Sampson. 1992. "A forest at any price? The Headwaters Forest Bailout," *Sacramento News & Review*, June 11, p. 14–15, 17–18.

NGO Networker is a newsletter published by the World Resources Institute.

Noponen, Heizi, Julie Graham, and Ann R. Markusen, eds. 1993. *Trading Industries, Trading Regions—International Trade, American Industry, and Regional Economic Development* (New York: Guilford).

Norgaard, Richard B. 1988. "Sustainable Development: A Co-Evolutionary View," *Futures* (Dec.):606–20.

———. 1987. "Economics as Mechanics and the Demise of Biological Diversity," *Ecological Modelling* 38:107–21

———. 1981. "Sociosystem and Ecosystem Coevolution in the Amazon," *Journal of Environmental Economics and Management* 8:238–54.

Norris, Frank. 1899/1964. *MacTeague* (New York: New American Library).

Noss, Reed F. and Allen Y. Cooperrider. 1994. *Saving Nature's Legacy: Protecting and Restoring Biodiversity* (Washington D.C.: Island Press).

Nuijten, Monica. 1992. "Local organization as organizing practices—Rethinking rural institutions," pp. 189–207, in: Norman Long and Ann Long, eds., *Battlefields of Knowledge—The Interlocking of Theory and Practice in Social Research and Development* (London: Routledge).

Oelschlaeger, Max. 1991. *The Idea of Wilderness—From Prehistory to the Age of Ecology* (New Haven: Yale University Press).

Offe, Claus. 1990. "Reflections on the Institutional Self-transformation of Movement Politics: A Tentative Stage Model," pp. 232-50, in: Russell J. Dalton and Manfred Keuchler, eds., *Challenging the Political Order—New Social Movements in Western Democracies* (New York: Oxford University Press).

Ohmae, Kenichi. 1990. *The Borderless World—Power and Strategy in the Interlinked Economy* (New York: HarperCollins).

Okolicsanyi, Karoly. 1992. "Hungary: Antall's Government Proves Less than Green," *REF/RL Research Report* 1, #33 (21 Aug.):67.

Oliveira Filho, João Pacheco de. 1988. "Frontier Security and the New Indigenism: Nature and Origins of the Calha Norte Project," pp. 155–78, in: David Goodman and Anthony Hall, eds., *The Future of Amazonia—Destruction or Sustainable Development?* (New York: St. Martin's Press).

Olson, Mancur. 1971. *The Logic of Collective Action* (Cambridge, Mass.: Harvard University Press).

Onuf, Nicholas Greenwood. 1989. *World of Our Making—Rules and Rule in Social Theory and International Relations* (Columbia: University of South Carolina Press).

Orgoványi, Anikó. 1991. "Hungary's Green Heart: A Youth-Movement for Nature Conservation," *Green Newsletter*, Dec., p. 5.

Ormánság Alapítvány. 1993. "Rural Sustainable Development Ormánság Programme," August, photocopy.

———. 1992. "The Ormánság Project," September, brochure.

Orr, David. 1992. *Ecological Literacy—Education and the Transition to a Postmodern World* (Albany: SUNY Press).

Ostrom, Elinor. 1990. *Governing the Commons—The Evolution of Institutions for Collective Action* (Cambridge: Cambridge University Press).

———. 1989. "Microconstitutional Change in Multiconstitutional Political Systems," *Rationality & Society* 1, #1 (July):11–50.

Ouchi, William G. 1980. "Markets, Bureaucracies, and Clans," *Administrative Science Quarterly* 25 (March):129–41.

Packenham, Robert A. 1973. *Liberal America and the Third World: Political Development Ideas in Foreign Aid and Social Science* (Princeton: Princeton University Press, 1973).

Padoch, Christine and Nancy L. Peluso. 1996. "Changing Resource Rights in Managed Forests of West Kalimantan," in: Christine Padoch and Nancy L. Peluso, eds., *Borneo in Transition: People, Forests, Conservation and Development* (Kuala Lumpur: Oxford University Press).

Pangestuti, Yunida. 1989. "*Birokrasi Sentralistis & Faktor-Faktor Penyebabnya: Sebuah Ilustrasi: Pembangunan Waduk Kedung Ombo,*" *Kritis* 6:1, 18–28.

Pannon Ecologists Club. 1994. "Report from the environmental monitoring project," Pécs, Hungary.

Passell, Peter. 1994. "For Utilities, New Clean-Air Plan," *New York Times*, Nov. 18 (nat'l. ed.), p. C1.

Pearce, David W. and R. Kerry Turner. 1990. *Economics of Natural Resources and the Environment* (Baltimore: Johns Hopkins University Press).

Peet, Richard and Nigel Thrift. 1989. *New models in geography—The political-economy perspective* (London: Unwin Hyman, 2 vol.).

Peluso, Nancy Lee. 1995. "Whose Woods are These? Counter-Mapping Forest Territories in Kalimantan, Indonesia," *Antipode* 27, #4:383–406.

———. 1993. "Coercing Conservation: The Politics of State Resource Control," pp. 46–70, in: Ronnie D. Lipschutz and Ken Conca, eds., *The State and Social Power in Global Environmental Politics* (New York: Columbia University Press).

———. 1992. *Rich Forests, Poor People—Resource Control and Resistance in Java* (Berkeley: University of California Press).

Pepper, David. 1993. *Eco-socialism—from deep ecology to social justice* (London: Routledge).

———. 1984. *The Roots of Modern Environmentalism* (London: Croom Helm).

Persányi, Miklós. 1992. "Red Pollution, Green Evolution, Revolution in Hungary," pp. 75–96, in: Duncan Fisher, Clare Davis, Alex Juras, and Vukasin Pavlovic, eds., *Civil Society and the Environment in Central and Eastern Europe* (London, Bonn & Belgrade: Ecological Studies Institute, Institut für Europäische Umweltpolitik, & Eko-Center, May).

———. 1990. "Environmental Policy in Hungary—Public Participation and Non-Governmental Organizations: Their Role in Environmental Protection," pp. 40–45, in: Don Hinrichsen and György Enyedi, eds., *State of the Hungarian Environment* (Budapest: Statistical Publishing House, 1990).

"*Peta Kemiskinan*". 1993. *Tempo* 23, #11 (May 15).

Peterson, M.J. 1992. "Whales, cetologists, environmentalists, and the international management of whaling," *International Organization* 46, #1 (winter):147–86.

Petit, Charles. 1994. "Off-Roader Helps Avoid Battle over Butterfly," *San Francisco Chronicle*, Sept. 17, p. A1.

———. 1991. "Foresters Say Wildlife Important," *San Francisco Chronicle*, Aug. 7, p. D–6.

Phinney, David and Andrea Torrice. 1994. "Large Dams: False Promises," video documentary (Berkeley: International Rivers Network).

Polanyi. Karl. 1957. *The Great Transformation* (Boston: Beacon Press).

Pollack, Andrew. 1993. "Commission to Save Whales Endangered, Too," *New York Times*, May 18 (nat'l. ed.), p. B8.

Porter, Gareth and Janet Welsh Brown. 1996. *Global Environmental Politics* (Boulder: Westview 2nd edition).

Pranomo, A. Hadi and Agus P. Sari. 1992. "Redefining Development in Non-Consumption Terms," *Environesia* 6, #3: 1–3.

Press, Daniel. 1995. "Environmental Regionalism and the Struggle for California," *Society & Natural Resources* 8, #4:289–306.

Princen, Thomas and Matthias Finger, eds. 1994. *Environmental NGOs in World Politics: Linking the Local and the Global* (London: Routledge).

Pryde, Philip R. 1991. *Environmental Management in the Soviet Union* (Cambridge: Cambridge University Press).

Putnam, Robert D. 1993. *Making Democracy Work: Civic Traditions in Modern Italy* (Princeton: Princeton University Press).

———. 1988. "Diplomacy and Domestic Politics—The Logic of Two Level Games," *International Organization* 42, #3 (summer):427–60.

Racz, Barnabas and Istvan Kukorelli. 1995. "The 'second-generation' post-communist elections in Hungary in 1994," *Europe-Asia Studies* 47, #2 (March):251–79.

Rawls, John. 1955. "Two Concepts of Rules," *Philosophical Review* 64:3–32.

Reagan, Tom. 1984. *Earthbound—Introductory Essays in Environmental Ethics* (Prospect Heights, Ill.: Waveland Press).

"Regal Springs Tilapia". 1993. Pamphlet published by P.T. Aquafarm Nusantara for distribution in the United States.

Regier, Henry A. 1993. "The Notion of Natural and Cultural Integrity," pp. 3-18, in: Woodley, Stephen, James Kay & George Francis, eds., *Ecological Integrity and the Management of Ecosystems* (Ottawa: St. Lucie Press).

Regional Environmental Center for Central and Eastern Europe. 1992. *Information Bulletin* 2, #1 (autumn):7–8.

Reiff, David. 1991. "Multiculturalism's Silent Partner," *Harpers*, August, pp. 62–72.

Reisner, Marc. 1993. "Valley of the Smokes," *New York Times*, Oct. 29 (nat'l. ed.), p. A17.

———. 1988. *Cadillac Desert—The American West and Its Disappearing Water* (New York: Penguin).

Repetto, Robert. 1990. "Deforestation in the Tropics," *Scientific American* 262, #4 (April):36–42.

Republika. 1994. "*Kuasa Hukum Presiden Patahkan Gugatan LSM,*" November 1.

Ribot, Jesse C. 1993. "Market-State Relations and Environmental Policy: Limits of State Capacity in Senegal," pp. 24–25, in: Ronnie D. Lipschutz and Ken Conca, eds., *The State and Social Power in Global Environmental Politics* (New York: Columbia University Press).

———. 1990a. *Markets, states and environmental policy: the political economy of charcoal in Senegal* (Berkeley: Energy & Resources Group, University of California, unpublished Ph.D. dissertation).

———. 1990b. "Sustainable Development? The Role of Urbanization and Market-State Relations in Africa's Rural Decline," paper prepared for a panel on "Sustainable Development," Association of American Geographers' Annual Meeting, Toronto, Ont., 19-22 April.

Rich, Bruce. 1994. *Mortgaging the Earth—The World Bank, Environmental Impoverishment and the Crisis of Development* (Boston: Beacon Press).

Riker, James W. 1992. "Linking Development from Below to the International Environmental Movement: Sustainable Development and State-NGO Relations in Indonesia," paper presented at the Fifth Annual Conference of the Northwest Regional Consortium for Southeast Asian Studies on Development, Environment, Community and the Role of the State, at the University of British Columbia, Vancouver, Canada, October 16–18.

River Watch Network n.d., "What's Wrong with this Picture?", informational brochure.

Robbins, William. 1990. "For Farmers, Wetlands Mean a Legal Quagmire," *New York Times*, April 24 (nat'l. ed.), p. A1.

Robertson, Roland. 1992. *Globalization—Social Theory and Global Culture* (London: Sage).

Robison, Paul. 1986. *Indonesia: The Rise of Capital* (North Sydney: Allen & Unwin).

Rochlin, Gene I. 1994. "Broken Plowshare: System Failure and the Nuclear Power Industry," pp. 231–64, in: James Summerton, ed., *Changing Large Technical Systems* (Boulder: Westview).

Roe, Sarah. 1995. "Plenty of studies and little action mar green effort," *Budapest Week*, March 16–22, p. 6.

Rogers, Everett M. and D. Lawrence Kincaid. 1981. *Communication Networks—Toward a New Paradigm for Research* (New York: The Free Press).

Rose, Debra A. 1993. *The Politics of Mexican Wildlife: Conservation, Development, and the International System* (Gainesville: Dept. of Political Science, University of Florida, unpublished Ph.D. dissertation).

Rose, Richard and William T. E. Mishler. 1994. "Mass reaction to regime change in Eastern Europe: Polarization or leaders and laggards?" *British Journal of Political Science* 24, #2 (April): 159-72.

Rosenau, James N. 1992, "Governance, Order, and Change in World Politics," pp. 1–29, in: James N. Rosenau and Ernst-Otto Czempiel, eds., *Governance without Government: Order and Change in World Politics* (Cambridge: Cambridge University Press).

———. 1990. *Turbulence in World Politics—A Theory of Change and Continuity* (Princeton: Princeton University Press).

———. 1986. "Before cooperation: hegemons, regimes, and habit-driven actors in world politics," *International Organization* 40, #4 (autumn):849–94.

——— and Ernst-Otto Czempiel, eds. 1992. *Governance Without Government: Order and Change in World Politics* (Cambridge: Cambridge University Press).

Rosenbaum, Walter A. 1991. *Environmental Politics and Policy* (Washington, D.C.: CQ Press, 2nd ed.).

Rubin, Charles T. 1994. *The Green Crusade—Rethinking the Roots of Environmentalism* (New York: The Free Press).

———. 1993. "That Obscure Object of Desire: `The Environment' and Contemporary Environmentalism," paper prepared for the panel "Environmentalism and Political Philosophy," American Political Science Association annual meeting, Washington, D.C., Sept. 2–5.

Ruggie, John G. 1989. "International Structure and International Transformation: Space, Time, and Method," pp. 21–35, in: Ernst-Otto Czempiel and James N. Rosenau, eds., *Global Changes and Theoretical Challenges* (Lexington, Mass.: Lexington Books).

———. 1983a. "Continuity and Transformation in the World Polity: Toward a Neorealist Synthesis," *World Politics* 35, #2 (Jan.): 261–85.

———. 1983b. "International regimes, transactions, and change: embedded liberalism in the postwar economic order," pp. 195–232, in: Stephen D. Krasner, ed., *International Regimes* (Ithaca: Cornell University Press).

———. 1975. "International Responses to Technology," *International Organization* 29, #3 (summer 1975):569–70.

Rush, James. 1991. *The Last Tree: Reclaiming the Environment in Tropical Asia* (New York/Boulder: The Asia Society/Westview).

Sachs, Wolfgang, ed. 1992a. *The Development Directory* (London: Zed Books).

———. 1992b. "Environment," pp. 26–37, in: Wolfgang Sachs, ed., *The Development Directory* (London: Zed Books).

———. 1992c. "One World," pp. 102–114, in: Wolfgang Sachs, ed., *The Development Directory* (London: Zed Books).

Sagoff, Mark. 1988. *The Economy of the Earth—Philosophy, Law and the Environment* (Cambridge: Cambridge University Press).

Sakamoto, Yoshikazu, ed. 1994. *Global transformation: Challenges to the state system* (Tokyo: United Nations University Press).

Salim, Emil. 1979. *Lingkungan Hidup dan Pembangunan* (Jakarta: Mutiara).

Salisbury, Robert H. 1993. "Must All Politics be Local: Spatial Attachments and the Politics of Space," paper prepared for presentation to the American Political Science Association, Washington Hilton, Washington, D.C., Sept. 2–5, Washington University (St. Louis) Political Science Paper No. 211.

Sample, V. Alaric and Dennis C. Le Master. 1992. "Economic Effects of Northern Spotted Owl Protection—An examination of four studies," *Journal of Forestry* 90, #8 (Aug.):31–35.

Sand, Peter. 1994. *The Effectiveness of International Environmental Agreements* (Cambridge: Cambridge University Press).

Sari, Agus P. 1992a. "Kuala Lumpur Declaration: The Sell Out Begins," *SEA News*, July-September, pp. 4–5.

———. 1992b. "Lessons Learnt: The Energy Case," *Environesia* 6, #3: 4.

Sayadi, Lili Hasanuddin and Kathy Quick. 1992. "Ravaging the Lake Toba Ecoregion," *Environesia* 6, #1/2:19–23.

Schapiro, Mark. 1990. "The New Danube," *Mother Jones* 15, #3 (April-May):50–52, 72, 74–76.

Schmink, Marianne and Charles H. Wood. 1992. *Contested Frontiers in Amazonia* (New York: Columbia University Press).

Schneider, Bertrand. 1988. *The Barefoot Revolution—A Report to the Club of Rome* (London: IT Publications, trans. A.F. Villon).

Schneider, Keith. 1992. "New Way to Fight Environmental Laws," *San Francisco Chronicle*, January 22 (*NY Times* wireservice), p. A2.

Schneider, Stephen H. 1990. "The Changing Climate," pp. 25–36, in: Scientific American, *Managing Planet Earth* (New York: W.H. Freeman).

Schöpflin, George. 1994. "Post-communism: The Problems of Democratic Construction," *Dædalus* 123, #3 (summer):127–41.

———. 1991. "Post-communism: constructing new democracies in Central Europe," *International Affairs* 76, #2:235–50.

———. 1988. Rudolf Tőkés, and Iván Völgyes, "Leadership Change and Crisis in Hungary," *Problems of Communism* (Sept.-Oct.):23–46.

Schreiber, Helmut 1991, "Inter-German Issues of Environmental Policy," pp. 135-43, in: Joan DeBardeleben, *To Breathe Free—Eastern Europe's Environmental Crisis* (Washington, D.C./Baltimore: Wilson Center Press/Johns Hopkins University Press).

Schurmann, Franz. 1974. *The Logic of World Power—An Inquiry into the Origins, Currents, and Contradictions of World Politics* (New York: Pantheon).

Seager, Joni. 1993. *Earth Follies: Coming to Feminist Terms with the Global Environmental Crisis* (New York: Routledge).

Sebenius, James. 1991. "Designing Negotiations Toward a New Regime—The Case of Global Warming," *International Security* 15, #4 (spring):110–48.

———. 1984. *Negotiating the Law of the Sea* (Cambridge, Mass.: Harvard University Press).

Seibert, Berthold. 1989. "Agroforestry for the Conservation of Genetic Resources in Borneo," *Forestry and Forest Products,* GFG Report No. 13 (Samarinda: Mulawarman University), pp. 55–72.

Seleny, Anna. 1994. "Constructing the discourse of transformation: Hungary, 1979–82," *East European Politics and Societies* 8, #3 (fall):439–66.

Serasi, published by the Ministry of Population and Environment, Jakarta.

Setiakawan 1989, no. 3, December (magazine published by SKEPHI, Jakarta).

Shabecoff, Philip. 1990. "U.S. is Assailed at Geneva Talks for Backing out of Ozone Plan," *New York Times,* May 10 (nat'l. ed.), p. 1.

SHARE, quarterly newsletter of the Shasta Alliance for Resources & Environment, Redding, California.

Shenon, Philip. 1994a. "As Indonesia Crushes its Critics, It Helps Millions Escape Poverty," *New York Times,* August 27 (nat'l. ed.), p. A6.

———. 1994b. "Indonesia Shuts Three Outspoken Magazines," *New York Times,* June 23 (nat'l. ed.), p. A7.

Shields, Rob. 1991. *Places on the Margin—Alternative geographies of modernity* (London: Routledge).

Shiva, Vandana. 1991. *The Violence of the Green Revolution* (London: Zed/Third World Network).

Showers, Kate B. 1994. "Historical Environmental Impact Assessment: Connecting Land Use History to Environmental Impact Assessment," Boston: Boston University, African Studies Center Working Papers, No. 174.

Shuman, Michael H. 1994. *Towards a Global Village: International Community Development Initiatives* (London & Boulder: Pluto Press).

———. 1992. "Dateline Main Street: Courts v. Local Foreign Policies," *Foreign Policy* 86 (spring):158–77.

Sibl, Jaromir, ed. 1993. *Damming the Danube—What the Dam Builders Don't Want You to Know* (Bratislava: Slovak Union of Nature & Landscape Protectors & the Slovak Rivers Network, April).

Sik, Endre. 1994. "From the multicoloured to the black and white economy: the Hungarian second economy and the transformation," *International Journal of Urban and Regional Research* 18, #1 (March):46–70.

Sikkink, Kathryn. 1993. "Human rights, principled issue-networks, and sovereignty in Latin America," *International Organization* 47, #4 (summer):411–42.

Sikorski, Wade. 1993. "Building Wilderness," pp. 24–43, in: Jane Bennett and William Chaloupka, eds., *In the Nature of Things—Language, Politics, and the Environment* (Minneapolis: University of Minnesota Press).

Simons, Marlise. 1994. "East Europe Still Choking on Air of the Past," *New York Times*, Nov. 3 (nat'l. ed.), p. A1.

———. 1992. "Investors Shy Away from Polluted Eastern Europe," *New York Times*, May 13 (nat'l. ed.), p. A1.

Singer, J. David. 1961. "The Levels-of-Analysis Problem in International Relations," pp. 77–92, in: Klauss Knorr and Sidney Verba, eds., *The International System: Theoretical Essays* (Princeton: Princeton University Press).

Singh, Gurmit. 1992. "The Climate Convention: A Global Sell Out" (statement by the leader of Malaysia's Environmental Protection Society), *SEA News* (Climate Action Network — Southeast Asia Periodical Newsletter), July-September, pp. 1–4.

Sirait, Martua Thomas. 1992. "Mapping Customary Land: A Case Study in Long Uli Village, East Kalimantan, Indonesia," in: J.M. Fox and A. Flavelle, eds., *Voices from the Field: Papers from the 5th Annual Social Forestry Writing Workshop*, Program on Environment Project Paper (Honolulu: East-West Center).

SKEPHI. 1990. "A Commitment to Forest Conservation, Biosphere Transformation and Social Justice" (Jakarta: SKEPHI).

——— and *Kelompok Solidaritas Korban Pembangunan Kedung Ombo* (KSKPKO, or Solidarity Group for the Victims of Kedung Ombo Development). 1990. *Kedung Ombo: Between Development Myth and Marginal Reality* (Jakarta: SKEPHI and KSKPKO).

Skocpol, Theda. 1985. "Bringing the State Back In: Strategies of Analysis in Current Research," pp. 3–37, in: Peter B. Evans, Dietrich Reuschemeyer, and Theda Skocpol, eds., *Bringing the State Back In* (Cambridge: Cambridge University Press).

Smith, Denis, ed. 1994. *Business and the Environment* (New York: St. Martin's Press).

Smith, Neil. 1990. *Uneven Development: Nature, Capital and the Production of Space* (Cambridge: Basil Blackwell).

Smith, R.J. 1981. "Resolving the tragedy of the commons by creating private property rights in Wildlife," *CATO Journal* 1:439–68.

Snyder, Gary. 1995. "Cultivating Wildness," *Audubon* 97 #3 (May-June):64–70.

———. 1992. "Coming into the Watershed," *San Francisco Examiner*, March 1–2.

Soemarwoto, Otto. 1989. *Analisis Dampak Lingkungan* (Yogyakarta: Gadjah Mada University Press).

Sørensen, Knut H. and Nora Levold. 1992. "Tacit Networks, Heterogenous Engineers, and Embodied Technology," *Science, Technology & Human Values* 17, #1 (winter):13–35.

Soulé, Michael E., ed. 1986. *Conservation Biology: The Science of Scarcity and Diversity* (Sunderland, Mass.: Sinauer Assoc.).

Specter, Michael. 1995. "Russians Are Dying Younger and Younger," *San Francisco Chronicle*, August 2, p. A10.

Steelquist, Robert. 1992. "Salmon and forests: fog brothers," *American Forests* 98, #7–8 (July-August):27–32.

Steffen, Donna. 1995. "Green party still struggles with divisive past," *Budapest Week*, March 16–22, p. 6.

Stepan, Alfred. 1978. *The State and Society: Peru in Comparative Perspective* (Princeton, N.J.: Princeton University Press).

Stern, Paul C., Oran Young, and Daniel Druckman, eds. 1992. *Global Environmental Change—Understanding the Human Dimensions* (Washington, D.C.: National Academy Press).

Stevens, William K. 1994. "Dwindling Salmon Spur West to Save Rivers," *New York Times*, Nov. 15 (nat'l. ed.), p. B7.

———. 1993a. "Want a Room With a View? Idea May Be in the Genes," *New York Times*, Nov. 20 (nat'l. ed.), p. B5.

———. 1993b. "Battle Looms on Plans for Endangered Species," *New York Times*, Nov. 16 (nat'l. ed.), p. B5.

———. 1993c. "Biologists Fear Sustainable Yield is Unsustainable Idea," *New York Times*, April 20 (nat'l. ed.), p. B10.

———. 1993d. "Interior Secretary Is Pushing A New Way to Save Species," *New York Times*, Feb. 17 (nat'l. ed.), p. 1.

Stevis, Dimitris. 1995. "Labor Politics, Labor Movements and State-Society Relations, 1864–1994," paper prepared for presentation at the 36th Annual Meeting of the International Studies Association, Chicago, Feb. 21–25.

Stone, Christopher. 1993. *The Gnat is Older than Man—Global Environment and Human Agenda* (Princeton: Princeton University Press).

———. 1987. *Earth and Other Ethics: The Case for Moral Pluralism* (New York: Harper & Row).

Stone, Deborah A. 1988. *Policy Paradox and Political Reason* (Glenview, Ill.: Scott, Foresman and Company).

Strassoldo, Raimondo. 1992. "Globalism and localism: Theoretical reflections and some evidence," pp. 35–59, in: Zdravko Mlinar, ed., *Globalization and Territorial Identities* (Aldershot: Avebury).

Suara Pembaruan, daily newspaper published in Jakarta.

Subhan, S.D., Este Adi, and Zeverina Retno Pujisriastuti. 1993. "*Hariman Siregar: Gue Mesti Ikut Campur*," *Jakarta* 360, May 29-June 4, pp. 28–35.

Susskind, Larry E. 1994. *Environmental Diplomacy—Negotiating More Effective Global Agreements* (Oxford: Oxford University Press).

"Sustainable Development—From Theory to Practice". 1989. A special issue of *Development—Journal of the Society for International Development* 2/3.

Swisher, Larry. 1993. "Timber plan moves beyond the trees into water," *The Daily Astorian*, July 21, p. 1 (*LA Times* wireservice).

Szasz, Andrew. 1994. *Ecopopulism—Toxic Waste and the Movement for Environmental Justice* (Minneapolis: University of Minnesota Press).

Szendrei, Tibor. 1993. "István Csurka: Keeping Hungary Hungarian," *Budapest Week*, Feb. 25–March 3, p. 5.

Szirmai, Viktória. 1993. "The Structural Mechanisms of the Organization of Ecological-Social Movements in Hungary," pp. 146–157, in: Anna Vari and Pál Tamás, eds., *Environment and Democratic Transition—Policy and Politics in Central and Eastern Europe* (Dordrecht: Kluwer Academic).

Tarrant, James, et al. 1987. *Natural Resources and Environmental Management in Indonesia: An Overview* (Jakarta: U.S. Agency for International Development).

Tarrow, Sidney. 1988. "National Politics and Collective Action: Recent Theory and Research in Western Europe and the United States," *Annual Review of Sociology* 14:421–40.

Thompson, Janice E. 1992. "Explaining the regulation of transnational practices: a state-building approach," pp. 195–218, in: James N. Rosenau and Ernst-

Otto Czempiel, eds., *Governance Without Government: Order and Change in World Politics* (Cambridge: Cambridge University Press).

——— and Stephen Krasner. 1989. "Global Transactions and the Consolidation of Sovereignty," pp. 192–219, in: Ernst-Otto Czempiel and James N. Rosenau, eds., *Global Changes and Theoretical Challenges—Approaches to World Politics for the 1990s* (Lexington: Lexington Books).

Thompson, John. 1984. *Studies in the Theory of Ideology* (Berkeley: University of California Press).

Thompson, Michael. 1979. *Rubbish Theory—The creation and destruction of value* (Oxford: Oxford University Press).

Thrupp, Lori Ann. 1989. "Legitimizing Local Knowledge: From Displacement to Empowerment for Third World Peoples," *Agriculture and Human Values* 6 (summer):13–24.

Timberland Task Force Staff. 1990. "California Timberland Task Force, Options for Task Force Action, Revised Work Plan," April 9.

Tinker, Catherine J. 1993. "NGOs and Environmental Policy: Who Represents Global Civil Society?" Paper presented at the International Studies Association annual meeting, Acapulco, March 24–27.

Tirtosudarmo, Riwanto. 1991. "*Mampukah LSM Menjadi* 'Counter Hegemonic Movement'? *Komentar atas tulisan George J. Aditjondro (GJA) dan Arief Budiman (AB), dalam Kritis No. 3, Tahun V, 1990*," *Kritis* 5:3, 105–108.

Todarova, Maria. 1995. "Identity (Trans)Formation among Bulgarian Muslims," Berkeley, CA: Center for German & European Studies, University of California Berkeley, March, Working Paper 6.5.

Trager, Louis. 1995. "All's fair in selling growth to cities," *San Francisco Examiner*, Jan. 22, p. C1.

Tsing, Anna Lowenhaupt. 1993. *In the Realm of the Diamond Queen—Marginality in an Out-of-the-Way Place* (Princeton: Princeton University Press).

U.S. Department of Agriculture (U.S. Forest Service), U.S. Department of Commerce (National Oceanographic and Atmospheric Administration, National Marine Fisheries Service), U.S. Department of the Interior (U.S. Bureau of Land Management, U.S. Fish & Wildlife Service, National Park Service) and U.S. Environmental Protection Agency. 1993. *Forest Ecosystem Management: An Ecological, Economic and Social Assessment—Report of the Forest Ecosystem Management Assessment Team* (Washington, D.C.).

U.S. Agency for International Development (AID). 1992. "Freedom, Fresh Air, and Free Enterprise," brochure, October.

———. n.d., Environmental Training Project brochure.

U.S. Bureau of Land Management (BLM). 1993. "Thinking Globally, Acting Locally," *Newsbeat* (Sacramento Office), May.

U.S. Environmental Protection Agency (EPA), Office of International Activities. 1992a. "Concept Paper: International Environmental Management Training Centers," Jan. 2.

———. 1992b. "EPA Programs in Central/Eastern Europe," March 16.

U.S. General Accounting Office (GAO). 1994. *Environmental Issues in Central and Eastern Europe—U.S. Efforts to Help Resolve Institutional and Financial Problems* (Washington, D.C., May, GAO/RCED-94-41).

U.S. Peace Corps. 1992. "Environmental Education-Building toward a Sustainable Future," September, brochure.

U.S. Senate. 1995. "Hearings on the Impact of US Forest Service Programs on Local Communities," Subcommittee on Forests and Public Land Management, Committee on Energy and Natural Resources, July 5, Hearing Summary.

Vari, Anna and Pál Tamás, eds. 1993. *Environment and Democratic Transition—Policy and Politics in Central and Eastern Europe* (Dordrecht: Kluwer Academic).

Várkonyi, Anna. 1992. "A Catalogue of Woe: the Environment," *New Hungarian Quarterly* 33, #126 (summer):90–99.

Varkonyi, Peter. 1989. "Hungary: recent political and economic developments," *The World Today* 45, #5 (May):83–85.

Vásárhelyi, Judith. 1991. "Hungarian Greens were Blue," pp. 205–15, in: Craig L. LaMay and Everette E. Dennis, eds., *Media and the Environment* (Washington, D.C.: Island Press).

Viviano, Frank. 1995. "World's Wannabee Nations Sound Off," *San Francisco Chronicle*, Jan. 31, p. A1.

———. 1994a. "Eastern Europe's Lost Generation," *San Francisco Chronicle*, Sept. 19, p. A1.

———. 1994b. "Old Enemies Join Forces in Hungary," *San Francisco Chronicle*, Sept. 5, p. A1.

Vukovich, György. 1990. "Trends in Economic and Urban Development and Their Environmental Implications," pp. 13–34, in: Don Hinrichsen and György Enyedi, eds., *State of the Hungarian Environment* (Budapest: Statistical Publishing House).

Wade, Robert. 1988. *Village Republics: Economic Conditions for Collective Action in South India* (Cambridge: Cambridge University Press).

———. 1987. "The management of common property resources: collective action as an alternative to privatisation or state regulation," *Cambridge Journal of Economics* 11, #2:95–106.

Wæver, Ole. 1995. "Securitization and Desecuritization," pp. 46–86, in: Ronnie D. Lipschutz, ed., *On Security* (New York: Columbia University Press).

Wahana Lingkungan Hidup Indonesia (WALHI). 1992. "Logging Rent Report," draft.

——— and others. 1994. Letter to the Head of the Jakarta State Administrative Court, August 23, signed by representatives of WALHI (Indonesian Environmental Forum); LATIN (Indonesian Tropical Nature Foundation); FORSIKAL (Foundation Forum for Population and Environmental Study); PLASMA (Human Resource and Environmental Development Foundation); ICEL (Indonesian Center of Environmental Law Foundation; and Pelangi Indonesia Foundation.

——— and Yayasan Lembaga Bantuan Hukum Indonesia (LBH). 1993. *Perjalanan Secarik Kertas: Suatu Tinjauan Terhadap Penga-embangan Industri Pulp dan Kertas di Indonesia* (Jakarta: WALHI and LBH).

———. 1992. *Mistaking Plantations for the Indonesia's Tropical Forest* (Jakarta: WALHI and LBH).

Walker, Laura. 1992. "Mattolia in the Early 1990s," pp. 225-30, in Laura Walker, ed., *Mattolia—Visions of Our Grandchildren's World* (Petrolia, CA).

Wallace, L. Tim, Jerry Moles, and Kim Rodrigues. 1993. "Proceedings of the Panel Discussion on Property Rights, Eureka, California, Jan. 25, 1993," Berkeley, Calif.: California Agricultural Experiment Station & Giannini Foundation of Agricultural Economics, June, Working Paper No. 678.

Wallick, Heidi M. 1992. "The Politics of Old Growth," paper prepared for delivery at the 1992 Annual Meeting of the Western Political Science Association, San Francisco, March 19–21.

Walton, John. 1992. *Western Times and Water Wars—State, Culture, and Rebellion in California* (Berkeley: University of California Press).

Walzer, Michael. 1992. "The Civil Society Argument," pp. 89–107, in: Chantal Mouffe, ed., *Dimensions of Radical Democracy—Pluralism, Citizenship, Community* (London: Verso).

———, ed. 1995. *Toward a Global Civil Society* (Providence: Berghahn Books).

Wapner, Paul. 1996. *Environmental Activism and World Civic Politics* (Albany: SUNY Press).

———. 1995a. "Politics beyond the State: Environmental Activism and World Civic Politics," *World Politics* 47, #3 (April):311–340.

———. 1995b. "The State and Environmental Challenges: A Critical Exploration of Alternatives to the State-System," *Environmental Politics* 4, #1 (spring):44–69.

Wells, Michael P. 1994. "The Global Environment Facility and Prospects for Biodiversity Conservation," *International Environmental Affairs* 6, #1 (winter):69–97.

Wendt, Alexander. 1987. "The Agent-Structure Problem in International Relations Theory," *International Organization* 41 (summer):335–70.

Wheelock, Jane. 1992. "The household in the total economy," pp. 124–35, in: Paul Ekins and Manfred Max-Neef, eds., *Real-Life Economics—Understanding wealth creation* (London: Routledge).

Wilmer, Franke. 1993. *The Indigenous Voice in World Politics* (Newbury Park: Sage).

Wilson, Edward O., ed. 1988. *Biodiversity* (Washington, D.C.: National Academy Press).

——— and Stephen R. Kellert, eds. 1993. *The Biophilia Hypothesis* (Washington, D.C.: Island Press/Shearwater Books).

Winner, Langdon. 1986. "Mythinformation," pp. 98-117, in: Langdon Winner, *The Whale and the Reactor—A Search for Limits in an Age of High Technology* (Chicago: University of Chicago Press).

———. 1977. *Autonomous Technology—Technics-out-of-Control as a Theme in Political Thought* (Cambridge, Mass.: MIT Press).

Wolfe, Alan. 1991. "Three Paths to Development: Market, State, and Civil Society," paper presented to the International Meeting of NGOs and the UN System Agencies, Rio De Janeiro, 6–9 August.

Woodley, Stephen, James Kay, and George Francis, eds. 1993. *Ecological Integrity and the Management of Ecosystems* (Ottawa: St. Lucie Press).

Woods, Lawrence T. 1993. "Nongovernmental Organizations and the United Nations System: Reflecting Upon the Earth Summit Experience," *International Studies Notes* 18, #1 (winter):9–15.

World Commission on Environment and Development. 1987. *Our Common Future* (Oxford: Oxford University Press).

World Resources Institute. 1994. *World Resources 1994–95* (New York: Oxford University Press).

———. 1992a. *World Resources 1992–93* (New York: Oxford University Press).

———. 1992b. "Policies and Institutions: Nongovernmental Organizations," pp. 215–34, in: *World Resources 1992–93* (Oxford: Oxford University Press).

——— and FAO. 1987. *Tropical Forestry Action Plan* (Washington: World Resources Institute).

World Wildlife Fund (WWF)—USA. 1992. "Central and Eastern Europe Program," July.

Wright, Will. 1992. *Wild Knowledge—Science, Language and Social Life in a Fragile Environment* (Minneapolis: University of Minnesota Press).

Yaffee, Steven Lewis. 1994. *The Wisdom of the Spotted Owl—Policy Lessons for a New Century* (Washington, D.C.: Island Press).

Yearley, Steven. 1991. *The Green Case—A Sociology of Environmental Issues, Arguments and Politics* (London: HarperCollins Academic).

Yoon, Carol Kaesuk. 1994. "Boom and Bust May be the Norm in Nature, Study Suggests," *New York Times*, March 15, p. C4.

Young, Oran R. 1994a. *International Governance—Protecting the Environment in a Stateless Society* (Ithaca: Cornell University Press).

———. 1994b. "The Effectiveness of International Governance Systems," pp. 140–60, in: *International Governance—Protecting the Environment in a Stateless Society* (Ithaca: Cornell University Press).

———. 1989. *International Cooperation—Building Regimes for Natural Resources and the Environment* (Ithaca: Cornell University Press).

———. 1982. *Resource Regimes—Natural Resources and Social Institutions* (Berkeley: University of California Press).

——— and Gail Osherenko, eds. 1993. *Polar Politics—Creating International Environmental Regimes* (Ithaca: Cornell University Press).

Zimmerman, Michael E. 1994. *Contesting Earth's Future—Radical Ecology and Postmodernity* (Berkeley: University of California Press).

Zisk, Betty H. 1992. *The Politics of Transformation—Local Activism in the Peace and Environmental Movements* (Westport, Conn: Praeger).

Zöld Szív. 1993. "The Danube Project," informational flyer.

Index